AF559635

# POLITICAL THEORY
# AND
# POLITICAL THOUGHT

# POLITICAL THEORY AND POLITICAL THOUGHT

N.D. ARORA, MA, PhD
Formerly of PGDAV College,
University of Delhi, New Delhi

S.S. AWASTHY, MA, PhD
PGDAV College,
University of Delhi, New Delhi

HAR-ANAND
PUBLICATIONS PVT LTD

HAR-ANAND PUBLICATIONS PVT LTD
E-49/3, Okhla Industrial Area, Phase-II, New Delhi-110020
Tel.: 41603490
E-mail: info@haranandbooks.com/haranand@rediffmail.com
Shop online at: www.haranandbooks.com



**Reprint, 2023**



Published by Ashok Gosain and Ashish Gosain for
Har-Anand Publications Pvt Ltd

Printed in India

# Preface to the First Edition

Political Theory, as a discipline of a wider subject, Political Science, has always been on march towards its heights. It has always enliven itself to newer challenges and has, in the process, offered remedies to the problems coming its way. From time to time, Political Theory has attempted to give new orientations to concepts such as democracy, liberty, equality, rights, justice, citizenship, property, adding to it terms such as 'identity' and 'civil society'.

Political Thought, both Western as well as Indian, ancient as well as modern, too has sought to view such concepts from time to time. It is interesting to discuss, for example, Mill's views on democracy together with what Nehru thinks about it. It is instructive to know what Kautilya thought of the state in ancient India on the one hand, and Marx on the concept of state on the other, in the nineteenth century.

The present study is an exercise on the concepts and terms which contemporary Political Science has opened up. It also deals with the views of some representative political philosophers (both Western and Indian) on their related concepts.

We feel grateful to a host of colleagues who have helped us in making the present attempt as fruitful as possible. We thank our publishers, Mr. Ashok Gosain and Mr. Ashish Gosain, the two brothers, who made it possible for us to complete the project in time.

**N.D. Arora**
**S.S. Awasthy**

# Syllabus in Political Theory and Political Thought

1. (a) What is Politics?
   (b) What is Political Theory?
   (c) The relevance of Political Theory
   (d) Why study the history of Political Thought?
2. (a) Concepts: Democracy, Liberty, Equality, Justice, Rights, Identity, Citizenship, Property, Civil Society and State
   (b) Western Thought: Thinkers and Themes
      (i) Aristotle on Citizenship
      (ii) Locke on Rights and Property
      (iii) Rousseau on Inequality
      (iv) J.S. Mill on Liberty and Democracy
      (v) Marx on State
   (c) Indian Thought: Thinkers and Themes
      (i) Kautilya on State
      (ii) Gandhi on Swaraj
      (iii) Ambedkar on Social Justice
      (iv) Nehru and Lohia on Democracy
      (v) Periyar on Identity
3. Introducing Political Argument
   (a) Understanding Political Argument
   (b) Is Democracy compatible with economic growth?
   (c) Is Censorship justified?
   (d) Does Protective Discrimination violate principles of Fairness?
   (e) Should the State intervene in the institution of the family?

# Contents

# CHAPTER – 1

# What is Politics?

## I. Introduction

Human beings are different from all other living creatures. For most part of their life and living, the other creatures depend on conditions of not their making, and hence do but very little in changing themselves through their efforts. Human beings, on the other hand, though too find themselves in situations of not their making, but do or can atleast do a lot in changing the environment they live in. This is because human beings have the ability and capacity to make their own destiny. Karl Marx had, therefore, rightly said that man, though is born in history, is also the maker of history.

Indeed, there were times when human beings too, like all other creatures, lived at the mercy of nature and were, to a great extent, powerless to affect changes. But as they developed intellectually better than the other creatures, they became conscious of their surroundings and with the passage of times set themselves to explain and plan modifications and improvements in their environment.

Human beings, because of their relatively more developed mental and intellectual faculties, were able to do much in all fields of activity as compared to the other creatures, who remained, and in fact still remain, at the initial stages of their physiological evolution. The relatively higher developed mental faculties of human beings helped them to understand, comprehend, explain, define, refine and investigate both their physical and social environment. As the human beings began to know nature, learn its laws, utilize its resources, they also began to evolve, frame, examine and question their beliefs, customs and traditions they built from time to time. Most of the early social rules of conduct, peoples' attitudes and their social institutions, we must remember, arose unintentionally, and for a long period of time developed unconsciously. It was only gradually did the human beings realise their existence and that through their deliberate and conscious efforts they could possibly bring changes and make improvements in all aspects of their life and living.

Of all the social institutions, the state, we all know, has been the most important, the most universal, and the most powerful. It must have emerged and its authority must have been asserted the time when human life must have settled. In the process of settling themselves, people might have begun investigating about the institution of the state, discovered its origins, examined and upheld its authority; might have disputed over the proper sphere of its functions, dwelt over issues relating to the relationship between the governors and the governed. It would have been about the beginnings of this time that the assumptions about politics would have emerged. It would have been from these times onward that political activities might have started; political phenomena and political issues might have caught attention, discussing, debating, examining and investigating all about politics. Indeed, politics came much before it came to be studied as an academic discipline.

### (a) *Politics: Negatively Described and Vaguely Understood*

Politics is a widely observed phenomenon. It is ubiquitous. To attribute any activity to 'politics' is not astonishing. In fact, it has become almost a fashion, if not a habit, to address any human activity as 'political'. That is why that there are references such as 'university politics', 'church politics', 'politics in sports', 'students politics'. So excessive and vague has been the use of the word 'politics' that it has lost its real meaning.

The negative meaning of politics is gaining currency. It is, quite often equated with 'cynicism', 'scepticism', 'mistrust', a 'dirty' word associated with 'self-seeking behaviour, hypocrisy and the manipulation of attitudes'. That is why that some describe 'politics' as 'the technique of compromise'. There are others who call it as 'the art of possible', 'the last refuge of the scoundrel', 'the art of looking for trouble, finding it—whether it exists or not—diagnosing it wrongly, and applying the wrong remedy', and the like. Though there is not much truth in the meaning of politics negatively understood, but this does not, and in fact, should not prevent us to know what politics is.

Consider politics ethically and one would say with Plato and Aristotle that it is a means to attain what is 'good' and / or 'just' life. Consider it legalistically as with the ancient Romans, one will find politics another name for 'administration'. With St. Augustine, politics becomes 'a city of man' acting as a bridge to 'the City of God'. Consider it as most of the traditionalist scholars do, politics becomes a study of the state, the government or both. Consider it as some of the modern scholars do, it emerges as the study of power. The liberals, over time, have ended up by regarding politics as the reconciliation of antagonistic interests and thereafter as the pursuit of common good. The Marxists, while describing "politics" as a class concept and therefore 'dirty' declare it as an instrument of social and political change. With Aristotle, some would say that politics is a 'master science', while with Buckle, others would pronounce it as 'the most backward of all the arts'. In short, politics is different to different people in different circumstances and at different times, means differently.

### (*b*) *Politics: As Many People, So Many Definitions*

Serious difficulties arise when attempts are made to give politics a meaning. Mary Hawkesworth rightly says, "Within the field of political science, there is no one definition of politics that holds the allegiance of all political scientists". As such, there are as many definitions of politics as there are the people. A survey of numerous definitions of politics makes the assertion worth notable.

(i) *Politics is* about *state:* Deriving politics from the Greek word 'polis', it is described as one that deals with 'state'. Garner says: "Politics begins and ends with the state". Gettell holds the view that politics is "the historical investigation of what the state has been, an analytical study of what the state is and a political and ethical discussion of what the state ought to be". Garies declares politics as one that considers "state as an institution of power in the totality of its relations, its origin, its setting, its object, its ethical signification, its economic problems, its life conditions, its financial side, its end, etc." Bluntschlli tells us that politics is concerned with the state....understand and comprehend the state in its fundamental conditions, in its essential nature, its various forms of manifestation and its development". According to

Laski, "the study of politics concerns itself with the life of men in relation to organised states". Pollock describes politics as "the study of man as a citizen in his relations to the state." Acton is of the opinion that politics is concerned with "the state and with the conditions essential for its development".

(ii) Politics is about the *government*. Seeley says that politics "investigates the phenomenon of government, as Political Economy deals with wealth, Biology with life, Algebra with numbers and Geometry with space and magnitude". Leacock describes politics as one that "deals with government—the Government used in its widest sense rests on the fundamental idea of that authority". According to Apter, politics "is about the relations between the rulers and the ruled, and the means and the ends each employs". The Macmillan Modern Dictionary says: "Politics deals with the organisation and administration of government."

(iii) Politics is about both the *state and government*. Paul Janet says that "politics treats of the foundations of the state and the principles of government". Zacharia holds the view that politics sets forth "the fundamental principles according to which the state as a whole is to be organised and the sovereign power exercised". According to Fairlie, politics is concerned with "the life of man as organised under government and law, in what is known as State. It includes a study of the organisation and the activities of the state and of the principles and ideas which underlie political organisation and activities". Gilchrist says that politics deals with the state and government. Appadorai defines politics as it "deals with the state or political society, meaning by the term a people organised for law within a definite territory".

(iv) Politics is about *power*. George Catlin describes politics in terms of power: politics is power. Lasswell says that politics is what explains "who gets, what, when and how". With Kaplan, Lasswell says politics means "the shaping and sharing of power". Dahl is of the opinion that politics deals with "power, rule and authority". Wasby regards politics as something that the politicians "do from 9.00 a.m. to 5.00 p.m.", and we may add "both during the day and/or night".

(v) Politics is about *political system*. According to David Easton, politics is all about political system which "authoritatively allocates values in the society". Almond and Powell say that "politics studies the whole political system".

(vi) Politics is about *conflict*, its resolution, consensus. There are others who describe it as conflict. Dahl says that politics and conflict are born twins. Lipson declares, "By politics, I mean active controversy". Greaves opines that politics is concerned among other things with conflicts—conflict over the proper use of force, power, authority". All the Marxists refer to politics as struggle for power. Vernon Von Dyke thinks of politics as conflicts and struggles whereas Myerron and Banfield consider politics as "the activity (negotiation, argument, discussion, application of force persuasion, etc.) by which an issue is agitated or settled".

(c) *Politics: Traditional vs. Modern*

For a long time in the history of political thought, politics has been regarded as a study of the state, government and/or both. High lighting the traditional meaning of politics, the *Dictionary of Political Science* describes politics as a systematic study of the state and of the processes governing its internal and external relations. No wonder if the political philosophers focussed on matters relating to political institutions, broadly. Plato built the ideal state; Aristotle argued on the best practicable state, St. Augustine spoke on the city of God through the city of man; Machiavelli and Hobbes favoured an omnipotent ruler. The point is that for centuries, politics has been regarded as something that is associated with political organisation —the way it is composed and the way it works/functions.

The traditional meaning of politics, concerned as it is with the state or government or both, takes into account the organisational view of politics: that politics is a matter of state or at best, a matter as to what the administration is all about. The emphasis, therefore, in the traditional meaning of politics, is on the organisation: politics as political society: how best it is composed of and how best it can be protected, and how best it makes people attain their good life. Politics, in the traditional sense stays away from the people, most of the people. What it means is that political activity, in the traditional meaning of politics, is confined to micro level in which a substantial section of the people do not participate in the affairs of the state or the government. To that extent, politics is 'external' to the vast majority of the people.

The modern scholars, mostly under the influence of science, attempt to give politics a meaning in which it is described as an activity. From Hobbes and Max Weber and down to modern political scientists, mostly Americans (men like Merriam, Lasswell, Shils, Catlin, Dahl, Easton and others), politics has been described as the study of power. These scholars define power as 'a relation among actors in which one actor induces other actors in some way they would not otherwise act' (Dahl) or as the ability to produce intended effects as directly involve other persons' (Lasswell) or 'a relationship in which one person or group is able to determine the actions of another in the direction of the former's own ends' (Easton). These scholars hold the view that the power of the state, in politics, lies in and with the state. Robert Dahl, therefore, concludes, "The government is any government that successfully upholds a claim to the exclusive regulation of the legitimate use of physical force in enforcing its rules within a given territorial area. The political system made up of the residents of that territorial area and the government of the area is a state." Lipset says, "Politics is the study of political aspect of organised human society". There are the scholars who, while voicing the modern meaning of politics, regard it as 'conflict', 'controversy', 'struggle', 'consensus' and the like.

The modern meaning of politics, concerned as it is with the 'process' aspect of politics, considers it as an activity, a political activity performed by the governmental officials as rulers and by the people and their organised groups as citizens and political parties and pressure groups. For the moderns, politics is an activity, the liberals regarding it a fundamental activity so to create a good society; the Marxists declaring it as a means for effecting political and social changes. Politics, as activity, makes it closer to the people and to that extent, politics becomes an action-oriented phenomenon, more process-related than purposive; more empirical than normative; more fact-laden than value-laden. The main weakness in the modern meaning of politics is that it takes away the very 'heart' from politics, makes it soulless.

## II. Meaning of Politics

The lack of a universally agreed upon definition of politics does not imply that the topic is indefinable, that it is a simple concept which admits of no further definition, and hence, must be grasped intuitively. Nor does it imply that political scientists do not know what they are doing. As people try to give politics a meaning, they confront themselves with numerous alternatives, especially the following:

(i) One alternative seeks to embrace, in the meaning of politics, a host of activities thought to be 'political' in nature. For some, politics consists of those human behaviours which are centred on the institutions and practices of government. There are others who see politics as the process by which human organisations solve their problems, i.e., with the obstacles they perceive to exist between their present conditions and the goals they wish to pursue. There are still others who think of politics as those human interactions involving the use, or the threat of use, of power or authority. David Easton hints at a perspective in which politics is regarded as a process by which scarce resources (human, or material) are allocated within a social unit (a city, a state, or a nation) for the purpose of providing for human needs and desires.

(ii) Another alternative worth consideration in the process of giving politics a meaning is to ask certain questions and find their answers in politics. Some such questions may be mentioned here: How do the artifacts of human organisation (formal groups, political parties, nation-states, international organisations, for example) persist through situations of strains, stresses and changing circumstances? How do some individuals or groups first achieve and then maintain preponderant influence or power? What social, cultural and economic conditions nurture different types of political order (e.g., anarchy, democracy, authoritarianism, totalitarianism)? The second alternative is less an attempt at defining politics than an endeavour to describe what it does.

(iii) The third alternative attempting to give politics a meaning concentrates on the major or important categories of activity or behaviour that constitute politics. According to some, conflict is the essence of politics. Dahl, therefore, says: "Politics and conflicts are born as inseparable twins". Likewise, power and influence demonstrate certain relationships and activities that become a part of the study of politics and therefore, are included in what constitutes the meaning of politics. Leadership, decision-making process and the like are the other categories of activities or behaviour among individuals and groups, and therefore, are considered while giving politics a meaning.

William Bluhm attempts to combine, as nearly as possible, three alternatives explaining the meaning of politics, when he says: "Politics is a social process characterised by activity involving rivalry and cooperation in the exercise of power, and culminating in the making of decisions for a group."

Politics, keeping its essence in view, means three things: political activity, political process and political power. Because it is an activity, it is a process, and because politics is both an activity as well as a process, it aims at attaining power.

(a) As a political activity, politics is an endless action. As political activity, politics means more than one thing: it includes conflict, controversy, struggle—all as forces of reasoning, persuasion, adjustments, agreements, compromises, diplomacy, use of peaceful means and at times those of forcible ones. Michael Oakeshott had once said: "In political activity, then, men sail a boundless and bottomless sea; there is neither harbour for shelter nor floor for anchorage; neither starting point nor appointed destination. The enterprise is to keep afloat on an even keel; the sea is both a friend and an enemy". Political activity, as an essence of politics, is only activity, an endless march.

(b) Politics implies political process. Political process is a next step of political activity. Political activity is performed in a frame, within the already prescribed procedures, through institutions both political and non-political. Participation, in elections, for example, is a political activity which is done in accordance with the norms set by political institutions. But in the processes of elections, some non-political institutions do play their role: there is a role of religion in politics; there is the role of castes during elections. Pressure and interest groups, as non-political institutions, participate in the electoral processes.

(c) Politics as political power is described as a 'certain kind of human relationship; so feels Carl Friedrich. It is a relationship characterised as the rulers on the one hand, and the ruled on the other.

It is a device explaining the coercive element, the government's authority to exercise its process as derived from the people in democracies. In that sense and to that extent, politics as political power is the constrained use of social power", as Goodwin and Klingemann rightly point out.

The above discussion leads us to identify characteristic features of what may constitute the meaning of politics:

(i) Politics implies activity, a practical activity done by the individuals in public life. It is, therefore, something related to public, the people, the group at large.

(ii) Politics is related to 'political' mainly or what influences politics.

(iii) Politics is about power, i.e., about the capacity of social agents, agencies, and institutions to maintain or transform their social or physical environment. Politics is, as David Held says, 'about the resources which underpin this capacity (power) and about the forces that shape and determine its exercise'.

(iv) Politics is found in a system which is 'political' in nature. It works where political system is found or where political action is undertaken. This means that the extent of politics extends to political patterns of human relationships.

(v) Politics implies a pattern of political relationship—those who command on the one hand and those who obey on the other.

(vi) Politics includes government and its institutions, rules and procedures but it, at the same time, thrives within a broader system, called the social system.

(vi) Politics as the study of political system, itself a part of social system, studies problems which affect the whole fabric of human society.

By way of conclusion, one may like to say with William Walsh: We study politics, then, as it occurs in political systems. These systems (though abstractions)—consist of persistent patterned sets of relationships among human beings, relationships that have to do with power, rule, or authority.

Owing to its omni-presence, it is easy to understand that politics is substantially influenced by many elements of the broader social system (and one may add, ecological system) of which it is a part.' Stephen Wasby rightly regards politics as one aspect of the society. He says: "Even if special institutions are developed to perform political functions, politics is never separate from the larger society. In a sense, it is simply a facet of social system...". He continues: "To study politics is to take the social whole in order to examine one part of its structure and operation. When we do this, we need to know what the political aspect of society—the political subsystem, or polity—does for the entire society".

Politics, as a word, has a connotation different from political science, political theory, political thought. It is essentially a practical activity as against political science, political theory and political thought which have the theoretical aspect too. Garner says that 'politics' is used "to describe the activities by which public officials are chosen and political policies promoted or in a wider sense, the sum-total of the activities which have to do with the actual administration of public affairs." It is, thus, the business or activity related to the actual conduct of the affairs of the state. It is the art of statesmanship, and as such is an art; it is the art of diplomacy, and as such is more of maneuvering art. It does not deal as much with the origin of the state as with its functioning; it does not relate itself as much with the forms of government as with its actual working; it does not concern itself as much with the theory and objects of legislation as with the making and unmaking of laws; it does not go into the details of party-systems as with the elections and the election-campaigns. It is the practice of the theory of politics.

## III. Politics: Classical, Institutional and Functional

Politics is described differently in different times. Its three perspectives reflect the varying epistemological and methodological aspects. Their brief discussion would help understand the meaning of politics rather more clearly, historically:

### (*a*) *The Classical Perspective*

The classical perspective of politics is best represented by Aristotle in his *Politics,* though there is ethico-religious fervour of politics demonstrated in the whole of ancient and medieval Western tradition from Socrates–Plato to Renaissance-Reformation days. For Aristotle, politics was more than the hierarchical relations of domination and subordination; it was a relation among equals.

Politics, Aristotle insisted, existed only in a realm of freedom, freedom being an atmosphere where equal people, i.e. citizens participate in collective decision-making. The essence of politics, in Aristotlian thinking, was the participation of equals, in achieving a mode of life characterised by human excellence. Human excellence, Aristotle said, was possible if the citizens shared a common system of values, are united in their perspectives of the just and the unjust, act cooperatively to achieve their common objectives. Human freedom, according to Aristotle, makes political life possible within the political community; equal citizens identify the values they wish to live by; they alone create rules and institutions to instantiate those values. Dubbing politics as the master art, Aristotle thought of politics involving a form of practical knowledge concerning both, what is good for the community and how to attain that good.

The essential characteristics of the classical perspective of politics as stated above can be summed up as under:

(i) Politics does not constitute activities of ruling; ruling activities do not, therefore, make the whole of what politics is all about; politics is not a relationship between the rulers and the ruled.

(ii) Politics exhibits a relationship, among the equal citizens. Indeed, everyone, in ancient Greece, was not a citizen. Citizenship, then, was a virtue associated with free men. Those who constituted citizens, though a very small in number, were equals among themselves. A vast majority of population in ancient Greece—women, aliens, slaves—were not citizens.

(iii) Politics was a relationship among the equal citizens; it was not a relationship between citizens and non-citizens. It was the domain of citizens, among themselves.

(iv) Politics as a relation among equal citizens was their participation in collective decision-making as to how they would lead the public life so to be able to attain human excellence.

(v) Political life in political community is a testament to human freedom.

(vi) Politics involves political knowledge on the part of the equal citizens who, through their efforts, identify values of human existence and create institutions and through them, the rules to instantiate those values.

(vii) What unites citizens is sharing of a common system of values and their efforts to act jointly and cooperatively so as to attain the common objectives.

The classical conception of politics is an activity among the people called the citizens: citizens who share the common objectives; objectives which demonstrate shared and common values; values that perpetuate the good of the community in which citizens live; the concept of good means human excellence, human freedom and valued human existence for which the citizens create corresponding institutions and rules. Aristotle's politics is limited to community life; community means practically the citizens, only the citizens; a microscopic, but the important part of the community; citizens who are the propertied people, mostly the feudals who hold the land but do not work on it.

*(b) Institutional Perspective*

For the larger part of the Western modern society, the 'institutional' perspective of politics dominated the discipline of political science. On this view, politics involves the activities of the official institutions as established by traditions and constitutions. It came to be understood as state, government, political system, through their organs together with the functions and powers as assigned by the written constitutions or the un-written traditions. Great efforts are made for the interpretation of specific constitutional provisions and to the historical investigation of the means by which such provisions are subtly expanded and transformed over time. Politics, thus, came to be known as explaining what constitutes sovereignty; what is the specific role of the monarchs, the rulers; limitations on the powers of the state; the structure of the governmental institutions and their functions and powers. Most definitions of politics, until the beginnings of the twentieth century, revolve around the state and the state machinery, heavily oriented towards law: formal, legalistic, structural. The definitions of politics given by Garner, Gettell, Garies, Pollock, Bluntschlli, Leacock, Seeley, Gilchrist and a host of others reveal the institutional meaning together with others like Bagehot (*The English Constitution*, 1865-67), Woodrow Wilson (*The Congressional Government*), James Bryce (*The American Commonwealth, Modern Democracies*, Vol. I, II), Arthur Bentley (*Process of Government*), Charles Merriam (*New Aspects of Politics*), Herman Finer (*Theory and Practice of Modern*

*Governments*), F.C. Strong (*Modern Political Institutions*), Truman (*The Governmental Process*).

The characteristic features of the institutional perspective of politics can be summed up as under:

1. Politics is an activity related to the state, government and their institutions.
2. It relates to processes concerned with the composition, powers and functions of the governmental bodies.
3. It is related to the procedures constituting the formation and working of governmental structures as prescribed by the traditions and constitutions.
4. It is related to elections, electoral processes, political parties, and the like.
5. Politics that emerges from the constitutional perspective is largely formal, mostly legalistic and usually structural.
6. It has no reference of the classical conception of values and ethics. Its constitutional and legalistic elements are rather obvious.
7. Its hyperfactualism robs its realism: The English political system looks, theoretically, absolute monarchical, constitutional limited government if we glance its form of government; actual democratic republic for all practical purposes.

David Easton describes the institutional meaning of politics as intuitive: we describe it as we want to describe as what strikes us as to what politics is. Furthermore, if politics is to be understood solely in terms of the state, what can be said of those societies in which no state exists; if the constitution provides a blueprint for the operations of the state, how about the states which have no constitutions, or how about those states whose constitutions mask the real distribution of power or how to know and explain the revolutionary movements if the governments are the locus of politics? The institutional perspective of politics conceals more than it reveals.

*(c) Functional Perspective*

Dissatisfaction with the institutional approach has given birth to a variety of interpretations with regard to the meaning of politics. But all these interpretations have, David Easton tells us, one quality in common: they all identify politics as a kind of activity, behaviour or function. That is why that all these meanings with regard to politics assign some functions to politics: some describe politics as power—how to attain it, maintain it and preserve it. By 1930s, Catlin, Merriam and later Lasswell and Kaplan, Key argued for an interpretation of politics as a set of power relationships. Some thought of it as a means for allocating authoritatively values in the society (David Easton). Some looked at it as 'conflicts' and their 'resolution' (Dyke and Odegard), while others describe it as an activity (Myerron and Banfield). The behavioural politics is committed to value-free political activities and the post-behavioural, to politics which is relevant and action-oriented. The Marxists regard politics as a means for class-struggle; it is considered as a pursuit of common good in developing countries. The post-modernists (Foucault—*The Order of Things*) regard politics as a productive force which creates a world in its own image.

The functional perspective of politics regards it as an activity which, in the liberal-pluralist tradition, seeks to conciliate common interest; in the Marxian tradition, politics acts as a means of class struggle culminating in its very abolition; in the communitarian and in the developing nations, politics works for the pursuit of common good. These may be discussed as under:

(*i*) *Politics as the Conciliation of Interests*: The conciliation of interests is characteristic of liberal political theory, either classical or contemporary. The classical liberalism took upon itself the task of resolving conflicting interests as they existed among the individuals, whereas, the contemporary liberalism attempts to bring about conciliation of antagonistic interests as they are found among the numerous groups. What was individualism in classical liberal political theory, so has been pluralism in contemporary liberal thought. It is not, therefore, surprising to equate classical liberalism with individualism and contemporary liberalism with pluralism. Within the framework of individualist theory, individual interests' weighted more than the social interest, whereas pluralism seeks to highlight what is "social" in the individual. In both, politics is an effort to bring about the rule of law in which power guarantees the general interest and the common good against the pressure of private interests. Maurice Duverger says: "Politics is a means of realising the integration of all citizens into the community and of creating the just state," a state that acts as an umpire in the resolution of opposing interests.

Contemporary liberalism is an improvement over classical liberalism, as pluralism is, over individualism. Between the state as essentially an evil and the one that is an institution of service, there had stood a state that was regarded a positive good. Between Locke, Smith and Bentham on the one hand, and Laski, Maclver, Barker, Lindsay and Tawney on the other, there had stood John Stuart Mill, rightly described as a philosopher in transition and Thomas Hill Green who provided a bridge between classical liberalism and contemporary liberalism. If Locke, Smith and Bentham took up the cause of *laissez-faire* state on the one hand, Laski, Maclver, Barker, Lindsay and Tawney thought of the state as a positively good institution necessary for the development of man's personality on the other. Between these two, Mill and Green removed all doubts about the evil nature of political power. Mill, as an individualist, was closer to classical liberals than to the modern ones and Green, on the other hand, as an idealist, was nearer the contemporary liberals than to the classical ones.

From late 1880s, liberalism entered a new phase. John Stuart Mill and more than him, Thomas Hill Green made possible, through their writings, what may be called 'social' liberalism. Social liberalism was different from 'individual' liberalism (i.e., early, classical, economic) in so far as the good of the individual came to be thought as tied to the good of the whole community. The atomism of the formal classical view came to be regarded as morally and sociologically naive. Poverty, unemployment and ill-health came to be regarded, no longer, as the concerns of the isolated individuals, but had become social issues which had to be dealt with by the state as well. Liberty was no longer a *laissez-faire* affair, but had come to be regarded as best only when regulated or controlled.

Social liberalism of the late 19th and the early 20th century had paved way for a pluralist society with contemporary liberalism as its philosophy. The period between the two world wars (1919-1939) and the one that followed them, as also the impact of the socialist movements, created a state that was to be welfare; a society that was to be pluralist and a politics that was to resolve conflicting interests of the groups. That is how liberalism, in its numerous shades (first as 'individual' liberalism, then 'social', and ultimately 'welfare') have reached 1960s and 1970s. This is not to say that liberalism, now, has attained its demise, for an attitude and a mental frame as liberalism is, never dies. The latest and probably the recent variation of liberalism goes a step backward and exalts 'individual' within a broader frame of the society. This, atleast, is the essence of what has come to us through the writings of John Rawls, Robert Nozick, Friedrich Hayek and a host of other scholars like them.

The liberals, particularly the classical ones, are formally committed to individualism. *Individualism* revolves around individual. For the individualists, individual is both more real, than and prior to society. The individual, in the classical liberal format, is usually understood as a single, self-enclosed being 'shut up in his own subjectivity.' In terms of natural rights, the individual, the classical liberals would say, 'own his own body', the 'proprietor of his own person', as Macpherson uses the term and is, therefore, linked with 'possessive individualism'. Individualism or the classical liberalism, is primarily a philosophy of man, about him by highlighting his individual interests and for him in so far as it demands the fulfillment of his interests. It, thus, begins with the individual and ends up with the individual. For the individualists, the individual is selfish because he has his particular interests; he becomes social because he finds others as instruments for the satisfaction of his interests. In this setting, he is social. Because he is social, he knows how to extract from others what he himself needs, and also because he can distinguish between what is good and what is bad, he becomes rational. The individualist argument runs like this: As the individual, with his particular interests, wants to satisfy and maximise his interests, he finds himself in the society of people. Before the individuals, eager to fulfil their interests, break their heads, a body of rules and regulations is brought in to set the conflicting interests to order. This is from where politics starts.

For the early liberals, politics acts as the arbiter and the balancer. It reconciles the antagonistic interests of the individual and attempts to bring a state of balance; the state, only doing limited functions and also possesses limited powers.

Positive liberalism, as a reaction to negative liberalism of the early liberals, sought to reconcile individuality with community—

individual good with general good. T.H. Green, as the most significant exponent of positive liberalism, argued that society was a means for individual self-realisation and development, and that politics exists to draw forth the potentialities inherent in the individual. Green emphasised that self-realisation and self-development, could be made possible only within the framework of social institutions, including state. Both Mill and Hobhouse propagated Green's point of view that in individual's own good also lies the good of the community.

We cannot divorce our own good from the good of others. Mill had rightly observed that if a government was to be a government for the people, it has to be a government of all the people, representing all the interests of the society. Thus, the way was paved for pluralism which was, more or less, a variety of the 20th century liberalism. Kariel says: "As the exclusively proper way of ordering and explaining public life, it (pluralism) remains the heart of the liberal ideology of the Western world." Hence, in the changed conditions of the 20th century, a welfare state and the concept of 'general interest' were to be, obviously, associated with the pluralist theory.

The pluralist politics is, essentially, group politics. *Pluralism* is no longer a theory against the absolute nature of state sovereignty as it has initially emerged in the writings of Laski, Maclver, Lindsay or Barker. It has come to incorporate, as the 20th century American scholars, like Robert Dahl would suggest, a network of groups competing for capturing political power. David Held says: "Pluralists put particular weight on the processes creating, and resulting from, individuals combining their efforts in groups and institutions in the competition for power." Hence, the pluralist politics is mainly concerned with sets of individuals maximizing their common interests.

As individual interests find expression in group interests for purposes of fulfillment, it is, therefore, natural that there must exist clash of interests among the groups. Pluralism is a political theory of competing and mutual opposing groups. If resolution of conflicting interests among the individuals has been a characteristic of classical liberalism, the conciliation of conflicting interests among the groups is characteristic of modern liberalism or what may rightly be called pluralism. Individuals, without owing anything to the society, attempt to fulfil their interests and in the process, maintain a balance in the society—all this in the *laissez faire* atmosphere. Groups, without owning anything to the society, attempt to compete and control power over other groups so as to promote their own interests, but in the process, create an equilibrium. Accordingly, if the individual good was the motive to cover the risk of wholesale violence in individualistic era, the general good is the motivating force to cover the risk of wholesale anarchy in the modern times.

From the pluralist point of view, as with the classical liberals too, the state appears to be a neutral arbiter, impartially controlling the conflicts of social groups. Politics, Schwarzmantel says, supervises and regulates social antagonism, without taking sides. Politics, Bernard Crick says is a process of "ruling divided societies without undue violence." In the words of Duverger, "Politics is an attempt to resolve the individual and group conflicts without physical violence." As the pluralist theory is a group theory, its politics, as such, is competitive and not consensual, but in no way restricts politics to act as an umpire, for the personnel of the state who do not favour any one set of social or economic interests. The pluralistic politics, being competitive, gets reflected in more than one way—in elections, in dialogues, in legislative debates. "The pluralist view sees politics as a process of choice and competition... is marked by choice between, and competition among, a variety of political parties and pressure groups" ensuring "the diffusion of power", says Schwarzmantel.

The neutrality of the state, as the axiom develops in pluralist theory, is oftenly linked with a view of the state as an agent of reform. The pluralist state is becoming, increasingly, *a welfare state* is no longer an instrument of the capitalist class, but is one that puts into effect schemes of social welfare and has, as in most of the European countries, assumed a more active and interventionist role than ever before. Hobson, Hobhouse, Dewey have viewed the state as an integral part of the economic and social life of the community. It was not just concerned, as in the heydays of *laissez faire,* with freeing individuals from obstacles to their economic activity, but was actively involved in the promotion of a better life for its citizens. This is, in fact, the essence of the welfare state as the pluralists view it.

The above discussion of politics as the conciliation of interests as represented in the liberal pluralist—neoliberal tradition has, as has been seen above, certain *characteristic features*. Some of these can be stated, briefly, as under:

1. Individuals or groups of individuals constitute the basic unit;
2. Individuals have their own interests;
3. It is natural that the interests of the individuals/groups may clash with one another;
4. Individuals/groups are autonomous and possess their rights protected unto themselves;
5. The state comes to bring conciliation of interests;
6. The state discovers the common interest, resolves conflicts arising out of the opposing interests;
7. Politics is a fundamental activity that helps create a state which acts as an umpire;
8. Between the individual and the state, politics is for the individual, for the promotion of his/her personality.

Politics, as the conciliation of interests, admits the capitalistic view of what politics is all about. Politics does not resolve interests, but protects and promotes the interests of the capitalist class. In the name of political liberty, the capitalistic politics ignores economic equality. Inequality remains as the basis of the capitalist society; politics is politics among the capitalists, the working/non-possessing classes either stay away or become victims of the capitalistic exploitation.

(*ii*) *Politics as Class Struggle*: Politics, as class struggle, is characteristic of the Marxist theory as the conciliation of interests has been that of liberation. The liberals, of either yester years or of today, consider individual and group interests, and conflicts among them as natural. The Marxists, on the other, regard these conflicts as man-made, and thus, not-natural. If the liberal, pluralists including, believe that the conflicts among the individuals or groups are resolvable, the Marxists hold the view that these conflicts are irreconcilable. So the Marxists, as Duverger tells us, declare that politics "is conflict, struggle, in which power allows those who possess it to ensure their hold on the society and to profit by it."

The basic assumptions of liberal politics as the conciliation of interests are unacceptable to Marxists. The Marxists, unlike the liberals, do not think that the conflicts among the individuals or the groups are natural; that there is something called as the general, common or social interest; that the state acts as the balancer of interests and is, therefore, non-partisan. On the contrary, the Marxists hold the view that the common interest, for all practical purposes, becomes, and always is, the interest of the economically dominant class; that politics is, and has always been, a class category. Politics, according to the Marxists, arose in class society and would remain until there exist mutually antagonistic classes in the society. The class society is represented by class politics where mutually opposing classes would continue to remain in the state of struggle against each other. It is only in the classless society that politics would disappear, wither away as Marx had once pronounced.

For the Marxists, the state is no impartial institution. They say that the state originated at a particular stage of social development, the stage when there emerged opposing classes. Until then, there was no state, no state apparatus, no political activity. Politics, the Marxists hold the view, was, thus the result of the class society. It arose to serve the economically dominant class and conversely, exploit the non-owning class. The state, in any class society, is a class institution, an oppressive organ, a partisan organisation, an executive machinery for purposes of exploiting the poor. The state, being a class instrument, remains as long as there remains the class society. The existence of the dictatorship of the proletariat in the socialist society, following the capitalist one, is a transitional phenomenon, existing until the overthrow of the capitalist system lock, stock and barrel and the establishment of the socialist society. That is why the Marxists regard politics not merely an instrument of class struggle but also a means for bringing about socio-economic changes in the society, transforming the class character of the society into its classlessness, from the capitalist society to the socialist one.

The characteristic *features* of politics as class struggle can be stated as under:

1. The conflicts, among the individuals and groups are not natural. They are the result of the class society.
2. The common interest is nothing more than the interest of the economically dominant class.
3. The state is never a neutral institution. It is what its base wants it to be. It is partisan in so far as it protects and promotes the dominant class and conversely oppresses the weaker ones.

4. Classes originate because of the origin of private ownership of the means of production.
5. As these classes stand in opposition against each other, they keep fighting. The change in the actors does not result substantially, in the nature of class war.
6. The class struggle phenomenon exists only in the class society. It is economic, political and ideological. In the classless society, there is no class struggle.
7. Revolutions, as the culminating stage of the class struggle, serve as the engines of social development, from the lower stage to the higher one.
8. The future of classes is their virtual abolition as and when the class society moves into classless society. In the interim period (the socialist society) between capitalism and communism, the working class would attempt to exploit the capitalists—the earlier expropriators.
9. Politics protects and promotes the dominant classes in class society.
10. It acts as a means of political and economic change and through the medium of revolutions, the outgoing class society gives way to in coming society: from lower stage of society's development to higher one.
11. In classless socialist society, politics, as the dictatorship of proletariat, would abolish capitalism and establish socialism, paving way for its complete abolition in the classless and stateless society of communism.
12. The communist society would be a society without the state; without politics.

Politics as class struggle has remained a subject of attack from many quarters. The *anti-socialists* emphasise, not on the class struggle, but on the natural harmonies of society. The *sociologists,* regarding the Marxian concept of class struggle as limited, highlighting numerous types of struggles in the society—racial, social, cultural, civilizational. The *revisionists* in Germany, the *Fabians* in England and the *syndicalists* in France dubbed the Marxian theory of class struggle as inadequate, parochial or not radical enough. The existence of politics as an instrument of class struggle on the one hand and as an apparatus for socio-economic transformation of society on the other: one negative and the other positive: one destructive and the other constructive makes confusion more confounded than removing it.

(*iii*) *Politics as the Pursuit of Common Good*: Politics invariably implies, among other things, political power—power to make laws, take decisions, enforce them and punish the guilty. But in doing all this, it does not and, in fact, cannot set aside its attempts to first search and then seek the fulfillment of common interest. No state, if it avows to be democratic, can survive for long unless it promotes what is in the interest of all or most of them.

To equate common interest with common good is not uncommon. The problem arises only when one endeavours to know as to what common good is. Common good may mean common interest, social justice, welfareism or good and just life for all alike. It may also imply good of all or/and good for all, actions done impartially or done without prejudice to others. Vague as the term is, common good means many things to many people.

The idea of common good is not new. The ancients, whether eastern or western, did point out as to what constitutes the common good. "If all communities (meaning here associations, numerous groups) aim at some good," Aristotle once wrote of the *polis* "the state or political community, which is the highest of all, and which embraces all the rest, aims and in a greater degree than any other, at the highest good." Much late Rousseau thought of common preservation and the general well-being the very essence of common good. But this is not enough!

Certain governmental functions such as defence, order, prevention of epidemic, good roads, though benefit all or nearly all, do not constitute the whole of common good. This is so because the idea of common good is associated, primarily and essentially, with services such as education, old age pensions, medical facilities and the like. The essence of common good lies in what is done in the interest and welfare of all the people. It is closer to the promotive, more than protective, functions of the state.

Surely, the properties of common good include the promotion of the interests of the people. We would not call a certain action of the government as promoting common good if it harms more than it benefits the people. None would challenge the fact that the idea of common good must incorporate in itself the realisation of some goal. There is yet something more to it. If common good means the realisation of some goal or aim, the question which assumes importance is the number of people whose interests are to be realised. Would we say that the promotion of the interests of majority is a common good? Benn and Peters say: "Neither is the common good merely the good of the majority; for we often think it right, for example, to tax the majority to relieve a needy minority; and we should condemn majority action if it took no account of suffering inflicted on the few merely because they are a few." For them, to seek common good means "to try to act justly," "deciding impartially between all claims and trying to satisfy those for which the best case can be made out."

So understood, common good is both an objective to be realised and a procedure to be followed. It is an objective in so far as it can be defined precisely and achieved through the medium of the state. It is a procedure in so far as it demands of the state to act in the most impartial manner.

Common good, both as an objective and a procedure, is closely associated with a state democratically constituted. Opinions may differ with regard to the contents of common good or what functions and services should or should not be enlisted as part of the common good, but unless a state is a state of all the people, it can not be a state for all the people. The idea of common good has emerged and developed with the evolution and growth of 'democracy'. To talk of 'common good' prior to our modern democratic age is a mere phantasm. In ancient times, the idea of common good was merely an ethical idea, a sheer ideal and a model to be adopted in real life. During the medieval monarchical days, 'common good' existed either in the religious precepts or in the philanthropy of the autocratic czars as expressed in certain relief measures. It is only with the advent of 'democracy' that the idea of common good assumes importance as a matter of peoples' claim on the state. The liberals touched the 'common good' mark after travelling through *laissez faire* and welfare state. The socialists, especially of the Marxian type, soon discovered the totalitarian state turning into an authoritarian one, and , therefore, pushing a step backward, contented themselves with the ideal of common good.

The goal of common good is more relevant to the developing nations than to the developed ones. The developed nations see in 'common good' state's efforts to act as impartially as possible. They find it in its procedure. The developing countries, economically and socially backward as they are, regard 'common good' as an objective as well as procedure. The tasks of nation-building and modernisation being undertaken in the developing nations, reflect, in ultimate, nothing but the realisation of 'common good'.

The notion of 'common good' has cut across all modern ideologies, for it has been the goal set to be achieved by all of them. The individualists like John Locke and Adam Smith saw good of the society emerging from the good of the individual. The utilitarians like Jeremy Bentham found common good in the 'greatest happiness of the greatest number.' T.H. Green, the idealist, held the view that common good is attained when the state becomes an obstacle against all obstacles. The utopian socialists like Saint Simon thought the good of community as a condition for the good of the individual. Marx insisted that common good could be realised only in a classless society.

The communitarians like Michael Sandel, Michael Walzer and Charles Taylor were not the first to invoke the idea of community as a reaction against the idea of 'individual'. Hegel, Green, Bosanquet, Tawney, Williams, Wolff had, in their different ways, provided their critiques on what was mischievous in liberalism. The communitarians can, at best, be regarded as the latest critics of liberalism.

The communitarians believe that common good cannot be determined by abstract reasoning, nor are they freely chosen by atomized moral agents, but rather arise out of and are implicit in the ways of life of particular communities. Condemning the liberals for having built individualism, subjectivism, atomism, instrumentalism, contract-based and market-oriented liberalism, the communitarians declare community as the source of political values and of common good. The communitarian argument can be summed up as under:

1. Common good, the communitarians say, cannot be developed by abstract philosophical reasoning. Nor is it the product of individual preference or emotional attitude. Rather, it is embodied in the community itself. So understood, community serves as the basis of practical reason and political judgement, including common good itself.

2. The liberal theory of the self and the conception of the human condition flowing from it have been criticized by the communitarians. They argue that the self does not exist in isolation and that it, atleast, is, in part, constituted by the values of community within which the self finds himself or herself.
3. The development of community cannot be, the communitarians tell us, secured by agreement on abstract principles, but rather has to trade on values which are implicit in the way of life in community as it exists. Walzer points out: "Justice and equality can conceivably be worked out as philosophical artifacts, but a just or egalitarian society cannot be. If such a society isn't already here—hidden as it were in our concepts and categories—we shall never know it concretely or realise it in fact."

The following characteristics of politics as the pursuit of common good are notable:

1. Politics is not merely an agency for reconciling the conflicting interests of the individuals. The emphasis is not on 'the individual' but on what is 'common' for all the individuals.' Politics discovers what is 'common' for all and thereafter, promotes the spirit of commonalty.
2. Politics is not 'class struggle' as the Marxists insist. If it were so, the dictatorship of the proletariat, howsoever transitional it might be, would not have been, as Lenin said, better than the bourgeois state quantitatively as well as qualitatively. Class permeation, and not class conflict, is the essence of the state.
3. The idea of common good presupposes a state that serves and not the one that orders. Benn and Peters say that the state alone is peculiarly fitted to achieve common good.
4. Politics exists to pursue common good. The range of common good lies between protection on the one end and development-conservation on the other. It begins with the establishment of social order and ends up in a state that serves all.
5. As an objective, the state has to achieve the common good; as a procedure, it has to act justly and impartially. The developed countries adopt common good more as a procedure than as an objective, whereas, the developing nations accept it both as an objective as well as a procedure.

6. Common good, as a concept, is a modern democratic phenomenon. Its geneses can be traced back in the writings of the individualists, utilitarians, idealists, socialists—both utopian and scientific. The latest to join the race are the communitarians.

Common good relates itself to the interests of the community as against those of the individual. Fairly old as the concept of common good claims itself to be, it has grown and developed with the idea of 'democracy. 'Common good' sets a goal and a way to achieve it. Politics, if it has to respond to the values of democratic norms, has to throw all its weight in pursuing the good 'common' to all.

The notion of 'common good', on both theoretical and practical grounds, is too weak to withstand its own vagueness. This is because the idea raises more questions than solves them. One is never sure as to where the boundaries of 'common good' start and where do they end. Again, one does not know the satisfaction of the interests of how many people in a society would constitute 'common good'. The government can always, including Rousseau's government based on general will, resort to arbitrariness in the name of 'common good'.

Despite all the limitations which the idea of 'common good' is supposed to contain, there is a ground and that too, a profound ground in favour of 'common good' both as a concept as well as a concrete category. The philosophers, by invoking the idea of common good, show a path to be followed by the rulers. Though 'common good' may be a distant goal, yet nothing stops any state to make an attempt approaching it. The notion of 'common good', like those of justice, equality, freedom and others, act as trend-setters and keep strengthening the idealist stream which is no less important in political theory.

## SUGGESTED READINGS

1. Bellamy, R., *Theories and Concepts of Politics: An Introduction,* (Manchester, Manchester University Press, 1993).
2. Blondel, J., *The Discipline of Politics,* (London: Butterworths, 1981).
3. Catlin, G., *The State and Method of Politics,* (New York: Archon Press, 1964).
4. Connolly, W.E., *Appearance and Reality in Politics,* (Cambridge: Cambridge University Press, 1981).

5. Crick, B., *In Defence of Politics,* (London: Weidenfeld, Nicholson, 1962).
6. Deutsch, Karl, W., *The Nerves of Government: Models of Political Communication and Control,* (New York: Free Press, 1963).
7. Duverger, Maurice, *Political Parties* (New York: Wiley, 1951).
8. Easton, David, *The Political System: An Inquiry into the State of Political Science,* (New York: Knopf, 1953).
9. Ealau, H., *The Behavioural Persuasion in Politics,* (New York: Random House, 1963).
10. Eulau H. and March J. (eds), *Political Science,* (Englewood Cliffs, NJ: Prentice-Hall, 1969).
11. Finifter A. W., (ed), *Political Science: The State of Discipline,* (Washington, DC: American Political Science Association, 1983).
12. Foueault M., *The Order of Things: An Archaeology of the Human Science,* (New York: Vintage Books, 1973).
13. Gray, H., *Liberalism: Essays in Political Philosophy,* (London: Routtedge, 1989).
14. Greenstein, F. and Polsby, N., (eds), *Handbook of Political Science,* Vol I to VII, (Reading, Mass: Adison-Wesley, 1975).
15. Key, V.O., Jr, *Politics, Parties and Pressure Groups,* (New York: Crowell, 5th ed., 1942).
16. Kymlica, W., *Liberation, Community and Culture,* (Oxford: Clarendon, 1989).
17. Lasswell, H., *Politics: Who Gets What, When and How,* (New York: P. Smith, 1950).
18. Leftwich, A., (ed), *What is Politics?* (Oxford: Blackwell, 1984).
19. Mouffe, C., *The Return of the Political,* (London: Verso, 1993).
20. Rosenblum, N., *Another Liberalism,* (Mass: Harvard University Press, 1987).
21. Sandel, M., *Liberalism and its Critics,* (Oxford: Basil Blackwell, 1989).
22. Tanenhaurs, J., and Somit, A., *The Development of Political Science: From Burgess to Behaviouralism,* (Boston: Allyn and Bacon, 1967).
23. Walzer, M., *Spheres of Justice,* (Oxford: Martin Robertson, 1983).
24. Wasby, S., *Political Science: The Discipline and Its Discussions,* (Calcutta: Scientific Book Agency, 1972).
25. Walsh, W., *Studying Politics,* (New York: Praeger, 1973).

# CHAPTER – 2

# What is Political Theory?

## I. Introduction

Nobody debates the demise of Political Theory today, for its resurgence has been a fact of history, or atleast of recent history. David Held observes that since 1970s there has been a revival of interest in Political Theory in Europe, U.S.A. and in other parts of the world. The key reasons for this revival are attributed to: (a) break-up of the post-war consensus, (b) the consequential clash of values, and (c) changes in the humanities and social sciences, particularly a renaissance in Political Thought. It is, therefore, important to know as to what Political Theory is, or what it is about, and a host of other questions relating to its evolution, development, nature and significance.

### (*a*) *What is Theory?*

Before one attempts to know the meaning of Political Theory, it is necessary to know first as to *what a theory is.* Originating from the Greek word 'Theoria', *theory* means a well-focused mental look taken at something in a state of contemplation with the intent to grasp or understand it. Arnold Brecht refers to the broad and the narrow meaning of the word 'theory'. In the broader sense, theory, he says, means 'a thinker's entire teaching on a subject (including description of facts, thinker's explanation, his conception of history, his value judgements, and his proposals of goals, policy and principles). In the narrower sense, theory, he continues, means 'explanatory' thought only or atleast primarily. It is the narrower meaning which Brecht prefers to assign to the word 'theory'.

Theory is oftenly confused with its related concepts for their boundaries overlap. Theory is not practice because, though we learn by doing, the latter has to work on some kind of base, the thinking. Theory involves a theoretical frame which practice lacks. Theory is not description because "describing" is only a part of "thinking"; its other parts include discovering, determining, augmenting, explaining and framing a phenomenon. Theory is not hypothesis, for hypothesis denotes a tentative assumption of facts and therefore, lacks what theory certainly has, definiteness. Theory is not philosophy because while theory is about 'something', philosophy is about 'everything'. Theory is not thought because it is a thought about thought and not an entire thought itself. There is much common between theory and reason, for both claim to be scientific, yet theory looks beyond reason, beyond science.

Accordingly, theory, as Karl Deutsch says, attempts to explain, order and relate disjointed data, identifies what is relevant and, therefore, points out what is missing in any phenomenon; predicts on the basis of observable facts. Theory is, therefore, a guide to practice, adds much to what is merely described, clarifies hypothesis, and as a part of philosophy explains an issue which meets the requirements of both reason and vision.

### *(b) Meaning of Political Theory*

Political Theory is a theory about what is 'political', the science and philosophy of something that is 'political'. A few definitions of Political Theory may be mentioned here:

1. "A body of thought that seeks to evaluate, explain and predict political phenomena. As a subfield of Political Science, it is concerned with political ideas, values and concepts, and the explanation of prediction of political behaviour. In this broad sense, it has two main branches: one is political philosophy or normative theory, with its value, analytic, historical and speculative concerns. The other is empirical theory, with its efforts to explain, predict, guide, research and organise knowledge through the formulation of abstract models, and scientifically testable propositions." (Political Science Dictionary)
2. Broadly it means 'as anything about politics or relevant to politics' and narrowly as 'the disciplined investigation of political problems.' (Sabine)
3. "Political Theory is an explanation of what politics is all about, a general understanding of the political world, a frame of reference. Without one we would be unable to recognise an

event as political, decide anything about why it happened, judge whether it was good or bad or decide that was likely to happen next." (Bluhm)

4. Political Theory is 'a combination of a disinterested search for the principles of good state and good society on the one hand, and a disinterested search for knowledge of political and social reality on the other'. (Andrew Hacker)
5. Political Theory is 'a network of concepts and generalizations about political life involving ideas, assumptions and statements about the nature, purpose and key features of government, state and society and about the political capabilities of human beings'. (David Held)

From the above definitions, we may specify the major aspects of the meaning of Political Theory as under:

1. The area in which Political Theory works extends to the realms of politics only—political life of a citizen, his political behaviour, his political ideas, the government he establishes and the tasks the government performs.
2. The methods, which it applies, include description, explanation, and investigation of any political phenomenon.
3. Though it is all about what is 'political', yet it attempts to understand 'political' in relation to 'social', 'economic' 'psychological', 'ecological', 'historical', 'moral' and the like.
4. Its ultimate objective is to build a good state in a good society and in the process create processes, procedures, institutions and structures historically tested and rationally attuned.
5. As a body of thought, it seeks to explain, evaluate and predict political phenomena, and in the process, builds not only scientifically testable models, but suggests values as rules of human conduct.
6. It is both prescriptive as well as explanatory.

To sum up, one may say that political theory is an overview of what the political order is about. It is a symbolic representation of what is 'political'. It is a formal, logical and systematic analysis of the processes and consequences of political activity. It is analytical, expository and explanatory. It seeks to give order, coherence, and meaning to what is described as 'political'.

(c) *Contents and Subject Matter of Political Science*

For a better understanding of the meaning of Political Theory, it would be instructive to turn to its subject-matter and content.

Politics as a political activity is usually associated with cynicism, and scepticism demonstrating self-seeking behaviour, hypocrisy, and manipulation of attitudes. Political Theory may, obviously, mean, then, a theory relating to all such negative connotations. But politics is neither politicking nor does Political Theory, a theory of political intrigues or subterfuge. If politics means what relates to 'political', then Political Theory may rightly claim to be a disciplined investigation of what constitutes political. If Political Theory deals with what relates to the domain of 'political', then its subject-matter is bound to vary from time to time. From the early Greeks to about the end of the eighteenth century, Political Theory concerned itself mostly with what politics "ought to be." Almost during the nineteenth century and the first half of the twentieth century, Political Theory dealt, largely, with the nature, and structure of government as a decision-making body. Then came a period when some of the American political scientists, under the influence of scienticism, declared the death of Political Theory as against those, mostly the British traditionalists, who kept advocating the value and usefulness of Political Theory as a guide to political action. With the culmination of debate about the decline and resurgence of political theory, the two sides came to realise the process and the purpose of political activity. As such, the concern of Political Theory, today, has been both the nature and the proper ends of government.

Political Theory, as a disciplined investigation of political problems, implies those problems which are associated with the institution of government. Indeed, Political Theory is closely related to the study of what, and why of a government, but it is, on the other hand, associated inescapably with the relationship between the government and the outer world. Political system is a part of social system and social system exists within a particular environment. The environmental bearings are to be understood to the extent they influence the social system. The social system, encompassing in itself the whole variety of social sciences, moulds and gets moulded by the political system. Political Theory, while examining any political phenomenon, has to take account of what is non-political; be it economic, moral, geo-political, cultural, ecological and what not. We need to place political theory within the realm of political system, political system within the realm of social system, social system within the period it exists and under the environment it breeds. If Political Theory, David Held says, is concerned with "what is really going on" in the political world and, thereby, with the nature and structure of political practices', then a theory of politics today must take account of the place of the polity within geopolitical and market processes, that is, within the system of nation-states, international law and global political economy.

Political Theory, being dynamic in its nature, takes deliberations on political issues which confront the world from time to time. In the pre-cold war period, Political Theory had to face several political problems, and hence its concerns and challenges were different. Now, the political problems are varied, the concerns are different and so are its challenges which it faces today. Broadly speaking, Political Theory deals with contents such as (a) social justice, (b) changing welfare activities, (c) varying democratic systems with emphasis on mass participation, (d) feministic challenges to change the whole of political theory today, (e) environmentalist problems and stress in green democracy, (f) post modernism, (g) terrorism and their impact on global politics, and (h) new social movements and their impact on civil society and the like.

Political Theory does not, and in fact, should not exist in isolation. It exists within a context. To understand political theory is to understand the context. The subject-matter of Political Theory includes understanding of what is really 'political', to link political within what is non-political, and to integrate and co-ordinate the results of the numerous social sciences for knowing its own nature. Its scope is not limited to what it constitutes, but to what exists in the periphery and beyond.

The focus of the content and subject-matter of Political Theory is what goes on in political world. Accordingly, its basic components must be determined. Arnold Brecht refers to some units of Political Theory, especially the following.

1. Group and not the individual is the real basic concept in Political Theory.

2. As Political Theory deals with group, it is natural that there should be clash of interests not only among the individuals, but also among the numerous groups. As a result, equilibrium or reconciliation of opposing interests has to serve the other component of Political Theory.
3. As group life lies at the heart of Political Theory, the concepts with which it concerns itself are, or should be, power, influence, control, legitimacy, justice and the like.
4. Another unit of Political Theory is action-oriented philosophy. No Political Theory can be successful without action.
5. To understand political theory is to know its agents and its actors, who are called the elite. Elite, therefore, constitutes another component of Political Theory.
6. Choice and decision-making are also the units of Political Theory because they help know the seat where power rests.

Suggesting that the task of defining what is political as a continual one, Sheldon Wolin includes the following in the contents of political theory: (a) a form of activity centering around the quest for competitive advantage between groups, individuals or societies; (b) a form of activity conditioned by the fact that it occurs within a situation of change and relative scarcity; and (c) a form of activity in which the pursuits of advantage produces consequences of such magnitude that they affect the whole society or a substantial portion of it in a significant way.

To make the contents of Political Theory relatively identifiable, it may be suggested that it needs to address itself to the following major themes:

(i) Institutions and laws that frame peoples' collective life: state, governments, political institutions and laws framed by them.
(ii) Resolution of peoples' ever-recurring conflicts and disagreements, wars, peace problems and the like.
(iii) Problems such as power competition, conflict, deprivation, violence and the like, threatening social/collective life.
(iv) Nature and proper ends of the state and government and political system.
(v) Politicization and the emerging problems associated with it: political socialisation, political culture, political development,

political communication, impact of social movements and of revolution, etc.

(vi) Political elite and leadership, political parties and pressure groups.

(vii) Concerns, such as social justice, equality, freedom, democratic participation, social movements relating to gender, environment and pollution-free society.

(viii) Modernisation and post-modernism.

(*d*) *Political Theory: Major Streams*

Three major streams are mentioned while explaining the evolution and growth of Political Theory. These are as under:

(i) Classical Political Theory

(ii) Modern Political Theory

(iii) Contemporary Political Theory

(*i*) *Classical Political Theory:* Political theory, in its classical tradition, is not related as much to periodisation as is to the major themes of study. The classification of political theory into classical, modern and contemporary is, indeed, thematic. What divides the classic or the traditionalist from the modern is the element of science in the latter and its absence in the former. Philosophy dominates the classical tradition of political theory whereas the science predominates the modernist. There may be an Aristotle and a Thomas, in the ancient and medieval periods of the West, who may emphasise on the science element while discovering the laws or public life and there may be a Strauss, in our times, who may see the utility of philosophy in the study of politics. Likewise modern political theory and contemporary political theory are to be distinguished. While all modern political theory may not be contemporary, most of contemporary political theory is always modern: modern political theory is empirical and scientific whereas contemporary political theory is philosophical and historical as well; modern political theory is present-oriented while contemporary political theory is future-oriented. Contemporary political theory attempts to synthesise the essence of both classical and modern political theory.

Political theory, in its classic form, emerged in ancient Greek culture, in the writings of Socrates, Plato and Aristotle, and continued until the beginning of the nineteenth century. The classical paradigm, according to Sheldon Wolin, relating to political theory, consisted of the following:

1. The classical political theory was the practice of systematic enquiry whose aim was to acquire reliable knowledge about matters concerning the people. As a philosophical pursuit, theory sought to establish a rational basis for belief, as a politically inspired pursuit, it sought to establish a rational basis for action.
2. The classical political theory identified the political with the common involvements, which men shared as partners. The Greek *Polis,* the Roman *res publica* and the medieval-times usage of *commonweal* denoted a sharing of what is common.
3. Its basic unit of analysis had always been the *political whole:* the *polis,* the *res public* or the commonweal and in the process, functioned and what their effect was on the quality of life in the political whole—the state. Political theory, in its classic form, emerged to view the state as composed of, and dependent upon, various inter-related structures, which denoted activity, relationships and belief. *Activity,* for example, may relate to ruling, warfare, education, religious practices, production of commodities; *relationships* may involve those between social classes, between types of superiority and inferiority, between the authorities and the subjects; *belief* may mean anything, i.e. concerning gods, justice, equality, natural law and the like.
4. The notion that political theory related itself to the political whole, the state, gave way to an idea of system, an order and the resultant conceptions of balance, equilibrium, stability and harmony. No wonder if classical political theory tried to analyse the sources of conflicts, anarchy, instability, anomies and revolution, it also attempted to enunciate the principles of justice to form a guide for the discharge of duties in the political community.
5. The classical political theory thrived on the significance of comparative studies for providing a more comprehensive explanation and a wider range of alternatives. Owing to this reason the classical political theory developed a classification for political forms (e.g., monarchy, aristocracy, democracy, their variants) and a set of concepts like law, citizenship, justice and participation to explain differences or similarities.

6. The classical political theory had been, largely, ethical in nature. Its response was rooted in a moral outlook: Plato advocated the ideal state, Aristotle, a state that can achieve the best possible, and St. Augustine, the city of God. The classical political theory undertook to appraise the various constitutional forms, to determine the best suited form for a particular set of circumstances, and to decide, if any, absolutely best form.
7. The classical political philosophers projected a bold and radical form of polity as the ideal. However, some dismissed the idea as utopian and visionary. The project of the ideal states was no idle pastime, but was an invaluable means of practising theory to acquire experience in its handling.

*(ii) Modern Political Theory:* Modern political theory encompasses a host of diverse trends which include the institutional-structural, scientific, positivistic, empirical, behavioural, post-behavioural and even the Marxist. Thus, when one talks of modern political theory, one talks of all these trends, which dominated the greater part of the 20th century. It is, since 1960s-1970s, that contemporary political theory started.

The classical political theory, by and large, was philosophical, normative, idealistic and to some extent, historical. Ideologically, modern political theory can be classified into two opposing divisions—the liberal and the Marxist. The liberal included the individualist, the elitist and the pluralist, liberal tradition, beginning from 15th-16th centuries, arose as a reaction against the classical political theory and after travelling through its institutional-structural voyage reached scientific-positivist-empiricist goals so to give way for the behavioural and the post-behavioural political theory. The Marxist political theory, dialectical- materialist in nature, offered diametrically opposite view to the one advocated in whole of the West.

As the classical political theory failed to position itself with the changing times of the 18th-19th centuries in the West, the modern political theory, with its institutional, behavioural and post-behavioural trends, dubbed the whole classical tradition as dull. Their advocates, from Merriam and Key and down to Dahl, Lasswell, Easton, deplored the historical-normative-evaluative tradition of the classical political theory. Instead, they laid emphasis on the scientific empirical-behavioural study as the most plausible one to understand the intricacies of politics. They stressed on 'present' rather on 'past', 'living' rather on 'dull', 'immediate' on 'remote': 'objective' rather on 'subjective': 'analytic' rather on 'philosophic': 'explanatory' rather on 'descriptive'; 'process-oriented' rather on 'purpose-oriented'; 'scientific' rather on 'theoretical'. They attempted to build a science of politics; objective, clinical, value-free, observational, measureable, operational.

Historically stated, modern political theory as it arose in the West, emerged from the shadow of positivism-empiricism. Until then, political theory, largely classical, was confined to a marginal role, being conceived at best as a body of classic texts of mostly historical interest, and usually found in philosophy, history, and logic. Positivism-empiricism denied the early political theory the status of a legitimate form of knowledge and enquiry. According to the positivist and empiricist outlooks, all knowledge is found in sensory observation; concepts and generalizations represent only the particulars from which they have been abstracted; values can not play any role in the formation of knowledge. As the meaning of concepts and theories, the positivist-empiricist believe, is directly tied to empirical observations, value-judgements, therefore, should not be accorded the status of knowledge. Accordingly, the normative statements of political theory may be characterized as mere declarations. Though positivism and empiricism was short-lived, its legacy thrived for a long time particularly in North America. This legacy was scienticism. The influence of scientism on the emerging behaviouralism and post-behaviouralism was both apparent and real. Behaviouralism, on its own, had certain features. It encouraged the systematic introduction of quantitative methods of analysis as the supreme methods of inquiry; it sought to displace the theoretical frameworks of normative political theorists by the development of empirical theory; and it decisively rejected the history of political theory as the primary source of interpretation. Post-behaviouralism was an extension of behaviouralism, adding the credos of 'action', 'relevance' and 'values' to behaviouralism. Thus, the challenge to behaviouralism came from within, from post-behaviouralism.

Modern political theory of the Western shade, as it developed over time, had certain features, particularly the following:

1. Facts and data constitute the bases of study. Facts are accumulated, explained and are used for testing hypothesis.
2. Human behaviour can be studied and regularities of human behaviour can be expressed in generalisations.
3. Subjectivity gives way to objectivity; philosophical interpretation to analytical explanation; purposive to procedural; descriptive to observational; normative to scientific.
4. Facts and values are separated. While in the early period, the facts were given all values, the values had no place in research, yet in the later period, values came to make the facts as relevant as possible.
5. The methods adopted for research and study are to be self-conscious, explicit and quantitative.
6. Political activity is an activity influenced by numerously other activities; social, economic, religious, moral, psychological, ecological and the like. Hence, inter-disciplinary synthesis is bound to yield better results.
7. "What it is" is more important than either "what it was" or "what it would be", for the present is nearer to either past or future.
8. Realism holds more weight than what is 'dull' or what is utopian. What and how and why a state does, is more relevant than what it had been doing or is likely to do.
9. Values are to support facts; substance, to forms; and theory, to research. This is the theme of post-behaviouralism.
10. The journey from behaviouralism to post-behaviouralism is a journey from status quo to social change.

The Western modern political theory combines the merits of its empirical, formal and normative shades. It is concerned with both facts and values, both description and prescription, both explanation and valuation.

At the other end of modern political theory stands the Marxist political theory. Its importance lies in change through the struggle between opposites: between relations of production and productive forces with a view to have a better mode of production; development from the lower stage to the higher one: from, say, capitalistic to socialistic and from socialistic to communistic.

The major characteristics of the Marxist political theory can, thus, be summed up as under:

1. That every phenomenon is in a flux.
2. It is in the nature of every phenomenon to attain its utmost development.
3. As such, the direction of movement is from lower to the higher stage of development.
4. The motion occurs through a dialectical method which is triple in essence. Hegel called it: thesis, anti-thesis and synthesis; Marx called it: relations of production, productive forces, and a new mode of production.
5. Between mind and matter, it is matter that dictates. Matter only produces while mind merely reflects.
6. Matter evolves because of its own law of evolution inherent in it.
7. At the roots of our whole superstructure, there is the base. The material base builds its own social, political, economic or educational super-structure. As is the base, so is the superstructure.
8. Man, labour and nature constitute the essence of social development.
9. Politics, as a class phenomenon, exists to justify the class character of a particular society. As and when class society is abolished, politics would lose all significance.
10. Politics works both ways: it destroys the fabric and values of the earlier society, and build the new society.

As such that politics, as a power, is an instrument of social and political change. The dictatorship of proletariat would abolish the capitalist society and build the socialist society. As socialism would turn into communism, politics, as state, would wither away.

*(iii) Contemporary Political Theory:* Political theorists, after 1960s and 1970s, have demonstrated the need of political theory in the fast changing world of ours. That is why that the interest in political theory is constantly growing in our times. This is partly because behaviouralism and post-behaviouralism, with their too much emphasis on science, have led us nowhere close to realities on the one hand, and partly because of the failure of the Marxism model in some parts of the world on the other. Soon, it came to be realized that political theory is more than a philosophy as it is also more than a science. Its mere reliance on philosophy robs it from being relevant and its over emphasis on science obviates it

from serving as a vision. It is not that we are parting away from our immediate past, but attempting to build on it.

If the task of political theory is, as it has been, to make us understand the political phenomenon, it is, therefore, necessary that it should confine itself to the explanation, investigation and ultimately comprehension of what relates to politics: concepts, principles and institutions. This is what contemporary political theory is doing. Brian Barry (*Political Argument,* 1965), while attempting to reconstruct and rediscover the role of political theory, attempts to 'study the relation between principles and institutions,' explanatory task of political theory should not lose sight of what it existed in the past. John Rawls (*A Theory of Justice,* 1971) refers to another task of contemporary political theory: a continuous search for truth, and suggests that the attempt can be made alongside the scientific-empirical methods. R. Nozick (*Anarchy, State and Utopia,* 1970), while rejuvenating on the recovery of political theory from its virtual demise, reverts to the individualist model of 'minimal' state and believes that contemporary political theory can solve many political problems by combining the classical ends with empirical means. The consensus, for example, (John Plamenatz; *Democracy and Illusion,* 1973) is that the empirical analysis and reflections of a logical and moral characters can co-exist in political theory.

Highlighting the characteristic features of contemporary political theory, David Held refers to the following:

1. To renew, as the history of political thought, and examining the significance of text in their historical context.
2. To revitalize the discipline as a form of conceptual analysis and in the process finding political theory as a systematic reflection upon, and classification of, the meanings of the key forms and concepts such as sovereignty, democracy, justice and the like.
3. Developed as the systematic elaboration of the underlying structure of our moral and political activities: the disclosure, examination and reconstruction of the foundations of political value.
4. Revitalized as a form of argument concerned with abstract theoretical questions and particular political issues.
5. As a critique of all forms of foundationalism, either post-modernists or the liberal defenders. It, accordingly, presents

itself as a stimulant to dialogue and to conversation among human beings.

6. Elaborated as a form of systematic model-building influenced by theoretical economics, rational choice theory and game theory, it aims to construct formal models of political processes.
7. Developed as the theoretical enterprise of the discipline of Political Science. As such it attempts to construct theory on the basis of observation and modest empirical generalizations.

David Held offers a number of distinct tasks of political theory: "first, the philosophical-concerned, above all, with the conceptual and normative; second, the empirical-analytic-concerned, above all, with the problems of understanding and explanation; and third, the strategic-concerned, above all with an assessment of the feasibility of moving from where we are to where we might like to be. To these, one must add the historical, the examination of the changing meaning of political discourse—its key concepts, theories, and concerns—over time."

The post-1970s, while witnessing new developments in Political Theory, has given rise to four distinct views:

1. With Rawls, political theory, as branch of moral philosophy has been described as essentially normative. Accordingly, the task of political theory is not only to develop general principles for evaluating the social structure, but also to design appropriate institutions, procedures and policies (see Ackerman, *Social Justice in the Liberal State,* (1980); Barry, *A Treatise on Social Justice,* (1989), and Beitz, *Political Theory and International Relations,* (1979).
2. Political Theory is primarily contemplative and reflective enquiry concerned to understand human existence in general. So understood, as was really viewed in its older form, it is neither a branch of moral philosophy nor normative in its orientation (see Taylor, *Philosophical Papers,* 1985) MacIntyre *After Virtue,* 1981; Connolly *political theory and Modernity,* 1988).
3. Political Theory is primarily concerned to articulate the self-understanding of a particular community, and that it is necessarily municipal in its scope and interpretive in its orientation (see Walzer, *Sphere of Justice,* 1983).

4. Political Theory needs to be tentative, exploratory, conversational, open-minded, ironic, sensitive. Such scholars draw inspiration from post-structuralist and post-modernist writers (see Rorty, *Contigency, Irony and Solidarity*, 1989).

## II. Nature of Political Theory

The nature of political theory is closely related to the meaning one gives to it. As there is no agreement on the meaning of political theory, there is, therefore, no agreement about the nature of political theory. There are some who describe political theory to denote the works of numerous thinkers. But this assertion makes political theory more of political thought. There are others, who equate political theory with political philosophy. While it is true, that political theory constitutes a part of political philosophy, a part can never be a whole and as part, it remains a part of the whole. There are still others, mostly the modernists, who, after incorporating science in political theory, prefer to call it political science. But, political science is the science of politics and as such it is not a history of politics, or a culture of politics, nor even a philosophy of politics whereas, political theory is a combination of all these. Political theory is usually confused with politics. The difference between the two is as much as is between theory and practice: a person may either be a politician, a political scientist, a political theorist, or a political philosopher, but he is never all in one, and seldom one in two or one in three.

### (*a*) *Political Theory: History*

That political theory, as history, has been emphatically advocated by men like George Sabine, but all history is not political theory. That political theory is a science has been forcefully emphasised by men like Robert Dahl and David Easton, but all science is not political theory. That political theory is a philosophy, has been sufficiently enunciated by men like Leo Strauss, but all philosophy is not scientific, which means that philosophy can be unscientific as well. This is not to say that political theory is devoid of history, science or philosophy.

Political theory without history is a structure without a base. In studying and analysing politics, what we learn to understand is a political tradition, and a concrete manner of behaviour. It is, therefore, proper that the study of politics should essentially be a historical study. History, we should know, is more than the tale of the dead and the buried, but is like a store-house of experience and wisdom, the sum-total, Rathore says, "and simultaneously the formation-head of a new development, something eternally significant and instructive, inseparably linked with contemporareity in the perpetual progress of mankind. Ignore history and the delight of political theory is never to be retrieved."

### *(b) Political Theory: Science and Philosophy*

Political theory without the quantum of science is unthinkable. If one defines theory as an explanation of a phenomenon, as Brecht really does, the phenomenon, without the element of science, would make it a matter of mere faith, a conviction or a belief. Theory has to have a 'science' in it, but only as much as theory needs. Too much scienticism in political theory robs the latter of its real essence. Its exponents, Rathore says, have not "succeeded in expending a cast-iron scientific theory of politics and what they have produced is a far–from–cohesive theory."

The sustenance of political theory depends on philosophy. Philosophy, as the sum-total of general laws (morals, norms, values etc. etc), has served political theory well through the ages. Philosophy, Kant says, has answered three questions: "What can I know?" "What must I do?", and "What can I hope for?" and this is what makes the philosophy a lodestar of life. Without philosophy, no political theory can ever hope to exist.

Science and philosophy, though stand on opposite poles, yet it is theory that combines the two. Theory, including political theory, has not only a philosophy, it also has a science. It is, therefore, in this background that one may say that a political theorist is both a political philosopher and a political scientist. It is, in this sense, that both political philosophy and political science are inadequate names for political theory. Brecht aptly says: "Political philosophy, political theory and political science are no longer interchangeable terms." With the emphasis placed on science and a distinction from political philosophy, political science now refers to efforts limited by the use of scientific methods in contrast to political philosophy, which is free to transcend these limits. Likewise, political theory, when opposed to political philosophy, now is usually meant to refer to scientific theory only, and when opposed to scientific theory, now is usually meant to refer to a mere philosophy.

### (c) *Political Theory: Change and Continuity*

In relation to history, political theory is the outcome of a peculiar set of historical circumstances, and as such, has a significance for all times to come. This makes the character of political theory respectable. In relation to philosophy, political theory is an attempt truly to know the nature of political things alongwith what is right, and good in them. In relation to science, political theory seeks to strive knowledge, as of facts or principles, gained by systematic study.

Contemporary political theory is more of continuity than of change. When the political scientists, in the West, were trying to bring in scienticism and empiricism, they were not rejecting all that was the essence of traditional political theory. To an extent, they were giving a new development to what is considered 'political', in a way, they were liberalising political theory from its descriptive-interpretative shackles. They did realize the utility of knowing what politics had been in a particular time and under a particular situation. They did acknowledge the teachings of a particular political philosopher and his legacy. As such, they did not dismiss as worthless in all philosophy. Seen in this sense, the empirical-scientific (behaviouralism and post-behaviouralism) trend in political theory was not a change, but a continuation of normative-philosophical tradition.

Likewise those, who attempted to look at political theory more from a sociological point of view (de Tocqueville, Graham Wallas, Bagehot and others) or more from a psychological point of view (Hobbes, for example), they were merely adding numerous dimensions so as to understand political theory more clearly. Taken as this, the emphasis laid by the American scholars during the greater part of the post-war period, in the inter-disciplinary approach in politics was not an attempt to denigrate it, but was an endeavour to give politics a fuller meaning, making it more understandable and relevant.

Similarly, recent efforts to reject scientific jargons, purely empirical-drawn conclusions and techniques-oriented models are measures to set the worthlessness of political theory aright. Contemporary political theory is not condemning all empiricism or behaviouralism. Its science element is being retained to point out beneficial in social sciences as its philosophical content useful for understanding sciences related to society. So understood, political theory is not, and has never been, a break with the past, but is one that is in the state of constant continuity. We may conclude with Isaiah Berlin, in a rather lengthy statement: "Neo-Marxism, neo-Thomism, nationalism, historicism, existentialism, antiexistential liberalism, and socialism, transportation of doctrines of natural rights and natural law into empirical terms, discoveries made by skillful application of models derived from economic and related techniques to political behaviour and the collusions, combinations, and consequences in action of these ideas indicate not the death of a great tradition, but, if anything, new and unpredictable developments."

## III. Relevance of Political Theory

A theory is described as one that enables us to organise our knowledge, orient our research and interpret our findings. But it is theory seen as a science, as a methodology and as a technique for reaching a goal. Seen as a philosophy, a theory is the enunciation of general-rules and laws as to how a man must live, a state be ordered and a society be organised. But theory, as we have seen earlier, is both a science as well as a philosophy. Defining political theory as the "critical study of the principles of right order in human social existence," Germino declares that political theory is "neither reductionist behavioural science nor opinionated ideology." It is, we must remember, a science but not a science which confines itself to propositions, capable of sensory verification, but a science that fulfills the requirements of any social science. As a political philosophy, political theory is not a utopian construction, but is one that finds out the truth of life. "Turning his back at distortions, over-simplifications, sloganeering, and demagoguery," Germino writes," the political theorist speaks out with honesty on the perennial problems confronting man in his existence in society." Political theory, as a philosophy, attempts to find out what the truth is in a particular situation, to generalize from that what the truth would be in a different state of circumstances and then to advocate views with all the passion at its command. Accordingly, political theory would continue to be needed as is needed science, or art, for it is, as

Plamenatz says, "not fantasy or the parading of prejudices; nor is an intellectual game. Still less it is linguistic analysis." For Plamenatz, political theory is "an elaborate, rigorous, difficult and useful undertaking," and "as much needed as any of the sciences."

The importance of a political theorist. Brecht says, "is to see, sooner than others and to analyse, more profoundly than others, the immediate and potential problems of the political life of society; to supply the practical politician, well in advance, with alternative causes of action, the foreseeable consequences of which have been fully thought through; and to supply him not only with brilliant ideas, but with a solid block of knowledge on which to build." He continues, "when political theory performs its function well, it is one of the most important weapons in our struggle for the advance of humanity. To imbue people with correct theories may make them choose their goals and means wisely so as to avoid the roads that end in terrific disappointment."

As a science, political theory can perform certain useful functions. David Easton mentions some such functions:

"1. To identify the significant political variables and describe their mutual relations. To ensure this, an analytical scheme is essential. This would render research meaningful and arrange facts leading to generalizations.
2. The existence, and wide acceptance of and consensus by workers in the field, on a theoretical framework, would enable the results of the various researches to be compared. It would help in the verification of conclusions drawn by the earlier researches and may also reveal the areas of research which require more empirical work.
3. Finally, the existence of a theoretical framework, or at least, a relatively consistent body of concepts, making research more reliable."

But this is what a theory does as a science. Though such functions of political theory, in themselves, are, indeed, important, yet they help understand a phenomenon, not the phenomena; a part and not the whole.

Theory is not merely a science, it is a philosophy as well; not a phenomenon, but phenomena as well; not a part, but a whole as well. Indeed, political theory does make people understand as to what the present is and for what the present exists. But it does more than that. Accordingly, it rises above being the attendant of the status quo: it deals with larger functions of how the present has come to stay, on what assumptions does it exist and where would it, in future, lead to. Political theory, no doubt, arises from a specific context, but its significance extends beyond that. It considerably contributes to the capacity of man to understand himself, his system, his society and his history. Its job is not merely to understand the system around him, but is one through which he is to take the command of his own affairs himself.

Political theory serves as a teacher, a guide and a philosopher of men in general in their attempts to comprehend and control the whole environment—both social and natural. It is worth-noting the significance of political theory as indicated by C. Wright Mills:

1. Political theory is itself *a social reality:* It is *an ideology* in terms of which certain institutions and practices are justified and others attacked, it provides the phrases in which demands are raised, criticisms made, exhortations delivered, proclamations formulated, and at times, policies determined.
2. *Second,* it is an *ethic,* an articulation of *ideals,* which, at various levels of generality and sophistication is used in judging men, events and movements, and as goals and guidelines for aspirations and policies.
3. *Third,* it designates agencies of *action,* of the *means of reform, revolution and conservation.* It contains strategies and programmes that embody both ends and means. It designates, in short, the historical levels by which ideals are to be won or maintained after they have been won.
4. *Fourth,* it contains *theories* of man, society, and history, or atleast assumptions about how society is made up and how it works; about what are held to be its most important elements and how these elements are typically related; its major points of conflict and how these conflicts are resolved. It suggests the methods of study appropriate to its theories. From these theories and with these methods, expectations are derived.

The relevance of political theory has never been in doubt, especially after its resurgence. Its strength lies in its change and continuity; in its growth and rise; in its understanding the milieu in which it operates; in its capacity to handle the present and guide the future. Its relevance lies in its contribution which we may, briefly, state as under:

1. Political theory keeps raising moral and ethical questions constantly; it not only raises questions, but it needs to give their answers as well. It investigates beliefs about ends, values and norms: it endeavours to explore what is right and what is good. In a word, political theory is normative; its normativism has never been in doubt; its relationship with values, though, was challenged by the behaviouralists, but later came to be restored. Political theory, now, works alongwith both 'facts' as well as 'values'.
2. Political theory, Vernon Dyke says, "is concerned with the normative, it is an error to think of its as limited to the normative". Indeed, political theory teaches, but it also describes and explains at the same time. It is normative, but it is narrative as well, it is explanatory and exploratory as well. It does talk about ideologies: idealism, socialism, liberalism; but it does explain their world view. It is a technique of analysis.
3. Political theory is not merely philosophy; it is not thought about thought only. It is also a framework, a conceptual framework, i.e., it is a set of interconnected concepts of politics. It is a theorising about politics. It is describing as to what politics is; it is explaining as to what it is all about; it is analysing as to what it can be. It offers conceptual clarification.
4. Political theory is not merely philosophy; it is pragmatism, rationalism: it is pragmatism in the sense that beliefs have a meaning and their justification stems from practical results. It is rationalism in the sense that whatever exists in politics; it exists through the power of reasons. Political theory is not, as Planenatz said, fantasy, but is an elaborate, rigorous, difficult and useful understanding. It is an activity as well.
5. Political theory, Germino explains, as a critical study of the principles of right order in human social existence, is neither reductionist behavioural science nor opinionated ideology. It is a science in the sense that it comprehends both the knowledge of facts and the insight with which this knowledge is comprehended and evaluated. To that extent, it is an experimental enterprise.

By way of conclusion, we may say that political theory builds a model of the political order, serves as a guide to the systematic collection and provides an analysis of political data. As science, political theory describes political reality without trying to pass judgement on what is being depicted, either implicitly or explicitly. As philosophy, it describes rules of conduct which help secure good life for all.

Political theory is no easy and simple an enterprise. It is an elaborate and a consistent exercise, at that, aiming to achieve a better world of politics. Philosophy and science have no privileged cognitive status in political theory. All political philosophy makes claims about the operation of the political world—claims which require detailed examination, within model of enquiry, which go beyond those available to philosophy alone. All political science raises normative questions, which, a dedication to the normative-explanatory does not eliminate. Political theory, if it has to be successful, requires the philosophical analysis of concepts and principles, and the empirical understanding of political processes and structures. Neither philosophy nor science, in their individual capacity, can easily replace the other in the projection of political theory. This is so, because systematic political knowledge embodying generalizations about patterns of political life is possible and that efforts to achieve it are the major tasks of political theory today.

## SUGGESTED READINGS

1. Brecht, Arnold, *Political Theory* (Bombay: Times of India Press, 1970).
2. Charlesworth, C. (ed), *Contemporary Political Analysis* (New York: Free Press, 1967).
3. Connolly, W., *Political Theory and Modernity* (Oxford: Blackwell, 1988).
4. Finifter, A. (ed), *Political Science: The State of Discipline* (Washington D.C. American Political Science Association, 1982).
5. Gould James, A. and Thursby, Vincent V. (eds). *Contemporary Political Thought: Issues in Scope, Value and Direction* (new York: Holt, Rinehart and Winston, Inc., 1969).
6. Held, D. (ed), *Political Theory and the Modern State* (Cambridge: Polity, 1989).

7. ________, *Political Theory To-day* (Cambridge: Polity 1991).
8. Kavanagh, D. *Political Science and Political Behaviour* (London: Allen and Unwin, 1983).
9. Kymlicka, W., *Contemporary Political Philosophy* (Oxford: Oxford University Press, 1990).
10. Leftwich, A. (ed.) *New Dimensions in Political Science* (Aldershot, Edward Elgar, 1990).
11. Lloyd, C. (ed), *Social Theory and Practical Practice* (Oxford: Clerendon, 1983).
12. Miller, David (ed), *The Blackwell Encyclopaedia of Political Thought* (Oxford: Blackwell, 1987).
13. Miller, D., and Siedentop, L. (ed), *The Nature of Political Theory* (Oxford: Clarendon, 1983).
14. Ricci, D.M., *The Tragedy of Political Science* (New Haven: Yale University Press, 1984).
15. Weisberg, H. (ed) *Political Science: The Science of Politics* (New York: Agathon, 1986).

# CHAPTER – 3

# What is Political Thought?

Politics, political theory and political thought are intimately related to each other. They constitute a fabric whose each part is connected with the other two. To understand politics without either political thought or political theory is to know it only casually; political theory helps explain what politics is all about or what political thought really possesses. Political thought is all about politics, as it functions, or, it is political theory in so for as it has a measure of theory in its framework.

## I. Nature of Political Thought

### *(a) Political Thought: Its Thematic Essence*

Political thought refers to the systematic reflection upon the practices and institutions of political life. It is about political life, about politics essentially. It is not about society, and hence, it is not social thought. Rather it is about society in relation to politics as is social life in relation to political life. It is not about economy, and hence, it is not economic thought, but it is about the impact of economics on politics. It is not about ethics, though it does contemplate about ideal political constitutions and ideal political life.

Political thought is an orderly reflection on the political institutions and political practices; it is about how people live under a political authority, obey it, resist it if it does not conform to what they think proper dispassionately; it is about how political life is influenced by the external world and how it is influenced by the world around; how does authority work as a system and how it is related to the sub-systems under it and outer systems of which it is only one part.

Political thought signifies, traditionally understood, political philosophy at the best. When, for example, we speak of the history of Political Thought, we generally focus on great texts of political philosophy, on Plato's *Republic,* on Aristotle's *Politics,* on Hobbes's *Leviathan,* or say, Marx's *Economic and Philosophic Manuscripts.* These texts/works deal with the broad-ranging explorations of politics which, in turn, relate to the general conditions of life and experience. Plato elaborated, we must remember, the nature of relationship, between knowledge, practical political life and philosophic understanding. Aristotle sought to relate the actual conditions then existing, to the ethical norms these conditions absorb in themselves. Hobbes related the necessity of the state to man's demand for an assuredly peaceful life. Marx highlighted the importance of materialism in our social life as well as in nature.

Political philosophy becomes the political thought of a particular philosopher of a particular time. But it is not political thought only or merely. So regarded, it is more than political thought in the sense that it reflects, too, on the political concepts which exist over a long period of times and circumstances. The concept of justice', for example, from Plato to Rawls, is a part of political philosophy, covering, thus, the theorisation of the concept of 'justice' as has travelled through the writings of numerous philosophers. Political thought as history has been emphatically advocated by scholars like George Sabine. Without history, political thought is a structure without a base; a body without life. In studying and analysing politics, what we learn to understand is a political tradition, and a concrete manner of behaviour. It is, therefore, proper that the study of politics should essentially be a historical study. History, we should know, is more than the tale of the dead or buried. It is tradition, experience, wisdom stored. Ignore history and with it the times and circumstances, we would not know Plato, the philosopher. Ignore the context, which is historical always, we would never understand what the text is.

Political thought, as history, is the thought of the whole society of a particular period, which includes, what a particular philosopher views politics and political life as a whole. It has, therefore, (i) the political thought of the whole people reflecting political vision they have on politics and political institutions. Professor Barker thought of the preamble of the Indian Constitution (1950) as the political thought of the Indian people; (ii) it is the sum-total of all the ideas, a particular political philosopher of a particulars time: so one talks about the political thought of Plato, Aristotle, Mill or Marx, wherein, each philosopher has his views on a variety of political concepts; it is about political life and political institutions, which political philosopher(s) reflect with political life and institutions of their times and in the process either defend them (Aristotle defending Stavery) or condemn them (Marx on the capitalist mode of production); and (iii) it is about the political thinking of a particular age: so we talk about the political thought of ancient times; or a medieval ages, or of the sixteenth century or of the twentieth century.

Political thought explains as well as speculates; narrates as well enquires; speaks, teaches as well as evaluates; understands a part together with the whole. It is both the parent and child of political viewing.

### *(b) Political Thought, Political Philosophy and Political Theory: Their Distinctions*

Political thought and political philosophy have been used interchangeably. When we talk of the history of political thought, we refer to the classical tradition that began with Plato and ended with Marx, though, both Germino and MacIntyre consider Hegel's political philosophy as the ending of the classical tradition, for, both see Marx as re-interpreting Hegel. The works of the great philosophers depict not only the problems faced in their respective times, but also reflect their examination, enquiry and experience. Political philosophy may, thus, be termed as the political thought of a particular philosopher of a particular age. But political philosophy is larger than the political thought of a particular philosopher; it is the political thought of an age or of a community. Political thought is also intimately linked with political philosophy. It amplifies and clearly states political ideas, puts them in a time frame. So, political philosophy does include political thought even though all political thought is not political philosophy. The difference between political philosophy and philosophy is not about the mood or method but about the subject matter. Philosophy, according to Wolin attempts to understand the "truths publicly arrived and publicly demonstrable" while a political thinker tries to explain the meaning of the political and its link with the public sphere.

Political thought is a historical narrative, descriptive to a large extent. Though political thought is historical in its approach, it is also, at the same time observational, empirical, operational, comparative and scientific.

Political philosophy, indeed, is larger than political thought. Although its area includes the methodological and substantive aspects of political thought, its thought comprises of a particular political philosopher or of a particular period. It also includes the rational synthesis of political speculation, maxims and norms. Political philosophy is more of a speculation than of a reality, which is not the case with political thought, or, for that matter political theory. Political philosophy is largely imaginative, philosophical and speculative; political thought is largely descriptive, analytical, explanatory and evaluative.

Political thought and political theory are related to each other, in so far as thought has a measure of theory with some amount of thought. The two are really inseparable with their thought and theory. In an attempt to change a phenomenon into abstraction, we attempt to build a theory that leads us to assume that political theory admits a measure of theoretical assumption, but it does not end up there. In fact, starting from this position, political theory covers a wide range of practical political activities, and, in the process, interprets, examines and relates them with one another. This is to say that political theory is as much related to theory, as to the practice of politics. It is both, a pure theory as well as a pure practice. C. Wright Mills (*The Marxists*) regards it a social reality, an ideology, an ideal as well as a theory. So widely understood, political theory, for Mills, becomes political thought. The latter explains politics and political life as it really exists; it defends or condemns and justifies or evaluates the political institutions, as they exist, at a particular point of time. It articulates, both at the levels of generality and sophistication, political events, and movements. Although it formulates a theory of man, society as well as state, yet the two, political thought and political theory are distinct.

Political thought explains and political theory speculates. Political thought is tied to a particular time frame; political theory is above time, in fact beyond all times. Political thought, by nature, is both historical and therefore, transitional; political theory is one that is future-oriented, developmental, and to that extent, has a measure of ideology. Political thought is both history as well as politics; political theory is politics, science, history, philosophy—all rolled into one. Political thought provides political theory, necessary data on which the latter contemplates and acts. It is the whole philosophy of a philosopher: Hobbes's political thought, for example, is the complete philosophy of Thomas Hobbes; political theory is concerned with, so far as Hobbes is concerned, taking Hobbes's political thought in view, a larger question of the Hobbesian thought—why do the people need a state or why must they obey the law?

*(c) Relationship between Political Thought and Political Science*

Political thought is the assemblage of the philosophies of the numerous political philosophers, wherein, each political philosopher theorises on political issues confronting his times. Each political philosopher discusses the political ideas of his times and the age he lives in. It is in this sense that the assertion is made that each philosopher is the child of his own age. It is history vertically, and history horizontally. Vertically in the sense, that a political philosopher theorises on concepts historically drawn. Plato discussed the concept of justice after having discussed the numerous notions of justice prevailing then: the father-son (Cephalus-Polemarchus) traditional view of justice; (Thrasymachus) the radical view of justice and the two-brothers' (Glaucon and Adeimantus) pragmatic view of justice. As against the historically-horizontal view of justice, political thought discusses the concept of justice vertically, when it examines the term 'justice' as it evolves in the writings of the subsequent political philosophers.

History is related to political science only casually, and to the extent it helps understand political phenomena. So understood, there is much that separates the two terms, political science and political thought. History is a characteristic feature of political thought; science, that of political science. The nature of political thought is philosophical, while that of political science is empirical. Political thought is a value-laden exercise; political science is value-free. Political thought understands the present through the help of the past and thereafter, builds future on the present; political science deals mainly with the present, and with the future, only marginally. These distinctions apart, there is much that both need from each other.

Political science depends on political thought in more than one way. Political thought places data at the disposal of political science for the latter's scrutiny. A political philosopher's philosophy is examined by a political scientist through scientific tools. The political ideas of a political philosopher are examined in a way that he is described as an idealist or a scientist. There is a valid point when Plato is said to be the father of political philosophy, and Aristotle, as the father of political science—political idealism owes its inspiration to Plato, political realism, to Aristotle.

Political thinkers do not ignore scientific methodology while putting forth their political philosophy. Aristotle is said to have adopted the comparative method of analysing and classifying states of his times—he is said to have read and examined 158 constitutions of his age. Hobbes, and before him, Machiavelli too, had followed the scientific method in expressing their ideas, if science means a study derived from intensive readings, experimentation, observations, leading to testable and consistent conclusions. Marx, to take another example, is said to have given a scientific theory of socialism. However, though all of them had reached certain finality in political theorising, the subsequent developments negated much of this claim. As such political theory is always a mixture of fact and value incorporating the subjective considerations of the thinkers and the prevailing climate of his age.

## II. Political Thought: Its Meaning

### *(a) Political Thought: Its Essential Ingredients*

To understand what political thought is, it is essential to know what it contains in it, what it explains and reflects on and what it is concerned with. Its major essential ingredients may be identified, briefly, as under:

1. It is about politics and political life; about political structure and institutions: almost all philosophers, venturing to write, reflect on the type of politics they confront and political life they live in.
2. It is the political commentary on the times and circumstances of the political philosophers.
3. In the course of their reflections on their age, the political philosophers deal with the theories and concepts, their

merits and weaknesses, such as, their views on the state, division of power, legal frameworks, types of polity and politics, kinds of society and environment.

4. Political thought is not only about politics or political life or political institutions, it is about their ideas and theories; it is not about politics only, it is about its speculation as a concept. It is not only about the government, but is also about the government that ought to be. To that extent, political thought contains normativism which, as we know, has dominated the greater part of political thought, especially the western political thought.
5. Political thought is not only a reflection on political life of a particular period, it is also a reflection on the society in which a particular political philosopher lives and reflects. When Plato was planning to build an ideal state, he had in view the ancient Greek society and the problems it was then confronting. When Marx and Engels condemned the bourgeois state as the committee for managing the common affairs of the whole bourgeoisie, they were reflecting on the characteristic features of the capitalistic society.
6. Political thought, as expressed through works and treatises, and writings and reflections, provides a body of knowledge through concepts and categories which alone help in understanding the subject or the subject-matter. It is, thus, the source of knowledge of political concepts and can be a key to formulate numerous models and categories.

Political thought is politics in so far as it makes it as its subject matter; it is history in so far as it represents an age; it is theory in so far as it examines on the concepts it works on; it is philosophy in so far as it speculates on political terms and categories.

### *(b) Political Thought: Its Framework*

The essential ingredients of political thought help formulate its framework.

Political thought is about politics or what is relevant to politics. It is an account given by numerous political philosophers relating to political institutions, political events, and political activities, their evolution and their growth. What has Plato discussed in his *Republic?* The *Republic* is about justice in the state and in the individual and thereby leading to the construction of an ideal state. Aristotle's *Politics* is about the possible, the desirable, and the best practicable state. Locke, in his *Two Treatises of Government,* stated to have given the chief end of people uniting into commonwealth, and that chief end of the state is the protection of the property of the people and about limiting the powers of a state. Marx, in his numerous writings, sought to foresee a classless and a stateless society from where, according to him, would begin the real freedom of man.

Politics implies political activity. It is an activity, which helps a citizen participate in the composition and functioning of the government. It is an activity which helps the political parties seek power and then rule the people. It is an activity through which political power is sought, maintained and retained. It is an activity of manipulation and bargaining, of seeking and exercising power. It is, therefore, rightly said to be an art of possible. It is about power, as Lasswell observed, who gets what, when and how. Politics, as an activity that helps secure political power, exercise it and retain it, is the central point of all political thought.

Political thought is thought about politics. When we take politics from its particularity to generality, we enter into the realms of political thought; when we take politics from its transitory and day-to-day form into its sustainable form, we tend to prepare the grounds of political thought. Political thought responds, in a general way, to the questions relating to politics, the state, political activities, state's policies and its functions, for various political philosophers, over the years, have done so. It seeks to find the permanent or near permanent solutions to the problems that confront politics. Political thought discusses not only the state, but also its highest form. It, through the philosophies of the political thinkers, not only examines the various theories of the origin of the state, but also seeks to develop a consistent theory regarding the origin of the state that appeals to our reasoning. The day-to-day issues relating to the nature of the state, forms of government, functions of the state, nature of political power become the issues discussed by the political philosophers. Machiavelli's reference of casual questions relating to the ruler's security became the characteristic questions of statecraft. Marx's attempt to analyse capitalism is a question of politics, but in the process of analysis, if Marx builds a socialist and communist society after capitalism, it becomes a part of political thought.

Political thought obtains data from politics. Politics introduces political activities for discussion by the thinkers. Political thought, on the other hand, gives a direction to the activities concerning politics. Politics, during the Stuart period in England, became the basis on which Hobbes and Locke built their philosophies—Hobbes trying to prefer authority to freedom and Locke, doing just the reverse, i.e., giving freedom, a predominant place to authority. Marx, while analysing and studying capitalism and in the process seeking to obtain more truth, and thereafter keeping in the medieval and early history, not only tried to know the functioning of the activities of capitalism, but was also built a new vision of political thought, creating history in what is known as the materialistic interpretation of history. Born in a particular political atmosphere, political philosophers study the atmosphere and in turn, build a new political environment, a new philosophy, and a new thought.

Politics assumes political activities; political thought studies them, seeks to know the objectives of those activities and gives them a shape, a vision and in the process, builds new concepts. Politics gives us the account of political activities; political thought gives us political education; politics is knowledge about the political conduct, political thought that of the theories of political conduct. Politics, therefore, identifies the way towards which political thought moves. Politics paves way for political thought, and political thought guides the future direction of politics. Marx's political theory inspired the Russians to launch the socialist revolution and, the earstwhile Soviet Union, sought to guide the socialist movements in the underdeveloped world. The ever-continuing direction of politics makes the basis for political thought. If politics provides political thought, political thought provides politics a vision to look to.

### *(c) What is Political Thought?*

It is the sum-total of ideas on matters relating to politics, state and government as expressed by the thinkers. It is historical in nature because it is described as history. It analyses, examines and evaluates issues that have a universal concern and are of perennial interest even though each political theorist responds to a particular political reality. It is written, keeping the larger public in mind and is not confined to ivory towers for an intimate link is established between the political process, institutions, events and actors. Usually, political theory flourishes in times of crises which act as stimulus though it is not necessary that all crises lead to political theorising.

Political thought is the description, analysis, expression, and evaluation of the philosophies of the philosophers of a political tradition. It is a tradition in so far as it comes to us as a body of thought. It is the sum-total of what stays on, and an accumulation of what is changed and what continues. It is what keeps responding to our circumstances. What becomes out-dated, is not the part of the tradition.

Political thought attempts to identify values and norms and makes them an inseparable part of a particular political trend. Western political thought, if we wish to identify its magic themes, evolves and revolves around values, such as, liberty and libertarianism, democracy and democratic tradition, equality and egalitarianism. Political thought, as it has existed and/or exists in India, for example, seeks to establish ethical/moral values in politics, spiritualism, cooperative living and the like.

Political thought is primarily the study of the state. It studies society in so far as society influences the state as political life and social life, though independent is inter-dependent. Similarly, it focuses on economic institutions and process in so far it influences the political order and process. It also takes into consideration ethical questions, for ultimately it is concerned with a just and good political order.

The characteristic features relating to what political thought can be stated, briefly, as under:

(i) Political thought is the systematic reflection upon the practices and institutions of political life; it is the commentary on the existing political institutions: how people have lived under a political authority, why have they obeyed it, why have they resisted it?

(ii) Political thought is not merely the description of political life and political institutions, it is also the analysis, examination and evaluation of the issues which concern political life. It is both science and philosophy: science in so far as it examines critically the concepts, and philosophy, in so far as it reflects on those concepts.

(iii) Political thought, in course of its discussion of political life and political institutions, helps identify ideas and concepts and issues of universal concern; political philosophers and theorists alike have debated the nature of state and peoples' obligations to obey the laws and will continue debating in times to come.

(iv) Political thought is history, as it relates itself to a particular time; as it relates itself to a particular time; as the political philosopher seeks to answer the problems that confront his/her times; and as it has the experience and richness of the time in which it is written.

(v) Political thought is ethics as it upholds the ideals and norms of the political tradition it belongs to.

(vi) Political thought is not merely the assemblage of the political ideas of a particular theorist (political thought of Mill or Marx, for example), it is also the assemblage of political ideas of a host of political philosophers (Political Thought: From Socrates to Stoics). It is also what may be related to a particular time. That is why that we hear about the political thought of the sixteenth century or of the twentieth century. There are, for example, references about political thought related to nations and states: Political thought in England, the US Political Thought, the Indian Political Thought, and the like.

## III. Western Political Thought

### *(a) Nature and Content*

It is impossible to imagine political thought of the West (for that matter, of any society) without history. Political thought is related to politics, but it is history that provides political thought its very basis. We do not mean to say that political thought can be studied without politics, but we certainly want to insist that we cannot study political thought without history. Understanding political thought in the historical context is, in fact, understanding political thought in the real sense. A political philosopher's political philosophy emerges in the age the philosopher breathes. In fact, his political philosophy is an answer to the times the philosopher lives in. His philosophy cannot be separated from history of his times. No political thinker builds up his political philosophy without taking an account of the age or his times. To put the point in another sense, it may be said that a political philosopher is understood only in his milieu. Plato, though an idealist, could hardly be separated from his soil; his classification of states depicted the classification as it prevailed then; his theory of education was drawn heavily from what existed in Athens and Sparta then. Machiavelli's whole methodology depicted his debt to history. The contractualists—Hobbes, Locke and Rousseau—made history as the basis of their social contract theory. Karl Marx went all the way to advocate the materialistic interpretation of history. The objective conditions of history always provide the foundations on which the political philosophers have built their philosophy.

Furthermore, we can understand the political philosophy of a political thinker only in the historical context. Separate a political philosopher from his times, one will always find a Popper condemning Plato as an enemy of open society. A contextual study is always a safer method of understanding a text. A text without a context is a structure without a base. Machiavelli is better understood in the context of renaissance. Hobbes and Locke, with their poles apart views, can be better studied in the background of the English civil war. Marx can be understood in the light of the growing capitalism of the European/Western society.

Western political thought is based on history, but its history, Professor Sabine rightly says, has no concluding chapter. It has grown and is growing, and in fact, will always keep growing. It has grown in a typical way; each subsequent philosopher condemns/criticises the philosophy or political ideas of an earlier philosopher, and in the process builds his own philosophy. Aristotle did so with Plato; Locke did so with Filmer; Bentham, with Blackstone; John Stuart Mill, with Bentham; Marx did so with Hegel, Adam Smith and Proudhon. So, Western political thought has grown; it proceeds on polemics, it changes, but it continues. It is continuing since the days of Plato and Aristotle. No wonder, if then, it is said that all philosophy is a footnote to Plato. Plato and Aristotle together gave the base, on which stands the whole fabric of Western political thought; for political idealism and political realism are the two pillars of the Western political philosophy from where arise numerous other related shades.

It is not easy to identify what the Western political thought contains or what its characteristic features and trends really are. However, major contents, features and trends of the Western political thought can, for the sake of making a point, be identified.

*(b) Characteristics and Trends*

*(i) Political Institutions and Political Procedures:* Western political thought deals, largely, with political institutions and procedures relating to them. If political theory deals with what is related to or is relevant to politics, political thought, coming as it is, from the writings of a host of political philosophers deals with political power, i.e., wherein it is vested and how it is exercised, and for what objects does it exist. The political thinkers from the earlier days to the present times have dealt with such questions relating to politics: Plato was more interested in the state as it ought to be, than Aristotle, who devoted all his energy on the best practicable state. The ancient Roman theorists talked about the nature and role of law in administration. With the medieval Church theorists, (Thomas Aquinas especially) political power was made to work under the divine law; the divine law under the natural law; the natural law under the eternal law. The early modern political theorists (Machiavelli and Bodin) were concerned with the supreme power (i.e., sovereignty) of the state or with actual and potential states. The contractualists (Hobbes, Locke and Rousseau) were eager to answer questions, as to how the state came into existence and as to why people obey laws. While political philosophy deals with institutions as they were, as they are, and as they need/ought to be. Marx saw them in materialistic terms. Sabine puts the point across when he says, "An important function of political thought (meaning the theorists or the political thought) is not only to show what a political practice (i.e., politics, political activity of his time) but also to show what it means. In showing, what a practice means, or what it ought to mean, political theory can alter what it is."

Political philosophers have sought to understand the political institutions of their times, have given them the meanings and, in doing so, have suggested ways of altering them. Thus, we may say that political thought deals with institutions. Further more, and it is important as well, subsequent philosophers have, after having suggested the changes in the institutions, maintained continuity. The political philosopher, to use Sabine's words, is a 'connector', a 'relator' who weaves the political fabric.

Western political thought is equally dominated, since the beginning, with an interest in the political procedures as to how and why political power is applied. Indeed, political thought deals with political institutions, but it is also related to the working of political institutions. The political philosophers were and are, primarily concerned not with what a state is or what it does, but also with how a state once entrusted with power, makes use of it. In other words, political thought has been, along with the study of political institutions, dominated with, if we want to give it a word, the rule of law, i.e., the procedure as to how the political power is put to use.

The rule of law is meant to rule the people, and not the man that rules. It is a negation of the coercive, arbitrary and totalitarian rule. It is a justification of power and its use. The rule of law, as a concept, has certain features of its own: the law is to be applied impersonally; it cannot be used as a means for attaining individuals ends; it must be applied indiscriminately, though it is an act of particular circumstances, has to be independent from the particularities. It forbids people to use coercive power over others and encourages to respond to the general norms of society and its equilibrium. It has to be in consonance with 'reason'. Plato's ideal republic was a construction of reason and one of the major concerns of the *Republic* was the development of leadership of rectitude to remain subservient to its rational law. Aristotle preferred the rule of law to the rule of man, howsoever wise these may be. The Romans and the medieval thinkers advocate the efficacy of law: temporal or ecclesiastical. The contractualists did refer to the natural law. The jurists, from Austin to Blackstone, and Coke, never lost sight of the juridical and legal power. The Marxists denounce the State as an instrument of exploitation while the anarchists reject externally imposed authority. No modern political philosopher, if any, preaches a system without making the rule of law as the foundation of society.

*(ii) Political Idealism and Political Realism:* The two major streams along with which the whole Western political thought keeps marching on are: (i) political idealism or as one may see political philosophy, and (ii) political realism, or as one may call it political science. Plato represents political idealism, and Aristotle represents political realism.

Political thought, as it has evolved in the West, represents political idealism (from Plato) and political realism (from Aristotle). In fact, the Western political thought has tossed between what ought to be and what is, the former stream led by Plato, and the later, by Aristotle that is what makes Wayper remark that the Western Political Thought begins with the ancient Greeks, particularly from Plato and Aristotle onwards.

Plato offers political idealism in so far as he regards the state not only natural but necessary as well. For Plato, the state was all in all, and apart from it, man could not attain the highest possible perfection. Looking at the state from the idealistic and moral point of view, Plato had a profound imprint on the later idealists. St. Augustine's the *City of God,* Rousseau's political ideas, Hegel's theory of the state, Green, Bradley and Bosanquet and a host of others were great followers of Plato's idealism. St. Augustine's the *'City of God'* was almost Plato's ideal state, though with a strong element of Christianity. Plato was a dominant influence in Rousseau's thought in whose the *Social Contract,* the state was a moral organism. Immanual Kant (1724-1804), a follower of Rousseau, Fichte (1762-1814), Hegel (1770-1831) were idealists in their own right, upheld idealism in the Western Political Tradition. The English idealists, such as, T. H. Green (1836-1882), F. H. Bradley (1846-1924), B. Bosanquet (1848-1923) were relatively moderate in their idealism who regarded the state not only natural and moral entity but thought of it as an organisation which commands respect from the people.

Aristotle offers political realism in so far as he proceeds from particularities to generalities, from the actual conditions of life to the desirable and possible ones. Unlike Plato, who adopts the deductive methodology, Aristotle pursues the inductive one. Plato moves with conclusions, Aristotle reaches at them. Like Plato, Aristotle too had left influence on the subsequent political theorists. We see Aristotle's imprint of political realism on Polybius (204-122 BC), Cicero (106-43 BC), Thomas Aquinas

(1227-74) hailed also as the Aristotle of the thirteenth century. Marsilio of Padua (1270-1342), Machiavelli (1469-1527), Locke (1632-1704), the behaviouralists and the post-behaviouralists who start always with Aristotle, and the recent theorists of the communitarian school such as Maclntyre, Sandel and Taylor.

(*iii*) *Philosophy and Science:* There are the characteristics of philosophy and of science as other elements as major components of Western Political Thought. If all later philosophy is a footnote to Plato, so is all science, a footnote to Aristotle. Plato is rightly called the father of the Western political philosophy, so is Aristotle, the father of political science. All philosophy is deductive, Plato follows the deductive method; all science is inductive, Aristotle follows the inductive method. Philosophy speculates and science observes. All philosophers who venture to write on politics proceed with pre-conceived notions; all those theorists who venture to write on politics reach their conclusions. The political scientists tend to be more interested in situations, in normative analyses of political systems as a whole, and more willing to think that politics is importantly distinct from other realms of ideals; political philosophers, on the other hand, are simply moralists who apply their familiar tools to new situations. Political philosophers are much more willing to be radical, whereas, the political scientists are much more likely to insist on remaining close to some core institutions.

Western Political thought has philosophers who urge to make politics more of a philosophy than science; it also has scientists who wish to make politics more of a science. Rousseau, Hegel, Kant, Strauss and the like are those who follow the philosophical approach of Plato. Hobbes, Locke, Bentham, Mill, the positivists, the empiricists, the behaviouralists who follow Aristotle in making politics a science.

(*iv*) *Political Ideologies:* Political ideologies constitute a considerable part of Western Political Thought. They also make a greater part of what the Western Political Thought is about Idealism is traced to Plato; realism, to Aristotle; liberalism has its advocates from John Locke to Robert Nozick; Marxism is associated with Marx and Engels and with their host of disciples; varieties of socialism belong to a variety of writers who include Berstein, G.D.H. Cole, Bernard Shaw, Nehru and Jai Prakash Narayan and Lohia; post-modernism, to Richard Rorty and Michael Foucault. Western

Political Thought is, indeed, enormously rich in providing theories and ideologies from time to time.

(*v*) *Political Issues:* Every political thought thrives on political issues; every age has its own share of political issues; political traditions go along with political issues. Contemporary political thought in the West has its issues with which it is confronting at present. David Miller identifies such issues which, in brief, can be stated as under:

1. *Social Justice:* The issue of social justice dominates political thought in one form or the other. Numerous liberal theories demand atleast the partial offsetting of the economic and social inequalities thrown up by an unfettered market economy. The Marxists give their own views on the subject while Rawls and Dworkin, their version; and the dissenting voice comes from Hayek and Nozick.
2. *Feminism:* The feminists, across the world, challenge the conventional liberal disparities between public and private spheres. They demand fundamental changes in personal relationships of men and women and advocate affirmative action policies.
3. *Cultural Identity:* Western Political Thought is confronted with the issue arising from what we call the new politics of cultural identity. The demands are being made to modify political institutions to reflect and express distinctive features of numerous cultures with a greater measure of self-determination in an age of post-colonialism and in an environment of multi-culturalism.
4. *Environmentalism:* Western Political Thought is alive towards issues arising from environmental degradation. The environmental movements are addressing themselves to urgent environmental concerns. They seek to establish green democracy, sustainability and environmental ethics.

(*c*) *Interpreting Classics/Works*

Charles Tayler defines interpretation as "an attempt to make clear, to make sense of an object of study." He continues: "The interpretation aims to bring to light an underlying coherence or sense." A work on political thought is, by definition, a structural of meanings and still it does not yield its coherent meanings to us until we interpret it. What it is prior to interpretation? It is nothing but a structure of words and so, is inconsequential. Whenever we attempt to grasp the meaning of a text coherently, we are only interpreting it. Karl Mannheim says that the three types of meanings—objective, expressive and documentary—emerge when we try to understand any phenomenon: the objective meaning is grasped from the text; the expressive meaning, from the unity of the subject and the text; the documentary meaning, from the unity of the text and the context.

To understand a philosopher is to know what he wrote and meant? But this is *one* way of understanding a philosopher—through what he wrote, reading only the text. John Plamenetz insisted an 'understanding through text'. *Other* way of understanding a philosopher is 'understanding text through the context'. Skinner, Pocock and Collini insisted on contextualism. Strauss and Wolin give us still *another* way of understanding a work. It is by placing a work in a tradition, say in the Western political tradition, the Indian political tradition or the like. The *logical or social-scientific* approach to understand a work insists on going into the internal consistency of the work and its comparison with the other works around. The *philosophical-moral* approach to know a work lays emphasis on what MacIntyre calls identifying differences immoral concepts' as developed in a work, i.e., evaluating the work.

Andrew Hacker refers to numerous ways of studying classics/ work. These are: (*i*) *Capital and Carbuncles,* the way the work came to be written, in a particular way: it is essentially a biographical approach, relating the *Capital* to Marx's carbuncles, the *Social Contract/Origins of Inequality among Men* to Rousseau's constricted bladder; the *Prince/Discourses* to Machiavelli's bad temper; (ii) *Hero Worshippers* or *Lost Laundry List,* again a biographical approach, relating everything to one's major work which a man writes, important and unimportant: Hegel is known not by an article he wrote on the English Constitution; he is known because he had written the *Philosophy of Right* or the *Philosophy of History;* Marx is known to the world as an author of the *Capital* and not as a poet having written—a poem in a college magazine; (iii) *Intellectual Plagiarism/Pursuit of Pedigrees,* connecting the indebtedness of a theorist to his predecessors and contemporaries: trying to interpret by finding similarities between two theorists, say, for example, Burke and De

Tocqueville; connecting the two philosophers (Hobbes's hedonism with Bentham's utilitarianism) without any concrete proof; (iv) *Who said it first* approach is another way of understanding a work, declaring Plato as the father of Political Philosophy; Aristotle, as the father of political science; Machiavelli as the father of modern political thought of the West; Comte, as the father of sociology; Marx may not have originated the word 'socialism', but he may rightly be called the father of scientific socialism; (v) *The Mind Readers,* giving the idea of what the theorist really desired to convey: by putting our words into the mouth of a philosopher hardly helps us understanding him: Sabine is a great scholar, but we are not sure as to what he wrote about John Stuart Mill was actually the same which J.S. Mill really had in mind; (vi) *The Camera-eye/Representative Reflection* relating one's ideas to having represented his times. This is to say that Plato's *Republic* reflected his times or Locke's *Two Treaties on Government* was a representative reflection of his days. Biographical approach, as this is, is largely a subjective one; (vii) *Influential Intellects,* interpreting one's thought with the corresponding event or connecting an event to one's thought. It amounts to saying that there could not have been the French Revolution had there been no Rousseau before it, or that Lenin's writings made possible the Russian October Revolution: theory guiding the action or the action making theory; (viii) *Influencing the Masses* linking a work to a political event: linking Locke's writing to the 1688 revolution; (ix) *The Logic-Book,* declaring the significance of the work for its logical nature; and (x) *Timelessness,* explaining the constant and continuing relevance of the work and stating its validity because of its weight.

### (*d*) *Why Study the History of Political Thought?*

Western political thought, since its beginning from ancient Greece, has dealt with diverse varieties of issues, and each philosopher has handled them from his own angle. Indeed, the political philosophers have, at times, disagreed on the solutions, but what is important is the continuity of the issues which have captured their intentions. The major issues relating to politics have given the concerns of political philosophers. By attempting to find solutions to these political issues, the political theorists have given political thought not only a direction, but also a unity of thought processes. The significance of political thought lies in the attempt of the political philosophers to identify political issues, and provide solutions, thus giving political thought a meaning and a vision. Sheldon Wolin puts a point, saying, "the designation of certain activities and arrangements as political, the characteristic way that we think about them, and the concepts we employ to communicate our observations and reactions ... none of these are written in the nature of things but are the legacy accruing from the historical activity of political philosophers". He states these political issues: the power relations between government and subject, the nature of political authority, the problems created by social conflicts, purposes and objectives of political activity, and the character and utility of political knowledge.

The works on political theory are written by political philosophers from time to time, and are related to a particular time, and yet they are timeless. They are timeless because they live in all times and live beyond their own times; they are relevant in all ages—past, present and future; they highlight problems which are problems for all times to come: corruption in politics had been a problem in Plato's times, and it is a problem even today. The works are timeless because they deal with issues confronting every age; the themes they touch reflect all times in all circumstances; and they live in perpetuity.

The works on political theory are not outstanding because what is expressed therein is original, a 'who-said-it-first' type. All the terms such as 'class', 'class struggle', 'proletariat', 'bourgeois', 'revolution', 'surplus value', which Marx used, Isaiah Berlin says, were not his, i.e., he was not the first person who used them, for they have been used by many scholars earlier. But that was not what goes to the credit of Marx. Marx's contribution lies in giving these terms new and definite meanings, and above all, a new political thought built on them. What is original may be an important factor, but what is more important is the understanding of a political situation and giving to the world, a new interpretation. That is where lies the importance of Marx, and, for that matter, of any political philosopher.

The political texts have contributed a great deal to the evolution of the specialised language, expressed through words, symbols, concepts and has become the vocabulary of political philosophy. The concept of 'general will' used by Rousseau is an example of such vocabulary. The words such as 'state of nature', 'civil society' and the like are other examples. These works in politics by numerous philosophers have enriched our literature.

Western political thought is political theory, spread over history. It is the embodiment of the writings of numerous political philosophers. These writings are works in the field of Political Science which have stood the test of time. They have survived through ages because of their intrinsic worth. They remain interesting and instructive because of their perennial themes, sound comprehension, subtle style and profound analysis. They wield great influence, and are, basically, suggestive.

The works of political thought are outstanding not because they are universally praised. In fact, they are neither praised nor denounced. Plato is rated very high by some like Barker, Wilde, Whitehead who go to the extent of saying (*Adventures of Ideas*) that all subsequent philosophy is a footnote to Plato, while others such as Popper, Crossman and Winspear, condemn him as fascist, totalitarian, and enemy of democracy (see Karl Popper, *Open Society and Its Enemies*, 1945). Machiavelli, to take another example, has been denounced by Catholic writers, such as, Butterfield, but has been admired by secular scholars, such as, Allen, Gramsci and Wolin. These works on political thought flourish because they are continuously studied, interpreted, and discussed, each subsequent reading gives a new and fresh orientation. They are a great aid to thinking. It is, in this sense that they are suggestive. Plato does not impose his 'communistic' devices for acceptance, but he does stimulate our mind and reactivate it to think of other possible devices. They are not only suggestive, but are essentially inspirational.

About the importance of the Western political thought, Sheldon Wolin writes: "In teaching about the past theories, the theorist is engaged in the task of political unitation, that is, of introducing new generations of the students to the complexities of politics and the efforts of the theorist to confront its predicaments, of developing the capacity for discriminating judgement, and of cultivating that sense of significance... which is vital to the scientific enquiry but cannot be furnished by scientific methods, and of exploring the ways in which new theoretical vistas are opened." Dilthey also says; "In studying classics, we construct our life experience with the aid of experiences of the great thinkers. Communication with their experiences enriches our own experiences of the great thinkers. Communication with their experiences enriches our own experience." Karl Marx writes "only music can awaken the musical sense in man."

The great tradition of Western political theory, from Plato to Hegel, deals exhaustively with the major contradictions and dimensions of the political process. Their importance is exhibited by the fact that though they were primarily concerned with the immediate problems besetting their contemporary situation, yet they were able to transcend their localism. In the process, they were able to provide a framework of analysis that would enrich other periods as well by their penetrating insights and thoughtful reflections on perennial problems of politics, power, authority, legitimacy, equity and order. They are masterpieces as they do not belong to any one culture, civilisation or time, but are cherished by the entire humankind.

The above discussion states the relevance of the study of political thought. To sum up, we may highlight the relevance of the study of political thought as under:

1. The study of political thought reveals the identification of certain political issues together with the solutions as discovered by the political philosophers. These political issues remain largely the same: the nature of political authority, problems of political obligation, the ongoing debates on what should be the rights of the people, the nature of corruption in administration. The solutions offered by the political philosophers act as our guide: we work on those solutions, we restate them and refine them. Their teachings remain suggestive always.
2. The reflections on the same political issues, time and again, make us understand these issues from numerous angles and in the process help us solve them from varying perspectives. Political thought places before us the age-old experience so to help utilize it. It helps converse us with history; a dialogue between different perspectives, between us on the one hand and the great political philosophers on the other. We communicate with the political philosophers of the past, and in the process, enrich ourselves.

3. Political thought is a key to understand the past. With political philosophers we go into their times, their situations and in the process, understand history as it existed then. A political philosopher not only writes history, i.e., his political philosophy, he interprets the history of his times. In the process, we, as the students of political thought, know not only the political philosopher of a particular time, but also the times in which the political philosopher lives.
4. Political thought contributes to the growth of certain political concepts and ideas. That is how we build the meaning of the concept of justice as it comes to us through the writings of numerous political philosophers. Our concept of 'liberty' has not been the same as it was during the times of either Hobbes or Locke, but whatever it is, it has grown since the days of Hobbes and Locke.
5. Political thought adds to our vocabulary and to our literature of political theory. It gives us new concepts, new meanings and new interpretations. It keeps adding to our corpus: 'social justice' here and 'feminism' there; 'terrorism' here and 'postmodernism' there.
6. Political thought is suggestive and therefore, inspirational and activating and reactivating. We may not agree with Plato's communistic diagnosis as devices to eliminate corruption in politics, but who stops us on thinking about other possible alternatives? Political thought is an aid to our thinking.
7. Political thought, by illustrating political institutions and political structures, helps us choose and build our own. It is through political thought that we have known numerous forms of government (parliamentary, federative) and of states (democracy, dictatorship, military regime) and have, in the process, chosen our own type of political system.

Political thought helps us enrich our knowledge, and our experience, train and broaden our responsibilities, sharpen our discriminating power and acquire sound judgement. Asirvatham writes: "It (Political Thought) gives precision and definiteness to the meaning of political terms. It is conducive to clarity and honesty of thought. It is an aid to be interpretation of history. A knowledge of past political thought is an invaluable help in understanding present day politics and international relations. Political thought represents a high type of intellectual achievement." Political thought is rich and therefore, is illuminative, and educative.

## SUGGESTED READINGS


1. Bagby, Laurie M., *Political Thought: A Guide to the Classics,* (Toranto: Wadsworth Group, 2002).
2. Bluhm, W.H., *Theories of Political System: Classics of Political Thought and Modern Political Analysis* (Englewood Cliffs, N.J.: Prentice-Hall, 1965).
3. Brecht, A., *Political Theory: The Foundations of Twentieth Century Political Thought,* (Bombay: The Times of India Press, 1965).
4. Carnoy, M., *State and Political Theory,* (Princeton: Princeton University Press, 1984).
5. Gunnell, J.G., *Political Theory: Tradition and Interpretation,* (Cambridge: Winthrop, 1979).
   __________, *Between Philosophy and Politics: The Alleviation of Political Theory,* Amherst Mass: University of Massachusetts Press, 1986).
6. Hacker, Andrew, "Capital and Carbuncles: The 'Great Books' Reappraised" in *APSR,* 48; pp. 775-786.
   __________ *Political Theory: Philosophy, Ideology, Science* (New York: Macmillan, 1964).
7. Hallowell, J.H., *Main Currents in Modern Political Thought,* (New York: Halt, 1960).
8. Held, D., *Political Theory Today,* (Oxford: Polity Press, 1991).
9. Kateb, G., *Political Theory: Its Nature and Uses* (New York: St. Martin's Press, 1979).
10. Kymlicka, W., *Contemporary Political Philosophy: An Introduction,* (Oxford: Clarendon Press, 1990).
11. Mcllwain, C.H., *The Growth of Political Thought in the West* (New York: Macmillan, 1932).
12. Miller, D., (ed.) *The Blackwell Encyclopaedia of Political Thought,* (Oxford: basil Blackwell, 1987).
13. Miller, J.D.B., *The Nature of Politics,* (Harmondsworth: Penguins, 1962).
14. Plamenatz, John; *Man and Society,* Vol. I, II (London: Longmans, 1963).
15. Pocock, J.G.A., "Review of Political Theory: Tradition and Interpretation", *Political Theory,* 8, 1980), pp. 563-567, 1980).

16. Portis., E.B., *Reconstructing the Classics: Political Theory from Plato to Marx,* (New Jersey: Chatham House, 1953).
17. Quinton, Anthony., *Thoughts and Thinkers* (London: Duckworth, 1982)
____________ (ed), *Political Philosophy,* (Oxford: Oxford University Press, 1989).
18. Sabine, G.H., *What is Political Theory?", Journal of Politics,* 1 (1), 1939, pp. 1-6.
____________, *A History of Political Theory,* (Delhi: Oxford and IBH Publishing Co., 1973).
19. Skinner, Q., "Meaning and Understanding in the history of Ideas," *History and Theory,* 98 (1969), pp. 5-53.
20. Strauss, L., *What is Political Philosophy and Other Studies?* (Glencoe, The Free Press, 1959).
21. Tannenbaum, D.G., and Sehultz, D., *Inventors of Ideas: An Introduction to Western Political Philosophy,* (New York: St. Martin's Press, 1998).
22. Van, Dyke V., *Political Theory: A Philosophical Analysis* (Stanford: Stanford University Press, 1960.
23. Vogelin, E., *History of Political Ideas,* 2 Vols (Columbia: University of Missouri Press, 1978).
24. Wayper, C.L., *Political Thought* (Delhi: B.I. Publication, 1974).
25. Wolin, S., *Politics and Vision: Continuity and Innovation in Western Political Thought,* (Boston: Little Brown, 1960).

# CHAPTER – 4

# Concepts: Democracy

Democracy is a very difficult word to understand. Its numerous connotations have so vastly been stated that there could hardly be a definition of democracy, containing all that it possesses. As a system of government, to some, it is a form of government while for others, it is a way of life. It is government of the people, for a member of the ruling class; but a narrow and indefensible oligarchy for the poor. As a form of government, as Burns tells us, democracy is another name for self-government. Lecky on the other, considers it as the government of the poorest, the most ignorant, the most incapable. And yet it is, by far, a better system of government as compared to monarchy, as the rule of one; oligarchy as the rule of the few, howsoever able they may be; dictatorship, either of one person or one party. As compared to the other forms of non-democratic systems, democracy is more educative, more responsive, more responsible, people-friendly, and less prone to revolution and violence. Its chief plus point is its basis; it is based on equality, liberty and welfareism.

## I. Democracy: Meaning and Definitions

### *(a) Democracy and its Essential Characteristics*

The political aspect of democracy emphasises everyone's share in the government; its economic aspect demands abolition of exploitation; its social aspect seeks elimination of all distinctions. A rather conservative definition of democracy is given by Professor Dicey: "Democracy is a form of government in which the governing body is comparatively a large fraction of the entire nation." Professor Bryce hints at a more liberalised definition of democracy: "Democracy is that form of government in which the ruling power of the state is vested not in a particular class or classes but in the members of the community as a whole". MacIver's definition of democracy, highlighting the representative system, says that it is not as much the way of governing as is "a way of determining who shall rule and how".

The word 'democracy' has a Greek ancestry (the Greek historian Herodotus coined the word democracy in the fifth century B.C.) *demos*, and *kratos* meaning a form of rule by a section of the populace as opposed to the rich or the aristocrats. The Greek meaning implies the rule of the commoners, the poor, the least intelligent. That is one reason that democracy, as Aristotle thought, was a perverted form of government, the rule of the mob. The Greeks, it may be noted, did not include in the ruling populace, the aliens, the women, the children, and the slaves.

The dictionary meaning, given to democracy, says that it is the rule of the people. But this does not make things clear unless we know what or who constitutes the people. If by people, we mean all the adults without any other qualification attached to it, we may not have the rule of the people, because all the people do not rule, and in fact, can not rule. If by people we mean those who participate in decision-making or administering or legislating, then such a system would be rule of the few, and not of all the people. So considered, the rule of the majority would also be not democratic (rule of the people) for it would exclude the few—minority. Any meaning of democracy must include the people, directly or indirectly, constituting the government. The role of the people in the composition of the government makes the government, the government of the people, but it would be a democracy if it is controlled by the people. What it means, is that government of the people is one constituent of its being a democracy, its another constituent is that it has to be government *by* the people, i.e., people must have control over what the government does. This would mean that the people should have freedoms and liberties and rights so to check the dictatorial tendencies, if any, of the government. There is yet another constituent of democracy, and perhaps an important aspect and that is: that the government has to be a government *for* the people, i.e., it exists for the welfare of the people. It is, in this context, that Abraham Lincoln's oft-quoted Gettysburg's addressed (1863) definition of democracy has any significance: democracy is the government *of* the people, *by* the people, and *for* the people.

A despot may rule in the interest of the people but nobody would call such a government democracy; a people's rule, either themselves or through their representatives, may not grant substantial freedoms, much less care for their comforts, would hardly be a democracy. An oligarchical rule, howsoever popular in terms of service to the people, would not be democratic unless it guarantees liberties to the people. The idea of democracy is the idea of **participation**, of **representation**, of **control**, of **accountability**, of **self-development**. Professor Lively (*Democracy*, 1975) summarizes the following *characteristics* in a democracy:

1. That all should govern in the sense that all should be involved in legislating, in deciding on general policy, in applying laws and in governmental administration.
2. That there is a need for people's participation in crucial decision-making, that is to say, in deciding general laws and matters of general policy.
3. That rulers should be accountable to the ruled; they should, in other words, be obliged to justify their actions to the ruled and be removable by the ruled.
4. That the rulers should be accountable to the representatives of the ruled.
5. That rulers should be chosen by the ruled.
6. That rulers should be chosen by the representatives of the ruled.
7. That rulers should act in the interests of the ruled.

Lakoff (*Democracy*, 1996) gives an elaborate definition of democracy, saying that, "Democracy is a process of self-government in which individuals operate upon their environment directly and indirectly-directly as they make decisions for themselves, pursue careers, enter into relationships with others, and otherwise live their lives and indirectly through political representatives accountable for them. The system of government makes possible centralized decision-making and rule-setting in matters that affect all citizens (the responsibility that accompanies all freedoms), and decentralized decision-making and rule-setting in those best addressed on the local level. It is, in short, a social and political system characterized by a high degree of personal liberty and equally high degree of political liberty, manifested in regular and free competitive elections, protected by a legal system based upon a constitution, and often articulated by means of federalism."

It is possible to give a few general *indicators* which sum up the totality of the meaning of democracy:

(a) Democracy is *commonality*; it is more than "one-person, one vote", it is the sense of awareness which allows a consensus to be maintained. Democracy is not majority, and if it is so, it becomes the tyranny of majority. Consensus make the out-voted feel that they are also part of the whole, the community.

(b) Democracy is *empowering*, for it enables the individual to exercise control over his individual life, and acting together with others, it enables the community to exercise control over the decisions of its collective life.

(c) Democracy is *accountability*. Where accountability lacks, the elected system becomes nothing short of an elected dictatorship. Those elected as rulers must be accountable to their electorate.

(d) Democracy is the *effective representation* of the collective will of the electorate. It is not only the people's will, it is also their concerns in the corridors of power. It is not simply to be a delegate for the political party, slavishly following its policy; it is the expression of the policy of the people.

*(b) Democracy and Other Forms of Government*

The meaning of democracy, as a form of government, can be understood if we are able to make distinction between democracy and other forms of government. Monarchy, as an absolute form, stands opposite to the democratic system. While monarchy is the rule of one person, democracy is the rule of all the people. Monarchy does not depend on the consent of the people in matters relating to the administration of the affairs of the people; democracy rests on the consent of the people. The monarch's accountability towards the people of what he is doing and has really done exists nowhere, while in a democratic system, those who rule are held accountable for their actions. Monarchy cares very little for the welfare of the people, not withstanding a few exceptions here and there; democracy and the welfare of the people are inseparable. Monarchy may well be described as the rule *of* one person, *by* him/her and *for* him/her; democracy is the rule of the people, by the people and for the people.

Oligarchy/aristocracy is the rule of the few, by them and for them. The few, howsoever the best and the most wise they may be, do not match with all the people, for the rule of all is anyway better than the rule of the few. The self-rule is relatively more educative, more responsive and more responsible . The classical elitist theory is what it preaches, historically saying that history is the graveyard of oligarchies', or 'the iron law of oligarchy'. As against oligarchical rule, democratic system is one that is people- oriented; its basis is people's consent; it is directed towards attaining peoples' interests, it functions as peoples' watch man. Democracy's relationship with people is as nearer as is oligarchy's/aristocracy's farther from them.

Democracy is the rule of the people, meaning thereby the *consent of the people* in the organisation of the government; *the control of the people* on those who, as people's representatives, rule the ruled. It is here that democracy differs from a dictatorship; either the rule of an authoritarian monopolistic political party or the rule of the military chief. The consent of the people is never sought or asked in any dictatorial regime; nor do the people control their rulers; the accountability towards the people is absent in all despotic systems. The more components of consent, control and accountability make a system democratic; their less components degenerate the system to dictatorship. To put the point rather clearer, the increasing consent (of the people), control (over the rulers), accountability (of the rulers towards the people) indicates the system as more democratic; their decreasing levels indicate the presence of a dictatorial regime.

If we consider 'Y' as democracy and 'X' as any type of dictatorship and 1 as consent, 2 as control and 3 as accountability, we would be able to make a relative comparison between democracy and dictatorship as in figure 1, as below:

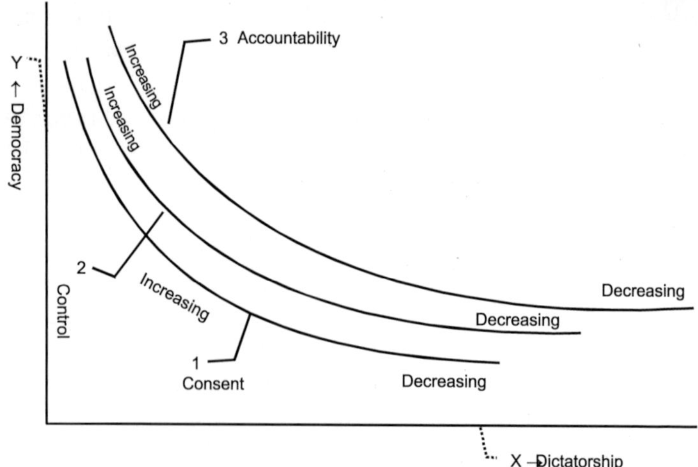


**Fig. 1.**

*(c) Democracy and its Ideals*

Some of the major ideals of democracy can be stated as under:

(i) Democracy, as a political system and as a way of life, differs drastically from other forms of government. In fact, democracy is no idle dream nor an aesthetic asylum. It is a *shared experience* which helps inspire and regulate thought and action, while in all other systems, the experience is imposed.

(ii) Democracy is not as old as monarchy is; it is relatively a phenomenon not very old. But its ethical conceptions are fairly old: *individuality, liberty, equality, fraternity*. These go to the days of the French Revolution (1789). These have given democracy ideals which, as Gordon Ziniewicz says, "have become the very basis of understanding clearly the human nature and individuality (equality), freedom of thought and action (liberty), and community and communication (fraternity)." Neither monarchy nor oligarchy and nor dictatorships, admit values of equality, of liberty and fraternity.

(iii) Democracy is one phenomenon that unites individuals with society. It binds them into one whole. So considered, the ideal of democracy integrates *individual fulfillment and social harmony*; it is where the personal good and the common good get mutually reinforced. It is an ideal of unity, of equilibrium within the personal and social movement, of unifying without uniformity.

(iv) Democracy identifies itself with scientific discovery; it is what strengthens free enquiry, free participation in free communication of ideas. The *democratic attitude* and the *scientific attitude* are *attitudes of flexibility and openness,* where thought and observation work hand in hand. Flexibility empowers the democratic ideal of tolerance and accommodation while openness relates itself with the democratic mindset.

(v) Democracy is *a unity in diversity*. It is an order within varieties, equilibrium within motion of diverse but freely cooperating individuals and interests. It is not the unity of the individuals surrendering their own individuality, but the unity of the individuals working together, i.e., 'joining forces'. It is a unity in a sense of harmony, within a wide range of ideas and interests, which is freely planned, freely engaged in, and freely communicated by and from individuals.

(vi) Broadly understood, the ideal of democracy hints *democracy as a way of life:* how people relate themselves towards one another, how they respect one another, how they bear with one another. Democracy, as Dewey says more oftenly, includes attitudes of sympathy, tolerance and respect ... such attitudes form character; they guide the intelligent reform of desires and interests, the framing of purposes which are inclusive, expansive, and social. The ideal of democracy brings home, is taken to heart, internalized, is made to intervene bruising and healing endearness of ongoing life.

(vii) Democracy is more than a 'political' phenomenon; it is *moral*, it is *social*. This is to say-that democratic political institutions, if they are to stay in power or have to be effective, are to be rooted in moral and social conceptions, attitudes and cultures. According to Dewey, political democracy is a means for realising overall moral and social democracy.

(viii) Democracy stands for *human development*. It means *growth*. Strictly speaking, there is no life without growth or say self-renewal. The choice is not between one way of life and another, it is between a way of growth and a way of decline. Democracy is neither monarchy nor dictatorship, for the latter do not respect human personality nor individual growth.

(ix) Democracy, like growth, is a sustainable *reconstruction*. As such, it is prospective, future-oriented plan-oriented. It is an open-ended moving power.

(x) Democracy is not a dogma, but *a creed*. It is a belief in the essential goodness of human nature; it is a confidence in human potentiality: human being as the master of his/her own destiny. Democracy is not the truth one boasts, but it is a truth worth seeking. It is self-corrective, self-educative and self-evolving and thus, is never complete. It is an evolution.

## II. Democracy: Evolution and Growth

### *(a) Western Concept of Democracy*

The western idea of democracy had its roots in ancient Greece. But the idea, then, was considered a perverted one. Plato and Aristotle had no word of praise for democracy. As Laski says: "It (democracy) was of course a limited democracy based on slavery; and in no Greek community (Athens including) did free citizens constitute the majority of the inhabitants." Aristotle's notions of citizenship, emphasising the virtues of being a legislator and a judge, and of polity, as the government of all in the interest of all, were not even labelled as democracy', for he had used the term in a perverted sense. During the period of ancient Roman empire, the ideas of good government and sound administration were important but the democratic element, then, was nominal in the republican period and non-existent in imperial. The idea of plebeians never had any democratic character, much less the power of legislation, the Senate, (or the patricians) had power and authority together with the emperors, but they were no commoners in the sense we use the term in democracy. Cicero, Seneca, Gaius and Ulpian expressed shadowy democratic ideas by pointing out equality of men at the time of their birth.

The Middle Ages had no conception of democracy. The dominance of faith over politics, of Christiandom over the kings and the feudal lords, of birth over merit, of extinct equality over dead liberty, made democracy and the democratic institution a far cry in the whole period of the medieval age. It was only during the late Middle Ages when the two swords (authority: ecclesiastical and temporal) came to be separated from each other that the ideas of benevolent rule, representation, contract appeared which prepared the basis for democracy that the West was to follow.

With renaissance, reformation and enlightenment, grew the present form of democracy in the West. Way back, the Magna Carta (1215) had voiced some freedoms; the Petition of Rights (1628) curtailed the absolute powers of the king, the Glorious Revolution (1688) followed by the Bill of Rights (1689) cut short the unlimited powers of the rulers on the one hand and made them accountable for their action (execution of Charles I and the fleeing of James II in England, for example) on the other. All these developments show the idea that government has to be a government *by* the people. The American War of Independence (1776) and the French Revolution (1789), emphasising on the Rights of Man and on "Liberty, Equality, Fraternity" and the revolutions of 1848 in most of the non-Anglo-French countries of Europe and later winning of the suffrage rights, brought in focus that the government has to be government *of* the people. The introduction of the welfare state, following the Soviet proletarian revolution, filled up the vacuum of the idea that democracy has to be government *for* the people.

*(b) The Evolution of Democracy: The Philosophers' Speak*

The original meaning of democracy, in the literal sense was in the ancient Greek days was "rule of the people" Herodotus, the Greek historian, included equality before the law, popular participation in decision-making, and popular control of public officials in the maxim 'rule of the people'. But thinkers like Plato and Aristotle were hostile to the idea of democracy. In fact, both the teacher and the pupil were typically elitists. Plato was in favour of the ruling class which represented 'reason'—the philosopher-rulers. Aristotle was well known for his sympathies towards benevolent monarchy: he was, as is known, the teacher of Great Alexander the Aristotle had taught Alexander for sometime though he regarded polity as the best form of government—a combination of aristo-democratic system.

The ancient Romans did admire constitutionalism with emphasis on the concept of law, binding both the rulers and the ruled, but they were monarchical in their views with fascination for far-flung empire. Slavery was an accepted norm in both ancient Greek and Roman societies. Cicero (106-43 BC) had not only systematised the concept of natural law but also formulated explicitly the idea of natural rights.

The middle Ages are significant for emphasising the conception of a moral law of nature, the quest for a universal society, and the belief in the dignity of the individual. And yet, Christianity propagated obedience to political authority as conditional: if the ruler defies the law of God, he may be lawfully overthrown. St. Thomas Aquinas (1225-1274), described as the Aristotle of the thirteenth century, did talk of human law, though inferior to the eternal law of God.

Feudalism, as a system, was a step backward in the annals of democracy, for it represented a series of relationships between the king, the lord, the vassal or the self: contractual, hierarchical and personal relationship, dominated and supported by religion. The Reformation, with religious, social, political and economic changes, pointed towards individualism which is regarded as one of the major steps towards democracy. Martin Luther (1483-1546) eliminated the Church as the intermediatory between the individual and the creator; John Calvin (1509-1564) thought salvation a question of individual effort and hard work. Calvinism found its supporters in the growing industrial, commercial, manufacturing and business classes whose very existence sought the emergence of a fairly permissive political environment and thereby the development of capitalism. This, in turn, was conducive to the development of the type of democracy that prized individualism and liberty. The Renaissance led to further the expression of individualism—the discovery of the human being and the emphasis on self-expression, self-realisation and self-fulfillment.

Reformation and Renaissance together contributed to the concept of the secular state. Niccolo Machiavelli (1469-1527) worked for the stability and instability of political orders; his main concern was the creation of a stable and secular state. Jean Bodin (1530-1596), Hugo Grotius (1583-1645) and Thomas Hobbes (1588-1679) developed the concept of state through its element of sovereignty: the ruler-as-sovereign or the state-as-sovereign, fitting neatly into the scheme of monarchical absolutism.

The seventeenth and eighteenth centuries challenged the notions of absolute sovereignty: The scene was England and France and the challengers were John Locke (1632-1704) and J. J. Rousseau (1712-1778). Their "social contract" proved to be of potential importance for the development of democracy. Both Locke and Rousseau laid emphasis on the intrinsic value of the individual (a democratic element), although the latter submerged individuality into collectivity. Both regarded the state/government as a result of individuals' agreement. Both insisted on the consent of the individual as a condition for an ordered political life. Both referred to rights as almost natural, inalienable and absolute: "Right to life, liberty, estate" (Locke) or that "Man is born free" (Rousseau). Both thought of the government as a trust—Locke declaring it explicitly and Rousseau, implicitly. For Locke, if the rulers exceed their political authority, they may be rightly overthrown through revolution. For Rousseau, it is the 'general will which is the basis of government; general will as more will for the people than of the people: the individual obeys the government, and if he does not, he may be 'forced to be free', meaning thereby that in obeying the government, he obeys himself.

There were numerous factors emphasising on the 'democratic' elements evident from the social contract theory—atleast of John Locke and J. J. Rousseau. Some among them were: (i) assertion on human freedom and dignity; (ii) emphasis on rights of the individual; (iii) the state as the result of individuals' consent and their agreement; (iv) the state to act as a means for the individual and community; and (v) a revolt against monarchy and tyrannical rule.

The English, the American and the French revolutions of the seventeenth and eighteenth centuries gave concrete reality to the social contract ideas as it came to be built in the West. In the later centuries, writers such as Thomas Jefferson (1743-1826), Alexis de Tocqueville (1805-1859), Abraham Lincoln (1809-1865), Jeremy Bentham (1748-1832), Edmund Burke (1729-1797), and John Stuart Mill (1806-1873) systematised and elaborated the concept of democracy, with writers and scholars, in the greater part of the twentieth century, building a case for representative or indirect democracy.

*(c) Democracy—Thematic or Models of its Growth*

For having a clearer idea of the growth of democracy, it would be instructive, if not informative, to give a summary of different models of democracy as stated by David Held (*Models of Democracy*, 1987).

1. *Classical Democracy:* In a small city-state and in slave economy, citizens, though limited, enjoy equality among themselves and participate directly in legislative and judicial functions. There is a provision for open assemblies with executive directly elected, by lot or by rotation—assembly's powers include all common affairs.

2. *Protective Democracy:* Politically better organised and existing in a society of patriarchal chiefs, citizens need protection from the rulers and from one another. It is a system where the rulers rule in the interests of the citizens only in name; in actuality they interfere in total governance. The model is protective because it protects the ruled from the arbitrariness of the rulers, protects the rulers from the infringement in one-another's sphere, protects the whole legal system from those who violate the rules.

3. (i) *Radical Model of Developmental Democracy:* The system visualises small, non-industrial communities with a society of independent producers where men are made free from work and politics. The citizens, in this model, enjoy political and economic

equality; no one masters the other; all enjoy equal freedoms; legislative powers with directly elected legislative bodies, executive with 'magistrates', either appointed, or elected directly or chosen by lot.

(ii) *Developmental Democracy:* The system visualises an independent civil society with a *laissez faire* state supported by competitive market economy; private ownership of means of production exists alongside the community or cooperative forms of ownership. In this model, participation in political life is regarded necessary for protection of individual interests, and development of informed, committed and developing citizenry. There is popular sovereignty with universal franchise along with proportional system of representation; the government is representative; the system of checks and balances exist so to avoid absolutism.

4. *Direct Democracy and the End of Politics:* The system visualises classless society with the working class coming victorious against the bourgeoisie where private property is abolished and market economy is destroyed. It aims at achieving freedom and free development for all; ensuring complete political and economic equality; providing equal opportunities for all according to their abilities. Public affairs are regulated by communes, all officials are elected and, therefore, can be recalled, economy is planned, and public affairs are collectively governed.

5. *Competitive Elitist Democracy:* The system visualises industrial society with competitive groups competing with one another for power and benefit. The electorate is poorly informed, and, therefore, is politically almost apathetic. In this model, the elite is reelected because it is skilled and is, therefore, capable of making decisions: political, and non-political. The essential features of such a model of democracy are: (a) parliamentary government with a strong executive or presidential government with an alert legislature; (b) competition between groups and political parties; (c) dominance of party politics; and (d) well-trained bureaucracy.

6. *Pluralist Democracy:* It visualises the existence of numerous communities in the society with their own culture, basis, strength and objectives and each attempting to achieve something for its own group. There exists active citizenry along with numerous passive body of citizens with full political participation. This model encourages government by minorities generally, prevents the development of powerful factions and hence, has almost unresponsive state. The essential features of such a model are:

(a) freedoms and liberties are available; (b) the device of checks and balances so to keep legislatue, executive, judiciary in their respective domains; (c) the presence of competitive electoral system; (d) the coexistence of diverse range and sometimes overlapping interest groups seeking political influence; (e) the law and the Constitution are respected; (f) the state, instead of being impartial, seeks to attain its own sectional interests.

7. *Legal Democracy:* The system visualises effective political leadership, guided by liberal principles; bureaucratic role and that of the interest groups are minimised. The essential features of such a model are: (a) a state that works on the basis of Constitution; (b) rule of law prevails over those of men; (c) free-market society; (d) a state with minimal functions and maximal individual autonomy.

8. *Participatory Democracy:* The system visualises a perfect and just society with material resources available to everyone and also an open order where informed decisions are ensured to each. This model ensures (i) an equal right to self-development; (ii) developing a sense of political efficacy; (iii) concern for collective problems; and (iv) contribution to the formation of a knowledgeable citizenry. The essential features of such a model are: (a) direct people's participation in each institution of society; (b) party leadership is made accountable to party membership; (c) an open institutional system is maintained to ensure the possibility of experimenting all political forms.

9. *Democratic Autonomy:* The system visualises the availability of an open information, ensuring informed decisions in all public affairs, setting of the government's priorities with extensive market regulation of goods and labour, minimization of unaccountable power centres in public and private life. This model expects individuals to be free and equal in the determination of the conditions of their own life; guarantees equal rights and demands equal obligations. The essential features of this model in respect of the institution of state are: (a) autonomy enshrined in the Constitution; (b) competitive party system; (c) central and local administrative services internally organised according to the principle of direct participation. In respect of society, the key features of such a model are: (a) existence of diverse institutions and groups; (b) self-managed enterprises; (c) community services (education, health, etc.) are internally organised on the

principle of direct participation; (d) private and voluntary enterprises to help promote diversity and innovation.

## III. Types and Kinds of Democracy

*(a) Democracy—Direct and Indirect*

The traditional forms of democracy are described as direct and indirect. In direct democracy, people are themselves the rulers; in indirect democracy, the people are the electorate and rule through their representatives, who are periodically elected. In direct democracy, there is no distinction between the ruler and the ruled: the ruled is the ruler, and the ruler is the ruled. In indirect democracy, between the ruler and the ruled, there stands the representative.

Direct democracy is possible only in countries where both population and territory are small. That is why it was there in city-states like Athens in ancient Greece and also in small town-like Cantons in Switzerland. There are devices like initiative and referendum and recall in most of the other cantons and in some states of the U.S.A. *Initiative* is the device through which the people make proposals for legislation or initiate proposals for amendment in the Constitution. It is, therefore, the first word with the people and a sort of sword through which people can attack to ward off any challenge to democracy. *Referendum* is the device through which the people approve or disapprove any legislation or proposed amendment. It is, therefore, the last or the final word with the people, and a sort of shield through which people can defend themselves in case democracy is threatened *Plebscite* literally means 'decree' of the people. It is a device, as Professor C.F. Strong says, to obtain a direct popular vote on a matter of political importance. *Recall* is a device by which elected representative can be recalled if the majority of the electorate so decide.

Indirect democracy is also known as representative democracy. It is usually in vogue in most of the countries today. In such a form of democracy, the electorate elect their representatives from constituencies: single or multiple through ballot system: open or secret. Representative democracy is expressed through devices, such as, territorial representing constituencies, functional representing interests, or proportional representation of minorities.

In non-socialist countries, democracy is known as liberal democracy as has come to be understood in elitist, pluralist or participatory form, to mention a few among many, and in socialist countries, the kind of democracy that prevails has come to be known as peoples' democracy.

Democracy, whether direct or indirect, ensures a form of government better than any other; educative, responsive, responsible. It seeks welfare of all; abhors violence and revolution, guarantees reforms and obedience of the laws; and upholds both equality and liberty. But it is also regarded as the government of the incompetent, of irresponsible multitude, which turns into petty party politics. It corrupts both the rulers and the ruled, which is generally unstable, and usually imaginary. And yet, democracy, as a form of government, has been admired by all. Burns concludes, rather rightly: "No one denies that existing representative assemblies are defective, but even if an automobile does not work well, it is foolish to go back to a farm cart, howsoever romantic it may be."

Democracy, indeed, is the best of all the forms of government, and yet it is the most difficult. It needs a conducive atmosphere for its sustenance, survival and success. Socially, there must be social justice, free from discrimination, and a sense of unity among the people. Economically, there has to be economic equality and economic security. Politically, there should be liberty, law and order, local institutions, judicious majority and cooperative minority, rule of law, free press, impartial periodic elections and so on. Equally, there has to be politically alert citizenry in whom duty-abidingness, common interest, sense of fair judgement and the like virtues are deep-rooted.

*(b) Democracy: The Elitist, the Pluralist Types*

*(A) The Elitist Theory of Democracy*

*(i) Background of the Theory:* The elitist theory of democracy is an amalgamation of two opposing, rather conflicting strands: elitism and democracy. Elitism implies the rule of the few, whereas democracy, in its direct form, means the rule of all. The elitist theory of democracy is not elitist in so far as it claims to be democratic; it is not democratic in so far as it traces its roots in elitism. The elitists, notably Vilfredo Pareto (1848-1927) and

Gaetano Mosca (1858-1941), both Italians, and Robert Michels (1876-1936), Swiss, never found democracy as a viable proposition. Their argument is: democracy in the sense of popular exercise of power and peoples' participation in society's public affairs can not be, in practice, realized; power is, and has always remained the privilege of the dominating few; democratic system is impossible and impracticable. The elitists, therefore, accept the view that democracy is a device that marks the harsh reality of elite rule and that history is nothing but the graveyard of oligarchies—or what Michels declared as "the iron law of oligarchy."

The classical elite theorists such as Pareto, Mosca, Michels together with the present-day elitists such as C. Wright Mills, (1916-1962), Schumpeter Mannheim, Sartori oppose the classical form of democracy as the direct rule of the people themselves. Mosca's words still serve an authoritative statement of the elite theory. "In all societies—two classes of people appear: a class that rules and a class that is ruled. The first class, always the less numerous, performs all political functions, monopolises power and enjoys the advantages that power brings, whereas the second, the more numerous class, is directed and controlled by the first...". In other words, the elitists hold the view that it is always the few who have ruled the many; the elite that rules the masses. Michels puts forth the elite argument by talking about "the political immaturity of the mass", 'the organic weakness of the mass', 'the need which the mass feels for guidance', 'the apathy of the masses and their need for guidance'. The elitist conclusion is: as the masses are incompetent, so there arises the need of the leaders; as the masses are politically immature, so the idea of mass sovereignty is always a myth; as the masses are apathetic, so they are not political; as the masses are disorganised, so they are irrational; and as the masses are irrational and manipulable, so there are possibilities of demagogic leaders destroying democracy and then turning it to fascism.

The elitist argument of the rule of the few over many never found favour with the exponents of democracy. The 'democracy' theorists, while lauding the will of the people, keep singing, with Rousseau, the chorus of the will of the people as the will of God. They are convinced that the people as a whole, have a will of their own, separate from and independent of the will of the individuals, whether individually or severally. The revolutionaries of the American War of Independence and of the French Revolution, as also the idealists (Hegel, Green and others) who followed them, kept alive the notions of 'Rights of Man' or of 'people' in the hearts of the theorists of democracy.

The 'democracy' theorists have been sceptical about elitism as have been the elitists, about classical democracy. Each knows its merits as also its weaknesses. The elitists know how practical they are, and how undemocratic they are at the same time. Similarly, the 'democracy' theorists know how great servants of the people they are, and how impracticable they are at the same time. The fusion of one into the other produces a form of government which is called 'elitist theory of democracy', 'democratic elitism', 'competitive theory of democracy', 'plebscitary elitism' as Max Weber would have called it. The necessity of the growing industrial society during the 18th-19th centuries necessitated the need of one by the other. The industrial society had thrown up diverse economic, industrial and other social groups wanting to have an edge in public affairs and hence competition among themselves. Elitism had to turn towards democracy as democracy towards elitism. Michels' 'iron law of oligarchy' comes to be accepted in the sense that direct democracy is considered not a possible pragmatic system; 'democracy' comes to be accepted in the sense that the people make a choice among the elites available and the system makes them democratic in so far as the elites are made responsive and responsible to the masses. Summing up the idea of democratic elitism, Schwarzmantel (*Structures of Power*, 1987) says: "The fact that masses have a choice between different elites, satisfies all the requirements of a democratic system. Organisation implies oligarchy, as Michels asserted; democracy needs leadership. In this sense, the elite-mass distinction is preserved and the analysis remains in the elitist tradition. On the other hand, it is a necessary and sufficient condition for a democratic system that, at stated intervals, the masses decide which elite is to rule".

(ii) *The Theory Explained:* Joseph Schumpeter (*Capitalism, Socialism and Democracy*, 1943) may rightly be called the most influential proponent of the elitist theory of democracy. He attacks democracy by saying that there is no such thing as 'the will of the people', that the masses, being ill-informed, do not formulate the agenda of politics, that the political issues are always raised, articulated and debated by the leaders, that initiative, in politics, travels from top to bottom and not from bottom to top. When the masses elect the leaders or a particular elite, the government is formed. In such a situation, Schumpeter says, the leaders should be free and autonomous to formulate and carry out policies of the government as composed by the people. The democratic element, in a situation like this, is preserved in (a) periodic elections of the leaders by the masses, and (b) in the accountability of the leaders towards the electorate. The elitist element is preserved in (a) enough autonomy of the leaders to formulate the policies, and (b) enough freedom to execute them. The elitist view of democracy may be summed up as Weber once described in a situation like this: "In a democracy, people choose a leader in whom they trust. Then the chosen leader says, 'Now shut up and obey me'. People and party are then no longer free to interfere with his business... Later the people can sit in judgement. If the leader has made mistakes—to the gallows with him."

For an order of democratic elitism, Schumpeter insists on the following conditions:

1. The calibre of politicians must be high.
2. Competition between rival leaders (and parties) must take place but within the prescribed norms.
3. There has to be a well-trained independent bureaucracy to aid and advise politicians.
4. Excessive criticism of government on all issues be permitted.
5. A political culture capable of tolerating differences of opinion be guaranteed.

In democratic elitism, the following features should constitute a broad framework of the elitist theory of democracy:

1. The elite's unflinching faith in democratic norms. It needs to realise that it possesses power as long as the electorate wants it.
2. The establishment of the elite-masses contact is the only basis of the elitist democracy.
3. Non-interference of the masses in elite's business: formulation of policies and in the conduct of administration.
4. The elite's capabilities and experiences in political and public matters is a matter beyond any doubt.
5. Effective and active competition among the groups—constant and always continuing.

6. Circulation of elite from among the masses.

*(iii) The Theory's Evaluation:* The elite theory of democracy has some inherent limitations.

(i) The theory is no longer democratic, if by democracy we mean a system where there is a substantial amount of popular power and citizens' involvement. In this sort of democracy, the masses only produce a government, they do not sustain it.

(ii) The elite theory of democracy does ensure a measure of responsiveness by the leaders to the led, but democracy, in its essence, is not just confined to responsiveness, nor is it limited to checking and controlling the executive. Democracy implies *people's participation* at each level of governance, from initiating a legislative proposal to vetoing the other.

(iii) The elitist thesis that the masses, in general, need not interfere in elite's public affairs and the insistence that the politicians may keep 'get on with the job' are not compatible with classical democracy and is, in fact, a surrender of sovereignty. Indeed, democracy does mean citizens' participation in politics, but it also means right of the citizens to judge or pass judgement on their rulers. Real democracy is not only descriptive in the sense of being a way of electing the governors, but is normative in the sense of being a way of judging the rulers and the existing power system.

(iv) Democratic elitism cuts out from democratic theory its very heart—the idea of participation. Schwarzmentel writes: "It (democratic elitism) takes a purely static view accepting the features of present-day mass society fixed for ever instead of envisaging a process that would transcend the elite-mass dichotomy. The stability of the existing order is, thus, made the chief value, and democratic involvement then appears to threaten that value."

(v) The democratic elitism alienates the ruled from the rulers. Despite the fact that the ruled can exercise control over the rulers, it does not imply that the ruled control the rulers. All the agencies and devices, through which the masses can possibly control the rulers, remain under the control of the ruled. The distance between the ruled and the rulers keep widening.

(vi) Democratic elitism is more elitist than democratic. The fact remains that the rulers—the elite–remain a class in themselves. As such, the theory is more elite-oriented, and its democratic convictions are both formal and imaginary.

(vii) The elitist theory of democracy is anti-liberal, for it does not recognise the individual a rational being. It is anti-socialist, for it has a theory of political democracy and has, in fact, no theory of socio-economic democracy.

(viii) The elitist theory limits democracy only to "governance" level.

(ix) In terms of progress, the elite theory of democracy is a step backward. It has removed, from its essence, the moral content of democracy, a feature the classical theory of democracy had possessed. What was the heart of the classical theory of democracy—democratic humanism—was replaced by the elitists with what they made—democratic mechanism. The elitist theory of democracy is retrogressive. Macpherson writes: "...democracy is reduced from a humanist aspiration to a market equilibrium society. And although the new orthodox theory claims scientific neutrality, its value judgement is clear enough: whatever works, is right."

The strength of the elitist theory of democracy lies in the fact that effective political power has always, in all societies and in all ages, remained in the hands of the few—a select minority. It also lies in the fact that such a system of democracy has, in reality, worked effectively well in Western political systems, that any other alternative of democracy could not and has, in fact, not worked, and that the socialist model as against the elitist one, has proved infeasible.

### *(B) The Pluralist Theory of Democracy*

*(i) Elitism, Pluralism and Neo-pluralism:* There is much that separate elitism, pluralism and neo-pluralism from each other, though they are parts of the larger frame of liberalism of either yesterday or today. Pluralism, as it developed especially in the United States of America in 1940s, 1950s or later, was a reaction against elitist theory of democracy. While the elitist democracy advocated the exercise of power by a dominant and relatively united group, one or strictly very few (C. Wright Mills, *The Power Elite,* 1956), the pluralist had an absolutely opposite thesis, saying that power is

held not by one or the other group, but by groups. Within the framework of liberalism, pluralism demonstrated a more democratic orientation than elitism. The elitist theory had a very poor view of the masses and were convinced that only the elite (the ruling class, the governing class, hence, only political) had the aptitudes and capabilities to rule. The pluralist democratic theory admits numerous groups of all shades, competing to obtain power of the state. The pluralists are more democratic than the elitists in so far as the former do not allow the state to act arbitrarily: for there is a network of parties, groups, associations, in the pluralist frame, exercising their democratic rights to check the absolutism of the state. The elitists do presume a fragmented society, but not the one in which numerous groups are equally powerful, but the one where there is the monopoly control of the more powerful. In pluralism, on the other hand, the state is highly responsive to numerous groups. In elitism, there is no group conflict; in pluralism, there is. In pluralist democracy, the people, though non-political, are not apolitical, but in elitist theory, the people are regarded apolitical, and, therefore, made to act as non-political. Elitism is a matter of containment; Pluralism, of democratization.

Following are the factors that separate neo-pluralism from pluralism. (a) neo-pluralism is an extension of pluralism, but the one in which the role of the business groups is relatively crucial; (b) in a pluralist democracy, groups are powerful, more or less, equally, whereas, in a neo-pluralist arrangement, dominant groups are seen distinct from secondary weak groups; (c) power is an observable phenomenon and is relatively dispersed in pluralism, whereas, in neo-pluralism, power is unobservable, hidden structurally and ideologically, and, therefore, is concentrated in big issues but dispersed in secondary ones; (d) in the pluralist theory, democracy exists through conflictual groups whereas in neo-pluralist theory, it exists, but very little; and (e) in pluralism, society is distinct and in a way, non-political; in neo-pluralism, society is distinct, but with limited influence.

*(ii) Development and Growth:* Pluralism, in the initial stages of its beginning, began as a reaction to the concentration of sovereignty in the nation-state. Experts, mostly Englishmen, argued that the state sovereignty, in the sense John Austin used the term, is merely a legal fiction, that its monopoly of individual's allegiance is

untenable, that the 'intermediate institutions, such as, churches, universities, economic organisations and the like are as important as the state on the one hand and the primary groups like the family on the other. The primary groups, including the intermediataries, play important role in the life of the individuals, and that they should be allowed to exist independent of the state. The English pluralism, fearful as it was of the state powers, urged for assurance that the state would not interfere in the functioning of these groups. That was, indeed, the message one gets from the writings of Figgis, Maitland, G.D.H. Cole, Hobson, Lindsay, Barker, Laski and Maclver.

Pluralism, as it grew and developed in the United States, was largely the result of the writings of Truman, Bentley, Dahl, Lindblom, though its ancestry is related to Schumpeter, Weber, Madison, and others. It has, in the Western political system, travelled through various phases and assumed the names of 'empirical democratic theory' 'a descriptive-explanatory account of democratic politics. With the changing times, pluralism has passed through its classical stage to reformed and then to neo-pluralist ones. Each subsequent stage of pluralism was a variant of the preceding one. To explain the point, one may examine the position of the groups in the changing pluralist variations, for pluralist democracy is, essentially, group democracy. With the classical pluralist theory, groups are easily formed in a society and they exist because they compete. In the reformed pluralist theory, certain groups gain privileged access over the ones, excluded in neo-pluralism, the role of the business interests becomes more crucial as compared to others, of mostly secondary importance. Furthermore, in the classical pluralist theory, the task of the government tends to mediate and adjudicate between the demands of the numerous conflictual groups. In the reformed phase, it responds to the groups, not equally but differentially; and in neo-pluralist phase, it becomes almost a tool in the hands of the business interests.

*(iii) Pluralist Democracy—Features*: Though there are numerous variations of pluralism, yet it is possible to state some recognizable features common to all. Pluralism is a process; a process of political action, and a process which, in Lasswell's phrase, settles who gets what, when and how. It assumes a multiplicy of groups/actors competing for power, influence, job, status and so on in a variety of political arenas. It minimizes the connections

between the different arenas and maximizes the openness of the contests. In it, democracy is competitive rather than consensual and where politics is pragmatically focussed upon "here and now" situation.

The characteristic features of pluralist democracy, common to all shades of pluralism, as summed by Schwarzmantel, are:

1. There is no single group which is able to exercise systematic and pervasive control over more than one range of issues. What it means is the existence of numerous groups in the society and the fact that each group is dominant in its own area—all trying, in varying degrees, to influence the government. More the issues, more the groups and more dispersed and varying is the influence.
2. The idea of countervailing power (as used by J.K. Galbraith) exists in pluralist scheme. Galbraith explains that in an advanced economy, there exists a balance between the capital and the labour with no one having an in-built advantage over the other. Both exist, not in a situation of perfect competition, but in one, that is imperfect, where both hold power and both can influence and restrain governmental action.
3. Though the pluralists do not have any coherent theory of state, yet it seeks a state which is neutral. Indeed, the role of the dominant business groups is growing fast, yet the pluralist democracy envisages a state which acts as an umpire, impartially controlling the conflicts of groups, supervising and regulating social antagonisms.
4. As the pluralist democracy survives in a multiplicity of groups with their own interests and demands, pluralism is not committed to any ideology. There is, thus, the plurality of ideas and, therefore, no uniformity of belief, any belief, "a society of publics" as C. Wright Mills would have used the phrase.
5. The pluralist democracy is a democracy of competition, consent and accountability. It is a democracy of competition because it allows competition among the numerous groups; it is a democracy of consent because it is run by a group which has a considerable support and consent, and it is a democracy of accountability because the elected representatives have to be responsible to the electorate for deeds.

6. The pluralist democracy is a democracy in the sense that it prevents the concentration of political power in the hands of few. It is also a democracy in the sense that it permits the numerous groups and all citizens their democratic right of participation in politics.

*(iv) Assessment of the Pluralist Theory of Democracy:* The pluralist theory of democracy remains within the ambit of the Western political systems: systems which allow economic inequality and political democracy, separation of powers, rule of law, constitutionalism, competitive society, citizenship rights, a system of freedoms and liberties, and a talented bureaucracy. Its strength lies in its effective application in the Western society, in whatever form it suits a system.

And yet its weaknesses can be highlighted:

1. The assumptions that a society has numerous groups, and that the groups play a significant role, are not empty assumptions. But, it is too much to assume that the numerous groups are powerful equally. Indeed, certain groups, mostly the economically dominant groups, have more resources and more means, and, therefore, hold more powers in the society at the cost of others. This makes the whole pluralist assumption undemocratic.
2. The pluralist theory of democracy, while making group as a political unit, ignores the emphasis on individual which was the hallmark of the classical democratic theory. The pluralists have reduced individual to a rhetorical sovereign: making him almost a slave to the groups around him and submerging his identity in that of the group.
3. As the pluralist democracy is a group democracy, it is always likely that politics may not be able to receive the attention of the problems and issues concerned with the average citizen or an ordinary group. To put the point the other way, power may prevent certain issues to come before open discussion. Bachrach and Baratz rightly point out that a group may be powerful enough to determine the "agenda" of politics, and to make sure that certain items are never put on that agenda. This kind of process may make the pluralist democracy as democracy of the dominant.
4. The pluralist view of the democratic state as neutral arbiter is countered by (a) ever-increasing power of the state, and

(b) imposing and influential business groups in the society. As the state assumes more powers, it becomes more bureaucratic and hence, less democratic. As the economically powerful groups exert influence on the state, they make the state as their instrument. And, if in a situation like neo-pluralism where the state comes to forge its own interests, it hardly remains neutral then.

In an unequal and market sort of society, where the power is captured through competition, the emerging victorious group not only holds the power but attempts to retain it. Power, in the hands of the small cohesive group dominating the society, fades the pluralist vision of dispersion of power and thus, makes the whole politics, oligarchical.

But upto a point, pluralism has a value and an appeal to those who believe in liberty and in democracy. To those who hate tyranny and concentration of powers and to those who favour dispersion of power, to them, pluralism must provide a workable system and to that extent, it may appear to be democratic.

*(c) Theory of Participatory Democracy*

Democracy has, indeed, been a puzzling concept. Its theoretical implications and its practical applications, keep throwing up newer problems day after day. The recent rethinking on the terms of reference relating to democracy has been put forth by Carole Pateman (*Participation and Democratic Theory, 1970; The Problem of Political Obligation: a Critique of Liberal Theory,* 1985), C. B. Macpherson (*The Life and Times of Liberal Democracy,* 1977), and N. Poulantzas (*State, Power, Socialism,* 1980). They all represent what may be called as 'participatory democracy'. Professor Held tells us: "'Participatory democracy' is the main counter-model on the left to the 'legal democracy' of the right",—counter model on the left, so far as it condemns closed society of the socialist societies, and a critique of the right in so far as it exposes the so-called 'equalities' which the Western societies claim to have won. Pateman questions the idea of 'free and equal' citizens and says that the existing inequalities of class, sex and race have gone to denounce the equalities among the citizens. She even challenges the impartiality of the state and goes on to say that the state, instead of removing inequalities, sustain and reproduce them. Poulantzas holds the view that the socialist democratic model has failed to train citizens in the art of democratic administration. Macpherson, while declaring the Western societies as liberal democratic—liberal first and democratic later—doubts if liberalism would succeed in shouldering the weight of democracy as seen in direct participation of the people in administration.

*(i) Participatory Democracy—Explanation of the Theory:* The Theory of participatory democracy, as advocated by Pateman, Macpherson and Poulantzas, can be, briefly, stated as under:

(a) Democratization of parliaments, bureaucracy, political parties and the like is the first condition of participatory democracy so to make them all more open and more accountable.

(b) Drastic decentralization of powers, both vertically and horizontally, so to enable the formulation of policies and decision-making run from the bottom to the top.

(c) Reorganisation of political parties, while making them less hierarchical, on the principles and procedures of participatory democracy.

(d) Accountability of the political administrators and managers to the people they represent.

(e) Direct participation of citizens in the regulation of the key institutions of society, including the workplace and the local community.

(f) Maintenance of an open institutional system to ensure the possibility of experimentation with political forms.

So understood, participatory democracy envisages an equal right to self-development; a type of society which fosters a sense of political efficacy, nurtures for collective problems and contributes to the formation of a knowledgeable citizenry, capable of taking a sustained interest in the governing process (Held: *Models of Democracy*, 1987). Birch offers, rather a relatively negative meaning of participatory democracy. He says in his work, (*The Concepts and Theories of Modern Democracy*, 1993): participatory democracy "means a system in which small local units, informally organised, would have a veto power over national decisions." Dahl (*A Preface to Economic Democracy*, 1985) goes on to give a list of conditions so to meet the criterion of collective decision-making and extensive involvement:

1. *Equal votes:* The rule for determining outcomes... must take into account, and take equally into account, the expressed

preferences of each citizen as to the outcome; that is, votes must be allocated equally among citizens.

2. *Effective participation:* Throughout the process of making collective decisions, every citizen must have an adequate and equal opportunity to express his preference to the final outcome.
3. *Enlightened understanding:* In order to express preferences accurately, every citizen must have adequate and equal opportunities for discovering and validating his preferences on the matter to be decided.
4. *Final control of the agenda by the demos:* The demos must have the exclusive opportunity to make decisions that determine what matters are and are not to be decided by processes that satisfy the first three criteria.
5. *Inclusiveness:* The demos must include all adult members except transients and mentally challenged persons.

The demands of the participatory democracy are, indeed, numerous. Notable among them, are: a constitution enshrining the principle of autonomy, and therefore, equal rights, equal rights to cast a vote, and equal rights to enjoy the conditions for effective participation, enlightening understanding and the setting of the political agenda. Participatory democracy, has to have a broad scheme of rights—political, to ensure effective participation; economic, to have an access to adequate economic and financial resources; social, to include childcare, health, education. Obviously, such a scheme of rights would specify obligations of the citizens towards one another and also the responsibilities of the state towards the citizens and their groups.

*(ii) Participatory Democracy—An Assessment*: The idea of participatory democracy is an attractive one, but falls short of practical application. It is an advance over all other strands of democracy—elitist, pluralist, socialist, but there are certain limitations which this theory of participatory democracy suffers from.

1. Participatory model of democracy fails to specify the conditions necessary for such a democracy, as also the means of securing such conditions.

2. Indeed, there is no better method of learning than practising what we want to learn. Accordingly, we learn to participate by participating, but there is no evidence to show that participation

would help, as Professor Held says, 'to trigger a new renaissance in human development.' It would be unwise to think that participation would make people cooperative and dedicated; it would, rather, be wise to presuppose that participation would not make people morally or intellectually better than what they are.

3. To count much on participation, is to demand more than what is possible. It is questionable whether participation would lead to desirable political outcomes and would reduce tensions resulting from distributional questions of social justice and democratic decisions.

4. Although participatory democracy attacks the principles of liberalism (i.e., citizens are free and equal and so on) yet it does not leave out the means through which liberalism works. It accepts competitive political parties, representative system, periodic elections, and so on. It is, thus, a theory which builds itself on bases, which it chooses to attack.

5. The crux of participatory democracy is the availability of specialised information and expertise to the decision-makers. "In such a situation, groups of amateur politicians," Birch says, "may lend themselves to manipulation by demagogues or by ideological factions." Open participation, he continues "may mean *domination by* those with strong ideological motivations, who are willing to give their time to it, but who would not necessarily be able to win a competitive election."

6. Paticipatory democracy envisages substantive involvement in all spheres and at all levels. The important question is, as to how these spheres and levels are to be connected with each other, and how the different aspects of these spheres and levels would come together. The participation theorists never thought that such problems would ever be there. To that extent, the terms of references with regard to participation theory have been too narrowly drawn.

7. Participatory theory is too demanding. It makes a politician out of each citizen. A chemist may not like to indulge in politicking; an astronomer may not find time for politics; a businessman may not have an aptitude to know as to what goes on in the debates of the municipal committees. Why demand so much from the people? Why seek so large changes in the lives of the common people? Why not leave politics to the politicians? Such are the questions, some even valid, of the critics of the participation theorists.

All that the critics of participation theorists say is not valid. Indeed, a chemist may not have a liking for politics, but it is too much to say that a chemist is only a chemist, and not a father, a resident, a cricketer, a citizen, a voter, and not a being because he keeps his shop open for twenty-four hours a day. True also, participatory democracy anticipates an alert citizen-body and a host of institutions of all sorts, but this does not mean that we should abandon the project because it is too expensive, too time-consuming, too demanding.

The merit of the theory of participatory democracy lies in the fact that (i) it focuses on the individual not in isolation, but in the context of co-operative effort, with others; (ii) it engages in finding out the means for achieving the ideal of self-rule, (iii) it provides, or atleast attempts to provide suggestions for remedying the ills of the existing societies, and (iv) it helps us to know or discover the limitations of the existing systems and thereafter, to envisage changes in the political economic, social conditions of the people.

*(d) The Concept of Peoples' Democracy*

'Peoples' democracy' is associated with the Marxian theory of democracy. The Marxists do not think bourgeois democracy as the real one. For them, it is the dictatorship of the capitalists: rule of the capitalists, by them and for them; it is a class democracy, i.e., democracy of a class, a dominant class, an economically dominant class; the rule of minority over majority. For that matter, no class society can even claim to be democratic. A class system, the Marxists say, is conflictive in nature, and therefore, is exploitative. In a situation of inequality and exploitation, there can be democracy only for the rich, the possessing class. Professor Held says: "Marx believed that democratic government was essentially univiable in a capitalist society; the democratic regulation of life could not be realized under the constraints imposed by the capitalist relations of production". Giving the Leninist account of Western democracy, Neil Harding says: "Western-style representative democracy was no more than a sometimes convenient constitutional form, through which the real economic dominance of the capitalist class was exercised. In the epoch of monopoly or finance capitalism, it had become redundant and potentially destabilizing for the maintenance of the cycle of production and reproduction of capital. During the war, it had finally become discredited and had been displaced by the direct rule of finance capital, that unabashedly utilized the state to maintain and extend its own power." "From all this," Harding continues, "it followed that representative democracy, with its elaborate division of power and its attendant separate jurisdictions for legislative, executive, judiciary, army, and police could not possibly serve as the political form of the realization of socialism. Liberal democracy had not merely preserved, it had refined and sanctified the age-old and basic division of society into governors and governed."

*(i) Explanation of the concept of Peoples' Democracy:* For the Marxists, democracy and its full form can only be found in a classless society, beginning from the socialist society onward. Revolutionary as Marx was, he saw in a revolution an engine of history, pushing history ahead to unfold an era of real human freedom. "The political instrument of their enslavement cannot serve as the political instrument of their emancipation", for 'a master of society' will not become 'a servant' on request, "so writes Marx (*The Civil War in France,* 1870). Once the bourgeois democracy is abolished by the working class, there would usher, the Marxists say, a transitional period of the dictatorship of proletariat which would eventually pave way for a classless and a stateless society—the real permanent democratic society. Lenin believed that though the dictatorship of proletariat would be a bourgeois state without the bourgeoisie, yet it would be, as compared to the dictatorship of the capitalists, under capitalism, democratic in so far as it would be the rule of majority (therefore by them and for them) over the minority, both quantitatively and qualitatively rule of the working class over the erstwhile exploiters.

The socialist state would be qualitatively different from the bourgeois state, for socialism would mean rule not of the rich, the capitalists, the few, but would mean rule of the common man, the workers, the people. Under socialism, after adopting the socialist economy, the power of the state would be reclaimed by the people; the people would debate, discuss and finally decide all public issues; they would implement what they decide and would adjudicate all their disputes themselves. Under socialism, the power of the people, as it really was under Bolshevism, for example, would be direct, immediate and unrestricted. Marx and Engels had stated, (*The Communist Manifesto,* 1848) that socialism would be "an association in which the free development of each is the condition for the free development of all."

Marx had thought that the discovery of the Commune (1871) was the political form under which the economic emancipation of labour could be evolved. The commune, it was argued, was to make a reality of democracy by involving all citizens in all aspects of the governmental process and it was to retain control over all its functionaries by electing them all. Under socialism, in the Bolshevik view, as Harding says: "Democracy was to be direct, participatory and transformative. Its purpose was to transform people from passive objectives of the purposes of the others into conscious and active subjects."

So considered, the features of the peoples' democracy, as stated by Professor Held, may be summed up briefly as under:

1. Regulation of public affairs by councils organised pyramidically in the socialist era, and leading ultimately to self-regulation under communism.
2. Election and recall of all the officials of the state under socialism while governance of the public affairs by the people collectively under communism.
3. People's militia to sustain the socialist society, leading to a system without coercion and with self-evolving norms under communism.
4. Defeat of the bourgeoisie, unity of the working classes and elimination of all class privileges of the socialist era to be followed by abolition of private property, scarcity, market system, and the establishment of a citizen-centric society.
5. Beginning with the free development of each, and ending with the free development of all would make way for a free society where each and all would have all freedoms, end of exploitation, and ultimately the achievement of complete political, social and economic equality.
6. People's democracy rests on the principle of what 'each can give' to the one that is extendable to 'receive what you need'.

The concept of peoples' democracy, as suggested by Professor Held, would make somewhat a picture like this: "The machinery of the state would be replaced by the commune structure. All aspects of 'government' would then be fully accountable: the general will of the people would prevail. The smallest communities would administer their own affairs, elect delegates to larger administrative units, and these would, in turn, elect candidates to still larger areas of administration. This arrangement is known as the 'pyramid' structure of direct democracy; all delegates are revocable, bound by the instructions of their constituency and organised into a 'pyramid' of directly elected committees."

*(ii) Assessment of Peoples' Democratic Theory:* One may be tempted to say that the concept of peoples' democracy, as has developed through the writings of Marx, Engels, Lenin and through its application in some of the socialist countries, reflects the characteristics of elitist democracy on the one hand, and participatory theory on the other. What the concept and practice of peoples' democracy shares with elitist democracy is the fact that the power of decision-making lies in the hands of the few—the elite in the case of elitist theory of democracy and the communist party or what may be called in Lenin's vanguardism. Both, somewhat realistically, believe that there is always an unequal influence of all the people over the decision-making. But this is not to say that the Marxian democracy shares with the elitists the idea that ordinary citizen is apolitical and illiterate in shouldering the responsibilities of managing the public affairs.

What the concept as well as the practice of peoples' democracy shares with the participatory theory is an aspiration to a much fuller participation (i.e., self-rule in all respects) by the whole populace in decision-making. But it is wider and more ambitious, to the extent of impracticability, in scope than participatory theory.

Peoples' democratic theory is the democracy of Marxism-Leninism, Marxian in theoretical terms and Leninist in practice. To that extent, the concept of peoples' democracy is more democratic if viewed from the eyes of Marx; less democratic if viewed from Lenin's point of view. Marx was, indeed, a theoretician *par excellence*. His analysis of fraudulent democracy was unparalleled; his description of the socialist society first and the communist society later, as the society of the whole people was fairly democratic. But, as the concept came to be handled from Marx's times of capitalism to Lenin's days of socialist revolution, there came up the institution of a new type of party, the party as the vanguard of the people. With that the people came to be eclipsed by the workers; workers, by the party; the party, by the leaders; the leaders, by the chief. Marx had created a democratic ideal, Lenin substituted it by a group and Stalin made it dictatorial, the personality cult. Plamenatz says that when one moves from German Marxism to Russian Communism, one moves from horses to mules.

This, of course, does not mean that the concept of peoples' democracy is flawless. One may identify some of weaknesses as under:

1. If what Marx thinks and in what Lenin modifies, there is, in such a classless society, a propensity of an authoritian form of politics, when it is led by a vanguard and that too in the name of the people. In such a society of the whole of the people, there is, Professor Held argues, "no longer a place of systematically encouraging and tolerating disagreement and debate about public matters... There is no longer scope for the mobilization of competing political views."
2. The society of the whole people or what may be called 'the commune structure', where there is no public discourse, and the procedure to protect peoples' autonomy, there is no guarantee that those elected by the people into high offices would like their action to be scrutinized or their behaviour checked. The limitless powers with the communes would generate and foster dictatorship.
3. The Marxian picture of the communist society as "an association of free men, working with the means of production held in common and expanding... in full self-awareness as one single labour force; ...an association in which the free development of each is the condition for the free development of all" are all good, good democratic words, but without practical application, only blueprints of the new society.
4. Numerous difficulties arise when the ideals of government of the people are replaced by 'the government of things', 'self-regulating' and 'self-evolving system'. Things do not and in fact, are not as simple as are viewed. There has to be someone to: initiate a tangible proposal; suggest as to where a steel plant is to be built; and make a beginning. To say that things would begin themselves is a position which is untenable.
5. There are severe limitations of smooth functioning of institutions in a classless society. The idea that the executive

tasks can be spread amongst the population, that the delegates act under and within instructions, and that the representatives are recallable—are all very attractive, but at the same time unworkable.

6. The classless society of the Marxist-Leninist type expects a citizen body which is highly political, highly social, highly effective, ready to accept all the responsibilities related to its status or position. The citizen of the peoples' democracy has to be a part of a larger part and at the same time, has to be a part connected with another. Given the differences of mental and physical differences as of cultural gaps, it is, indeed, impossible and even undesirable to assume that a person would do all his different roles equally well, and that all the people, do so. And then, it is really impossible to assume that the people would become accustomed to observing the elementary conditions of social life.
7. The assumption that a person can be trained to become active through Lenin's vanguardism is a position which stands in direct opposition to what Marx and Engels, repeatedly, held: "We cannot ally ourselves, therefore, with people who openly declare that the workers are too *uneducated* to free themselves..."
8. Marx did not, Professor Held thinks, produce an adequate theory of institutional structures of the classless society. He reduces political institutions to an undifferentiated type, to a complex of organisations which are not clearly separated, makes power conceal in a hierarchical form and then, assumes the new system would be transparent, open and accessible to all. All this is a gamble, "a gigantic gamble". A.J. Polan (*Lenin and the End of Politics,* 1984) says, "the gamble that it will be possible to set about constructing the state 'in the best of all possible words'. The odds against the gamble are astronomic... It demands, in short, ...an absence of politics."

## IV. Democracy: Principles, Merits and Demerits, Conditions of its Success

### *(a) Characteristics Features of Democracy*

Democracy has its characteristic features—the principles around which democracy rules. Democracy alone possesses such principles which no other form has. Some of these principal features may be briefly, stated as under:

1. *Equality* is one of the characteristic features of democracy, more specificality, political equality. What it means is that all the people are equal, none having any privilege. Political equality means equal political rights, equal protection of law, equality before law. Negatively, it means absence of all types of discrimination. All forms of democracy must respect the principle of equality: one person-one vote. Professor Hearnshaw says: "Democratic society is merely one in which the spirit of equality is strong and in which the principle of equality prevails."
2. *Liberty* means freedom to hold an opinion, express it, voice it against injustice, against oppression, against repression. It is freedom of thought, of expression and of faith. It is pursuing one's own good in one's own way without violating the similar liberties of others. It is choosing one's own rulers, combating the corrupt authority.
3. *Participation* means exercising every opportunity to elect the rulers, to take part in decision-making directly or indirectly. If people are to participate in all public affairs, citizens ought to be entitled to contest election without any discrimination, ought to possess a vote, and that all votes ought to be of equal value: "one person, one vote; one vote, one value."
4. *Principle of Majority* is a characteristic which democracy alone possesses. It means that all decisions are taken on the basis of majority: majority decision becomes the decision to be accepted by all. It is a principle of judicious majority and cooperative minority, a principle, where the minority has the right to change itself into majority. It is a principle where political questions are resolved by the strength of support calculated in numerical terms. In effect, government by the people, means government by the majority, who thereby claim the right to speak for all. The substitution of majority for 'people' does possess the danger of 'majoritarianism', the tyranny of the majority as James Madison fears.
5. *Constitutionalism* means rule, through well-defined established procedures. It includes a written constitution, governance through the procedures enshrined in the constitution, whether written or unwritten rule of law rather than of men, representative system based on periodic and free elections, accountability towards people, decisions through debates,

discussions and ballots, free and fair elections, free public opinion devices and the like.

6. *System of Rights and Liberty* is another characteristic of democracy. Autonomous individual with rights and liberties is the essence of democratic government. Rights and liberties and duties make citizens as they ought to be; they make democracy as it ought to be. No other form of government ensures rights to the people than what democratic system does. Democracy is government of the citizens in so far as they constitute it freely and run it effectively through exercising their rights and liberties.
7. *Public Interest* is the fact that the democratic government takes into account what is in the general interest of the people. It serves more than it orders; it owes more than it owns. Though the meaning of 'public interest' is different with different people, and though some even denounce the very existence of public interest (for example, Bentham), yet the idea of public interest alone is democratic in essence.
8. *Companionship* lies at the very heart of democracy. Democracy, as Hollingshead says, is more than a political organisation; it is a social relationship, an associated living, a conscious striving on the part of each member to seek along with others the advancement of the common welfare. It is a cooperative society, a comradeship and not a competitive one; it is a society where people strive to aid rather than exploit.
9. *Justice* is also a principal characteristic of democracy. Democracy alone ensures justice, whatever meaning we may give to the word 'justice'. Democracy abhors injustice; it rejects all forms of discrimination; it stands against tyranny, oppression and absolutism; it fights for social justice: against the wolf and in favour of the lamb; against the exploiter and in favour of the exploited. Gettell writes." Since it is based on the general principle of equality, it is likely to promote justice as one of the main purposes for which the state exists."
10. *Fraternity* emphasises on universal brotherhood/sisterhood. It is only democracy which is in tune with the nature of man. It is one that coordinates man with man, nation with nation. Professor Maxey rightly says that democracy is a way of life in which "the voluntary and free intelligence and activity of man can be harmonised and coordinated with the least

possible coercion and it is the belief that such a way of life is the best way for all mankind; the way most in keeping with the nature of man and the nature of universe."

The above chief characteristic features of democracy show it both as an ideal as well as a procedure. As an ideal, democracy is a theory of equality, of freedom, of autonomous individual, of rights and liberties, of fraternity, of companionship, of justice, of public interest. As a procedure, it seeks to establish a government based on constitutionalism, participation, rule of law, decentralisation, freedom of press and of judiciary, fair and free elections, majority rule, accountability. For a government to be called a democratic one, it should pass the following procedural democratic test:

(i) control over government decisions about policy constitutionally vested in elected representatives;
(ii) elected representatives chosen in frequent and fair elections;
(iii) elected representatives exercise their constitutional powers without facing overriding opposition from unelected officials;
(iv) all adults have the right to vote in elections;
(v) all adults have the right to run for public office;
(vi) citizens have the right to express themselves on political matters, defined broadly, without the risk of state punishment;
(vii) citizens have the right to seek out alternative sources of information, such as the news media, and such sources are protected by law;
(viii) citizens have the right to form independent associations and organisations, including independent political parties and interest groups;
(ix) government is autonomous and able to act independently from outside constraints; and
(x) there is no discrimination among the citizens on any ground whatsoever.

*(b) Merits and Demerits of Democracy*

Democracy, as a form of government, has its merits which outscore it against all other forms of government. It also has its limitations as well.

(i) *Merits of Democracy*: Some of the chief merits of democracy are as under:

1. *Best of all Forms of Government:* The merit of democracy lies in its being the best of all forms of government. Monarchy denies all tenets of equality and liberty; absolute monarchy results in autocracy. Aristocracy thrives on discrimination and favoritism. Dictatorship, either of military regime or of a certain political party, is absolutism personified. Democracy, as an ideal, is the best of all systems; it is, as a procedure, another name of popular government based on equality, liberty, participation.
2. *Democracy—an Ethical concept:* Democracy is much more a broader concept than merely a political status. It is a faith in the common man. Lindsay argues that democracy implies that all beings have a worth in themselves. No one is a mere means to another's end." No other form of government respects individual as democracy does.
3. *Alike considerations for all citizens*: Democracy is a government which alone guarantees that the will of every one in the community shall be duly considered, recognised and respected. It also ensures that no one shall be neglected in what is done by the government. Asirvatham writes, "In a democracy, at least in theory, there is not a single man who can suffer without the rest of the community sharing in his suffering." Lowell says: "In a complete democracy, no one can complain that he has not a chance to be heard."
4. *Cooperation between the Specialists and Laymen:* Democracy alone has the qualities of the specialist and the laymen together. The mere specialisation brings about soulless efficiency and that was what had killed the ancient Rome. The laymen alone know what exactly is that they require: he who wears the shoes knows where the shoe pinches. Democracy brings together the benefits of specialisation and peoples' requirements. To be governed only by a specialist is nothing short of a calamity as Hocking rightly says. To be governed only by a layman is nothing short of being led by an incompetent.
5. *Public Education:* Democracy is an experiment in public education. It is only democratic polity that stimulates interest; it is only democracy that is informative. During elections, issues are raised; speeches are delivered, articles are written, programmes are outlined, and policies are proposed, and with the result of all this, the general understanding rises

phenomenally. Burns rightly writes: "All government is a method of education, but the best education is self-education; therefore, the best government is self-government which is democracy."

6. *Ennoblement of the People:* Democracy, Asirvatham says, ennobles people; it makes them better qualitatively. It is based on the assumption that what one does himself is better than what is done for him by others. It is the best aid to self-help, initiative and self-esteem. It is conducive to the development of all-round man. It alone makes possible self-realisation of the individual.
7. *Patriotism:* Democracy promotes patriotism. It, being the rule of the people, creates a feeling among the people that their loyalty to the state is their loyalty towards their country and not towards the king/queen who heads the state. Laveleye says, "The French people never really loved France until after the revolution (1789)...." Mill says: "Democracy strengthens the love for country because the citizens feel that the government is their own creation."
8. *Reduction of the Danger of the Revolution:* Democracy reduces the chances of revolution. It is a government by persuasion and not by coercion. It reduces the possibilities of coups and smoothens the transfer of power from one set of rulers to another, peaceful and without any violence. It is a government, where laws are obeyed simply because the people think of government as their own. This itself reduces the dangers of revolt against the government. Gilchrist says: "Popular government is a government by common consent; from its very nature, therefore, it is not likely to be revolutionary."
9. *Responsiveness:* Democracy is a government which is responsive. It is responsive to the public opinion; to the changing conditions; to the point of being so flexible that it responds when the situations so demand. To that extent, democratic polity is neither rigid nor stale.
10. *Responsibility:* Democracy is a responsible government. Those who hold the power, they are responsible to those who elect them. The rulers' accountability is the essence of democratic polity. In other forms of government, there is no accountability of the rulers: the monarch, in a monarchy, is responsible to God, as James—I of England would say. Those who rule in

aristocracy are accountable to none. So is the dictator, in a dictatorship, responsible to none, not even to himself. Democracy ensures both accountability to what the rulers do and responsibility to what they are supposed to do.

*(ii) Demerits of Democracy:* The demerits of democracy can be summed up, briefly, as under:

1. *Rule of the Irresponsible Multitude:* Democracy is described as the rule of the irresponsible multitude. Aristotle thought of it as a perverted form of government. Mill feared the tyranny of majority. Lecky felt of it as opposed to liberty. The greatest defect of democracy is its undue importance on quantity: Votes are counted and not weighed. It exalts multitudes, making majority supreme.
2. *Oligarchy of the Worst Type:* Democracy is the rule of the majority, which boils down to nothing but minority. Talleyrand described it as the "aristocracy of blackguards". This aristocracy is nothing but the 'demagogue', 'the grafters' and 'the bosses'. Maxey writes that democracy easily falls prey to demagogism, bossism, and vicious pressures of politics.
3. *Rule of the Political Parties:* Democratic rule becomes eventually the party rule. As representative democracy functions through elections, political parties decide on candidates, conduct election campaigns, form government and formulate governmental policies. Ultimately democracy becomes an arena among the political parties. Indeed, party system is indispensable to democracy. It, as Bryce says, (i) encourages hollowness and insincerity, (ii) carries the national divisions into local elections, (iii) leads to the spoils system, and (iv) debases moral standards.
4. *Rule of Ignorance:* Democracy, usually, is described as the cult of incompetence—the government of the amateurs. As the common people do not reason much, they elect the most common representatives, who choose the rulers, usually as common as are the electors. Incompetence marks the rule in democracies. Intellectually, democracy becomes the rule of the poorest, the poor of the poorest; rule of the most ignorant.
5. *Cult of Incompetence:* Democracy rests upon a multitude which is usually ungrateful, largely emotional and eventually passionate. The common people have much less to reason. "Today," Asirvatham says, "they laud a man to the skies and tomorrow they cast him down is the mire; they are inconstant

and fickle in their attachment, both to principles and to persons." "At times, they are given to idealism and hero-worship," he continues, "at other times, they become obscurantists and obstruct all progress."

6. *Psychological Case against Democracy:* Democracy has been attacked on psychological grounds. Maxey says that the people are sheep-minded, ape-minded and wolf-minded, and accordingly, "they are credulous, impulsive, panicky, intolerant, unconscionable, cruel, unjust, stupid, and everything but rational." Under such circumstances, the democratic government is, Maxey says, "prone to indecision, fickleness, instability, and stupidity because of the violability, irrationality, and ineptitude of the masses."
7. *Government of the People—not-practicable:* Democracy, as the government of the people is theoretically true, but for all practical purposes, democracy is seldom, and in fact, never government of the people. Everything, in democracy, is decided by the majority: democracy is too oftenly the rule of majority and, as such, it is not the rule of the people. The voice of the people may very well be the voice of the devil. To assume that the representatives always 'represent' the people is a mistake: they, consciously or unconsciously, may misrepresent the people.
8. *Expensive:* Democracy is a very expensive form of government. We all know that democracy means organisation of opinion, propaganda, and frequent elections. All this means a lot of expenditure. Democracy, Maxey rightly says, is extravagant. Those who have money, are able to rule in democracies. To that extent, democracy can be rightly described as plutocracy.
9. *Bribery and Corruption:* Democracy's common abuses, among others, are bribery and corruption. Bryce has shown that there are several instances of electors, members of legislatures, administrative officials and even judicial officials succumbing to the temptation of illicit gains. In India, the opportunities for illicit gains have grown and so, the numbers taking advantage of them.
10. *Ill-education:* Democracy ill-educates more than it educates. It flatters people; produces a pretentious proletariat; conceals realities; inculcates in people a false sense of equality and attempts to survive on conservative attitude of the people.

Burns is of the opinion that the civilisation which a democracy produces is said to be "banal, mediocre or dull."

Lord Bryce sums up the chief faults observable in modern democracies as follows:

1. 'The power of money to pervert administration or legislation.
2. 'The tendency to make politics a gainful profession.
3. 'Extravagance in administration.
4. 'The abuse of the doctrine of equality and failure to appreciate the value of administrative skill.
5. 'The under power of party organization.
6. 'The tendency of legislators and political officials to play for votes in the passing of laws and in tolerating breaches of order.'

*(c) Essential Conditions for the Success of Democracy*

Democracy, indeed, is the best of all forms of government. "No one denies that the existing representative assemblies are defective, but even if an automobile does not work well, it is foolish to go back on a farm cart, however romantic it may be," so says Burns. Likewise Smith too says: "If one cannot gain heaven, it is foolish to despair, if there still remains in one's hands the means of avoiding hell. "Carpenter declares: O'Disrespectable Democracy, I love thou."

The defects of democracy are not its defects; they are of those who use democracy. We may give below the conditions necessary for the success of democracy: first, those as suggested by the scholars, and thereafter, suggestions as need to be there.

*(i) Prof. Hearnshaw lays down the following conditions:*

1. *A high standard both of honesty and of honour.* Moral soundness is absolutely necessary. Without clean hands and a pure heart, particularly in the leaders, democracy is bound to fail. A corrupt democracy is the vilest and most hopeless of political organizations. There should be equal rights for everybody, equity in law, and equality of opportunity.
2. *A high level of intelligence and a sound system of education.* Lack of common sense is dangerous in a democracy. Without a spirit of 'normal reasonableness on the part of the people at large', democracy will degenerate into mob rule or lead to dictatorship.

3. *A clear consciousness of the community*. Democracy calls for a strong sense of solidarity, an intense conviction of unity, a pervasive feeling of communal life. Racial feuds, religious schisms, class conflicts, and social cleavages are bound to weaken democracy.
4. *A sound public opinion, a sensitive social conscience, and an effective general will.* Democracy cannot be much better or much worse than the prevailing public opinion. Therefore, when and where democracy fails, one of the potent causes for it is unsound or ineffective public opinion.
5. *Social and industrial democracy.* If democracy is to succeed, it should invade man's social relationships as well as his economic life. Maxey rightly observes that an industrial democracy should be set up within, or parallel to, political democracy. It is a welcome sign that Indian democracy stresses the importance of democracy in both the political and the economic fields.

*(ii) J.W. Garner lays down the following as the essential conditions of democracy:* (a) 'a relatively high degree of political intelligence and abiding interest in public affairs, a keen sense of public responsibility, and a readiness to accept and abide by the decision of the majority' coupled with respect for the rights of minorities; (b) facilities for elementary education; (c) education in political matters and training in the habits of government; and (d) a high moral level.

(iii) Putman says: "Civic responsibility, social connectedness, individual accountability, associated membership, civic management, social trust and social justice are traits that have an important role in a democratic society."

(iv) Lothian suggests: "(a) that government should be conducted under guarantees of freedom of speech and criticism, and political and economic initiative for the individual; (b) that it should be changeable without violence, at the ultimate decision of an adult electorate."

(v) Bryce gives the following conditions necessary for the success of democracy: (a) more emphasis on the protection of the interests of the poor; (b) encouraging patriotism and courage; (c) establishing public order with a view to protect the individual liberties of the citizens; (d) minimising expenditure; (e) maintaining public satisfaction in the country; (f) having sound international and power systems; (g) eradicating the adverse effects of corruption and property; and (h) able and honest public servants.

Conducive atmosphere necessary for the success of democracy can be stated as under:

(i) *Social Conditions:* Social justice, social unity and social education constitute the social conditions necessary for the success of democratic polity. The members of the society should not be discriminated on any ground—of caste, creed, colour, sex, race, place of birth and the like. The social life of the people has to be peaceful and orderly; social strifes eat away the very vitality of the unity of the democratic society. Social education, in the form of social obligations as a member of the society, is a very important condition required in a democracy.

(ii) *Economic Conditions:* Economic equality and economic security, constitute the economic conditions necessary for the success of democracy. "Where there are great economic inequalities," Laski said once, "there the relations among the people as of those between the masters and the slaves." By economic equality what we mean is the minimum gap between the rich and the poor, an assured standard of living for everyone, absence of exploitation: 'sufficiency for all, before there is superfluity for the few' as Laski says, economic security implies security of what one prossesses: property in the form of capital and also in the form of labour.

Only in a relatively prosperous society, in which a reasonably fair distribution of the national wealth has taken place, do the people have the leisure, information and education necessary to participate in political affairs

(iii) *Political Conditions:* Democracy requires a conducive political atmosphere. An atmosphere of *liberty, equality, justice* is a condition required in any democratic polity. There has to be *judicious majority* and a *cooperative minority* to make democracy a success. "Local self-government institutions," Bryce had once said, "are the best schools of democracy." Written constitution removes any ambiguity which may come up as an obstruction in the path of democratic functioning. Constitutionalism, the free and fair elections, rule of law, sound public opinion, well-organised nationalistic political parties, are some of the other political conditions for the success of democracy.

(iv) *Moral Conditions:* The people and their leaders have to possess sense of common interest, of duty-abidingness, and of honesty. They have to exercise franchise more as a matter of duty than of right. The leaders, ministers, bureaucrats, the legislators have to serve more as public servants rather than the masters of the people.

(v) *Intellectual Conditions:* Those, who exercise their rights in the democratic set-up, whether as citizens or as rulers, have to have common sense ready enough to make right choice at appropriate times. They have to have the sense of justice. There has to be a democratic culture characterised by openness, tolerance, empathy, adaptiveness and flexibility. There has to be a democratic person characterised by virtues such as tolerance and cooperation, in particular.

## SUGGESTED READINGS

1. Burnheim, J., *Is Democracy Possible?* (Cambridge: Polity Press, 1985).
2. Cohen, J., and Rogers, J., *On Democracy* (New York: Penguin 1983).
3. Diamond, L. *Developing Democracy,* (Baltimore: The Johns Hopkins University Press, 1999).
4. Duncan, G., (ed.) *Democratic Theory and Practice* (Cambridge: Cambridge University Press, 1983).
5. Held, David, *Models of Democracy* (Oxford: Polity Press, 1987).
6. Held, D., and Pollitt, C., (eds.), *New Forms of Democracy* (London: Sage, 1986).
7. Lakoff., S., *Democracy* (Boulder, Colo: Wesview Press, 1996).
8. Lively, J., *Democracy* (Oxford: Basil Blackwell, 1975).
9. Macpherson, C.B., *The Real World of Democracy* (Oxford: Oxford University Press, 1966).
10. ________, *The Life and Times of Liberal Democracy* (Oxford: Oxford University Press, 1977).
11. Pateman, Carole, *Participation and Democratic Theory* (Cambridge: Cambridge University Press, 1970).
12. ________, *The Problem of Political Obligation: a Critique of Liberal Theory* (Cambridge: Polity Press, 1985).
13. Rodewald, C., (ed.) *Democracy: Ideas and Realities* (London: Dent, 1974).

14. Schumpeter, J., *Capitalism, Socialism and Democracy* (London: Allen and Unwin, 1976).
15. Yankelovich, D., *The Magic of Dialogue: Transforming Conflict into Cooperation*. (New York: Simon & Schuster, 1999).

## CHAPTER – 5

# Concepts: Liberty

Liberty or its synonym, freedom, is one of the most discussed concepts in Political Science. Liberty has also been an ideal for which thousands of people have sacrificed their lives. For these people, liberty or freedom has a romantic connotation, to achieve it at any cost and not to surrender it, come what may. Liberty has also been used in the national sense, i.e., national liberty, which means to achieve freedom from foreign rule, as India achieved it on 15th of August 1947. We are here concerned with liberty as a concept.

Historically speaking, liberty is a modern concept. The Greek city–states had no concept of liberty. The Athenian ideals had no sympathy for the slaves. The Greek citizens had certain privileges which helped them attain the ideals of citizenship. The famous Greek statesman Pericles said that freedom meant advancement and political activity for full citizens. The Stoics believed that liberty is necessary for the development of individual's personality. The Stoics thought of liberty relatively in modern sense. In the medieval times freedom was considered a privilege. It meant an exemption from tax, toll, duty or jurisdiction of a lord. Those, so exempted and privileged, joined the ranks of the nobles and the honourables. In fact, till the end of sixteenth century, freedom was synonymous with gentle birth or breeding, nobility, generosity, magnanimity and all the traits which were claimed by the nobles as a reason for their superiority over others. The inadventation of modern age saw the rise of middle class or capitalist class which invoked the slogan of liberty against the feudal society. John Locke declared that man has a natural right to life, liberty and property. The U.S. Declaration of Independence (1776) viewed life, liberty and pursuit of happiness as inalienable right of man, given by God. The French Declaration of the Rights of Man and Citizen (1789) says that "Men are born and remain free and equal in rights" and that "The aim of every political association is the preservation of the natural and imprescriptible rights of man. These rights are liberty, property, security and resistance to oppression." It also declared that "liberty consists in the power to do anything that does not injure others; accordingly, the exercise of the natural rights of each man has no limits except those that secure to the other members of society, the enjoyment of these same rights. These limits can be determined only by law..."

## I. Meaning of Liberty

A precise and generally acceptable definition of liberty is very difficult. Liberty has been understood differently by different people. Let us briefly understand some of these interpretations of liberty. *Firstly,* liberty or freedom is defined *as social relation* or social freedom. As Zygmunt Bauman says, "For one to be free, there must be atleast two. Freedom, as social relation means, social difference and social division. I am free, means that there is a form of dependence from which I want to escape." Freedom of movement means that there are people whose movement is not free. If being free means acting without restrictions, it implies that actions of some others are constrained. Hobbes said liberty depends on the silence of law; Locke said that 'where there is no law there is no freedom.' Liberty as social relation, does not find any inconsistency in both definitions, because we are socially free to act in a certain way, if there is no law prohibiting that act and if this is the case, then others are unfree to hinder me from doing so. *Secondly,* liberty as *social freedom* means freedom of one person against others who are unfree to hinder his enjoyment of freedom. Freedom also refers to freedom of choice. Hume defines liberty in this sense. According to him, liberty is the power of acting or not acting, according to the determinations of the will. Freedom of choice means there are many alternative actions and the individual is free to choose from them. *Thirdly,* freedom refers to free will. Freedom as *free will* has been advocated by the religious preachers like Pelagins, St. Augustine, St. Thomas Aquinas and John Calvin. According to them, God has made human beings free, and human beings are free to choose between good and bad, according to their will. They are free to work towards salvation or doom and they are responsible for their deeds. Freedom has also been interpreted as free actions. It means that freedom consists in voluntary action which is not motivated by fear of punishment.

Freedom in this sense also refers to actions which are determined by a man himself without any influence of others. J.S. Mill said, "the only freedom which deserves the name is that of pursuing our own good in our own way". Freedom has also been defined as free persons. Here, freedom refers to a characteristic of persons. A person is free to the extent he is able to develop his capacities to the fullest. Freedom here means self realisation. Laski uses liberty in this sense. He says, "By liberty I mean the eager maintenance of that atmosphere in which men have the opportunity to be their best selves." Marx also talked in the similar way when he discussed the communist society "in which the free development of each is the condition for the free development of all". Freedom also means feeling free. It means doing what one desires. A person feels free to the extent that he does what he wants. Here freedom is the state of mind. It can also be state of affairs. We derive a feeling of freedom when we are free to choose one of the several alternatives. Still, there are people who feel free when they escape from freedom and submit themselves to others and act according to their will. Often freedom is identified with a free society. Here, freedom is a characteristic of a group. A society in which liberties are evenly distributed, is called a free society. This means democracy. Freedom is considered as synonym to democracy. These different interpretations of liberty give a descriptive meaning of it. Liberty also has valuational meanings which means freedom is a value which can be estimated.

Freedom is also defined as protection of basic rights. Classical liberalism advocated this kind of freedom. It believed that a free society is based on *laissez faire*. Individuals have rights and liberties and the individuals who are enjoying such rights are free. The government can restrict a person's freedom only when necessary to protect other person's freedom. This view does not take into consideration the poverty or other factors which hinder the enjoyment of rights. Another interpretation of freedom takes care of this aspect, which advocates freedom as satisfaction of basic needs. According to Sidney and Beatrice Webb, "Personal freedom means, in fact, the power of the individual to buy sufficient food, shelter and clothing." This concept of freedom requires restriction on individuals freedom for the common good of the society. It means state regulation concerning public health, education and welfare. Here, freedom includes desirable social unfreedom and excludes undesirable social freedom. Freedom is also defined as government by consent. This persuasive definition of freedom says that the government should be representative of the people, who have given their consent to be governed by the government. Rousseau took this argument to another extreme. He said individual may be forced to be free. The individual is free when he obeys the laws reflecting the will of the majority or the "General will." His concept of freedom gives individual no choice but only to act according to the wishes of the authority.

Liberty or freedom mean different things to different people. By way of conclusion, some such meanings may be summed up as under:

(i) Freedom means freedom of choice when an individual has to choose between a series of alternatives.

(ii) Freedom means free will, the actual choice of an individual despite or irrespective of available alternatives.

(iii) Freedom means free action, the voluntary actions which an individual performs.

(iv) Freedom means free persons, unslaved, a quality of self-realisation as Marx would like to put.

(v) Freedom means feeling free, when a person does what he desires to do without any hesitation or compulsion.

(vi) Freedom means a free society when the people make their own destiny, independent of any external control.

## II. Definitions of Liberty

In addition to the various definitions of liberty given in the above discussion, some others are:

- Liberty consists in 'absence of restraints'.

—*Hobbes*

- "Freedom consists in a positive power or capacity of doing or enjoying something worth doing or enjoying".

—*T.H. Green*

- "Liberty is the freedom of individual to express, without external hindrance, his personality."

—*G.D.H. Cole*

- "Liberty means to secure enjoyment by the individuals and by the association of the power to think their own way under the shelter of the law, provided they do not impair the corresponding rights of others."

—*Ramsay Muir*

- Liberty is 'the opposite of over government.'

—*Seeley*

- Liberty is "the absence of restraint upon the existence of those social conditions which in modern civilization are the necessary guarantee of individual happiness." —*Laski*

- "Freedom is not the absence of all restraints but rather the substitution of rational ones for irrational". —*McKechzie*

- Liberty means, "that the state treats each and every moral person as a free agent, capable of developing his own capacities in his own way and therefore, capable of enjoying and exercising the rights which are the conditions of such development".

—*Barker*

These definitions of liberty, spread as they are, over a long history of Western political thought, refer to 18th-19th centuries' concept of liberty on the one hand, and the 20th century and its post-period concept on the other. The 18th-19th centuries' concept of liberty is one that is relatively closer to individual's initiative, autonomy and choice. Any attack on this kind of liberty, as associated with the individual by the state, is regarded an attack on the individual. As the laws of the state put premium on the individual, this kind of liberty, for want of better terminology, may be described as *negative liberty*. The 20th and the post - 20th centuries' concept of liberty is relatively liberalised in so far as it seeks from the state an atmosphere where the individual is able to make use of his/her own faculties so to help build one's own personality. This kind of liberty is described as positive liberty. The negative liberty is liberty as non-interference whereas the positive liberty is self-realisation or self-mastery. Isaiah Berlin also talks about the negative and positive aspects of liberty in his *Four Essays on Liberty*.

## III. Two Concepts of Liberty: The Negative Liberty: Liberty as Non-interference

The early liberals advocated the negative concept of liberty. The important thinkers in the category are Locke, Bentham, Jefferson,

Burke, Adam Smith and J. S. Mill to some extent. Here we will discuss some of these thinkers.

To Locke, life, liberty and property are the natural rights. They are pre-state rights as they existed even before the creation of state. The state was created by people because their natural rights were in danger. Therefore, the state and government are subservient to the natural rights. Government is a trust and remains in power till the people's wishes. Locke advocated a limited government and maximum liberties to the people, the state to interfere as minimum as possible.

Hobbes and Locke belonged to the era of possessive individualism of seventeenth century which comprised of the following seven propositions according to Macpherson:

(i) What makes a man human is freedom from dependence on the wills of others.
(ii) Freedom from dependence on others means freedom from any relations with others except those relations which the individual enters voluntarily to further his own interest.
(iii) The individual is the master of his own person and capacities, for which he owes nothing to society.
(iv) The individual cannot alienate the whole of his property in his own person, he may alienate his capacity to labour.
(v) Human society consists of a series of market relations.
(vi) The freedom of an individual can only be limited to secure the same freedom for others.
(vii) Political society is a human management for the protection of individual's property and, therefore, for the maintenance of orderly relations of exchange between individuals.

Adam Smith advocated a policy of *laissez faire* in which he stood for non-interference of government in economic activity. The market is self-regulative and the law of demand and supply takes care of both the capitalists and the labourers. The worker is at liberty to sell his labour and the capitalist is free in his economic ventures. Thus, a free market ensures maximum liberty to both capitalists as well as the workers. The state has no role to interfere and protect the weak. Here the classical liberals advocated the theories of struggle for existence and the survival of the fittest. In nature, there is a struggle for existence and in this struggle only the fittests survive, rest perish. In society also there should be struggle for existence in which the fittest will survive. The state has no business to protect the weak and poor who cannot survive the struggle.

The negative view of liberty regards state as a necessary evil. It is an evil because it restrains and all restraints are evils. It is necessary because of the selfishness and capacity of individual. Without state, there cannot be peace and order in the society and this constitutes state activity. The state should not undertake welfare activities because it is not meant for these purposes. The state should not undertake welfare activities because it is not meant for these purposes. The state should concentrate only on its political functions for which it is created. The functions of state according to liberals are three: (i) maintenance of law and order to protect individuals; (ii) to protect society from outside aggression; and (iii) to maintain the sanctity of contract between the individuals. Thus, the state is a limited state, the object being maximum liberty to the individuals. Bentham too favoured a non-interventionist state.

### *(a) J.S. Mill on Liberty*

John Stuart Mill is one of the greatest exponents of negative liberty. He lived at a time when the functions of state began increasing. Mill saw this expansion with suspicion and a threat to the freedom of individuals. The importance of Mill lies in his refusal to compromise with individual's liberty.

According to Mill, individual's activities are divided into two parts—self-regarding and other regarding. Self-regarding activities are exclusively his concern which do not affect others, while in other activities individual has to interact with others. In the self-regarding sphere like choosing a career, there should not be any control. He says, "In the part which merely concerns himself, his independence is of right, absolute. Over himself, over his own body and mind, the individual is sovereign." The individual's liberty cannot be curtailed on the basis of physical and moral goodness. He cannot be compelled to do certain act, because it is better for him or it will make him happier or it is wise or even right for him. Individual himself is the sole judge as to what constitutes right for him. Individual himself is the sole judge as to what constitutes right or wise or happiness and what is better for him. One may reason with him, or persuade him, not to do a particular act, but he cannot be compelled. Only when his conduct harms others, his liberty can be curtailed. Mill aptly remarks. "That the only purpose for which power can be rightfully exercised over any member of a civilized community, against his will, is to prevent harm to others."

The objective of individual in his life is to develop his personality, which is possible only when he has complete freedom in self regarding activities. Any restraint here, will hamper the development of individual's personality. Therefore, restraint is evil. However, in other regarding activities, Mill does not mind restraints because liberty is to be enjoyed by each and every person of the society and, therefore, it may be limited and restricted.

Mill also defined the contents of liberty. It comprises *firstly*, the inward domain of consciousness, which means liberty of conscience, thought and feeling, absolute freedom of opinion and sentiments on all subjects practical or speculative, scientific, moral or theological. *Secondly*, the principle of liberty requires liberty of tastes and pursuits; one should be free to plan one's life; of doing all actions as one likes without harming others even if others think that such action is foolish, pervert or wrong. *Thirdly*, freedom of association for any purpose which does not involve harming others.

Mill stands for an absolute liberty of expression. The government has no right to suppress it. He asserts, "If all mankind minus one were of one opinion, mankind would be no more justified in silencing that opinion than he, if he had the power, would be justified in silencing mankind." Mill reminds us of Socrates and Jesus Christ, whose freedom of opinions were suppressed. He says, "Mankind can hardly be too often reminded that there was once a man named Socrates between whom and the legal authorities there took place a memorable collision." An opinion is not to be suppressed because it may be voicing truth as was the case with the opinions of Socrates and Christ. If the opinion is right, we lose the opportunity of correcting the false opinion that we hold and if wrong, we lose the benefit of viewing a cleverer perception and livelier impression of truth produced by its collusion with a wrong opinion. Mill further says, "Those who want to suppress it, of course, deny its truth; but they are not infallible. They have no authority to decide the question for all mankind and exclude every other person from the means of judging. To refuse a hearing to an opinion because they are sure that it is false to assume that their certainty is the samething as absolute certainty. All silencing of discussion is an assumption of infallibility."

Mill is also aware of tyranny of majority and society. Though he favours democracy, he is also very clear that the majority may become as tyrannical as the despotic rulers and tyrants were in the past. Liberty may be threatened by the exercise of powers by the majority. Therefore, government's powers in a democracy should also be limited for the sake of liberty. He says, "The people who exercise power in a self-governing state are not always the same people with those over whom it is exercised... The limitation, therefore, of the power of government over individuals loses none of its importance when the holders of power are regularly– accountable to the community,..." In political speculations, 'the tyranny of the majority is now generally included among the evils against which society requires to be on its guard.' Liberty is to be protected not only from the tyranny of majority but also from that of the society. Society tries to impose its own ideas and practices on individual. It restricts those who do not obey the social order. The objective is "to fetter the development and, if possible, prevent the formation of any individuality not in harmony with its ways, and compel all characters to fashion themselves upon the model of its own." Mill stands for the autonomy of individual, who is not responsible for his actions to the society, so far his self-regarding actions are concerned. Individual is to be given a free atmosphere to develop his different faculties.

Mill also advocates certain limitations on individuals's liberty. We have already mentioned the first limitation i.e. liberty is subjected to the condition of not harming others. In case of self regarding functions also in some circumstances, the liberty may be curtailed. Nobody can be allowed to commit suicide. Individual can be prevented from consuming poisonous food. *Secondly,* Mill justifies these interventions because in such cases, individual does not know his interest well while the society knows it better. *Thirdly,* the children are exempted from the enjoyment of liberty because liberty is available only to human beings in the maturity of their faculties'. *Fourthly,* the backward people or races cannot have liberty. Mill advocated a despotic government for them. Needless to say that this is the objectionable assumption liable to be used by imperialism to justify despotic rule over the colonies.

*(b) Negative Liberty and Modern Libertarians*

In modern times, the concept of negative freedom has been propagated by many writers in the West. They defend liberty as the absence of restraints. Among its forceful advocates are Isaiah Berlin, Robert Nozick, F.A. Hayek, Rawls, Pennock and Milton Friedman.

According to Berlin, liberty counts in doing what one desires to do without interference from other persons. He says, "You lack political liberty or freedom only if you are prevented from attaining a goal by human beings. Mere incapacity to attain a goal is not lack of political freedom." Thus, there is no lack of liberty, if a person is not able to use his rights because of poverty or ignorance. On the contrary, Berlin says, there is an absolute loss of liberty if my liberty rests on some one's misery and my liberty is curtailed to relieve him of his misery and there is no increase in other person's liberty. The relief of misery cannot be termed as increase in liberty. According to Berlin, the concept of negative liberty has historically, justified tyranny, in which state stands outside the actual individual human being and that is dangerous. He says, "I wish my life and decisions to depend on myself, not on external forces of whatever kind. I wish to be the instrument of my own, not of other men's acts of will." Berlin's definition of a free man is of a man who is not in irons, not imprisoned in a jail nor terrorised like a slave by the fear of punishment; it is not lack of freedom not to fly like an eagle or swim like a whale. Freedom means non-interference by others. "The wider the area of non-interference, the wider my freedom." Says Berlin.

Berlin sees no particular connection between negative liberty and democracy. An individual may have more negative liberty under an easy-going despot than in an intolerant democracy. Berlin, here, is reminding us of Mill's views on the tyranny of majority. The sovereignty of the people can destroy the sovereignty of the individual liberty. It does not involve any logical commitment to 'some frontiers of freedom which nobody should be permitted to cross.' Berlin believes in the autonomy of individuals and 'if the essence of men is that they are autonomous beings... then nothing is worse than to treat them as if they were not autonomous, but natural objects." The reformers do exactly that. They treat the men as objects who have no wills of their own. Thus, they degrade men. Berlin also finds no relation between liberty and the conditions required for the realisation of liberty. When we try to create necessary socio-economic conditions of real freedom, we forget freedom itself. In fact, absence of necessary socio-economic conditions for the realisation of liberty does not mean absence of liberty. Liberty is present even there, where there is no justice and equality.

*Lastly,* it is to be remembered that Berlin stands for what Graham Wallas calls two spheres view of liberty. It means man's life can be divided into two spheres; in one sphere man should be completely free, where there should not be any control or coercion. There is still the second sphere where control and interference in man's life is necessary. The liberty may be curtailed here. Berlin, in fact, is advocating Mill's division of man's actions—self-regarding and other regarding. Like Mill, the negative liberty is available in self regarding activities of an individual, while restraints may be necessary in other regarding activities, so that the others are not harmed. Nozick, following John Locke, advocates individual rights as natural, so natural that even the state has no power to interfere. He favours a minimal state. Hayek, too, is a libertarian like Nozick. With Hayek, any act of coercion on individual amounts to denial of liberty.

Rawls and Pennock have followed Berlin in their conceptions of liberty. Pennock says, "Liberty is the opportunity for spontaneous and deliberate self-direction in the formation and accomplishment of one's purposes." Opportunity, to Pennock, means 'the absence of external control of threats, physical impediments or moral or legal obligations.' Therefore, if I am not able to enjoy liberty because of social circumstances, it does not mean absence of liberty. Rawls is more concerned with the relative value of different liberties. He is not concerned with negative or positive liberty. Like Berlin and Pennock, he also refuses to count poverty or social reasons as factors restraining liberty. They do affect the worth of liberty, its value to an individual but do not determine whether that individual has liberty. Rawls bases his argument on the basis of twin principles of justice. The first principle is that everyone is to enjoy the most extensive liberty which is to co-exist with similar liberty for others and secondly that socio-economic inequalities must work to everyone's advantage. These two principles divide the society into two spheres—the political sphere, as a citizen where liberty is inviolable and equal, and socio-economic inequalities must work to everyone's advantage. These two principles divide the society into two spheres—the political sphere, as a citizen where liberty is inviolable and equal, and socio-economic sphere where considerable inequality may prevail.

Milton Friedman also supports the concept of negative liberty. Liberty means, according to Friedman, "the absence of coercion of a man by his fellowmen." Further he asserts, 'Freedom... has nothing to say about what an individual does with his freedom; it is not an all embracing ethic.' To Friedman, economic freedom is a necessary condition of political freedom. He praises competitive capitalism, which alone can guarantee civil liberties. The restrictions on economic freedom constrains political freedom because they are not wholly distinct. Decisions made in one also affects the other. Friedman advocates free economy which should be constraint-free in the operation of free market and state should not undertake pension schemes and exchange control. To Friedman, capitalism is a pre-condition for political freedom. Free market economies like as existed in Athens and early Roman period and in certain nineteenth and twentieth century societies can be possible without tyranny, servitude and misery. The operations of a free market economy disperse the concentration of political power. He is against positive view of liberty, because it does not accept a free market society. He is also against socialist state on the same ground. He criticises the concept of democratic socialism because any form of socialism is incompatible with individual liberty. Friedman says, "A society which is socialist, cannot be democratic in the sense of guaranteeing individual freedom."

The modern libertarians advocate freedom of speech, assembly and association and liberty of thought and conscience very vehemently. These liberties should be protected from the interference by other individuals through political or legal provisions. Thus, modern libertarians regard civil liberties as sacrosant. But why civil liberties be given more importance than other socio-economic rights? Modern libertarians have advanced three arguments in this respect.

1. The civil liberties are basic. They are key to other liberties. If they are lost, others will also be unsecured.

2. These civil liberties do not harm others who also enjoy the same liberties. Thus they can be widely distributed among the people.
3. The civil liberties are connected with rationality. Men make decisions and it is not necessary that every decision may be right. Therefore, we should be open to criticism. Hence freedom to express one's views and criticise those of others is absolutely necessary.

The concept of negative liberty are summed up in following:

(i) Liberty means absence of restraints.
(ii) Liberty is necessary for the development of individuals' personality.
(iii) Man's activity can be divided into two spheres—self-regarding and others-regarding. In self-regarding activity, man should be given full freedom, which include freedom of expression, and thought, to assemble and to form association. In others-regarding activities, the state needs to interfere, but to the minimum.
(iv) The state should have a very limited function, as it is a necessary evil.
(v) Liberty is to be protected from the tyranny of majority.
(vi) Political and civil liberties are to be protected at any cost. They cannot be sacrificed in the name of equality and justice.
(vii) Mere incapacity to use liberty does not mean absence of liberty.

*(c) Criticism*

The concept of negative liberty was in vogue in the eighteenth and first half of nineteenth centuries in England and other parts of the Europe. There is no doubt that it brought prosperity in the society. However, very shortly its ill effects were also noticed. The concept of negative liberty furthered the liberties of propertied class at the expense of the liberties of the weak, who virtually became slaves. Macpherson aptly states that a formulation of negative liberty furthered the liberties of propertied class at the expense of the liberties of the weak, who virtually became slaves. According to Macpherson any formulation of negative liberty which takes little or no account of class-imposed impediments, deliberate or unintentional, is not entirely adequate. *Secondly,* Mill's division of human activities into two—self regarding and other regarding, is questionable. Human activities cannot be divided in such a manner. Mill himself puts drinking and gambling in self-regarding activity of a man. But a little understanding of effects of drinking and gambling will make it other-regarding activity. A worker wastes his money in drinking and gambling. Consequently, he cannot look after his family and children, who live a life of misery and poverty. Besides there are other social effects of drinking and gambling, like crime. Thus, all talks of self-regarding activities are but insignificant. This mistake has also been committed by Berlin, Pennock and Rawls. Mill (and his followers) as Barker puts it, separate the inseparable. "The conduct of any man is a single whole; there can be nothing in it that concerns himself only, and does not concern other men; whatever he is, and whatever he does, affects others and, therefore, concerns him". Therefore, Barker calls Mill as the prophet of empty liberty and an abstract individual. The same is true of the concept of negative liberty as advocated by modern libertarians.

## IV. The Concept of Positive Liberty: Liberty as Self-Realisation

Historically speaking, the concept of positive liberty emerged as a reaction to the concept of negative liberty. It was realised that the negative liberty which defined liberty as absence of restraints led to a social situation in which only a few were able to enjoy it while the majority in a cesspool of misery and deprivation had no relations with liberty. The later half of the nineteenth century gave way to positive liberty which meant power of the individual to work for oneself. T.H. Green, Bosanquet, Barker and Laski are the principal architects of positive liberty.

### *(a) Views of Green*

According to T.H. Green, positive freedom means, "a positive power or capacity of doing or enjoying something worth doing or enjoying, and that, too, something that we do or enjoy in common with others". It means that freedom possesses two qualities. *Firstly,* it is the freedom to do or enjoy what is worth doing or enjoying along with others. Freedom is to be enjoyed not in isolation but in common with others. To Green 'it is the liberation of all the powers of man for the social good.' It means a power of the individual by which he has a share in the goods that society produces and an ability to contribute in the common good. *Secondly,* freedom is determinate or definite. Freedom is not licence, to do anything as one wishes. On the contrary, it is the power to pursue those objects which make our lives better. It is the quality of doing what is worth-doing. To Green, freedom means self-perfection, which a man does by contributing to the welfare of social whole. It is a moral freedom.

Green is highly critical of the policy of *laissez faire* and its effects on the social system. Real freedom cannot exist in the midst of ignorance, poverty and moral deprivity. He said, "To an Athenian slave who might be used to gratify a master's lust, it would have been a mockery to speak of the state as the realisation of freedom; and perhaps it would not be much less so to speak of it as such to an untaught and underfed citizen of a London yard, with gin shops on the right hand and on the left." In other place, he says, "If the ideal of true freedom is the maximum of power for all members of a human society alike, to make the best of themselves, we are rightful in refusing to ascribe the glory of freedom to a state in which the apparent elevation of the few is founded upon the degradation of the many, and in ranking modern society, founded as it is, on free industry with all its confusion and ignorant license and waste of effort above the most splendid of ancient republics." Thus, Green's effort is, in the words of Barker, "to reintegrate the individual into those socially created values which the unhistorical Benthamites had ignored." He demonstrated that, if the source of all spiritual values is the individual, the individual should be considered in his universality that is, in those aspects that join him to other individuals.

The object of state, according to Green, is to remove hindrances to freedom. Here, he emphasises a wide role for state. Ignorance, drinking and poverty are hindrances to good life and he wants state to remove these evils. He also advocates state action in housing and labour welfare. He, in fact, wants all the hindrances to good life be removed by state action. Yet the state remains a negative state, whose functions are limited. Wayper says, "The negative form in which Green speaks of state is nevertheless significant. It is a reminder that in the final analysis what matters most in life must remain within the province of the individual—the development of his moral nature." Green belongs to the idealist tradition which regards state as a natural institution necessary for the moral realisation of the individual. The state creates conditions necessary for good life. But it cannot be an absolute state.

### *(b) Views of Laski on Positive Liberty*

Defining liberty Laski says, "By liberty I mean the eager maintenance of that atmosphere in which men have the opportunity to be their best selves. Liberty, therefore, is a product of rights. Without rights there cannot be liberty, because without rights, men are the subjects of law unrelated to the needs of personality." To Laski, liberty is a positive thing. It is not just absence of restraint. It means certain action or conduct of individual can be prohibited in common interest and such prohibition does not constitute an invasion of liberty. Thus, liberty is not in danger if someone is refused permission to commit murder or, if someone is asked to obey traffic rules. But the problem is that sometimes the government claims that it is acting in common interest and invades liberty. No prohibition is justified just because government has ordered it. For example, the restriction of the franchise to the owners of property was an invasion of liberty. Laski wants that all the prohibitions imposed by the state 'should be built upon the wills of those whom they affect.' To Laski, all such restraints are evil which stop a person doing something which he thinks worthwhile to do. Similarly, we have a life of spiritual enrichment and any restraint is evil when it frustrates such life. We also have a right to personal initiative in the things that add to our moral stature and this cannot be restrained. Laski wants liberty of thought, expression, will and conscience.

Laski does not agree with Mill's division of human action into two spheres—self regarding and other regarding. He says, "All conduct is social conduct in the sense that whatever I do has results upon me as a member of society." Liberty involves, in its nature, restraints. One cannot enjoy liberty at the expense of other's liberty.

To Laski, liberty means presence of opportunity. We can create channels; we cannot force men to take advantage of those channels. Laski cites an example to prove his point, "A man may feel that all that he cares for in life depends upon success in love; we can remove the barriers of caste or race or religion which, in the past, have barred his access to that love. But we cannot guarantee to him that his plea will be successful."

Laski has discussed three aspects of liberty—private, political and economic. These rights, we have covered in forms of liberty, in this chapter.

According to Laski, there are three conditions of liberty without which it cannot be secured for the general masses. They are as follows:

(i) *Absence of special privileges*—The presence of special privileges leads to frustration and kills the habit of creativeness. They give a life of deprivation to those who do not possess special privileges. They lose the ability to realise their own good. Laski declares, "Special privilege is incompatible with freedom because the latter quality belongs to all alike in their character as human beings." The common good can only begin by the abolition of special privileges.

(ii) *Universality of rights*—Laski says that there cannot be liberty, where the rights of some depend upon the pleasure of others. Here, he advocates state control for the protection of political and economic freedom. My rights as a citizen should not be encroached upon. Similarly he wants state regulation in the distribution of wealth, in matters of livelihood and other welfare measures.

(iii) *The state should be impartial*—State action should be aimed at securing benefits to all. However, it is very difficult because state is compelled to support the interest of a small section. Therefore, we must try to seek that system which will minimise the bias involved. Rights are, therefore, important because they are the guarantees of a minimum bias. A citizen today should guard the rights of man and must react whenever he sees that the state is acting in a biased manner for the secret of liberty is courage.

However, later on Laski changed his views. In his preface to the second edition of *A Grammar of Politics,* he says, "In 1925, I thought that liberty could most usefully be regarded as more than a negative thing. I am now convinced that this was a mistake and that the old view of it as an absence of restraint can alone safeguard the personality of the citizen."

The concept of positive liberty can be summed up as follows:

(i) Liberty is not merely absence of restraints. It is more than that.
(ii) Liberty includes private, political and economic liberty.
(iii) Liberty cannot be realised where there is existence of special privileges, where there is no equality of rights and when state action is biased.
(iv) Rights are necessary for liberty.

(v) The state activity should be extended to include welfare of the individuals. For the purpose, individual liberty may be curtailed.

Scholars have started referring to third concept of liberty. It is described as liberty as non-domination. The intellectual roots of liberty as non-domination may be traced to the republican tradition of ancient Rome, the Italian Renaissance and the period leading up to the American Revolution. Liberty, as non-domination involves, what Cicero had said: 'being subject to no master." It is, as Livy would say, "to stand upright by means of one's own strength without depending on the will of anyone else." Pettit affirms that liberty as non-domination is possible only in a political system, where there are no discretionary powers and where the enjoyment of right is not contingent upon either the goodwill of anyone else or one's ability to elicit someone's goodwill.

## V. The Marxist Concept of Freedom

In order to understand Marxian view of freedom, it is necessary to know Marx's views on man and his essence. Marx refuses to accept liberal view of atomistic man. An isolated self-seeking man to Marx is a fiction. Man is intrinsically connected with other fellow-beings. Human essence is the totality of social relations. Therefore, man's purpose is not to seek his self interest. Man, in Marxism, is defined by his capacity to work and is distinguished from other creatures by his ability to produce freely. Man is a creator and has ability to enjoy his creation. Being social, his creative activities are directed not only for himself, but for the development of all the members of the society. Man can thus be understood in terms of human values of love, sympathy, art, culture, music, games, literature, knowledge of philosophy and sciences.

Freedom follows from such a comprehensive understanding of man and his essence. Marxism has no intention of getting involved in the liberal's understanding of liberty in terms of negative and positive freedom. The Marxists take freedom in a wider context. Freedom means living life to the fullest. Not only individual's minimum economic requirements are to be realised, but he should also be able to cultivate human values and be creative and develop his personality. Petrosyan rightly remarks, "Marx's understanding of freedom implies activity aimed at creating real conditions for the free all-round development and flowering of man's individuality." True freedom can be found only in a free society. The problem is that the free society does not exist in a class-divided society. It only existed in primitive communism, where there was no private property. With the origins of private property, a class divided society came into being, which is still continuing. Marx wants to eliminate the root cause of class-divisions which is private property. Only with the elimination of private property, classes will disappear and a free society will emerge in the form of communism, where the individual will really be free. A detailed analysis of Marxist notion of freedom can be done under following heads:

(i) Freedom as recognition of necessity
(ii) Freedom as social action
(iii) Freedom in a capitalist society
(iv) Freedom in a socialist society
(v) Freedom in communist society

(i) *Freedom as recognition of necessity:* According to Marxists, man is governed by certain objective laws which he does not create. They emerge independent of his will. Freedom consists in understanding these laws and using them for his benefits. That is what Engels means when he says "Freedom is the recognition of necessity." These objective laws consists of two types—one works at the level of nature like laws of gravitation and the other being the laws of social development. The objective laws of nature are determined by the nature itself while the objective laws of society are determined by the means of production. In both cases man cannot change them. But he can study them and in their study he is free. Initially when man came on to this earth, he was highly ignorant. He was a slave of the nature. Slowly, he learnt many things about the nature and used them to his benefit and became free to that extent. Engels writes, "Freedom does not consist in an imaginary independence from natural laws, but in the knowledge of these laws and in the possibility which is thus given of systematically making them work towards definite ends... Freedom of wills, therefore, means nothing but the capacity to make decisions with knowledge of the facts... Freedom, therefore, consists in command over ourselves and over external nature, a command founded on knowledge of natural necessity; It is therefore, necessarily a product of historical development. The first men who separated themselves from the animal kingdom were in all essentials as unfree as the animals themselves, but each step forward in the field of culture, was a step towards freedom." By understanding of the objective laws, man becomes the master of nature and society and gets benefits out of them. Thus, by understanding rules of water, one swims in a river or by understanding the natural cycle of rains, the farmer organises his agricultural activities. Similarly, man has to understand the social laws of development which will make him clear that the property creates classes which are antagonistic to each other; a class divided society only results in exploitation and obviously, where there is exploitation, there can be no freedom. These conclusions are based on objective laws of society which cannot be changed by man. In this context freedom lies in understanding these objective laws and use them to benefit us. Marx declared, "The true realm of freedom... can blossom forth only with this realm of necessity as its basis."

(ii) *Freedom as social action:* The existence of objective laws, which are free from man's control, does not mean that there is no role for man. Marx declared, "Man makes his own history, but he does not make it out of the whole; he does not make it out of conditions chosen by himself, but out of such as he finds close at hand." Philosophers have only interpreted the world, but the point is to change it. The freedom comes when man after understanding the objective laws involves himself in revolutionary activity. There is, no doubt, that the ultimate cause of revolution is the conflict between forces of production and relations of production, a conflict which is outside of human will. But once this conflict emerges it creates man's consciousness it and also the will to revolt. The human will is the immediate cause of revolution. Engels said, "Freedom of the will consists in nothing, but the ability to come to a decision when one is in possession of a knowledge of facts." Antonio Labrida declared that volitions are a result of necessities. To Marx, revolutionary activity itself constitutes freedom because as Cornforth puts it, "A passive slave is simply a slave but slave in revolt is acting as a freeman even though he still wears his chains. Such people are pioneers of human freedom" Man is not merely a slave in the hands of material circumstances, he can also alter them.

(iii) *Freedom in a capitalist society:* In a class-divided society freedom is always a relative concept. It means different things to different classes. In a capitalist society freedom to capitalists means freedom to exploit the workers, while workers starve. Freedom to them means freedom to be exploited. In fact, in the capitalist society freedom is limited to a small section of population while the majority is always unfree. However, in another significant manner neither the worker nor the capitalists are free. This, Marx explained, in his theory of alienation. To Marx human essence lies in the pursuit of human values. Man is a creator and wants to enjoy his creation, but in capitalist society he cannot do so because he is suffering from alienation. According to Marx, the roots of alienation lie in the private ownership of means of production, where the profit motive dominates. The capitalist becomes a machine whose purpose is to make more and more money. Money, a dead thing, dominates the living thing. The capitalist feels alienated from the production. The workers also suffer from alienation. Marx writes, "The bourgeoisie... has converted the physician, the lawyer, the priest, the poet, the man of science into its paid wage labourers. It is torn away from the family its sentimental veil, and has reduced the family relation to a mere money relation... The labourers must sell themselves piecemeal, have been reduced to mere commodity, like any other article of commerce... Owing to extensive use of machinery... the worker becomes an appendage of the machine. Not only the workers are the slaves of the bourgeois class, and of the bourgeois state; they are daily and heavily enslaved by the machine, by the individual bourgeois manufacturer himself." Marx finds man's alienation in capitalist society in four ways— (a) from his product, (b) from nature, (c) from his species, and (d) from himself. A detailed study of Marx's theory of alienation has been made in the Marxist concept of property. An alienated being cannot be free. Hence, Marx advocates elimination of private property.

(iv) *Freedom in a socialist society:* Socialist society is, to Marx, the first phase of communism. Trotsky termed it as the most ruthless form of state. It is also called the dictatorship of the proletariat. Lenin said, "The purpose of the dictatorship is to establish socialism, to put an end to the division of society into classes, to make the exploitation of one human being by another for ever impossible. This end cannot be achieved at one stride... The reorganisation of production is a difficult matter. Time is requisite for the radical transformation of all departments of life."

Lenin claimed that dictatorship of the proletariat is better than the bourgeois democracy, because here the majority rules over the minority. The workers are free while the remnants of capitalism are unfree. All the means of productions are nationalised and become government property. But what about the freedom? Marx and Engels viewed socialism as a transitory phase and they did not give much thought to freedom. Moreover, socialism was not achieved in any state during their life time. However, the experiences of socialist states in twentieth century proved that the political system provided political, social and economic rights but it could not provide freedom. The political rights were available for only those who were the yes-men of the regime. The people always felt the loss of freedom. The economic performance was also less than satisfactory. This all led to the death of these socialist states with the exception of Cuba and China.

(v) *Freedom in a communist society:* According to the Marxists, the communist society will be a free society where man will be able to develop his personality in all its multi-dimensional form. The production will be for consumption and not for profit. The state shall wither away and the society will be a vast association for production and all work will be performed as a habit. There will be no landowners, no capitalists, no wage workers, but only human beings. Classes will disappear as there will not be private property. Thus, there will be no exploitation, no oppression and no alienation. The communist society will be characterised by abundance of wealth, where each will contribute according to his ability and will receive according to his needs. Engels said, "On the one hand, no single individual will be able to shift his share in productive labour, in providing the essentials of human existence, upon another, and on the other hand productive labour, instead of being a means of slavery will be a means towards human freedom, in that it offers an opportunity to everyone to develop his full powers, physical and intellectual, in every direction and to exercise them so that it makes a pleasure out of a burden." This is a society, as Marx prophesied, "in which the free development of each is the condition for the free development of all." Man will be able to develop both, as a person and as an individual. The human energy, which hitherto was being wasted in class struggle, will be devoted to social purposes. Man will really become creative and will enjoy his creation. Engels asserts,

"Then for the first time, man, in a certain sense, is finally marked off from the rest of the animal kingdom, and emerges from mere animal conditions of existence into really human ones. The whole sphere of the conditions of life which environ, and which have hitherto ruled man, now comes under the domination and control of man, who for the first time becomes the real conscious lord of Nature, because he has now become master of his own social organisation. The laws of his own social action, hitherto standing face to face with man as laws of nature foreign to, and dominating him, will then be used with full understanding, and so mastered by man. Man's own social organisation, hitherto confronting him as a necessity imposed by Nature and history, now become the result of his own free action. The extraneous objective forces that have hitherto governed history, pass under the control of man himself. Only from that time will man himself, more and more consciously, make his own history—only from that time will the social causes set in movement by him, have, in the main, and in a constant growing measure, the results intended by him. It is the ascent of man from the kingdom of necessity to the kingdom of freedom." It is this freedom of man which is the objective of Marxian ideology.

The main points of Marxian view of freedom is as follows:

(i) Freedom is a comprehensive concept which is to be seen in terms of man's essence, purpose and values.
(ii) Freedom means all-round development of human personality.
(iii) Freedom means the understanding of objective laws of Nature and society and to use them for man's benefits.
(iv) Freedom also means involving oneself in revolutionary activity.
(v) In a class-divided society, freedom is impossible. Freedom cannot exist where there is exploitation, oppression and alienation.
(vi) Elimination of private property is necessary for the achievement of freedom.
(vii) Freedom does not exist in a socialist society.
(viii) Freedom can only exist in a communist society.

### VI. Forms of Liberty

There are three forms of Liberty:

1. Civil Liberty

2. Political Liberty
3. Economic Liberty

1. *Civil Liberty:* It refers to such liberties which are available to a man in society. *Firstly,* it means right to life. Appadorai aptly puts it, "The most fundamental of all rights is the right to life, the foundation on which the superstructure of other rights can be built up." Therefore, all the constitutions recognise this as a fundamental right. The assumption is that man is basic to nature; without him the world has no meaning, therefore, his life is sacrosant. Any attempt to kill any individual or murder is taken very seriously and law provides rigorous punishment in many countries even capital punishment. Man has no right to take away his own life also. Suicide is also a crime and accordingly dealt with by law. *Secondly,* it is private liberty. Laski says, "By private liberty, ... I mean the opportunity to exercise freedom of choice in those areas of life where the results of my efforts mainly affect me in that isolation by which, atleast ultimately, I am always surrounded". The right to follow one's religion comes under private liberty. There should neither be penalty nor any advantage in following one particular religion. *Thirdly,* individual has a right to privacy. This is the right to be left alone and it means protection from governmental authority or any private individual to intrude into one's home, correspondence, or thoughts. Individual has a right to protect his abode, communications, even his free time from unauthorised intrusion. A major complaint of citizens of socialist countries has been that they are not left alone by the government. *Fourthly,* civil liberty also includes freedom of speech and expression. The democratic principle believes that you may not like my views, but I have a right to be heard. This means right to criticise and oppose governmental policies. It also means a free press, which is the most important platform for the expression of ideas. *Fifthly,* civil liberties include right to form association. In modern pluralist society, the individual can develop his personality and contribute to the common good through associations only. *Sixthly,* right to assemble peacefully and without arms. *Seventhly,* freedom of movement. In fact a list of civil liberties would be very long and would depend upon specific political conditions in different countries. To Blackstone, civil liberty consists in three articles—personal security, especially of movement; and personal property, or the free use, enjoyment, and disposal of all

acquisitions. However, we will still describe one more important type of civil liberty which is right to equality. As we know, equality does not mean complete equality in an egalitarian society; it only means elimination of discrimination based on colour, caste, creed, religion, belief, sex and other factors. We may conclude civil liberty with Barker. According to him, "Civil liberty consists in three differently expressed articles: physical freedom from injury or threat to the life, health and the movement of the body; intellectual freedom for the expression of thought and belief, and practical freedom for the play of will and the exercise of choice in the general field of contractual actions and relations with other person." Civil liberties are generally available to all persons living in the state, irrespective of whether they are the citizens or aliens.

(ii) *Political Liberty:* Political liberty is available to a man in his capacity as a citizen of the state. To Blackstone, it is a negative liberty which means the power of curbing government. He viewed government as something external to man, which is not true. As Barker says, "Government is not external; it is in us, or springs from us." Therefore, Laski is correct when he says, "Political liberty means the power to be active in affairs of state." The universal adult franchise stems from this assumption. Right to vote is a valuable right with which people elect their government. Individual also has a right to get elected, subject to limitations imposed by the provision of the constitution. Political liberty also means right to political dissent through peaceful means. It also means that the powers of the government are limited. The government is responsible to the people who are sovereign and are the very source of governmental authority. People have a right to participate in governmental activities and have access to the positions of authority. People elect their government on the basis of election and control it. As Barker aptly puts it, "by a general and continuous process of discussion, in which we all freely share according to our capacities." Gladstone, therefore, identifies political liberty as synonymous to democracy. According to Laski, two conditions are essential for the political liberty to become real. First is education. "I must be educated to the point where I can express what I want in a way that is intelligible to others." Our education system is defective which trains the children of the rich to habits of authority and the children of the poor, habits of submission. Such a division of attitude can never produce political freedom because 'a class trained to govern will exert its power' (as it is conscious of it) while the other class will 'not fulfill its wants because it does not know how to formulate its demands.' "It is only when men have learned that they themselves make and work institutions that they can learn to adjust them to their needs." The second condition of a real political liberty is the free flow of information and news. Laski says, "A people without reliable news is, sooner or later, a people without the basis of freedom." Therefore, the mass media, press, radio and television should be free and give impartial and reliable news.

(iii) *Economic Liberty:* The whole idea of civil and political liberties become superfluous and futile if they are not accompanied with economic liberty. A poor man can never be a responsible citizen as deprivation makes him incapable of enjoying his liberties. Therefore, individual must be free from poverty. This means that the minimum economic requirements of food, clothing and shelter must be available to all. Right to work must be given to all. Individual should also be entitled to a decent wage. In modern times, in almost all. Individual should also be entitled to a decent wage. In modern times, in almost all the countries, the governments fix a minimum wage for both the skilled and unskilled workers. This does not mean that there should not be private property. It certainly exists but highly regulated. Economic liberty also does not assume equality of income. It definitely stands for the elimination of wide economic disparities. A state with wide economic disparities becomes two states: of the rich and the poor, in which, stability and democracy will never acquire permanence.

Laski advocates democracy in industry for economic liberty. The worker cannot be treated like commodity who can be bought and sold in market like coal, tools and chairs. He should have dignity in the industry. He must not live at the mercy of capitalists. He must have a role both in setting up of the standards and application of standards by which his contribution is to be judged. Otherwise, he will work only under fear, the fear of being thrown out of job and the resultant starvation. Laski rightly states, "A system built upon fear, is always fatal to the release of the creative faculties and it is, therefore, incompatible with liberty." The best course is the worker's participation in the management of industry.

The three forms of liberty may conflict with each other and the experience proves that so is the case. The enjoyment of civil liberty of expression sometimes conflicts with the democratic state which in the name of political liberty, ban expression on the plea that it might give rise to hostility towards the government or promote hostility between castes or classes. Similarly, the workers demand for more wages, restricts the employers freedom of contract. The reservation of seats in legislative assemblies and jobs restrict other's liberties. In some cases, political liberty has to rescue economic liberty, like in the case of conflict of interest between the employers and employees. In some cases political liberty is to be curtailed for economic liberty. Barker rightly states that liberty is a complex notion, which, at once unites men in allegiance and divides them by its division. Here the principle of justice is to be introduced. Liberty should be taken as one of the principles of justice. Justice demands that the law should not only reconcile the liberty of one man with that of others, but it should also bring about a reconciliation between different forms of liberty.

## VII. Safeguards of Liberty

Liberty is the condition for any civilized existence. Without liberty, the individual loses his potentiality to develop his personality. Therefore, liberty has a sacrosanct value which is to be protected at any cost. The government, social and individual attitudes are some of the factors which may encroach upon and limit liberty. Hence the question before us is—how to protect liberty from various encroachments? The following are some of the safeguards of liberty:

(i) *Rule of Law*—As we have seen earlier that the early liberals believed that state is a necessary evil because it restrains and every restraint, constitutes a limitation upon liberty. The anarchists dismiss state as an unnecessary evil. According to them, all laws are bad and, a free people and a free society can only exist when all the laws are abolished. But these views are negative and cannot be accepted. Liberty cannot be a licence to do anything. If liberty becomes synonymous with licence then the law of jungle will prevail in the society where crude physical force, deceit and fraud will rule the social order. In such a situation, there cannot be liberty, only chaos and confusion will be the characteristics of human organisation. Montesquieu rightly suggested that it is principally by the nature and preparation of punishments imposed by law that liberty is established or destroyed. The purpose of law is to put restraints on one person's liberty so that others can also enjoy liberty. There cannot be absolute liberty, only a limited liberty. The limitations imposed should be for a fair social order, in which, each and every person is allowed to develop his faculties.

(ii) *Democracy*: The only system that can guarantee a free and fair opportunity to develop individual's personality is democracy. Lincoln rightly defined democracy as a government of the people, by the people and for the people. It is the people's welfare which is supreme because people are sovereign. A rule by dictator or a monarch gives freedom only to a person and his henchmen. Oligarchy gives freedom to a particular section of the people. Only in democracy the entire population enjoys the high principles of liberty. No doubt, democracy has loopholes. There cannot be perfect democracy but then the human beings are also imperfect. Perfection is an ideal which cannot be accomplished in the imperfect world. Given the imperfect world, democracy is the most perfect system of government, which has no alternative. This does not follow that democracy does not need any safeguards for liberty. In democracy also, there are innumerable threats to liberty which must be checked.

(iii) *Independent Judiciary*: The independence of judiciary is absolutely necessary for the protection of liberty. The judges must be free from the executive control because they have to protect individual's liberty from any invasion, caused not only from other individuals, but also from the government. Therefore they have to act fearless and impartial. This means only persons of high integrity should be appointed as judges. Their salaries should be protected by adequate constitutional provisions. Their dismissal and terms of office should be subjected to extreme care. Therefore, all the democratic constitutions provide a cumbersome procedure for their removal. In India, judges of the Supreme Court and the High Courts can be removed only on grounds of proven misbehaviour or incapacity by a special majority of both the Houses of the Parliament. Similar provisions we find in the U.S.A. and some other countries. J. Kent rightly says, "To give the judges the courage and the firmness to do their duty fearlessly, they ought to be confident of the security of their salaries and station."

(iv) *A bill of rights*: A bill of rights is also essential for the safeguard of liberty. A detailed and written bill of rights helps citizens in understanding their rights. It also puts specific limitations on governmental authority. In the U.S.A., individual's rights have been incorporated through constitutional amendments. The Indian Constitution also provides a detailed list of fundamental rights of the citizens. These rights can be modified only by a special procedure provided in the Constitution.

(v) *A democratic social order:* One of the important safeguards of liberty is a democratic social order. It means that democracy should prevail in society as well. It means existence of the attitude of tolerance and a fellow feeling for each other. It means that every person has a dignity which has to be respected. A society divided in terms of class and caste prohibit the development of such conditions as are necessary for the enjoyment of liberty. There should not be any discrimination on the basis of caste, class, creed, religion or sex. Similarly, liberty cannot be enjoyed in a society which has widespread economic disparities. The minimum economic requirements of food, clothe and shelter should be available to every person in the society.

(vi) *Vigilance*: Eternal vigilance is the price of liberty. One can be free only when he wants to be free and is ready to pay price for it. The people would protect their liberties. They should carefully watch the programmes and actions of the government and voice their protest whenever they feel their liberties are being threatened. The existence of such a people will deter a government from undue interference in their liberty.

## Conclusion

Liberty, it may be noted, is the essence of democratic life. Both the liberals and the Marxists lay emphasis on the importance of man's life: the liberals, limiting it to the individual's political life; the Marxists, extending it to the entire universe: individual, society, nature. Nevertheless, liberty constitutes an important ideal worth cherishing. Its quality lies in strengthening democratic polity, and man's endeavour to lead a rich life.

## SUGGESTED READINGS

1. Adler, Mortimer J., *The Idea of Freedom,* 2 vols (Garden City, N.Y. Doubleday, 1958–61).
2. Bay, C., *The Structure of Freedom* (Stanford, California: California University Press, 1958).
3. Berlin I, *Two Concepts of Liberty* (Oxford: OUP, 1988).
   _______*Four Essays on Liberty*, (Oxford: OUP 1969).
4. Cranston, Maurice, *Freedom: A New Analysis* (London: Longmans, 2nd Edition, 1955).
5. Friedrick, Carl J., (ed.) *Liberty* (New York: Atherton, 1962).
6. Laski, Herald J., *Liberty in the Modern State*. (London, George Allen & Unwin Ltd.).
   ________ "Liberty" in *Enclopaedia of Social Services*, Vol9, (New York: Macmillan, 1933).
7. Mill, J. S., *On Liberty* (London, Watt & Co, 1948).
8. Marx, Karl, *Economic and Philosophic Mansucripts of 1844* (Moscow: Progress Publisher, 1970).
9. Muller, Herbart J., *Issues of Freedom: Paradoxes and Promises* (New York; Harper, 1960).
10. Oppenheim, Felix E., *Dimensions of Freedom: An Analysis* (New York: St. Martins, 1961).

## CHAPTER – 6

# Concepts: Equality

The U.S. Declaration of Independence declares, "We hold these truths to be self-evident, that all men are created equal..." The French Declaration of the Rights of Man and Citizen explicitly recognised that men are born and remain free and equal in rights. Article 1 of the Universal Declaration of Human Rights, also accepts that 'all human beings are born free and equal in dignity and rights.' The Preamble of the Indian Constitution talks about equality of status and opportunity. The concept of equality is a fundamental basis of modern democratic state.

However, it is very difficult to define equality. Laski aptly puts it, "No idea is more difficult in the whole realm of political science." The concept of equality has such varied facets and a multitude of implications, that even after an exhaustive study on the subject, one really feels of not having mastered it. Let us understand the various meanings of equality.

### I. Meaning of Equality

An important difficulty in understanding equality, stems from the fact that nature has created men as unequal. This inequality can be very obviously observed in terms of physical and intellectual strength, capacity and beauty. The human society has further accelerated inequality including on grounds of caste, colour, creed, property, sex and many other factors. Appadorai, therefore says, "The statement that all men are equal is, then, as erroneous as that the surface of the earth is level." Burke condemns equality as a monstrous fiction', Coleridge as a infeasible proposition', Bentham as 'an anarchic fallacy' and Carlyle as a 'palpable incredibility and delirious absurdity.' Still we talk of equality of men and it constitutes the foundation of modern democracy.

Equality is sometimes referred to as equality of characteristics in men. The obvious inequality among men in terms of intellectual and physical strength, sex, colour, character traits, natural endowments, religion, age, social rank, property and other factors do exist. But the task is to identify certain properties that are similar in men. The men are equal means that men share certain qualities which must be specified. Hobbes said that the nature has made men so equal, in the faculties of the body and mind, that even the weakest can kill the strongest and no one can outwit the other. He postulated two kinds of equality between men, equality of ability and equality of expectation of satisfying their wants. Understanding equality in terms of equality of characteristics means that the resemblances among men are more significant than the obvious differences.

Equality is also understood as equality of treatment. This means that men, irrespective of their differences are of equal worth and dignity, therefore, they are entitled to be treated equally. According to Locke, men are equal because every man has equal right to his natural freedom. But to Laski, "Equality does not mean equality of treatment." A mathematician and a brick labour cannot be given equal treatment. It cannot be identity of rewards either.

According to Barker, "the principle of equality means that whatever conditions are guaranteed to me, in the form of rights, shall also and in the same measure, be guaranteed to others, and that whatever rights are given to others shall also be given to me." This notion of equality is essentially a legal notion which demands equality before law. However even today, Barker rightly states, this is a 'notion difficult to grasp and hold in its own true shape and form'. In the past, the powerful sections of the community have stated their claim of superiority before law on the basis of their standing in terms of wealth or social rank. We are different in general capacity; our wealth means a larger stake in the country, and our culture a great grasp of affairs; it is only fair that our superiority in general capacity should be accompanied by superiority in legal capacity, and that we should have something more than an equal standing before the law.' In modern times principle of legal equality has been accepted and the less wealthy and other less powerful sections, to quote Barker again say, "We are now equal to you in legal capacity; it is, therefore fair that we should also be equal in general capacity—in wealth and the opportunities it brings; in the general equipment and endowment of our faculties—and that legal equality should thus be crowned by social equality." The result has been, class conflicts in many political systems.

According to Laski, equality is a coherence of ideas and it implies a certain levelling process. "It means that no man shall be so placed in society that he can overreach his neighbour to the extent which constitutes a denial of the latter's citizenship." In simple words equality means men should be treated equal socially, economically and politically. According to Laski equality means the following:

(i) "The absence of special privileges. There should not be any individual or class who have special privileges. Politically, nobody enjoys a superior position and nobody can be denied access to the avenues and authority.

(ii) Adequate opportunities are available to all. It does not mean equal opportunities because that is not possible in modern societies which are characterised by so many disparities. Children who come hungry to school cannot, on average, profit by education in like degree to those who are well fed." Further 'the native endowments of men are by no means equal'. Some people are in better position in their lives because of the atmosphere in which they are born. Laski says: "Children who are brought up in an atmosphere where things and the mind are accounted highly are bound to start the race of life with advantages no legislation can secure. Parental character will inevitably affect profoundly the quality of children whom it touches. So long, therefore, as the family endures—and there seems little reason to anticipate or to desire its disappearance—the varying environments its will create make the notion of equal opportunities a fantastic one."

Bryan Turner, in his book, *Equality*, gives a comprehensive meaning of equality by highlighting its following characteristics:

1. That all men are fundamentally equal as persons.
2. That all must have equal opportunities.
3. Equality of conditions, for all social groups.
4. Equality of outcome and/or results

Equality means both negative and positive equality. Negative equality means absence of discrimination on the basis of birth, caste, creed, colour or religion; positively, it means creation of circumstances in which men are really free. It means, as Laski says that talent does not perish for want of encouragement. It means, "one man is not entitled to a house of twenty rooms until all people are adequately housed. It also means that minimum economic requirements of food, shelter and cloth be guaranteed to each and every member of the society. In fact the claim for equality is a protest against unjust, undeserved and unjustified inequalities." Therefore, on the one hand it means that all people are not the same; inequalities are obvious but on the other hand it also means that weaker should be protected from various types of exploitation; he should be promoted as he also possesses a right to decent living. But the basis of discrimination should be reasonable. The Indian Constitution is the best example of the modern concept of equality, the characteristics of which are as follows:

(a) The state cannot deny to its citizen 'equality before law and equal protection of law'.
(b) The state has also been prohibited from discrimination on grounds of religion, race, caste, sex or place of birth.
(c) Equality of opportunity in matters of public employment and no discrimination on grounds of religion, race, caste, sex, descent, place of birth, residence or any of them.
(d) Abolition of untouchability and prohibition of its practice in any form.
(e) Abolition of titles, except those of military and academic distinctions.

At the same time reasonable restrictions have been placed, which provide for special provisions for women, children and, Scheduled Caste and Tribes, and backward classes. The Constitution also provides directive principles of state policy in which the state has been directed to work in such a way so as the citizens of India really become equal and the objective of socio-economic justice is attained.

The Constitution of India treats all alike, but it treats some specially. These some are unlike the rest—backward socially, politically, economically, intellectually. The Constitution regards them the weaker sections of society and declares legal and constitutional discrimination in their favour so to help them rise so high that they become equal to all the rest.

The above discussion on 'equality' brings further its following major themes:

(i) *Impartiality:* This means impartial allocation of some benefits as also impartial application of laws.
(ii) *Equal shares to all:* this means that the same benefits/rights be given to all irrespective of any distinction.
(iii) *Equal shares to equals:* this means that equals should be treated equally.
(iv) *Proportional equality:* this means that the treatment be given in proportion to men in equality
(v) *Unequal shares corresponding to relevant differences:* this means that the state must discriminate so to benefit those who need benefits.

Equality is, thus, not perfect or absolute equality. It is equality of treatment, thus legal equality; it is equal satisfaction of basic needs, thus economic equality in so far as it fulfills the basic necessities of life; it is 'to each according to his merit', this is proportionate equality; it is 'to each according to his need', this is economic equality in so far as it speaks of sufficiency for all before it is superfluity for few.

## II. The Concept of Equality—Growth of the Concept

The Marxists believe that the origin of inequalities are to be found in the rise of private property. This view was also held by Rousseau. In the primitive society, there was a complete equality as there was no discrimination on any ground. Man for his survival was dependent upon the nature which provided for in plenty. But with the rise of private property, the society was divided into haves and have-nots and thus inequality entered into the human society. The Marxists, therefore, believe that real equality can be achieved only with the eradication of private property. We tend to agree with the Marxists that man has practised inequality, though we also witness in history, theorists and different movements advocating the objective of equality. Both Plato and Aristotle accepted and promoted inequality as a basis of their ideal states. Aristotle even justified the institution of slavery. The Greek city-states were based on inequality, the slaves had no political or social rights. Generally, the slaves were not even regarded as human beings. They were one of the forms of property. However, in the same Greek tradition we find the Stoics and other philosophers who supported the idea of equality among men. Stoics opposed slavery and advocated universal brotherhood and citizenship. Spartacus, who was the leader of slaves, asserted that the blood of all men belong to the same colour. He waged a war for the purpose which did not succeed. Another leader of slaves, Aristonicus, did the same thing with similar fate. The Romans juristic construction of *Jus Jentium* was a great step forward towards the conception of equality of people. However, the Romans also practised inequality, especially in their attitude towards the non-Romans. The medieval feudal order was totally based on inequality. The society was divided into three groups—the clergy, the nobles and the common people; the first two groups only enjoyed the rights while the third was supposed to be unequal.

The Christian vision of universal brotherhood clearly proclaimed the idea of equality to be realised in heaven, not in this world. In modern times the concept of equality was given special emphasis by the bourgeoisie in their struggle against the theory of divine rights of the kings. Hobbes declared that men are equal. Locke wrote, "To understand political power a right, and derive it from its original, we must consider... A state also of equality, where in all the power and jurisdiction is reciprocal, no one having more than others."

Rousseau differentiated between two kinds of inequality—natural inequality and conventional inequality. Natural inequality, like intellectual and physical strength, age, health, beauty, etc. are the creation of nature and therefore unalterable. However, conventional inequality i.e. discrimination based on caste, creed, colour, sex, property, etc. is man-made and therefore alterable. The liberal tradition raised the slogan of equality, and practised inequality at the same time. After demolishing the absolutist powers of the king and achieving democracy, they created a negative state with the objective of maintaining law and order for the benefit of property-owners. The ideology of Marxism arose against this trend; it stood for the emancipation of proletariat. Marxism emerged as a powerful movement; it also became official ideology of the Soviet Union and other socialist states. However this experiment failed. But what is important is that even the so-called socialist states failed to move towards the concept of equality. As a result of onslaught of Marxism, the liberal state modified and became a positive state. But it is still far away from the ideals of equality. The teeming millions of people in the various parts of the world live below poverty line, devoid of minimum basis of survival, while a few prosper.

## III. Dimensions of Equality

There are three dimensions of equality:

(i) Political Equality
(ii) Economic Equality
(iii) Social Equality

### (*i*) *Political Equality*

The dimension of political equality stands for democracy and universal adult franchise. There have been various forms of government. However democracy is the only form of government which believes and promotes equality among the people. Therefore, we have no alternative to democracy despite its obvious weakness. This democracy has to be based on universal adult franchise. There should not be any electoral qualifications based on caste, colour, creed, sex, or property for a voter. It should be based on general rules which must be applied to every body. Viewed in this context, the concept of political equality is a phenomenon of this century. In England and other Western countries, the universal adult franchise was gradually achieved; the women in England got the right to vote as late as 1918. Political equality also means absence of special privileges and no man or a body of men should be excluded from access to the avenues of authority. In other words, it means right to participation in the governmental affairs. The terms of such participation must be universal and reasonable. Political equality also includes legal equality which means all the citizens are equal in the eyes of law and enjoy what Barker calls "an equal degree of legal personality'. However political and legal equality is still a dream, as Barker aptly remarks, "All may possess equal rights; but all have not an equal power of vindicating rights, so long as the vindication demands expenditure, and so long as the same are more able than others to meet the expenditure demanded. In the actual operation of the courts, as distinct from the rule of the law of the land, inequality still remains, though it is steadily being diminished by reforms in their operation."

### (*ii*) *Economic Equality*

Laski also agrees with Barker when he says that "political equality is never real unless it is accompanied by virtual economic equality;

political power, otherwise, is bound to be the handmade of economic power." Historically speaking, the political power has always been monopolised by those who possessed economic power. Aristotle pointed out the equation between democracy and the rule of the rich. In modern times, Karl Marx gave an economic interpretation of history which powerfully suggested that political power has always been owned and controlled by the propertied class. Bryce, however, holds a different view. He remarks in his *Modern Democracies* that since democracy "is merely a form of government, not a consideration of the purpose to which government may be turned, (it) has nothing to do with Economic Equality... Political Equality can exist either along with or apart from Equality in property." But we cannot agree with Bryce. The fact is that political power is intrinsically related with economic power even in democracies. According to Laski, "A state divided into a small number of rich and a large number of poor will always develop a government manipulated by the rich to protect the amenities represented by their property."

The principle of *economic equality*, according to Laski, means that "the urgent claims of all must be met before we can meet the particular claims of some one. The differences in the social or economic position can only be admitted after a minimum basis of civilisation is attained by the community as a whole." It means the fulfillment of minimum economic requirements of food, cloth and shelter. For the purpose, the weak are to be protected and power of the strong be limited because the common welfare includes the welfare of the weak as well as of the strong. The quality of any state depends upon the extent to which it is able to achieve the minimum economic requirements of its people. *Secondly,* economic equality means approximate equality of wealth. This does not mean equal pay to all. It only means, as Laski suggests, none should, by virtue of differences in rates of payment, exert undue pressure upon the fabric of institutions. 'Where there are great inequalities of fortunes, there is always inequality of treatment.' Unfortunately this is happening today. The people who have nothing but their labour to sell, are being victimised. Laski notes that the desire of the great iron masters of France to dominate the heavy industries of Europe may well send the next generation to die on the battlefield. Similarly, in the expansion of imperialism, thousand of soldiers have died to protect or secure the markets for the capitalists. Laski says that the great inequalities of wealth make impossible the attainment of freedom. It means that the rich will always manipulate the state machinery for their own benefits and to the disadvantage of the poor. Therefore, monopolisation of wealth in few hands should be done away with. *Thirdly,* Laski advocates democracy in the industrial world. The decision should be rational which can be explained. 'It means the abrogation of unfettered and irresponsible will in the industrial world'. There should be workers' participation in the management of industry. The problem is that the employer always thinks in terms of self interest. He may dismiss a worker who refuses to adulterate or falsify his accounts. *Fourthly,* Laski wants key industries like coal and electric power, transport and banking, the supply of meat and the provision of houses should be controlled by the government. If left to the private enterprise, they should work under the rules which should be very strict.

According to Barker, the modern state faces two-fold problems in relation to economic equality. It is partly a matter of status and partly a matter of property and income. The mater of status means whether it is possible for the state to create a system in which workers and capitalists stand on more equal footing. In the matter of property and income, the issue is as to what extent the state corrects inequality in their distribution. The state has imposed taxes on riches and increased the wages of the workers. However, much has to be done in this field for the sake of economic equality.

### (*iii*) *Social Equality*

The dimension of social equality wants the extension of equality into society in general. Here also, it does not mean the uniformity in social status, because as Barker opines, equality is 'a derivative value', it being derived from the supreme value of the development of human personality—'in each alike and equally'. But then every personality has its own system and therefore uniformity, if imposed, will defeat the spontaneous development of all the varieties of human personality. Social equality means that there should be absence of discrimination in terms of caste, creed, colour, religion and descent. It means social harmony in which all the individuals have equal opportunities to develop their personality. It also means absence of special privileges in the society. The segregation of a people from the general population in terms of untouchability is a big blot on the Indian society. The concept of social equality would demand emancipation of women, children, untouchables and other economically and socially backward communities. However, the social inequalities cannot be eradicated in a short time. It takes a fairly considerable time. A combination of legal, economic and persuasive factors can be a good direction. However, the fact remains that no society till-to-date has been able to achieve complete social equality.

## IV. Liberty and Equality: Relationship

Regarding the relationship between liberty and equality, there are two views. The first view regards liberty and equality as incompatible, while the other view regards them compatible to each other. Let us examine the first view first.

The first view regards liberty and equality as opposed to each other. De Tocqueville, Lord Action, Bagehot, Hayek, Friedman, Mosca, Lukas and Pareto are some such writers who believe the two concepts as anti-thetical. The basis of their argument is that liberty and inequality are natural. Therefore, by nature liberty and equality are contradictory to each other. *Secondly,* every advance in equality diminishes freedom; every protection of freedom effectively hinders the promotion of equality. For achieving the objective of equality would mean curtailing the freedom. Lord Action said, "the passion for equality has made vain the hope for freedom." In order to develop the poor, the government not only taxes the rich but also puts constraints on their freedom to develop further. Therefore, whenever there is a state legislation on equality, freedom of others is restricted. The early liberals also believed that liberty is absence of restraints. They advocated total freedom to individuals which cannot be restricted in the interests of equality. According to Friedman, liberty means maintenance of capitalism because historically speaking the rise of capitalism restricted the absolute powers of the kings. Thus capitalism checks the power of state whereas the ideals of equality presupposes overthrow of capitalism. Thus, liberty and equality cannot go together. Keith Dixon points out that there have been many governments which deliberately pursued anti-egalitarian policies and justified their actions on the basis of the argument that long-time inequalities of reward and status increase efficiency and raise the standards of those lower in hierarchy. But this argument cannot be accepted as Dixon himself has rejected it. The interest of the poor can never be enhanced by giving economic freedom to the rich. There are certain writers like Scruton who attempt to bring about reconciliation between liberty and equality. Scruton is a pluralist and argues that no person should be dominant in one sphere of social life by virtue of his dominance in another. To him priority of freedom over equality would be determined within relatively distinct spheres of the human good. Thus, security and welfare would be governed by the concern for equality, while reward and punishment is the area where liberty should rein. But this view of dividing human activities and identifying certain autonomous areas for liberty is highly complicated and difficult to put into practice.

The fact of the matter is that liberty and equality are not opposed to each other. The objective of both is the same i.e. development of individual's personality. Dixon rightly puts it, "Inequalities themselves are a form of constraint. If I am denied access to education, for example, by virtue of my class origins, my sex, or the colour of my skin, my choices are thereby diminished. If I live my life continuously subject to hierarchical authority I am denied a sense of personal autonomy and control. My wants and needs become subject to definition by others and hence my freedom is restricted." In a society of unequals, the freedom only exists for the property owners, while the rest are denied the fruits of liberty. Liberty can only be useful in the society when there is equality; atleast where the minimum economic requirements are guaranteed to individuals. This view demonstrates the relationship between the two. Its advocates are Laski, Tawney, Pollard, Barker and the like. According to Laski, "There cannot, in a word, be democratic government without equality; and without democratic government there cannot be freedom." He further says, "Political equality, therefore, is never real unless it is accompanied by virtual economic equality; political power, otherwise is bound to be the handmaid of economic power... the state must dominate property, or property will dominate the state." This takes us to another aspect of relationship between liberty and equality. A society, where liberty is devoid of equality will be a society of strife and class conflicts. Laski quotes Madison who wrote. "The only durable source of faction is property." But it is obvious that to base the differences between men on a contest for economic wealth is to destroy the possibility of a well ordered commonwealth. It is to incite all the qualities in men-envy, arrogance, hatred, vanity which prevents the emergence of social unity. In fact, both the concepts of equality and liberty demand check on property. Equality that aims to end gross economic inequalities is the true basis of liberty. Tawney is right when he says, "A large measure of equality, so far being inimical to liberty is essential to it." Pollard aptly puts it, "There is only one solution to the problem of liberty. It lies in equality." According to Barker, we should dismiss any general policy of economic equality because in such a situation we lose the diversity and the dynamic process of movement, which are necessary conditions of the best society, in which each of us can be at his best. A static and immobile society of economic equality is not the environment in which the greatest number of persons can achieve the greatest possible development of the capacities of personality. Such achievement is a dynamic process which involves a dynamic society, with a rich variety of stations and functions and an easy movement of coming and going among those stations and functions." Therefore, our effort should be in the direction of progressive correction of economic inequality.

In conclusion, we may say that equality and liberty are not incompatible to each other. Both are essential for a harmonious development of individual and society. The concept of liberty, as Dixon says, should be committed to the principle that 'other things being equal individuals have the right to define and pursue their own wants and satisfactions, unhindered by authority or by the tyranny of orthodox opinions.'

### V. Equality and Justice

Justice is derived from *Jus* which means bond or tie. Justice is a social system in which men are bound together. However, justice is also a very complicated concept like equality in Political Science. In ancient times, Plato defined justice as doing one's duty and non-interference in other's affairs. He divided people on the basis of reason, spirit and appetite, as the rulers, soldiers and the producing classes and justice concerned with the observance of duties related to one's station of life. However, in modern times we cannot accept such a view of justice. According to Barker, "The end of any legal association or State... is to assemble and establish the external conditions required by every citizen for the development of his capacities; and this end is the justice." According to Robert Tucker, "The idea of justice connotes a rightful balance in a situation where two or more parties or principles are in conflict." According to Benn and Peters, "To act justly, then, is to treat all men alike except where there are relevant differences between them." Merriam says, "Justice consists in a system of understandings and procedures through which each is accorded what is agreed upon as fair." To Rees, justice requires that if two persons are equal they should have equal shares; if they are unequal they should have unequal shares in proportion to their inequality. This is the concept of distributive justice based on proportionate equality. However, disagreeing to this explanation, Marxists are the opinion that private property is an evil and should be eliminated, then only a truly just society will emerge.

Thus justice is a relative concept which means differently to different people depending upon their view of society. However, in a general sense, it means a just society which provides opportunities to the individuals to develop their faculties. Viewed in this context, equality and justice are intrinsically related. Real justice can be available in a society of equals. But a complete equality is impossible nor it is needed as we have explained earlier. In a society of unequals, as we have in modern times, justice in the context of equality would mean following things: (i) absence of special privileges; (ii) equality of opportunities; (iii) equality before law and equal protection of law; (iv) provision for political, social and economic rights; (v) fulfilment of minimum basic requirements of food, shelter and clothing and negation of wide economic disparities; (vi) absence of discrimination in terms of descent, age, caste, creed, colour, sex, property religion, etc; (vii) protection of the weak and for the purpose the rich may be restrained. Socially and economically backward be given special consideration in politics and economy; (viii) a balanced view of industry and economy where interests of labour and capital are subject to a just reconciliation; and (ix) the purpose is not to achieve complete equality but equality.

To conclude, justice stands for a harmonious development in the society in which the modern objectives of equality are to be realised. Thus both the concepts are inter-related and together they satisfy the ideals of modern polity.

## SUGGESTED READINGS


1. Albernethy, Georg L. (ed.), 1959, *The Idea of Equality*, Richmond: John Knox.
2. Anderson, Elizabeth, 1999, "What Is the Point of Equality?" *Ethics* 109, pp. 287–337.
3. Arneson, Richard, 1993, "Equality," in: R. Goodin & P. Pettit (eds.), *A Companion to Contemporary Political Philosophy*, Oxford: Blackwell, pp. 489–507.
4. Benn, Stanley I. & Richard S. Peters, 1959, *Social Principles and the Democratic State*, London: Allen & Unwin 1959.
5. Berlin, Isaiah, 1955–56, "Equality", *Proceedings of the Aristotelian Society* LVI, pp. 301–326.
6. Dworkin, Ronald, 1977, *Taking Rights Seriously*, Cambridge: Harvard University Press.
7. Dworkin, Ronald, 1981a, "What is Equality? Part 1: Equality of Welfare," *Philosophy and Public Affairs* 10, pp. 185–246, reprinted in: R. Dworkin, *Sovereign Virtue. The Theory and Practice of Equality*, Cambridge: Harvard University Press 2000, pp. 11–64.
8. Dworkin, Ronals, 1981b, "What is Equality? Part 2: Equality of Resources," *Philosophy and Public Affairs* 10, pp. 283–345, reprinted in: R. Dworkin, *Sovereign Virtue. The Theory and Practice of Equality*, Cambridge: Harvard University Press 2000, pp. 65–119.
9. Dworkin, Ronald, 2000, *Sovereign Virtue. The Theory and Practice of Equality*, Cambridge: Harvard Univeristy Press.
10. Kymlicka, Will, 1990, *Contemporary Political Philosophy*, Oxford: Clarendon Press.
11. Lakoff, Sandford A., 1964, *Equality in Political philosophy*, Oxford: Clarendon Press.
12. Lakoff, Sandford A., 1964, *Equality in Political Philosophy*, Cambridge: Harvard University Press.
13. McKerlie, Dennis, 1989, "Equality and Time," *Ethics* 99 (1989) 274–296, reprinted in L. Pojman & R. Westmoreland (eds.), *Equality. Selected Readings*, Oxford: Oxford University press 1997, pp. 65–75.

14. McKerlie, Dennis, 1996, "Equality," *Ethics* 106, pp. 274–296.
15. Pojman, Louis P. & R. Westmoreland, (eds.), 1996, *Equality. Selected Readings*, Oxford: Oxford University Press.
16. Rae, Douglas et. al., 1981, *Equalities*, Cambridge: Harvard University Press.
17. Rousseau, Jean-Jacques, 1755, *A Discourse on Inequality*, London: Penguin 1984, partly reprinted in L. Pojman & R. Westmoreland (eds.), *Equality. Selected Readings*, Oxford: Oxford University Press 1997, pp. 36–45.
18. Sen, Amartya, 1992, *Inequality Reexamined*, Oxford: Clarendon Press, Cambridge: Harvard University Press.
19. Thomson, David, 1949, *Equality*, Cambridge: Cambridge University Press.
20. Williams, Bernard, 1973, "The Idea of Equality," in: B. Williams, *Problems of the Self*, Cambridge: Cambridge University Press, pp. 230–249, reprinted in L. Pojman & R. Westmoreland (eds.), *Equality. Selected Readings*, Oxford University Press 1997, pp. 91–102.

# CHAPTER – 7

# Concepts: Justice

The word "Justice" is, indeed baffling. It is so not because of what it includes, but what it excludes. So, with numerous shades of people it has a different connotation. For a man of law, justice means the judgement pronounced by a judge; for a man of religion, justice means a set of morals and values which we should follow: for a poor man, justice means abolition of poverty; for a Cephalus, justice means keeping one's word; for a Polemarchus, justice means helping a friend and harming the enemy; for a Thrasymachus, justice means the will of the stronger to be imposed on the weaker; for a Glaucon, justice means the protection of the weak. The list is endless. What it means is that 'justice' depends on our view of society and its various aspects as also our existence in the society. For a worker, justice would include, among other things, adequate wages; for a subaltern, absence of outrages committed on him; and for a feminist, abolition of masculinist repression.

Let us make an attempt to understand the concept of justice as it has developed over the ages especially in the West.

## I. Etymology and Development

Derived from the Latin word 'jus' and also included 'justus' and 'justitia', and connected with the word 'jungere', again a Latin word justice means, what Professor Barker says 'primarily a joining or fitting a bond or a tie,' gliding into a sense of binding or obliging. Defining the word 'jus' Professor Barker remarks that in its original form, it means something "what is fitting and therefore, also binding." Elaborating the etymological meaning, he says that the word 'jus' conveys "the idea of valid custom to which any citizen can appeal, and which is recognised and can be enforced by a human authority." It is clear that Professor Barker, while largely drawing from the original Latin word, goes on to give justice a legal connotation. So, he says, the word 'jus' in its developed form, would mean, "a body of binding or obliging rules which—the courts recognize as binding, and not only recognize but also enforce." But for Professor Barker himself, justice is not merely a relationship between man and man (as about law and as in courts), but is a relationship between value and value. He, therefore, concludes. "...the function of justice may be said to be that of adjusting, joining or fitting the different political values. Justice is the reconciler and the synthesis of political values: It is their union in an adjusted and integrated whole."

The meaning given to the word 'justice' has been different in different times. With the Sophists of ancient Greece, justice meant the interest of the stronger... of the social group which is militarily stronger and economically rich to impose its will on the other groups. As against this, Plato emphasised on the moral and ethical element in justice by saying that it means performing one's duties with all abilities and capacities towards the social whole. Aristotle, on the other hand, holds the view that justice means equal share to the equals and unequal to the unequals, distributing power and position proportionately to the worth or contribution of the individual: flutes to be distributed among those who know flute-playing, as Aristotle had once put it. The Romans, known for their contribution of law to the Western political thought, used 'jus' therefore, justice so to denote the body of laws and the courts which enforce them, laws emanating from customs, legislative declarations and judicial pronouncements. During the medieval period, owing to the dominance of Christianity and the institution of the Church, the idea of justice came to be related to the idea of the rule of right, the idea of morality, the idea of righteousness, the idea of justness. It is interesting to note four categories of law in the hierarchical form in the writings of St. Thomas Aquinas. St. Thomas talks of the *lex aeterna*, the eternal law, the supreme and the one that exists in God: the *lex divina*, the divine law which is below the eternal law and one that exists in the scriptures; the *lex naturalis*, the natural law which is at number three below the eternal law and the divine law and the one that exists in the reason implanted in man by God. And below the natural law, is the *lex humana*, the human law which expresses itself in accordance with all the higher types of law, is made and imposed by human authority. Justice, during most of the medieval period, meant a body of ethical rules emanating from the scriptures, man's sense of morality and those made by man conforming to the principles of eternal, divine and natural law.

The natural rights theorists of the early modern period viewed justice as the rule of reason, a bridge between the medieval religious notion of justice and the ethical notion of justice as developed by a modern rationalist being. Locke and his followers held on to this concept of justice. That law is the expression and embodiment of justice was the meaning given to the word 'justice' by theorists in most part of the eighteenth-nineteenth centuries, declaring law as the declared will of the state and as the most obvious dimension of justice. With the development of democracy and democratic processes and institutions, justice came to be understood as equal participation of all the sections of society in political and public matters. The liberals, till date, identify justice with legal and political equality, including in it the rule of law, equality before law, equal protection of laws, one person—one vote. Again, with the development of industry, economic dimension of justice began to be advanced by socialists, syndicalists and anarchists with whom justice meant the establishment of a just social order, an order without economic exploitation and without political enslavement. Later, the Marxists developed the idea of socio-economic justice in which there were to be not only just laws, but also a just society. Social justice, a recent phenomenon, is associated with an egalitarian order with social ownership of major means of production, if possible, and without private property if necessary. Justice, in the Marxist sense, means distribution of burden according to our capacity and of benefit according to our needs. It, in the contemporary liberal and libertarian sense, means sufficiency for all and thereafter competition for greater benefits.

## II. Justice—Its Dimensions

Numerous dimensions of justice include, legal, political, social, economic and socio-economic. The *legal* dimension of justice assumes (a) that law is the declared will of the state; (b) that it includes both the customary and statutory law; (c) that it is issued by a defined authority and is enforced and imposed by the court; (d) that if violated, it is accompanied by a corresponding punishment; (e) that it is limited by the provisions of the Constitution or the conventions; and (f) that the Constitution is its supreme form, regulating the activities of the government and prescribing the rights and duties of the people. The *political* dimension of justice is an extension of the legal dimension for both, the legal and political dimensions, are advocated by the liberals, both of yesteryears and modern, its features include; (a) establishment of a democratic order without any discrimination; (b) political equality; (c) one person—one vote; (d) rule of law and not rule by peoples' whims; (e) enactment of the Constitutional provisions; (f) free press and democratic rights, and (g) fair and impartial periodic elections. The *social* dimension of justice reflects a just social society; its peculiarities would include: (a) elimination of all kinds of discrimination; (b) abolition of privileges based on birth, race, caste, creed, or sex; (c) social roles to be determined by capacity; (d) social mobility to be an alternative to rigid stratification; (e) equality of each with each and of each with all; and (f) universal brotherhood. The *economic* dimension of justice attempts to discover justice in the economic structure of the society; its features, as expressed in the writings of socialists, anarchists, syndicalists, are: (a) establishment of a social order as the principle of mutual cooperation; (b) attainment of maximum production achieved through voluntary and independent economic enterprises; (c) equitable distribution of commodities so produced; (d) abolition of exploitation of man by man; (e) social security in the event of accident, illness and old-age; and (f) prohibition of concentration of material resources in the hands of the few. The *socio-economic* dimension of justice is, by and large, a Marxist connotation of justice. Its features include: (a) a classless society, (b) abilities be matched to work; (c) work to be matched with needs; and (d) an exploitation-free and oppression-free social order.

## III. Justice and Its Relation with Liberty and Equality

Justice is a unifying force, a force that unites person to person, and value to value. It is, as Professor Barker rightly says, a synthesis, a final principle that regulates the general distribution of rights, as one's share in the whole system, and it thus 'adjusts' person to person. Adding to his argument, he continues: "...it (justice) gives to each principle of distribution (liberty, equality and cooperation) its share of weight in determining the distribution actually made, and it thus 'adjusts' principle to principle."

The idea of justice is the general right ordering of human relations or the final adjustment of persons and principles. It resides in all minds and, as such, is no abstract conception but is a social reality. It is neither morality nor ethics, for it relates itself to the outward life. But that outward life needs a set of conditions as also a set of norms which only are provided by morality. Professor Barker, thus, concludes: "If justice is not morality, it is based upon it. If its code is not that of ethics, it is a code which—is ultimately derived from ethics."

Explaining the relationship of justice with liberty and equality, Professor Barker points out: "Justice is a joining or fitting together not only of persons, but also of principles. It joins and knits together the claims of the principle of liberty, with those of the principle of equality; it adjusts them to one another in a right order of their relations." Equality may quarrel with liberty; for, if its application be pushed to the length of what is called a "classless" society; with absolute equality of possessions, it is at once brought into conflict with the liberty of each to try himself out in the effort of acquiring for himself some individual equipment."

The job of justice is to adjust, balance and reconcile person to person, principle to principle, value to value, and claim to claim. Professor Barker rightly regards justice as the holder of balance, saying that justice holds in the balance, both the claims of persons to rights and the claims of different principles to determine the distribution of rights, "measuring them by the standard of the maximum development of the capacities of personality in the maximum number of persons."

## IV. Socialist Theories of Justice: Marxist, Anarchist, Democratic-Socialist

There is a point in bringing the anarchists, the Marxists, and the democratic socialists together and clubbing them all as socialists (we are slipping out syndicalism, utopian socialism, radical socialism, evolutionary socialism, fabianism, guild socialism and the like, for each is either a variant of one or of two or more). Though, all of them are not socialists of the same shade, yet they are *the socialists* in their own right. Hence, there is something common among them so far as some aspects of socialism are concerned. What is important to note is what exists in each that is related to the other and that is what makes them the socialists. If socialism, in its essence, means, as it really is, not a very favourable attitude towards capitalism, all of them are the socialists: the anarchists, for example, condemn capitalism as a charter of economic exploitation; the Marxists provide a severe critique of capitalist mode of production; the democratic socialists see, in capitalism, the worst form of moral degradation. If socialism is the political philosophy of the working class or a doctrine that claims to fight for the cause of the workers, then all of them—the anarchists, the Marxists and the democratic socialists—are socialists. If socialism regards exploitation as the consequence of uneven distribution of social wealth, then all of them can, and in fact should have, claim to be socialists. If socialism means justice for the worker, the poor, the lowly, the downtrodden, then all are, indeed, socialists. If socialism means equal opportunities for all and a system without discrimination, then all of them are socialists in the sense we use the term. There is, thus, some degree of socialism in each—anarchism, Marxism and democratic socialism.

This is not to say that anarchism, Marxism, democratic socialism have nothing in uncommon. There are very important differences among them; differences about the objectives; differences about the strategy to be adopted in the realisation of those objectives. An anarchist would like to abolish state first and capitalism thereafter; a Marxist would, on the contrary, abolish capitalism first and state thereafter; a democratic socialist would neither at any point in future, abolish state nor capitalism. With regard to the means to be adopted for the attainment on the stated objectives, the anarchists would not mind using violence; the Marxists would adopt peaceful methods if possible and violent, if necessary; the democratic socialists would seek to bring about socialism, through peaceful democratic means and with the help of the state.

On the right-hand side of democratic socialism, stands anarchism and its variants, those which want to abolish the institution of the state in one go and those that accept socialism willy-nilly. On its left are Marxism and its variants, those which wish to abolish capitalism lock, stock and barrel, and those which believe in the indispensability of socialism as a higher, though not the highest, state of society's material development. Democratic socialism with its variants hold the view that capitalism can be regulated, workers' cause can be taken care of, socialism can serve to be an end in itself.

With socialists of all shades, justice exists where there is no injustice. This commonly understood meaning of justice does not explain much, but it is from where all the socialists start. The chief concern of all the socialists has been injustice meted out to the workers, peasants, poor, unemployed, the lowly and so on, in the system that exists in the society in general, and the capitalistic one in particular. That is why the socialists are more vocal, and even furious, in explaining what is unjust than in describing what justice really is. So, the socialist idea of justice springs from the realms of injustice, and therefore, justice, according to them, would exist where the individuals are free. For the Marxists, justice in the class societies is always a class justice, justice for the capitalist and conversely injustice for the workers. Hence, the Marxists find justice only in a classless society. The democratic socialists are both socialists as well as democratic, and therefore, for them, justice exists in a just order and in a just society.

(a) *The Marxist Theory of Justice*

The Marxists are vocal about uneven distribution of income as an example of injustice. While advocating their theory of justice (to be more specific as something that is opposed to injustice), the Marxists go much beyond the anarchists. Proudhan rightly remarked once that all property is theft, but Marx and his followers relate property to class society, class society of antagonistic classes—one owning the means of production, the exploiters and another without the means of production, the exploited, and antagonistic classes into a class concept of justice—justice for the rich. For the Marxists, justice is not merely just laws, but also just laws emanating from just society; it is not merely economic or social in nature, but also socio-economic in its ramifications.

According to the Marxists, justice is, more or less, a relative term; it is different for the rich and different for the poor; different for man, and different for woman; different for the capitalist and different for the worker. For the Marxists, justice, like property and law and politics, is a reflection of commodity relations, especially under capitalism. They say that under a communist society, justice would reflect different relations than those in a capitalist system. The bourgeois justice, the Marxists would declare, is bourgeois in the sense that it protects bourgeoisie and exploits the workers; it legitimises the capitalist's profit on the one hand, and the labourer's wages on the other; it legalises inequality. But, in a communist society, because of the social ownership of the means of production, justice would mean equality of all and equality for all. It would mean absence of all discrimination, all exploitation and all oppression. It would mean work for all in accordance with their abilities as also fulfillment of all the needs of all the persons in return to what each of them does. Hence, the idea of justice, in the Marxian scheme, is associated with the nature of the society itself. In a slave-owning society, justice would highlight something that is most impracticable—the ethical ruler; the medieval European society saw justice in Christianity; the capitalist Western society seeks to find justice in the justification of private property system. In a communist society, justice is just society and its corresponding just rules—a justice without coercion, without repressive state machinery, a justice where people obey laws as a matter of habit rather than any threat of punishment. The Marxian justice is one which springs from within the socialistic and cooperative relations among the people.

The Marxists do not believe that the idea of justice is the idea coming from the sky, hence eternal; sprouting from the deep sea, hence hidden. It, they say, exists in the system it finds itself; it is the system that gives it a meaning; it would mean different things in different systems of relations of production. If in the capitalist system, the Marxists seem telling us, the principle of justice would and in fact, is "take as much from the society as you can," in the Marxian society, if it could really be built, the principle of justice would mean: "give as much to the society as you can". In the capitalist justice, rights have an edge over the duties, whereas, in the Marxian justice, duties override the rights. The capitalistic notion of justice is more close to liberty than equality while the Marxian idea of justice is more close to the idea of equality than that of liberty.

(b) *The Anarchist Theory of Justice*

Even the anarchists are of various types, mention may particular be made about William Godwin (1756-1836—*An Enquiry Concerning*

*Political Justice and its Influence on General Welfare and Happiness*), Pierre Joseph Proudhon (1809–1865—*What is Property*?) and with them the Russian Bakunin (1814–1876), Kropotkin (1842–1921) and Tolstoy (1828–1910). One may, however, be tempted to include, among the anarchists, Mahatma Gandhi and Bertrand Russell. All these anarchists regard the state as a negative institution, some to the extent of abolishing it altogether. All of them take the disdainful view of the present capitalist society and dub it most exploitative, oppressive and unjust. They see justice in the absence of political coercion: political authority, in its any form, is all evil, and therefore, not only unnecessary but also undesirable. They, therefore, declare that the only way to establish justice is to abolish the state completely and replace it by an entirely "free organisation of society." For the anarchists, justice is not to be found in the presence of the government, but in its absence; not in the submission to any political authority above, but in the existence of free individuals with their independently arrived agreements; not in their natural quarrelsomeness, but in their natural cooperativeness.

Proudhon found in property negation of social justice, and therefore, he was opposed to it—property that creates further property. He found in state a supporter of property and therefore he was against all types of political authority. Proudhan's anarchist society is a free society where freedom is united with order, order with reason, and reason with justice. Bakunin finds injustice in the framework of private property, political authority, and religion: where these exist, there exists injustice; where they are absent, there alone we have justice. Kropotkin was a naturalist, and therefore, believed that if people are left to themselves to work out for their way of life, they would develop a number of voluntary associations to make social existence possible, maintain peace, practise mutual aid and create, in the last analysis, justness. Unlike Godwin and Proudhan who were individualistic anarchists, Bakunin and Kropotkin who were communistic anarchists, Tolstoy was a Christian anarchist; Mahatma Gandhi, a spiritual and a moral anarchist; and Russell is a humane anarchist.

For the anarchists, justice lies where there is no state, no property and no religion, and where there is free individual, voluntarily willingness and the reign of liberty. Justice finds expression not in bondage, but in freedom. It is a sense of liberty and not of slavery; of emancipation and not of exploitation, and of acting in accordance with free will, and not of the will dictated by any external force.

(c) *Democratic-Socialist theory of Justice*

This theory is neither Marxian nor anarchist. It is a mid-way concept of justice.

Unlike Marxists and the anarchists, the democratic-socialists do not regard, all laws as bad and all state as an instrument of class exploitation. On the contrary, the democratic-socialists, like all the liberals and the libertarians, hold the view that justice exists where the law exists, but the kind of law that is an embodiment of 'social service' and not, of awful majesty. Indeed, they think that police is necessary but it need not be extensively armed; that law, as an expression of justice, must regulate the conduct of the people, but it need not be more than enough; that courts have to dispense justice, but they need not be subject to those who hold political power. The democratic-socialists find the idea of justice in the idea of rule of law and hence, they provide for the courts, a heavy agenda such as diffusion, decentralisation, federalisation of political and economic power. They regard justice as a frame, as a system, as a goal to be set and attained by laws, and laws which have to be made by the state democratically structured. Hence, the democratic-socialists do not throw the baby (of justice) along with the bath-tub (of liberal-capitalism). Justice exists as does liberalism-capitalism: what does not exist in the bathwater is the filth and the dirt. For the democratic-socialists, justice cleans the dirt, shines as gold in the society, reconciles man with man, principle with principle, value with value. They believe that justice exists in a democratic order, for undemocratic system is always unjust; it exists in the framework of equality, for inequality is never just. Where people participate more, there is more equality, and where there is more equality, there we find the idea of justice.

But for the democratic-socialists, justice is not merely a matter of equality, it is also a matter of liberty—liberty which is not licence to do anything, but an atmosphere in which one grows without impeding the liberty of any other. The democratic-socialist theory of justice reconciles, rather adjusts, the two extremes as are provided by the liberals and the Marxists. They are liberals in so far as they see—justice in some infrastructure—laws, courts; they are Marxists in so far as they see it in a system which is exploitation-free.

In conclusion, we may find that the Marxist view of justice is: "Share the burden according to your capacity; and benefits, according to your needs." The anarchists, on the other, regard justice as a principle which says: "Share at will, take as you can." And the democratic-socialist view of justice is: "Take in proportion to what you give."

## V. Libertarian Justice: Hayek, Rawls and Nozick

The notion of justice, as has developed over the ages, is really very old. It has moved in its nature say, from Plato's ethical to Aristotle's distributive, then religious, utilitarian, socialist and down to the libertarians—F.A. Hayek (*The Constitution of Liberty:* 1960), J. Rawls (*A Theory of Justice:* 1972), Robert Nozick (*Anarchy, State and Utopia*: 1974) to name a few among them. The libertarian justice stands opposite to any and every socialist view of justice, and hence is an argument against social justice. It has nothing to do with any moral, ethical, intrinsic, eternal and natural values. It is individualistic, for it revolves around individual; libertarian, for it follows the notion of liberty. In economic terms, the libertarian justice demands: "no more redistribution"; in political terms, it asks for a minimal state; in social terms, it admits the claims of inequality.

### *(a) Hayek—Fallacies of Social Justice*

Friedrich Hayek, (1899–1992) an Austrian-born British economist, is a philosopher of freedom. He feels that the freedom of individual has been reduced by an activist state. His answer to the onslaughts of ever-increasingly powerful state is a limited state based on spontaneous order in society, a state providing essential condition for preservation of an overall order. Freedom as the condition of man in which coercion is most minimum, Hayek says, goes well along the limited state.

For Hayek, justice, in its nature, seeks to attain individual good, rather than the one that is called the social good. He argues that social justice does not secure liberties for the individual through which he/she can pursue his/her own good. He also says that as social justice stands for a particular purpose (of distribution of goods, or/and services to be given to the individuals in society), it is concerned more with the procedure than with the result—patterning the norms of distribution so that people share goods/services equitably, forgetting as to what an individual should get in return and as reward to what he/she gives to the society. So, for Hayek, justice seeks, not this or that purpose but a spontaneous order that helps develop rules of conduct, in short, the rule of law generally. His theory of justice, therefore, is a procedural justice: Justice must be sought in a rule of law, treating individuals equal disregarding their position, if any; all state-directed policies are incompatible with the principle of rule of law. The Hayekian justice is freedom, all freedom for the individual, all that he/she wants to obtain for his/her good. Conversely, for Hayek, injustice occurs when an individual interferes with the domain of freedom of another person, when this is secured by just and universally observed rules; injustice meaning the existence of coercion. Condemning social justice, Hayek offers two adverse consequences of the idea of distributive social justice: *Firstly,* an attempt to secure a particular pattern of justice will mean that one set of values related to human purposes will be given a preference to others in a society and this is incompatible with a liberal and free society in which the diversity of ends is recognised. *Secondly,* owing to a lack of clarity and precision about these values reflecting social and moral diversity, an attempt to distribute goods and income and services according to one or the other of these criteria, will be a very indefinite enterprise. This will empower the officials who will, of necessity, have to exercise power in a discretionary way. He, therefore, concludes that the claims of social justice would ultimately lead to the arbitrariness of government. In the name of the government's responsibility of securing just rewards for the individuals, it would usher in an era where the government would act unjustly and would ultimately yield before the interest groups that stand for private and not for public interest.

The idea of social justice does not only, in practice, end up in a sort of civil war among the numerous interest groups where the government itself becomes a party, it also helps transform a free society into a totalitarian one. His solution, therefore, is:

(i) a state that acts neutrally between the competing interests of numerous groups;
(ii) a set of abstract laws which will secure optimum individual freedom from minimum coercion; and
(iii) a free market unconstrained by the distributive principles of social justice.

Hayek's views, on the subject, cannot be accepted in toto. His over-dependence on the free market and its rules do not prevent, and in fact, cannot prevent the economically strong groups to act in their own interests. Such a situation would ultimately demand some norms of distribution and this would not indeed be, unjust. Furthermore, it cannot be predicted in a free market as to what would be the economic benefits for an individual, as also for a group, which is relatively weak. It is also difficult to accept Hayek's arguments that the state seeking social justice is illegitimate and that the market is always legitimate, for the state is not always wrong, and the market, not always right.

*(b) Rawls—the Contractarian Justice*

John Rawls, (born 1921) is an American philosopher. His work *A Theory of Justice* has been regarded as a significant contribution to liberal political theory. His interest in the liberal state and in the concept of justice has led him to formulate and reformulate his theory of justice for about four decades. In 1958, justice, for him, is fairness, one that became the part and parcel of Rawlsian vocabulary on justice. A revised version of Rawls's theory was published in "Distributing Justice" (1967). The most elaborate and comprehensive argument of his theory was presented in *A Theory of Justice* (1971).

Rawls's view of justice refers to 'original position' in which rational contractors under a 'veil of ignorance' decide how they wish to commit themselves to being governed in their actual lives and wish to cooperate with one another so to obtain mutual benefits, 'social primary goods' to all the members of society in just and 'fair' manner. Invoking on Kantion rationalism, Rawls deliberately explains the intellectual or theoretical motivation behind construction, and the two principles (specified below) of justice that he argues would be agreed upon under the contractual condition he specifies represent a kind of egalitarian political liberalism.

John Rawls' views on justice can best be summed up in his own words by highlighting the following:

*"First Principle"*

Each person is to have an equal right to the most extensive total system of equal basic liberties compatible with a similar system of liberty for all.

*"Second Principle"*

Social and economic inequalities are to be arranged so that they are both:

(a) To the greatest benefit of the least advantaged—and
(b) Attached to offices and positions open to all under conditions of fair equality of opportunity.

**First Priority Rule (The Priority of Liberty)**

The principles of justice are to be ranked in lexical order and therefore, liberty can be restricted only for the sake of liberty. There are two cases:

(a) a less extensive liberty must strengthen the total system of liberty shared by all;
(b) a less than equal liberty must be acceptable to those with the lesser liberty.

**Second Priority Rule (The Priority of Justice over Efficiency and Welfare)**

The second principle of justice is lexically prior to the principle of efficiency and to that of maximising the sum of advantages; and fair opportunity is prior to the difference principle..."

Stated simply, Rawl's conception of justice demands;

(i) The maximisation of liberty subject only to such constraints as are essential for the protection of liberty itself;
(ii) Equality for all, both in the basic liberties of social life and also in the distribution of all other forms of social goods, subject only to the exception that inequalities may be permitted if they produce the greatest possible benefit for those least well off in a given scheme of inequality ("the difference principle");
(iii) "Fair equality of opportunity" and the elimination of all inequalities of opportunity based on birth or wealth.

Rawls' contractarianism is not essentially of Hobbes, Locke or Rousseau. It is so only to show that certain moral principles are binding upon us because they would be acceptable by rational beings like us in the "original position". Justice, for him, is not law of nature or something based on reason, but is fair distribution on fair procedure This is what justice, for Rawls is: Justice as fairness.

Rawls admits that all individuals are not equal: say, equal in knowledge; all do not live in similar conditions: say, in similar social and economic conditions. There are some, Rawls declares, who are subject to what he calls "a veil of ignorance" and this veil excludes them not only from others, but also from themselves—the least advantaged members of society. Justice demands, so far as Rawls is concerned, due care for the least advantaged members of the society as well. It is the distribution of benefits among all the members of the society not in proportion to what one does, but in such a manner that the weakest of the weak is duly benefitted. Such a distribution of benefits, Rawls feels, is not only fair, but is also in accordance with the norms of justice.

Thus, we may conclude with summing up Rawls' notion of justice as under:

(a) Justice, for Rawls, is fairness.

(b) It assumes a view of society as a fair system of cooperation between free and equal persons.

(c) Its object is to find out appropriate principles which help realise liberty and equality.

(d) These appropriate principles, attempting to seek liberty and equality are the result of an agreement among the people concerned in the light of their mutual advantage.

(e) As the people see themselves free and equal, they soon realize that they need the same primary goods so to pursue their own conception of good.

(f) These primary goods include, among others, the basic rights, liberties, opportunities, income, wealth, self-respect.

(g) Justice would mean that all the primary goods are to be distributed equally unless an unequal distribution of any or all of these goods, is to the advantage of the least favoured.

Rawl's theory of justice was well-timed. It was presented at a time (1971) when liberalism was becoming infashionable and was facing serious challenges. In his own country (USA), dominant values and political institutions were being questioned by various movements led by students, black and anti-Vietnam war activists. The utilitarian tradition, till then so popular, seemed an inadequate basis for the protection of minorities. Sarangi writes: "There were questions about proper use of political power and just distribution of liberties and other social goods. Perhaps Rawls was responding to these historical developments and trying to present a persuasive theoretical alternative to utilitarianism."

Rawls' theory of justice is, indeed, important atleast in (a) providing, as Chantal Mouffe says, a defence of political liberalism which establishes its autonomy from economic liberalism; (b) providing an alternative to utilitarian thought. One of Rawls' important contributions, as Bhiku Parekh says, consists in giving liberalism a new foundation and a new vitality. He gives liberalism a moral depth which it has always lacked. Parekh writes: "He (Rawls) shows that men are not only materially, but also morally and ontologically interdependent, that they grow together and complete one another and that the full development of each is inseparable from the full-development of all within a just society. In taking this view, Rawls is able to relate liberty, equality and justice and to elucidate the radical dimension of liberalism."

And yet, the *shortcomings* in Rawl's theory, cannot be overlooked (i) His account of the original position is far from clear: why people who are not in the original position should adopt principles chosen by those who were? If there is a bias in the original position and if, as a consequence of that bias, the principles chosen do not respond to the norms of fairness. Sandel says that Rawl's notion of original position "contains a strong individualistic bias... —The original position seems to presuppose not just a neutral theory of the good, but a liberal, individualistic conception—...." (ii) His difference principle' is not without some demerit. Admitting the differences, i.e., inequalities, Rawls believes that an agreement would be reached between people. But will the wealthy share, and cooperate? (iii) Rawls gives priority to liberty and this, in itself, is another attack on him. Rawls says that a person in the original position will choose "the basic liberties" in priority to any distribution of income wealth and power because by so doing he would have better chances of obtaining primary goods. If that is so, what would happen if the basic liberties conflict or how, at all, can they be restricted? Rawls has no answer to such questions except that he assumes a state of cooperation among them. (iv) There is a clear contradiction between the first principle which demands equal liberty, liberties for all and the second principle which justifies inequalities—inequalities between the most favoured on the one hand and the least advantaged on the other. (v) It is difficult to assume, as Rawls wants us to assume, liberty for all in a system of inequalities: Liberty among the unequals is liberty of the stronger, his power to control the weak. (vi) Rawls' argument is more favouring the principle of liberty, whatever tall claims he may insist on with regard to the principle of equality. The fact that Rawls' first principle relates to the principle of liberty demonstrates his choice for this principle: Liberty comes first, everything else follows it (vii) Rawls' theory of justice is largely individualistic and libertarian. It is social in a very limited sense in so far as it does not exclude the weaker sections of society in his arrangement of justice.

*(c) Nozick—the Entitlement theory of Justice*

Like John Rawl, Robert Nozick (born 1938) is an American libertarian political pholosopher, known for his restatement of classical liberal case for a minimal state and his rejection of both economic management and social welfare. He is for a state which is like a "night-watchman", one which is limited to the narrow functions of protection against force, theft, fraud, enforcement of contracts, and so on.

Nozick's theory of justice stands opposite to that of Rawls in an important respect. Whereas, in Rawls' theory, justice is seen as particular pattern of social arrangements adjusting entitlements and resources in as neutral and fair manner as is possible, in Nozick, it is a view that individuals have rights and that those rights be respected at all costs and in all circumstances. According to Nozick, justice is not a matter of attempting to organise or reorganise society and its institutions to achieve some distributive pattern, but is one of respecting basic rights which limit what may be done to someone without consent and the entitlements which such rights yield. For Nozick, rights are so fundamental and the constraints upon others' actions are so strong that only one can justify a minimal state: a minimal state means most minimum laws and conversely most maximum liberties and rights of the individual as individual. This is a position which takes Nozick close to Hayek, and farther back to Locke.

We may briefly outline Nozick's theory of justice which is 'entitlement' theory as against the distributive theory. His argument is that if the state does something against the individual for which he is entitled, it is a case of injustice: individual is entitled to certain rights, already with him, and if the state takes them away, it does something which is not just. Nozick's assumption is that individual's rights are with the individual because he is an individual, no state had ever given these rights to him and no state through any arrangement can ever take them away from him. Justice, for Nozick, lies in not disrupting individual's entitlements; any thing that disrupts them through any patterned device is illegitimate and unjust. As against the Marxian principles: 'from each according to his ability to each according to his need' which, for Nozick, is a patterned device, he offers justice as one 'from each as they choose, to each as they are chosen.'

Nozick's entitlement theory of justice has the following characteristics:

(a) There is no social entity with a good that undergoes some sacrifices for its own good. There are only the individual people, different individual people with their own individual lives.
(b) Individuals have rights, and there are things no person or group may do to them. So strong and far reaching are these rights that they raise the question of what, and if anything, the state and its officials may do.
(c) The fact that there are different individuals with separate lives, means that no one may be sacrificed for others.
(d) The idea of basic rights implies their enjoyment by the individual and also constraints on the others not to coerce the rights of the fellow-individual.
(e) Justice has historical essence in that it came about in course of time and not through any set formula or pattern.

(f) Justice seeks to protect the rights of the individual, rights which individual has because he/she is an individual "Things come," Nozick says, "into the world already attached to people having entitlements over them". Individuals have rights because, as individuals, they are entitled to them.

(g) All and any type of interference in the entitlements or rights of the individual are illegitimate. Nozick's justification of property right is based on the principle that it is an entitlement of an individual. In this context, the buying and selling of property, in the market, is merely the transformation of property rights.

(h) Following Locke, Nozick believes that person is inviolable, that he/she has an absolute property right in his/her own person, powers and capacities that he/she comes to possess unquestionable property right in unowned things (extending Locke's argument), and that no one else has the right to question or coerce an individual's rights, property right including.

In Nozick's view, justice is not a matter of how the distribution should be made. If it means so, then it becomes a type of patterned distributive justice which, according to Nozick, would "involve appropriating the actions of other persons". It is a matter of how the distribution has come about; it is a matter of what one is entitled to; and finally, it is a matter of protection of one's entitlements. Such a type of justice is compatible with a minimal, and not with an extensive state.

There is much that separates Nozick from Rawls. Rawls favours distributive scheme; Nozick opposes it; Rawls' state is relatively more than a minimal', Nozick's merely minimal; Rawls is a defender of liberal-democratic and to some extent, a welfare state; Nozick, on the other, argues in favour of a libertarian minimal state; for Rawls, justice is always distributive; for Nozick, it is not justice if it is distributive and he says that a society is just so long as its members possess which they have a right to.

Nozick's entitlement theory of justice is more a theory of rights, especially that of property than a theory of justice. He extols the virtues of eighteenth-century individualism on the one hand, and the nineteenth-century *laissez-faire* capitalism. He isolates individual from other individuals, forgetting that individual does possess sociality, howsoever lone he may be. There is, above individual private interest, a social interest as well. Indeed, individual rights are inviolable, but Nozick goes on to make them absolute. His concept of minimal state and his passion for individual's basic rights make him a defender of Locke's theory in the present century. His notion of justice is vague, if not abstract. He throws away all the norms and principles normally associated with the idea of justice and brings it to mean the protection of status quo.

## VI. Justice: Subaltern and Feminist Perspectives

The idea of what constitutes justice is always different for different people. In fact, it goes with the status or position of the individual. If, for a ruler, it denotes the maintenance of law and order, it would mean, from the point of view of the ruled, the existence of certain rights and their protection. The liberals find justice in the existing system of things; the socialists, in the absence of exploitation and discrimination; the anarchists, in anarchy; the libertarians, in liberties and rights; the communitarians, in public good. The unemployed would see justice in the provision for employment; the subalterns, in the elimination of deprivation; the women, in the abrogation of men's dominance.

### *(a) Subaltern Perspective of Justice*

The dictionary meaning of subaltern is 'subordinate' 'lower in rank', particularly 'below the rank of captain'. In social sciences, it would, broadly speaking, mean an individual or a group standing lower in the social pyramid: the poor, the lowly, the downtrodden, in short, the weaker sections of the society. In broad sense, subaltern would include the tillers, the tribals, the agricultural labourers, the scavengers, the leather workers, in Gandhiji's terminology, 'the Harijan', the Dalits, the weakest of the weak.

The fact of social inequality is the fact of high and low; the rich and the poor; men of higher castes and those of lower; the socially favoured and the socially boycotted; in Marx's terms: the master and the slave, the lord and the serf, the bourgeoisie and the proletariat, the exploiter and the exploited.

History provides ample evidences of discrimination, deprivation, degradation of the people belonging to the lower strata of society. In the name of justice, injustice is inflicted on them; the law, as the incarnation of justice, is made by and exists to serve the interests of the superior; conversely, the law denies justice to the inferior.

It is interesting to note differences between the Marxian notion of opposing classes at different stages of history and the subaltern grouping. Whereas, in the Marxian thesis, these antagonistic classes are economically determined groups, in the subaltern connotation, the groupings are socially and culturally determined as well. That is why that we talk of the Dalits in the Indian caste system and of the tribals in the context of regionally backward tribes of India. But in both cases (Marxian and the subaltern), the disadvantaged are always exploited, discriminated, denied. The subaltern as also the exploited classes are denied the benefits of the basic necessities of life, are looked down upon as out-castes, are never given opportunities to better their conditions. Each type of society, at any given time, throws up the exploited lot as mere slaves. Obviously, for the deprived, justice is not what it is for the comfortable.

For the subaltern, justice is not the rule of law, much less a code of morals. For the tiller of the land, grant of land is justice; for a socially boycotted individual, social equality is justice; for a culturally underdeveloped, elimination of all impositions is justice; for a slave, emancipation is justice. If the subalterns rise in arms, it is understandable, for their revolt is the expression of their outrages against the system itself, their non-conformity speaks of their alienation.

The subaltern perspective on justice demands social justice for the disadvantaged. It demands two-fold objective at the same time; (i) elimination of all types of discrimination; and (ii) provision for special care so to attain social equality. The subaltern perspective of justice is not merely economic, but is also social, cultural, educational, and even psychological. The subaltern has not to be developed, but is made to feel that he/she is developing. The subaltern perspective of justice would, among other things, seek to remove traditional disabilities, eliminate exploitation in all forms, reserve positions in all public sector enterprises as in legislatures, make available all facilities required for social development. It would be unjust if the law does not protect the weaker, if the society does not embrace the lowly, if the government denies the deprived, basic necessities of life. The subaltern perspective on justice does not content itself with a job for the unemployed, an assistance for the aged, medicine for the sick, but goes further to include a complete transformation of society into one that can rightfully claim to be equalitarian. The subaltern justice is not libertarian and therefore, does not sacrifice equality for liberty. It is rather a phenomenon of protective discrimination, a discrimination in favour of the weak for purposes of not only raising the quality of life, but also taking advantages of the fruits of equality. It is heartening to note that the subaltern studies are being taken up both at macro-level and micro-level, in India as well as elsewhere.

*(b) Feminist Perspective on Justice*

The feminist philosophy, including its political theory, speaks of man's domination of woman as a curse inflicted on her by a socially-structured-male society. What is actually a natural sex-inequality is made a social gender inequality and then follows all sorts of values (if at all they, really, are) associated with masculinity. The female, feminism believes, is regarded inferior to male in all qualities. Physically she is dubbed as dull and dud; intellectually, as a being with less or no wisdom; socially, she has a place lower than man. She is considered ineligible for all public activities; her life is confined to the private life of the family—mothering the babies. Even in the family, she is not only second, but is always secondary. All her miseries, the feminists say, are the result of man's atrocities. Because she is physically weaker than man, she is made to lead a subordinate life. Almost half of humanity lives and has, in the past, lived in servitude, dependent always, at one or the other time, on man: be he a father, brother, husband or the son. Until recently, public or political life had been an area out of her bound. This is the situation in most part of the world to-day for most of the female folks. The rise and development of feminism have helped in not only understanding women's woes but also in bettering their conditions—social, economic, familial. Indeed, there have been cases of dowry deaths, brides' burning and of Sati, yet the woman, to-day is no more a commodity to be bought and sold at man's whims. Worth quoting are the few lines from a feminist icon Simone de Beanvoir to Chicago writer Nelson Algren: "I'll be good. I'll do the dishes. I'll sweep and I'll go buy eggs and rum cake myself. I won't touch your hair, your cheeks or your shoulder without permission."

The basis on which feminism lies is the idea of equality. Feminism abhors inequality between man and woman, and conversely, demands equality as the very core of society. Because woman is regarded unequal to man, she is made to suffer throughout her life: her subordination, powerlessness and oppression are the consequences of male dominance. Justice, in feminist perspective, demands escapism from woman's internalisation of female gender, and the low self-esteem, apathy and sense of helplessness that goes with it. What is needed, the feminists say, is not merely equal rights which man possesses, but also, as the socialist feminists insist, communalisation of domestic and childcare functions: the male superiority would have to be abolished; patriarchal culture would have to be demolished; gender socialisation would have to be imbibed; women's liberation from male oppression would have to be fought out. The feminists do not regard law to be neutral in disputes between man and woman; the idea of justice is, by its very nature, male-structured. Mackinnon says: "When law (in the male-structured society) is made ruthlessly neutral, it will be most male." It is as Mill rightly thought, foolish to think that a woman's interests can be incorporated in her husband's and that is why that he insisted on exposing the myth of male protection. Most feminist scholars felt, very strongly indeed, that women are as rational as men are, and therefore, they are entitled to the same legal and political rights. The feminist perspective on justice means, among others, elimination of all male domination, equality of rights, bridging the public and the private spheres, and creation of society, culture and politics in new, rather non-patriarchal forms.

Janet Radcliffe Richards, in her remarkable essay, *The Sceptical Feminist* (1982), provides a thought provoking feminist perspective on justice. She says that justice is bound up with individual's freedom to pursue his own destiny and this is what women are, currently, denied systematically. Drawing largely from Rawls' *A Theory of Justice* (1971), she like Susan Moller Okin (*Justice, Gender and the Family*: 1990), uses the idea of a model of the just society in which women would be as free to explore their own potential as men. She argues that a sexually just society would require a radical restructuring of work, increase the choices available to women, and ensure that the benefits and the burdens of having children were shared more equally between the sexes. Equally convincing is Okin's argument. She says, and with this we may conclude the feminist perspective on justice that at present, women are systematically disadvantaged in all areas of life; that her ideal is a society in which child-rearing and domestic work are shared equally; that this equality within the home would make possible gender equality in all other areas of life; that a just society would be one without gender. Arguing Okin's case, Valerie Bryson says."... it is within the home that children learn the values on which they will base their adult life," and that such values of democratic citizenship cannot be learned in a family based on domination and inequality" as the present male-constructed society, really is.

## SUGGESTED READINGS

1. Ackerman, B., *Social Justice in the Liberal State* (New Haven: Yale University Press, 1980).
2. Barry, B., *The Liberal Theory of Justice* (Oxford: The Clarendon Press, 1973).
3. Engels, F., *Anti-Dubring* (Moscow: Foreign Languages Publishing House, 1954).
4. Galstan, W.N., *Justice and Human Good* (Chicago: University of Chicago Press, 1981).
5. Goldman, A., 'The Entitlement Theory of Justice', *Journal of Philosophy*, 73, 1976.
6. Hayek, F.A., *The Constitution of Liberty*, (London: Routledge, 1960).
7. ________, *The Mirage of Social Justice* (London: Routledge and Kegan paul, 1976).
8. Miller, D., *Social Justice* (Oxford: The Clarendon Press, 1976).
9. Nozick, R., *Anarchy, State and Utopia* (Oxford: Blackwell, 1974).
10. Okin, S.M., *Justice, Gender and the Family* (New York: Basic Books, 1990).
11. Rawls, J., *A Theory of Justice* (Oxford: The Clarendon Press, 1972).
12. Richards, J.R., *The Sceptical Feminist* (Harmandsworth: Penguin, 1982).

13. Sankhdhar, M.M. and Mukherjee, Subrata (eds) *Essays on Fabian Socialism* (New Delhi: Deep and Deep Publications, 1991).
14. Stammler, Rudolf, *The Theory of Justice* (New York: Macmillan, 1925).
15. Jucker, Robert C, "Marx and Distributive Justice" in Fredrik Carl J. and Chapman, J.W. (eds.) *Justice* (New York: Atherton, 1963).
16. Walzer, M., *Spheres of Justice* (Oxford: Martin Robertson, 1983).

# CHAPTER – 8

# Concepts: Rights

Right are social claims which help individuals develop their personalities. If democracy is, as Lincoln had once said, a government of the people and also a government for the people, it must, then, exist to serve the individual. Such a democratic government can best serve the people if it maintains and provides a system of rights. States never give rights, they only recognise them; governments never bestow rights, they only protect them. Rights emanate from society and belong to the individuals as members of the society but they exist to help individuals attain the development of the human personality. State comes in to provide an atmosphere for the due enjoyment of the rights. It is in this sense that the functions of the government provide conditions for the exercise of rights and it is also in this sense that rights exist to provide a source, from where all governmental activities begin.

## I. Rights: Meaning and Nature

Right is a claim, a social claim necessary for the development of human personality. It is not an entitlement a person is possessed with. In the ancient and medieval times, people—some people—were entitled to enjoy privileges, but we do not call them rights. Rights are not privileges because they are not entitlements. There is a difference between rights and privileges: rights are our claims against others, as are rights of others' claims on us; entitlements are, privileges granted to some but denied to others; rights are universal in the sense they are assured to all who live in the society, privileges are not universal in the sense because they are possessed by the few; rights are granted to all without any discrimination, privileges are showered on some, the selected few; rights are obtained as a matter of right, privileges, as a matter of patronage; rights are social, because they exist in society and because they are available to all to be exercised for the good of all, including the holder, they are democratic in character, always.

To prepare a list of democratic rights for all times is to prepare a list, however, exhaustive, which would both be incomplete and inadequate. This is so, because the levels of democracy differ from society to society, as also from time to time. Hence, such an exercise is left as it is.

(a) *Rights: Meaning and Definitions*

While giving meaning to rights, some writers relate it to claims. Bosanquet says that "right is a claim recognised by society and enforced by the state." Wilde describes right as a "reasonable claim to freedom in the exercise of certain activities." Bosanquet and Wilde see a claim in the concept of right, though Bosanquet insists that the claim has been a recognised fact by the society and one that is enforced by the state and Wilde finds in a right the reasonableness of the claim. In both cases, a right is described as a claim, a claim that is individual's: rights, in this sense, belong to the individuals; they come in the domains of the individuals. Rights are claims, but every claim is not a right; every claim is not recognised and that every claim is not reasonable. Only those claims, which are recognised by others, by the society, are rights; only those claims which are reasonable, and that is what recognition makes them reasonable are rights. Laski makes a point when be says that in any system of rights, there is always the interest of the individual, always, at least, ultimately, finally isolated from his fellow men; and together with this, there is the interest of various groups (we may say, society), in and through which his personality finds channels of expression.

Rights are claims which belong to the individuals, and which are 'reasonable' and therefore, are recognised by others i.e., by society. These rights are claims, but claims which are social; social because they help reinforce the social good; social because they do not go against the society. It is here that Laski introduces the third essential aspect (the first two have been discussed above) which includes the interest of the community, i.e., the interest must not go against the good of the society: our rights are ours, but they are not those which harm others. Green rightly defines rights as those which "contribute to common good."

Right is a claim possessed by the individual which benefits him as well as the society. It is not a power. Rights do not constitute physical force at the disposal of an individual. There can be no rights based on force. Rights belong to the individuals as social beings and not to those who are isolated. Rights are with the individuals as members of the society; it is in this sense that they are 'the one-way traffic' affair; it is not that they are with the individuals who have the power, physical force with them. Rights are rights because they are not might; it is right as might, and not the might as right. Rights are social claims, and in this sense, they constitute power recognised as being socially necessary for the individuals. Hobbouse puts it as this: "Rights are what we may expect from others and others from us, and all genuine rights are conditions of social welfare. Thus, the rights anyone may claim are partly those which are necessary for the fulfillment of the function that society expects from him. They are conditions by, correlative to, his social responsibilities. The same idea has been emphasised by Gilchrist, in some what different sense. He says: "Rights arise, therefore, from individuals as members of society, and from the recognition that, for society, there is an ultimate good which may be reached by the development of the powers inherent in every individual."

(b) *Nature and Features of Rights*

As rights are rights of the individuals in relation to their fellow beings, they are always constituted into a contract. Rights are, by nature, contractual. They are contractual in so far as they are legal; they are legal because they are the result of the contract among men and between them as individuals. They are, therefore, obligational. Every contract confers rights and obligations on those who are part of the contract. By its very nature, the contractual rights are legal and therefore, binding, and have behind them a measure of force and compulsion.

There are the *positive as well as the negative rights*, maintained by the laws of the state. A right is positive when it expects a citizen to participate in political activity; it is negative when it refrains the individual from doing anything. Such rights, positive and negative, are contextual in nature for they are stated on the particular people by a particular authority and in a particular situation. It is, in this sense, that rights are always dynamic, their contents change with the changing circumstances. These rights like the contractual rights are both social, and civil.

There are *moral rights* as well, deriving their authority from a code of morality shared by the members of a community. These rights are not enforced by the state, but by the conscience of the individual or the customs which prevails in a community at a given time. Like the positive and negative rights, moral rights are also contextual, exist within the context of a particular frame. The Muslims, residing in Britain are not permitted to have four wives, although they belong to societies where such is the right of a Muslim. The context in Britain is different, and hence, a different moral right. Likewise, the British in Saudi Arabia cannot, and in fact, do not celebrate wedding with champagne.

Rights are not the *products of the state*, though there are rights given to us through laws. But the rights from legislation are merely a recognition of what already exists in the society. Our rights are social in the sense that they emnate from society at any given point of time; they are social because they had never existed before the emergence of society; and they are social because they cannot be exercised against the common good perceived by the society.

What is, then, the role of the state? As our rights are inviolable, it is the duty of the state to maintain, extend and protect them. The state is not the originator, but is the defender of our rights. If it were to be the 'giver' of our rights, it would grant them to us through a law made by it. By the same logic, the state would become the 'taker' of our rights by passing just another law. In that case, our rights are our rights, but to be exercised at the mercy of the state.

Our rights are the result of our membership of a political community as also the return of our service, say the obligation, done to the society. Rights are the rewards given to us by others in response to the performance of our duties towards others. Duties are the seeds of which rights constitute a crop.

Rights constitute the sum-total of those opportunities which ensure the enrichment of individual personality. Rights relate to the individual, to the development of his personality. "Rights are, thus, those conditions of social life", Laski says in his *A Grammar of Politics,* "without which no man can seek, in general, to be himself at his best". Rights arise in society. They originate in society. There are no rights before, beyond and against society. There are no rights before the emergence of society. Rights emanate from socially desirable conditions. No man, for example, has a right to murder or theft. Rights are social, because they promote social good or social welfare. The state does not create or grant rights, so it cannot take away them. The state only recognises rights, so it only secures them. Society grants rights and the state maintains them.

So understood the *characteristic features* of rights are:

1. Rights are related to the individual. Rights are rights of the individuals. They are related to the individual in the sense that they promote the development of the individual in the sense that they promote the development of the individual and his personality;
2. Right are social by nature. This means that rights are given by the society. It also implies that rights originate in society. There are, therefore, no rights where there is or there was no society;
3. Rights are social in another sense as well. They are social because rights are not, in their contents, against social good. That is why that there have never been rights which are either antisocial or immoral;
4. Rights are granted by society while the state recognises them, maintains them and secures them;
5. Rights emanate in social framework. Rights are granted by society only after obligations are fulfilled. Before rights, duties are performed. Rights and duties go together in the sense that rights come after duties. Because duties are offered, so rights are given; and
6. Rights are never permanent. They change with the changing time. As such, they are dynamic in nature. It is, therefore difficult to present any list of rights once for all, and for all times to come.

## II. Theories of Rights

Various theories with regard to rights have been there from time to time. Some such theories are:

### *1. Theory of Natural Rights*

The theory of natural rights had been popular during the 17th-18th centuries and mainly in the writings of Hobbes (*Leviathan*, 1651), Locke (*Two Treatises on Government*, 1690) and Rousseau (*The*

*Social Contract, 1762).* These contractualists say that there were natural rights possessed by man in the state of nature. Rights, the contractualists believe, were independent of organised society because they were the possession of man in the state of nature. Rights, according to them, were attributed to individuals as if they were essential properties of men as men. They are, the contractualists declare, inalienable, imprescriptable and indefeasible rights.

The theory of natural rights is criticised mainly on the following grounds:

1. The theory of natural rights is basically non-juristic. The natural rights are not basically sanctioned claims enjoyed by a man in a politically organised society;
2. The natural rights, as this theory emphasises, exist in pre-social period. The fact is that rights can never exist before or beyond society because rights before society are mere physical energies;
3. The contractualists say that men had natural rights in the state of nature and that society was organised to guarantee their realisation. This is basically wrong in the sense that it is society that grants rights and it is the government or the state that maintains and secures them.

The theory of natural rights had exercised a great influence during the days of American and French Revolutions. Yet, the theory came under attack later. Bentham denied the existence of pre-social rights. Rights, he insists, exist only in an organised society. Laski criticised the natural rights for their being a permanent bundle of privileges and held, "no permanent and unchanging catalogue of rights can be complied". The idea of rights is essentially dynamic, and changing with the social changes.

### *2. The Legal theory of Rights*

The legal theory of rights holds the view that the rights are granted by the state. It says that it is the state, the government that grants rights to the people. Among the various advocates of this theory, the names of Bentham, Hegel and Austin can be mentioned. The theory regards right as a claim, which the force of the state grants to the people. The essential features of this theory are: (i) that the state defines and lays down the bill of rights. Rights are not prior or anterior to the state, because the state is the source of rights; (ii) that the state lays down a legal framework which guarantees rights and that it is the state which enforces the enjoyment of rights; (iii) that as the law creates and sustains rights, so whenever the content of law changes, the substance of rights also changes.

The legal theory of rights suffers from various defects such as:

1. The state does maintain rights, it does not create them. Our rights emanate because of our membership of the society. The state comes to give the rights their guarantees and realisation;
2. If for once, it is admitted that the state creates rights as this theory affirms, it would have to be admitted that our rights are what the state wants them to be ours' and not what we want for ourselves; and
3. If the state grants a right through one law, it can take away that right through another law. Under such circumstances, our rights would be on the mercy of the state.

*3. The Historical Theory of Rights*

The historical theory of rights regards the rights as products of a long historical process. It holds the view that rights grow from traditions and customs. As traditions and customs stabilise owing to their constant and continuous usage, they take the shape of rights. The historical theory of rights originated in the 18th century in the writings of Edmund Burke and was later adopted by various sociologists.

The historical theory of rights is important, in so far as it condemns the legal theory of rights, which suggests that the rights are the creation of the state. It is also important because it denies the theory of natural rights. The state, the advocates of the historical theory emphasise, has only to recognise those rights of men which have already come into vogue through long usage.

But the historical theory of rights suffers from its own difficulties. It cannot be admitted that all our customs have resulted in our rights. In that case, the Sati system should have been the right of the Indian women and the child-marriage, the right of the children. Again, it is also not true that the present rights have all been derived from traditions and customs. The economic rights, right to work, right to social security etc., can not be related to any tradition or custom.

### *4. The Social Welfare Theory of Rights*

The social welfare theory of rights presumes that rights are the conditions of social welfare. The theory believes that the state should recognise only such rights as go to promote the social welfare. Among the modern advocates of the social welfare theory, Roscoe, Pound and Chafee are worth mentioning. Chafee believes that law and custom and natural rights etc. should all yield to what is socially beneficial or essential. Rights should be determined through the dictates of the social conditions.

Apparently, the social welfare theory of rights seems to be valid theory, but it presents certain practical difficulties. If only these rights have to be recognised which promote the social welfare, then the question arises: as to who would decide as to what and wherein the social welfare lies. Then the social welfare theory of rights suffers from all weaknesses as the legal theory of rights suffers.

### Conclusion

Various theories with regard to the rights speak about the changing liberal mood from one century to the other. Each theory of rights suffers from its own demerits, but each theory has its own importance. The theory of natural rights is important, in so far as it indicates that rights are natural to men as men. The legal theory of rights is important because it sets the state behind the rights, for the protection of rights. The historical theory of rights is important in so far as it gives rights the sanction of the past experience. The social welfare theory of rights is important is no far as it makes rights as socially desirable values.

## III. Laski on Rights

Harold J. Laski (1893-1950), a British political scientist and a leader of the Labour Party, had an eventful career. Starting as a pluralist (1916-20), he turned to be a socialised Benthamite (1920-25), a Fabian (1925-32), a Marxist (1932-42) and finally ended up as a liberal among the socialists, and a socialist among the liberals between 1942-1950.

Laski has definite views on rights which speak of his liberal-socialist stances. In his description of what rights are and what their nature is, Laski seems to be a liberal, but when he speaks of specific rights, Laski is, more or less, a socialist.

## Definition and Meaning of Rights

Laski's work, *A Grammar of Politics*, first published in 1925 but which had many editions and revisions till his death in 1950, gives an elaborate explanation of rights. According to Laski, "Rights are, in fact, those conditions of social life without which no man can seek, in general, to be himself at his best". Laski does not agree with Hobbes when the latter means by rights as the power to satisfy desires. The rights, according to Laski, are not the means for the satisfaction of one's desires, but they are social conditions necessary for the development of one's desires; they are social conditions necessary for the development of one's personality. The institution of the state, Laski says, maintains rights rather than grants them. Rights are, he continues, given by the society; they exist because society exists. They are prior to the state because society is prior to the state. Laski says that rights are neither natural nor historical: they are not natural because they did not exist in the state of nature as the advocates of the social contract theory claim; they are not historical because they had existed at one time or the other in history. Rights are, Laski argues, social in the sense that they are socially beneficial and socially essential. The state, he says, only recognises rights and ensures them to every citizen. Rights relate, Laski affirms, to the individual, to the development of his personality. It is a right because it helps individual seek what is best in him. Our rights are our rights because of our membership of the society. Rights, Laski emphasises, are not independent of society, but are inherent in it. "We have them", he says, "not only for ourselves but also for the protection of the society we are members". Rights and functions, Laski says, are corelative. Rights exist because there exist functions, duties and responsibilities. We have rights so that we may develop, so that we may contribute something to the society, so that we are useful to others.

## Nature of Rights

Laski's discussion on rights reveals certain features which are:

1. *Rights are given by society:* Rights arise in the society. Men have these rights because they are members of the society.

One who is not a member of the society, has no rights. That is why that the theory of natural rights is not acceptable to Laski, a theory which is condemned on the grounds that it specifies certain rights before the emergence of society. Rights are, Laski says, prior to the state but they are not prior to the society.

2. *Rights and man's personality:* Rights signify our progress. They are signposts of our development and progress. They are facilities which help man's personality to grow and develop. They add to man's values, ways, and quality of life. Without rights, it is difficult for the people to attain the development of their personality.
3. *Rights are social:* Our rights, Laski says, are social in nature. They are claims which are allowed by the society. There are, thus, no rights against the society. Society does not, and actually would never, grant us any right which is against society itself. There are no rights which destroy the very values on which a society is based. There are no rights that challenge the very existence of society. It is in this sense that our rights are moral in character. The individual has no right of killing or thieving.
4. *State protects rights:* Society grants us rights and the state protects them. Laski declares, "A state is known by the rights it maintains". The state, therefore, has a definite role to play in this respect. Certainly, the state, while maintaining rights, neither denies them nor can take away them. What at best, the state can do is that it restricts and suspends them. In no case the state can deny them. The task of the state is to recognise rights, maintain them and protect them.
5. *Rights are dynamic:* Rights are always changing in their character. They change with the changes in the social conditions. There can, therefore, be no permanent rights for all times to come. As circumstances change, so change our conditions, so also change our claims on the society, and therefore, so would change our rights as well. That is why that Laski emphasises that our rights have a content which changes with time and space.
6. *Rights and duties go together:* Laski does not think of rights without duties. We own rights because we owe duties. It is only after the performance of our duties that we have any

valid claim on our rights. The relationship between rights and duties is so close that it is difficult to separate the two. Our rights are duties of the others and others' rights are our duties. Indeed, rights imply duties. We have the right to free speech but we have the duty that we use such a right within the framework of the social order and public good.

**Citizens' Specific Rights**

The meaning and nature of rights given by Laski make him to be a liberal in his thinking. But when he comes to speak of specific rights, he seems to be a socialist, even a Marxist.

1. *Right to work:* A citizen, Laski says, has a right to work. His asusmption is that a citizen is born in a world where he can live only by the sweat of his brow. Society owes him the occasion to perform his functions. To leave him without access to the means of existence is to deprive him of that which makes possible the realisation of personality.

2. *Right to be paid adequate wages:* Closely related to the right to work is the right to be paid an adequate wage. By the work that he performs, he must be able to secure a return capable of purchasing the standard of living without which creative citizenship is impossible. The right to an adequate wage does not mean equality of income, but it does mean that a person should be able to satisfy his basic needs through the wages he gets.

3. *Right to reasonable hours of labour:* Related to the right to work and right to be paid an adequate wage is right to reasonable hours of labour. A citizen must, Laski says, "so distribute the period of labour that he may have the pleasure for creative tasks. The right to reasonable hours of labour implies right to rest and leisure. It is the right to discover the land of mind'. In other words, this right is the key to the intellectual heritage a man can devote himself to.

4. *Right to education:* The citizen has the right to such education as will fit himself for the task of citizenship. He must be provided, Laski says, "with the instruments which make possible the understanding of life. He must be able to give expression to his wants". Certainly, in the modern world, the citizen who lacks education is bound to be the slave of others. Such a man would not, if he is uneducated, rise to the full heights of his personality.

5. *Right to political power:* From the right to political power, Laski derives three rights: (i) right to franchise for everyone, (ii) right to be chosen as a governor, (iii) right to freedom of speech and expression.

6. *Other right:* Laski holds the view that on the foundations of these rights, there can be other rights as well. Freedom of religion, of equality and the like help people develop their personality. As to the right to property, Laski is of the opinion that one can not have property to the extent that he exploits others. So long as property, Laski says, is beneficial for the promotion of man's personality, it is allowed. In fact, he feels that property is essential for man's development, for his initiative to take up challenge, and for making his life more comfortable.

## IV. Concept of Human Rights

Human rights are rights worthy of human beings as human beings. S. Ramphal has very rightly stated that the human rights were not born of men but they were born with men. They are not as much a result of the efforts of the United Nations as are the emanations from basic human dignity. They are human rights because they are with the human beings as human beings or atleast they should be their rights as citizens of this world.

### *(a) What are Human Rights?*

Human rights may generally be defined as those rights which are inherent in our nature and without which we can not live as human beings. They are essential because they help us to develop and use our human faculties, talents, intelligence, and seek to satisfy our spiritual and other needs. They base themselves on mankind's increasing demand for a life in which the inherent dignity and worth of each human being will receive respect and protection.

Human rights lay at the roots of all organisations. These permeate the entire UN Charter. In the Preamble of the UN Charter, there is its determination "to affirm faith in fundamental Human Rights, in the dignity and worth of the Human person, in the equal rights of men and women and the nations, large and small".

Apart from the Preamble, the Charter contains a reference to the promotion of universal respect for the Human Rights in

Articles 13, 55, 62, 68 and 76. It may be noted that the Charter does not contain any Bill of Rights which was set up by the Economic and Social Council in February, 1946.

The *Commission on Human Rights* was directed to submit proposals, recommendations and reports concerning an international bill of rights, the status of women, freedom of information and similar matters, the protection of minorities, the prevention of discrimination on grounds of race, sex, language or religion.

The Commission divided its work in three stages:

1. Declaration: defining the fundamental rights and freedom;
2. An international convention or treaty setting forth in precise terms the provisions which governments were willing to accept as legally binding; and
3. To ensure observance of Human rights and to deal with violations.

The Commission after spending two and a half years of labour under the chairmanship of Mrs. Roosevelt drafted Universal Declaration of Human Rights. This declaration was to serve as a common standard of achievement for all people and all nations. The Declaration was approved by the General Assembly on December 10, 1948.

The Universal Declaration of Human Rights consists of a Preamble and thirty articles.

The Universal Declaration of Human Rights (UDHR) may be categorised into six families: *security rights* that protect people against crimes such as murder, massacre, torture, and rape; *liberty rights* that protect freedoms in areas such as belief, expression, association, assembly, and movement; *political rights* that protect the liberty to participate in politics through actions such as communicating, assembling, protesting, voting, and serving in public office; *due process rights* that protect against abuses of the legal system such as imprisonment without trial, secret trials, and excessive punishments; *equality rights* that guarantee equal citizenship, equality before the law, and nondiscrimination; and *welfare rights* (or "economic and social rights") that require provision of education to all children and protections against severe poverty and starvation. Another family that might be included is *group rights.* The UDHR does not include group rights, but subsequent treaties do. Group rights include protections of ethnic groups against genocide and the ownership by countries of their national territories and resources; and their use for the benefits of the world community.

*(b) Defining Features of Human Rights*

(i) Human rights are *political norms* dealing mainly with how people should be treated by their governments. The governments are directed into ways by rights against discrimination. Rights forbid governments to discriminate in their actions and policies, and they impose duties on governments to prohibit and discoverage both private and public forms of discrimination.

(ii) Human rights exist *as moral* and/or *legal* rights. A human right can exist as a shared norm of actual human moralities as a justified moral norm supported by strong reasons, as a legal right at the national level or as a legal right within international law.

(iii) Human rights are *numerous* rather than *few*. Locke's right to life and liberty, and property were few and abstract, but human rights address specific problems (e.g., guaranteeing fair trials, ending slavery, ensuring the availability of education, preventing genocide.) They protect people against familiar abuses of fundamental human interests. The fact is that the formulations in contemporary human rights documents are neither abstract nor conditional. They presuppose criminal trials, governments funded by income taxes, and formal systems of education.

(iv) Human rights *are minimal standards*. They are concerned with avoiding the terrible rather than with achieving the best. Their focus is protecting minimally good lives for all people. Henry Shue suggests that human rights concern the "lower limits on tolerable human conduct" rather than "great aspirations and exalted ideals." As minimal standards they leave most legal and policy matters open to democratic decision-making at the national and local levels.

(v) Human rights *are international norms covering all countries and all people living today*. They are the sorts of norms that are appropriately recommended to all countries. International law plays a crucial role in giving human rights a global reach. We can say that human rights *are universal* provided that we recognize that some rights, such as the right to vote, are held only by adult citizens; that some human rights documents focus on vulnerable groups such as children, women, and indigenous peoples; and that some rights, such as the right against genocide, are group rights.

(vi) Human rights *are high-priority norms*. "A human right is something of which no one may be deprived without a grave affront to justice." This does not mean, however, that we should take human rights to be absolute. As James Griffin says, human rights should be understood as "resistant to trade-offs, but not too resistant."

(vii) Human rights *have robust justifications that apply everywhere and support their high priority*. Without this they cannot withstand cultural diversity and national sovereignty. Robust justifications are powerful but need not be understood as ones that are irresistible.

(viii) Human rights *are rights, but not necessarily in a strict sense.* As rights they have several features. One is that they have right holders—a person or agency having a particular right. Broadly, the right holders of human rights are all people living today. More precisely, they are sometimes all people, sometimes all citizens of countries, sometimes all members of groups with particular vulnerabilities (women, children, racial and religious minorities, indigenous peoples), and sometimes all ethnic groups (as with rights against genocide.) Another feature of rights is that they *focus on a freedom, protection, status, or benefit*. A right is always to something which is the focus of the right holders' interest. Rights also *have addressees* who are assigned duties or responsibilities. A person's human rights are not primarily rights against the United Nations or other international bodies; they primarily impose obligations on the government of the country in which the person resides or is located. The human rights of a citizen of Belgium are mainly addressed to his government. International agencies, and the governments of countries, other than one's own, are secondary or "backup" addressees. International human rights organizations provide encouragement, assistance, and sometimes criticism to states in order to assist them in fulfilling their duties. The duties associated with human rights typically require actions involving respect, protection, facilitation, and provision. Finally, rights *are usually mandatory* in the sense of imposing duties on their addressees, but they sometimes do little more than declare high-priority goals and assign responsibility for their progressive realization. For example, the International Covenant on Economic, Social, and Cultural Rights (United Nations 1966c), which covers rights to basic human needs such as food, clothing, housing, and education, commits its signatories to "take steps... to the maximum of...available resources, with a view to achieving progressively the full realization of the rights.

*Description of Human Rights:* Human rights as they appear in Universal Declaration of Human Rights (UDHR) may be discussed as (1) Civil and Political Rights; (2) Economic and Social Rights; (3) Minority and Group Rights; and (4) Environmental Rights.

*1. Civil and Political Rights:* These rights are familiar from historic bills of rights such as the French Declaration of the rights of Man and of the Citizen (1789) and the United States Bill of Rights (1791, with subsequent amendments). Contemporary sources include the first 21 articles of the UDHR. These rights fit the general idea of human rights. First, they are political norms that primarily impose responsibilities on governments and international organizations. Second, they are minimal norms in that they protect against the worst things that happen in political society rather than setting out standards of excellence in government. Third, they are international norms establishing standards for all countries—and that have been accepted by more than 140 of the world's countries. Finally, it is plausible to make claims of his priority on their behalf, and to support these claims of importance with strong reasons. Consider the right to freedom of movement. One approach to justifying this right and its high priority would argue the importance of free movement to being able to find the necessities of life, to pursuing plans, projects, and commitments, and to maintaining ties to family and friends. A related approach argues that it is impossible to make use of other human rights if one cannot move freely. The right to political participation is undermined if a person is not permitted to go to political rallies or to the polls.

Civil and political rights are not absolute, and they may sometimes be suspended. Some civil and political rights can be restricted by public and private property rights, by restraining orders related to domestic violence, and by legal punishments. Further, after a disaster, such as, a hurricane or earthquake free movement is often appropriately suspended to keep out the curious, to permit access of emergency vehicles and equipment, and to prevent looking.

2. *Economic and Social Rights:* Besides the "civil and Political" rights just discussed, the UDHR includes "economic and social" (or welfare) rights. These include equality and nondiscrimination for women and minorities, access to employment opportunities, fair pay, safe and healthy working conditions, the right to form trade unions and bargain collectively, social security, an adequate standard of living (covering adequate food, clothing, and housing), health care, and education.

3. *Minority and Group Rights:* Concern for the rights of minorities is a long standing concern of the human rights movement. Human rights documents emphasize that all people, including members of minority ethnic and religious groups, have the same basic rights and should be able to enjoy them without discrimination. The right to freedom from discrimination figures prominently in the UDHR and subsequent treaties. It includes respecting and protecting people's rights "without distinction of any kind, such as race, color, sex, language, political or other opinion, national or social origin, property, birth, or social status."

Some standard individual rights are especially important to ethnic and religious minorities, including rights to freedom of association, freedom of assembly, freedom of religion, and freedom from discrimination. Human rights documents also include rights that refer to minorities explicitly and give them special protections.

Minority groups are often targets of violence and human rights norms call upon governments to refrain from such violence and to provide protections against it. This work is partly done by the right to life, which is a standard individual right. But the right against genocide protects groups from attempts to destroy or decimate them. The Genocide Convention was one of the first human rights treaties after World War II.

4. *Environmental Rights:* Environmental rights can be understood as rights to an environment that is healthy and safe. Such a right is human-oriented: it does not cover directly issues such as the claims of animals, biodiversity, or sustainable development.

The right to a safe environment can be sculpted to fit the general idea of human rights. It calls on them to regulate the activities of both governmental and non-governmental agents to ensure that environmental safety is maintained. Citizens are secondary addressees. This right sets out a minimal environmental standard, safety for humans, rather than calling for higher and broader standards of environmental protection.

**United Nations Human Rights Treaties**

Efforts to create international human rights treaties also went ahead within the United Nations in spite of the Cold War. *The Genocide Convention* was approved in 1948, and now has more than 130 signatories (United nations 1948a). It defines genocide and makes it a crime under international law. It also calls for action by UN bodies to prevent and suppress acts of genocide and requires states to enact national legislation prohibiting genocide, to try and punish persons or officials who commit genocide, and to allow extradition of persons accused of genocide. *The International Criminal Court*, created by the Rome Treaty of 1998 is empowered to prosecute genocide, along with crimes against humanity are was crimes at the international level.

For making the rights in the UDHR into the norms of international, two treaties were prepared, the *International Covenant of Civil and Political Rights* (ICCPR; United nations (1966) and the *International Covenant on Economic, Social, and Cultural Rights* (ICESCR; United Nations 1966c). These treaties embodying the UDHR's rights were not approved by the General Assembly until 1966 and only received enough ratifications to become operative in 1976. The ICCPR contains most of the civil and political rights found in the UDHR. The ICESCR contains the economic and social rights found in the second half of the UDHR.

There are many other UN human rights treaties that are implemented in roughly the same way as the ICCPR. These include the *International Convention on the Elimination of All Forms of Discrimination Against Women* (United Nations 1966), *The Convention on the Elimination of All Forms of Discrimination Against Women* (United Nations 1979), *The Convention of the Rights of the Child* (United Nations 1989), and *The Convention against Torture and other Cruel, Inhuman or Degrading Treatment or Punishment* (United Nations 1984).

**Other Human Rights Agencies within the United Nations**

Human Rights treaties are only one part of the UN's human rights program. There are a number of UN agencies that are charged with promoting human rights independently of the requirements imposed by human rights treaties. These bodies include the UN High-Commissioner for Human Rights, the Human Rights Commission, and the UN Security Council.

The *High Commissioner for Human Rights* coordinates the many human rights activities within the UN. The High-Commissioner receives complaints about human rights violations, assists in the development of new treaties and procedures, sets the agenda for human rights agencies within the UN, and provides advisory services to governments. Most importantly, the High Commissioner serves as a full-time advocate for human rights within the United Nations.

The *Human Rights Commission* is a standing body, created by the UN Charter, composed of 53 state representatives. Its main job is to deal with gross violations of human rights, wherever they occur. Because its members are state representatives rather than independent experts or jurists, the Commission is more of a political body than the Human Rights Committee established by the ICCPR. If the Human Rights Committee established under the ICCPR deals with human rights issues as a matter of international law, the Human Rights Commission deals with human rights issues as matters of international politics and diplomacy. The Human Rights Commission's achievements include authoring the UDHR and many human rights treaties, as well as the extended and successful campaign against apartheid in South Africa.

The *Security Council's* mandate under the UN Charter is the maintenance of international peace and security. The fifteen-member body can authorize military interventions and impose diplomatic and economic sanctions. During the Cold War, the Security Council tended to avoid human rights disputes other than apartheid in South Africa. But since the early 1990s the Security Council has dealt with many issues pertaining to human rights and war crimes. It authorized the use of military force in Somalia, the former Yugoslavia, Rwanda, Haiti, and East Timor, and sponsored a number of peacekeeping missions. It also established international criminal tribunals for Rwanda and Yugoslavia.

**Promotion of Human Rights by States**

States sometimes act, individually or with other states, to promote and protect human rights in other countries. For example, Portugal attempted to defuse the crisis in East Timor. And Australia led the military effort to restore peace and respect for human rights in East Timor. Methods include diplomacy, publishing reports and statements, conditioning access to trade or aid on human rights improvements, economic sanctions, and military intervention.

Efforts by states help to add real power to the international human rights system. The countries of Western Europe, Canada, Australia, and the United States, have been the pillars of the human rights establishment. They have lent their considerable support and clout to the system, keeping it going during hard times and helping it expand and flourish in better times. Although they have not always risen to the challenge of human rights emergencies, they have sometimes done so at considerable cost to themselves in money and lives. They have often worked closely with the Security Council. They do not, however, have a standing legal commitment to do this, except their commitment in the UN Charter to support the actions of the Security Council.

**Suspension and Limitations of Human Rights**

The Universal Declaration of Human Rights affirms that the exercise of a person's rights and freedoms may be limited—the limitations must be determined by law—but only for the purpose of securing due recognition of the rights of others and of meeting the just requirements of morality, public order and the general welfare in a democratic society. Rights may not be exercised contrary to the purposes and principles of the United Nations, or if they are aimed at destroying any of the rights set forth in the Declaration.

The Covenant on Economic, social and Cultural Rights states that the rights in that document may be limited by law, but only in so far as is compatible with the nature of the rights, and solely to promote the general welfare in a democratic society.

Unlike the Universal Declaration and the Covenant on Economic, Social and Cultural Rights, the Civil and Political Covenant contains no general provision applicable to all the Covenant's rights authorizing restrictions on their exercise. However, several articles in the Covenant provide that the rights being dealt with shall not be subject to any restrictions except those provided by law and those which are necessary to protect national security.

The Covenant on Civil and Political Rights allows a state to limit or suspend the enjoyment of, certain rights in cases of officially proclaimed public emergencies which threaten the life of the nation. Such limitations or suspensions are permitted only "to the extent strictly required by the exigencies of the situation" and may never involve discrimination solely on the ground of race, colour, sex, language, religion or social origin. These limitations or suspensions must also be reported to the United Nations.

Certain rights, however, may never be suspended or limited even in emergency situations. These are the rights to life, freedom from torture, freedom from enslavement or servitude, protection from imprisonment for debt, freedom from retroactive penal laws, the right to recognition as a person before the law, and freedom of thought, conscience and religion.

## Conclusion

The United nations and the other international organisations are pledged to promote "Universal respect for our observance of Human Rights and Fundamental Freedoms for all without distinction as to race, sex, language or religion."

Justice P.N. Bhagwati, while evaluating Human Rights, refers to three generation of Human Rights. He says: "It started with civil and political rights which have been termed first generation Human Rights which were followed by economic, social and cultural rights (as also civil and political rights) and which are described as second generation of Human Rights. We have now reached the third generation of Human Rights namely the Right to development." Right to development involves, Justice Bhagwati says, effective access to

— tangible resources to achieve their basic needs of productive and equitably paid work, sufficient nutrition, health care and hygience, shelter, energy resources, clean water and air;
— the necessary intangible resources, especially education and information, to enable them better to utilise resources, and to participate freely in the process of development;
— structures of production and government to assure the fair and equitable allocation of the above resources; and

— facilities and services to organise themselves to participate, monitor, evaluate and review development programmes and processes, and to hold accountable those responsible for their implementation.

The universal as Human Rights are, they are to be extended equally to all persons regardless of any distinction. Accordingly they are to be upheld by all the states, whatever their ideologies. To that extent, Human Rights make us the citizens of the world. The eseence of Human Rights lies in defining the essential moral conditions which ought to be guaranteed to citizens of any social and political order. The significance of Human Rights may briefly be summed up as under:

1. The Declaration and the Covenants of Human Rights were the first of its kind in the history of International Organisation.
2. They are a sort of statement of rights considered as essential for the development of human personality. Indeed, they, though not binding on the members-states, provide a yardstick to know the progress of the states.
3. They have served a very useful purpose. They are often cited in support of Human Rights.
4. They exert a profound influence on the Constitutions of new Nations and regional agreements. Though not vested with any legal force, they serve as useful instrument in defending human dignity.

Because human rights are universal, they are, therefore, abstract. They are in the nature of norms; ideals which ought to be achieved. What they lack are the institutions which could make them operative.

What they have are the ideals, the hopes and the appeals that numerous states could possibly give them some shape or validity. Obviously they are, because they are abstract, not real. The signatories of the UN Declaration, as we know, are different in more than one way, and as such it is difficult' to expect the application of these human rights with equal fervour by all. If examined closely, the human rights do not sound democratic in the sense that they may conflict with the policies determined by a democratically constituted authority.

But this is not to undermine the utility of the UN human rights. In fact, they aim to offer a meta-political moral framework for politics and social interaction among the states; the human rights ensure a just treatment of the individuals and the groups; they help evaluate the activities of numerous governments, and take them to task through world opinion if they violate them.

## SUGGESTED READINGS


1. Alston, P. and Crawford, J., eds., *The Future of UN Human Rights Treaty Monitoring*, Cambridge: Cambridge University Press, 2002.
2. Bailey, S. *The UN Security Council and Human Rights*, New York: St. Martin's Press, 1994.
3. Brandt, R.B. "The Concept of a Moral Right," *Journal of Philosophy* 80: 1984, 29–45.
4. Cranston, M. 1967. "Human Rights, Real and Supposed," in D.D. Raphael, ed. *Political Theory and the Rights of Man*. London: Macmillan, 1967.
5. ________. *What are Human Rights?* London: Bodley Head, 1973
6. Feinberg, J. 1973. *Social Philosophy*, Englewood Cliffs, NJ: Prentice-Hall, 1973.
7. Hart, H. "Are There Any Natural Rights?" *Philosophical Review* 64: 1955, 175–191.
8. Holmes, S. and Sunstein, C. *The Cost of Rights: Why Liberty Depends on Taxes*. New York: Norton, 1999.
9. Katayanagi, M. *Human Rights Functions of United Nations Peacekeeping Operations*. The Hague: Kluwer, 2002.
10. Kymlicka, W. *Liberalism, Community, and Culture*. Oxford: Clarendon Press, 1989.
11. Nickel, J. *Making Sense of Human Rights*. Berkeley and Los Angeles: University of California Press, 1987; revised edition forthcoming, Georgetown University Press, 2004
12. ________. 1993. "The Human Right to A Safe Environment," *Yale Journal of International Law* 18: 281–295.
13. Nozick, R. *Anarchy, State, and Utopia*. New York: Basic Books, 1977.
14. Rawls, J. *The Law of Peoples*. Cambridge, MA: Harvard University Press, 1999.
15. Shue, H. *Basic Rights*. Second edition. Princeton: Princeton University Press, 1996.

16. Steiner, H. and Alston, P. eds. *International Human Rights in Context*. Oxford: Oxford University Press, 2002.
17. Sumner, L. *The Moral Foundation of Rights.* Oxford: Clarendon Press, 1987.
18. Thomson, J. *The Realm of Rights.* Cambridge, MA: Harvard University Press, 1990.
19. Wellman, C. *Real Rights*. Now York: Oxford University Press, 1995.
20. ________. *The Proliferation of Rights: Moral Progress or Empty Rhetoric?* Boulder, CO: Westview Press, 1999.

## CHAPTER – 9

# Concepts: Identity

There has been, in recent years, an intense interest in questions relating to *identity* among scholars belonging to social sciences and humanities. In Political Science, the concept of *identity* is at the centre of debates in every branch of our discipline: in politics, much research is being done in 'identity politics' of race, gender, and sexuality; in comparative politics, 'identity' plays a central role in works on nationalism and ethnic conflict (see Horowitz, *Ethnic Groups in Conflict*-1985, Smith, *National Identity* 1991; Deng, *War of Visions* 1995; Laitin, *Identity in Formation* 1999). In international relations, the idea of 'state identity' is at the centre of constructionist critiques of realism and analyses of state sovereignty (see Wendt, "Anarchy is what states make of it 1992," also, *Social Theory of International Politics* 1999; Katzenstein, *The Culture of National Security*, 1996; Lapid and Kratochwil, *The Return of Culture and Identity in International Relations*, 1996; Biersteker and Weber, *State Sovereignty as Social Construct* 1995). In political theory, the questions of identity point out numerous arguments in gender, ethnicity, nationality and culture in relation to liberalism on the one hand and its alternatives, on the other (see Young, *Justice and the Politics of Difference*, 1990; Connolly, *Identity/Difference;* 1991; Kymlicka, *Multicultural Citizenship*, 1995; Miller, *Nationalism*, 1995; Taylor, *The Sources of the Self*; 1989). However, Political Science is much behind other disciplines in its treatment of the concept of *identity*.

Despite the fact that there has been a lot of interest in 'identity', the concept remains something of an enigma. What was said about identity 15 years ago, Phillip Gleason says, remains the same even today. Even the dictionary meaning of the word 'identity' has not captured the meaning scholars are trying to project now. Our present day idea of identity is a fairly recent social construct, though complicated as it is.

## I. Identity: Definitions, Meaning and Characteristics

'Identity' has come to mean, Gleason says, so many things that, by itself, it means nothing. The wholesale chaotic spread of 'identity talk' has, in fact, deprived it of any meaning at all. The Oxford English Dictionary (OED) defines identity as the sameness of a person or a thing at all times or in all circumstances, the condition or fact that a person is itself and not something else; individuality, personality." In this definition, there is no meaning that gives an idea of 'national identity' or 'ethnic identity'; it states identity as one that fulfils personality traits. The OED definition also fails to capture what we intend by declarations of the form "my identity is such as such", although "individuality" does come close, 'personality' is, of course, clearly way off. In one word, we may say that the OED reports an older meaning of the word "identity."

There is a second older meaning of "identity" that needs not apply to persons and that is also still in use—for example, "an identity of interests." This sense is defined in the OED as follows: "The quality or condition of being the same in substance, composition, nature, properties, or in particular qualities under consideration."

In our present meaning of the concept, we refer to Erik Erikson's concept which David do Levita presents, in a rather interesting manner, as follows:

"In Hiddesen, a charming little German town, a meeting was held in 1951 to discuss 'Health and Human Relations,' sponsored jointly by.... At that conference Erik H. Erikson spoke on 'The Sense of Inner Identity.' I was deeply impressed by Erikson and the exposition of his brilliant ideas.... We all felt that this 'concept of identity' was extremely important, *but it was not clear what the exact meaning was, so loaded with significance was the new term.*"

Erikson's meaning *has* made it into dictionaries, and is defined in one as follows: "the condition of being uncertain of one's feelings about oneself, especially with regard to character, goals, and origins, occurring especially in adolescence as a result of growing up under disruptive, fast-changing conditions" (see Webster's *New World Dictionary*).

Some definitions of 'identity' are given below:

1. Identity is "people's concepts of who they are, of what sort of people they are, and how they relate to others."

—*Hogg and Abrams.*

2. "Identity is used to describe the way individuals and groups define themselves and are defined by others on the basis of race, ethnicity, religion, language, and culture." —*Deng*
3. Identity "refers to the ways in which individuals and collectivities are distinguished in their social relations with other individuals and collectivities." —*Jenkins*
4. "The term [identity] (by convention) references mutually constructed and evolving images of self and other." —*Katzenstein*
5. "Identities are ... prescriptive representations of political actors themselves and of their relationships to each other." —*Kowert and Legro*
6. "My identity is defined by the commitments and identifications which provide the frame or horizon within which I can try to determine from case to case what is good, or valuable, or what ought to be done, or what I endorse or oppose." —*Taylor*
7. "Indeed, identity is objectively defined as location in a certain world and can be subjectively appropriated only *along with* that world. ... [A] coherent identity incorporates within itself all the various internalized roles and attitudes." —*Berger* and *Luckmann*

The above definitions of 'identity' clearly highlight its *characteristics*, chief among them are as under:

(i) It denotes how people think of themselves and how they relate themselves to others;
(ii) It is a process of how others think about us, about our status, religion, language, ethnicity and the like;
(iii) It is not something which is natural, inherent or immutable; it is rather something that is constructed, socially constructed;
(iv) It is labelling of themselves as members of particular group with characteristics of their own;
(v) It is what distinguished people from other peoples; group from other groups; a collectivity from other collectivities;
(vi) It is a way of describing oneself through what one likes, what one is, what one believes in, and what one seeks to ask for;
(vii) It is a frame of organising physical characteristics, beliefs, accumulated knowledge and experience, abilities and personality into attributes, the particular mix of which makes each individual unique and thus identifiable;

(viii) It is identification of self through differences; 'identification' in so far as it has characteristics of its own, and 'difference' in so far as it is distinct from others.

The word 'identity' is used in more than one ways. It is used to refer to the culture of a people, characteristic of its own; it is also used to refer to common identification with a collectivity or social category; it is used to refer to certain differences from others; it is also used to parts of a self-composed meaning, attached by persons to the multiple role they typically play in a highly differentiated contemporary societies; it is also used to refer to certain shared culture, values, ideals individuals cherish; it is also used to refer to human beings as self-contained unitary individuals who carry their uniqueness deep inside themselves like pearls hidden in their shells.

## II. Growth and Evolution

The contemporary history of the term 'identity' in its positivist and social-psychological sense spreads from the Scottish Enlightenment, but its growth and evolution can be traced in numerous branches of sciences. John D. Ely, in his essay "Community and the Politics of Identity: Toward the Genealogy of a Nation-state concept," describes the growth of the concept of identity in a unique way. His description goes as follows.

The characteristic metaphysical meaning for identity, or any theoretical meanings of a philosophical, theological, or scientific sense, referred, for centuries, to the quality or state of sameness in contrast to difference. Identity referred to maintaining a specific "thing-ness" through time. The term appeared in a largely metaphysical context influenced by a mathematical-geometric understanding of the heavens as a model for understanding the first principles of thinking. This mixture of mathematics, stars, and neo-Platonism stretches from Plato, extending by way of Plotinus and neo-Platonism through Augustine and Aquinas, Cusanus, Pico delle Mirandola, and Desecrates, up to Kant and the German idealists. It is characterized by the attempt to relate everything to one, the problem of the one and the many. "The one and the many, abstractly conceived as the relationship of identity and difference, is the fundamental relation that metaphysical thinking comprehends, both as logical and as ontological: the one is both axiom and essential ground, principle and origin." This mathematical-astral sense, tied to the age-old problem of the one and the many, characterized the neo-Platonic meaning of identity, of course, as a primal, essentialist, and ideal concept separated from the duration of sameness.

This mathematical-metaphysical sense has different types of meaning. In particular, in an Aristotelian context, the concept of sameness and species unity has a biological, qualitative sense. Aristotle uses sameness with respect to species of things. Sameness is only reduced to terms of a mechanically conceived universe in Hume's *Treatise on Human Nature*. This sense of qualitative distinction is even more strongly evident in his distinction between theoretical and practical science, between psychology and ethics. However, the term identity itself tends to remain much more purely metaphysical in its appearance, meaning, above all, something like one-to-one sameness or congruence in the Euclidean sense of *tautotes*, "same-ity." In Aristotle, the term *tautotes* occurs, though surely, is a general term, used as comparison or similarity with respect to one thing.

For centuries a relative obscure post-classical term in mathematics, the application of identify to the psychology and jurisprudence of the modern state begins with the scientific revolution and the Enlightenment, with John Locke saying in his *Essay on Human Understanding*: "The identity of the same Man consists... in nothing but a participation of the same continued Life, by constantly fleeting Particles of Matter, in succession vitally united to the same organised body." In developing his epistemic meaning, Locke took the old sense of 'that which persists' and applied it inwardly to consciousness of retaining one's sameness through time, remaining, thus, English in origin and empirical in nature.

Personal identity at first remains an English term in this new psychological sense. Though the terms 'self' and 'individual' develop conceptually in parallel on the continent, especially in Desecrates' psychological theory of the "I" of "Ego," Desecrates does not actually use the term identity to describe the ego. Locke and Hume elaborate the self with its personal and unique identity as part of the discourse of empirical and utilitarian philosophy and its understanding of the state.

It bears noting that the use of the term personal identity in the *Essay on Human Understanding* and the *Treatise on Human Nature* fits in the general psychological system elaborated by Locke and Hume. Neither writer, however, uses the term yet as a central, psychological, much less group-psychological, category at all. Personal identity is never synonymous with the self or applicable in place of terms like character or person. It remains an aspect or quality of the person. Indeed, both thinkers are traditional theorists of virtues and character; and when Hume discusses things that we would consider to be group identity, such as national identity, he speaks not surprisingly of national character instead. However, the term becomes a decisive epistemological one in empirical psychology, and it is within this tradition of thinking that we can trace its main development, which is the result of an interplay between the metaphysical-mathematical concept of identity, applied increasingly to the outer world, and the new psychological one; or the flowering of the social-psychological meaning of identity out of the development of the empirical-utilitarian concept of the self or individual developed by Locke, Hume, Jeremy Bentham, the Mills, and H.L.A. Hart.

James Mill, the economist, using the word 'individual' or 'character' in psychological terms, introduced the legal concept of identity, in the sense of identity of interest, though in the process moved towards 'groups' identity, mediating by a concept of the economically interested bourgeois–hedonist Benthamite psychology. Only in John Stuart Mill does the term identity begin to appear completely as a term for group identity as national identity, not surprisingly in the chapter of his book *On Representative Government,* which deals with nationality as connected with representative government. Mill refers to those things that unite a portion of mankind as a nationality—"common sympathies" that can be caused by the 'effects to identity of race and descent," by "community of language and community or religion, or by geographical limits." "But the strongest of all is identity of political antecedents: the possession of a national history, and consequent community of recollections; collective pride and humiliation, pleasure and regret, connected with the same incidents in the past. When Mill enumerates the various characters or qualities determining identity in this sense, we find the catalog of ascriptions that we have already seen in Amelie Rorty and the standard contemporary ascriptive accounts of the individual's identity. Identity becomes the central, ascriptively determined mode of describing the modern individual's psyche or personality, covering the various ways in which the legal-compulsive monopoly of the state and its various subsidiary compulsory institutions serve ascriptively to define individuals. The term simultaneously establishes itself as a unique characterization of the individual in British individualist philosophy. It expresses the specificity or uniqueness of that individual.

This particular character of the term evolves in the nineteenth century in those countries in which the nation-state and national feelings develop earliest: first in England, then in France. For Voltaire, it retains an old metaphysical meaning; Rousseau uses the verb *identifier*, occasionally, with regard to the confusion of special or partisan interest with communal. By the mid-nineteenth century, "Old identity," in English, contrasts older residents of a colonial region to new arrivals. Through means of frontier control, identity papers, and even photo-identification that begin to appear in the context of the French Revolution, a true system of national identification makes a relatively late appearance. Identity plaques were introduced as a means of identifying soldiers in the French Army in 1882, following the early origins of photo-identification in the wake of the repression of the Paris Commune. Identity cards were issued to British soldiers at the turn of the century, and identity disks—early dog tags—in 1909. Identity cards appear even later, after the general introduction of passports following World War I, in the Larrouse Dictionary only in 1929. Such usages are first clearly military; it is only later, in the 1950s, that identification extends to general identification cards or what we now call IDs.

The development, of a modern state, bureaucracy, political economy, and technical science form the background for the decisive emergence of the term identity. As later writers, especially in French psychoanalytic discourse, argue, the development of identity in this sense centers on an entity called the subject that "draws its position, its isolation ... from the ... absorption of material discontinuity into affirmation and symbolism," that is, "from its abutment against the constraint of state control."

If the major meaning of identity refers to state formulation of the bureaucratically identified subject, the social psychological sense continues to develop as well: through the nineteenth century, the term identification begins appearing in the most intimately private group sense, e.g., of "identification of husband and wife in feeling... and family" or as when "two lovers are spoken as being 'one.'" It is, indeed, precisely this meaning that Freud will adapt, with his determinist instinct-hedonism of primary process, to his theory of psychological development via identification. Thus, through the twentieth century, these two meanings begin to converge: (1) the idea of a self modified by national character inscribed by the mobilization of the state's subjects for purposes of military service, and (2) identification as the idea of becoming a oneness or unity through familial socialization. The two most important figures in this regard are the jurist Carl Schmitt, who develops the term as part of his anti-democratic and illiberal *Constitutional Doctrine* in 1928, and Erik Erikson, who develops the occasional use of identification in Freud's theory of psychological development into a theory of psychological identity and identity crisis following World War II.

Carl Schmitt was a conservative German jurist, whose writings became famous during the Weimar Republic, but who later joined the Nazi party, and whose influence is frequently underestimated in an Anglo-American context. Though largely unheralded outside of Germany, he developed such terms as the political and Eurocentrism, as well as coining the terms decisionist and juridification. He is important in the elaboration of identity as a legal and constitutional concept. In his writings dating from the early 1920s, the term crystallizes as a juridical ideal defining the modern state in ascriptive identities.

Identity appears in his writings in several meanings. Above all, however, he uses it as part of his understanding of democracy as the image or representation [*Vorstellung*] of an homogeneous unity of "ruler and ruled, governor and governed, state and people." It is one of two competing forms of constitution, along with representation, of the modern state as a "closed political unit." The term identity appears here, in a context of complete ascription. Schmitt imagines only a world of ascription by states or by political orders and the politizations of these. Politics, more precisely, the political, is for Schmitt the only non-ascriptive mode of orientation, since it is the means of adjusting those ascriptive orders to one another vis-a-vis the "friend/enemy relation." But politics is not thus a meritocratic, voluntary, or practical alternative to ascription. Schmitt's concept of the political is as anti-republican as his characterization of democracy as identity of ruler and ruled. Schmitt's use of the political, following the particularly German grammatical construction of an adjective used as a noun, erases the possibility of substantive public life or filled political space by dropping the noun that political modifies, while reducing the meaning to a means of regulating essentially ascriptive identities.

In Schmitt's view, a polity is constituted as a democratic political unit via the democratic presence of the citizens as identity of ruler and ruled, requiring a maximum of homogeneity. (He contrasts this term with representative forms, modes of the *Standestaat* or "estate-state," which require less homogeneity, e.g., Imperial Austria-Hungary contrasted with Republican France.) Homogeneity here, is the mode of ascription that characterizes the state and state system. Maximum homogeneity of pure identity democracy leads to an intensification of the political or "friend/enemy relation." When the political unity is composed not as pure but as mixed identities, in estate-state fashion, various groups of humans based on 'national, confessional, and class difference" can exist together in less intensified form. The world of Schmitt's politics, however, is that of his ascriptive identities in different historical modes: religious identity, national identity, class identity, and civilizational identity. What characterizes all these forms of identity is that they produce a unity of ascription. Schmitt himself preferred national homogeneity because it appeared to him as part of a system of national states that hedged war, where identity and intensification based on class or economic interest led to uncontained war inside and outside established political units, to global civil war. His sympathy with fascist, corporatist solutions in the early 1930s rested on the possibility of restabilizing such class issues in corporate national units with distinctive particularity, opposed to the universalist economistic attitudes of the liberals and left, which provoke global civil war. However unappealing this view is, many of his students and devotees continue to invoke ethno-cultural homogeneity or identity in an ethnopluralist fashion, that is, national identity as the basis of a stable and secure state, while blaming abstract universalism and socialism for provoking fascistic responses. Politics in this view is not some other, practical mode of being, some mode of continuing and shared practice in collective judgment, but a means of calming or intensifying ascriptive modes of existence that are as present in an estate-state as a modern, homogeneous one, but which in any case form, as it were, an iron cage of ascription and ascriptively based conflicts. He adapts not a critical, mediated concept of identity from German dialectics, but a version of unmediated, mathematical identity from British utilitarianism and its homogeneous, unified, and territorial concept of sovereignty for this purpose.

Schmitt's version of identity as ascribed versions of national homogeneity radicalizes and elaborates inhering concepts of ascribed identity appearing with the growth of the powers of the bureaucratic nation-state and its ability to register, mobilize, and regulate the specific identities of its nationals. This process was largely completed with the establishment of national identification for means of conscription in the first two decades of the twentieth century. Investigating the development of identity in Erik Erikson's social-psychology illustrates this nation-state-based ethnoterritorial mode of ascription in an apparently more benign fashion. At the same time, Erikson is important in understanding the terms of the modern debate over identity politics. He is the great popularizer of the term and its development as a social-psychological category. He illustrates the means of adapting Freud's concept of the ego and ego identification with the empiricist concept of the individual psyche as a personal identity; and he underscores the manner in which this additionally ascriptive Freudian impulse is tied to the twentieth-century development of the term identity to mean ethnic or national identity.

The term is developed by Erikson as a way to address perceived difficulties of immigrants assimilating in a majority culture and thus, retains its central role in managing state-building via ascription. Identity as a social-psychological category emerged in the early 1960s, as a means of explaining identity crises and problems of ethnic minorities in New York City in the humanist terms of psychology. Minority identity problems were contrasted to the identity of native U.S. Citizens. Minorities, in contrast to the unified identity of the majority culture, will tend to both identify and counter-identify with the majority culture. The central meaning is thus in terms of culture or the structure of nations, if we look at the context in which Erikson introduces the term identity. He explicitly transforms the term national characters into national identities.

Erikson's focus on unconscious features of development by which our religious and ethnic sensibilities are formed emphasizes how the psychoanalytic function here is designed specifically to explain those parts of our character formation *of which we are least aware or conscious*, thus those most ascribed, most unconsciously constructed in our head, by the categories of social existence. Equally important are the ethnic and state-building premises of the term in his social psychology. The migrant, in terms of religious confession, language, ethos, and increasing registration and control of populations by states via passports, is particularly important for Erikson, since the identity of an ethnic minority in the United States has already been defined or generated by the nation-state from which that individual or his parents originally stemmed. Given that ethnic and religious difference formed the core of his contrast between kinds of identities, Erikson draws a contrast between general identity (a kind of assumed national-cultural-ethnic normality) and the "super-identity" made up "out of all the identities imported by its constituent immigrants..."

The development of the idea of identity as a metaphysical, epistemological, juridical, and social-scientific term underscore the role of mobilizing myths or ideas of the nation or ethnos in the formation of national states, a process of legal ascription occurring *coincident* with the development of the nation-state. That the primary meaning of identity is a psychological meaning, that is, a social meaning, is not coincidental. This meaning veils the role of the state in the construction of social identities, namely via the introduction of identity papers that establish *Staatsangehorigkeit* or nationality.

### III. State of Identity Over-time

Identity is the identification of an individual as an individual; it is a recognition of an individual who belongs to a group different from others; it is a status with which a person/group of persons is recognised so on grounds of having peculiar traits; it is both a matter of identification and of difference.

In **traditional** societies, identity, both as a personal category or a social one, was fixed, solid and stable. Identity was a function of predefined social role, the traditional systems of myths religion and the like circumscribing the realm of both thought and behaviour. One was born and lived and died as a member of one's clan and a tribe; one was a member of a fixed kinship system. In the ancient times, both in the Western and Eastern societies, there was no problem with regard to 'identity'; people would hardly reflect on it or it would hardly be a topic for discussion; identify was taken for granted. Kellner, therefore, declared; "Individuals did not undergo identity crises, or radically modify their identity. One was a hunter or a gatherer, and member of the tribe, and that was that."

In **our times**, identity has become mobile, multiple, personal, self-reflective, and subject to change. This means that we, in modern societies, are caught up in so many different, sometimes conflicting, roles; we do not exactly know, what we really are. That is why that identity, and the issue of identity have become problematic in our times.

There is hardly truth in the fact that the identity is always fixed and stable. Jacques Lacan is of the opinion that the individual is decentralised; there is nothing which is called the autonomous self. A central thesis in Lacan's theory, is that the ego or the personal identity is constituted in relation to others, say parents, friends, relatives, the mass media etc. Identity is, thus, constantly undergoing changes which are dependent on our relations with others.

If we accept Lacan's thesis, modern identity is formed in relation to the different agents of socialisation: family, school, work, peergroup, the mass media and so on. In our society, therefore, individuals play a multitude of different roles. They are constantly occupied with developing their own unique personality. It might be said that there is a gap between so called personal identity and social identity and this gap leads to a constant quest for a meaningful way of integrating these different poles. Moreover, there is also the need to be a personality and a member of the special group at the same time.

## IV. Forms of Identity: Social and Personal

The two forms in which 'identity' is designed may be called 'social' and 'personal'. Thus, identity has two forms: (i) social and (ii) personal. In the former, an identity is just a social category, a group of people designated by a label or labels. This is used when one is labelled as 'Indian', 'father' 'worker' or 'citizen'. The latter, i.e., 'personal' identity is the meaning involved in declarations such as 'my identity'. Personal identity is a set of attributes, beliefs, desires or principles of action that a person thinks distinguishing her/him in socially relevant ways, and that (a) the person takes a special pride in; (b) the person takes no special pride in, but which so orient his/her behaviour that she/he be at a loss about how to act and what to do without them; or (c) the person feels she/he could not change is she/he wanted to. Used in this sense, 'identity' has become a partial and indirect substitute for 'dignity', 'honour' and 'pride'.

Social identity presupposes identity as a social category. To ask about identities of such and such people is often to ask about the social categories in which they place themselves or how they think about their content or rules of membership. Social identity is a category; it is also socially constructed. It, as a social category, in what has been socially produced over a period of time. That is what makes social identity socially constructed. Social identity does not exist in isolation; it exists, as a matter of identification, in relation to each other, and as a matter of difference in relation to others outside their domain.

The two classes of identities with regard to social identity are role identity and type identity.

Role identities refer to labels applied to people who are expected to perform some set of actions, behaviors, routines, or functions in particular situations. For example, taxi driver, toll collector, mother, father, president, professor, businessman, student. Type identities refer to labels applied to persons who share some characteristic or characteristics, in appearance, behavioral traits, beliefs, attitudes, values, skills (e.g., language), knowledge, opinions, experience, historical commonalities (like region or place of birth), and so on.

Taylor explains in his *Sources of the Self: The Making of the Modern Identity* as to what personal identity is. He says: "... the question of identity... is often spontaneously phrased by people in the form: Who am I? ... What [answers] this question for us is an understanding of what is of crucial importance to us" (p. 27). This can't be right as stated, since oxygen, the Clean Air Act, and lots of other things may be important to me but not be part of my identity." Taylor proceeds by putting restrictions on the things identity consists of and the sense in which they are important: "My identity is defined by the commitments and identifications which provide the frame or horizon within which I can try to determine from case to case what is good, or valuable, or what ought to be done, or what I endorse or oppose" (p. 27). Thus, in Taylor's interpretation, personal identity is a personal moral code or compass, a set of moral principles, ends, or goals that a person uses as a normative framework and a guide to action. Additionally, personal identity needs to include something which distinguishes an individual from other individuals. It is something that states individual as another individual in relation to others, and also an individual as a part of the social whole where other individuals do make their existence. Personal identity, we may sum up, consists of a set of of aspects or attributes of a person. These may be physical attributes (e.g., being tall or red-headed might figure into a personal identity), membership in social categories, person-specific beliefs, goals, desires, moral principles, or matters of personal style. Furthermore they must be aspects or attributes of the person that the person is conscious of, and which distinguish the person from at least some others.

Summing up the two forms of identity, we may conclude that identity means either as a social category, defined by membership, rules and allegedly characteristic attributes or expected behaviours, or (b) a socially distinguishing feature that a person takes a special pride in or views as unchangeable but socially consequential (or, of course, both (a) and (b) at once).

Identity, in its current, historically novel complex of meanings derives most of all from Erik Erikson's work in the 1950s. By 1970s, the word used in the above sense had acquired a healthy successful, life of its own in ordinary language and in many social science disciplines. Under the influence of post-modesnism and debates over multiculturalism, the late 1980s and 1990s found historians, anthropoligists, and most of all humanities scholars relying ever more heavily on 'identity' as they explored the cultural politics of race, class, ethnicity, gender, citizenship, sexuality and other social categories.

## V. Identity: Cultural-National, Communitarianism and Multiculturalism

The three perspectives, though differently stated, focus on identity. These are (i) Cultural Nationalism, (ii) Communitarianism, (iii) Multiculturalism.

(i) *Identity and Cultural-Nationalism:* The ideal of national identity with regard to the concept of identity has been articulated by the German far right of its ascendancy throughout the 1980s. National identity, for German rightists, invokes an ideal of national cultural-ethnic unity. These rightists have recognised and amplified the nationalist, ethno-cultural resonance in the meanings of identity. Their emphasis is that identity is a term denoting a nation-hood, a culture, and on ethnicity. Their view of politics is not only culturally conservative, it is also regionally nationalistic. How can we distinguish the calls for a 'politics of identity' or a community of "shared collective goods"—to use terms of post-structuralism, African American national or communitarians such as Charles Taylor or William Gallston—from anti-democratic cultural nationalists? Neo-nationalism is a version of identity politics evident not only in existing nation-states but also in nationalist separatism such as in Baskenland, Wales, French Canada, Belgium, Northern Italy, and the former Yugoslavia. As Taylor emphasizes, communitarianism resonates with regionalist, particularist, and rightist viewpoints. Given this convergence of terminology, how can communitarians avoid invoking the ideal of "shared collective goods," such as religion and language, that overlaps with the strong cultural nationalism of the far right? Rootedness is culture; it is found in the homeland or *Heimat*. Depending on differing registers of images and rhetoric, such community discourse can be shared by the far right. How can multicultural defenders of a "politics of identity" avoid invoking a political version of difference—one which, however *cultural,* overlaps with the rhetoric of difference used by the new right? Pierre-Andre Taguieff and Etienne Balibar develop concept of neo-racism illustrating this problem. Neo-racism, to use their term, no longer depends on positive scientific or biological demonstration of difference. It depends rather on the *cultural* reality of difference itself, articulated within a global system of particular *national* states. In so far as identity develops as a term integrating the psyche of the individual in the state system as a hierarchy of core and periphery, it will serve to reinforce this system. There is little doubt that the new-right invocation of national identity serves this project. The issue is the degree to which participation in the discourse of identity politics by multiculturalists and communitarians may also unwittingly serve this end.

(ii) *Communitarians and Identity:* Communitarians are today at the center of political theory debates in the United States. As critics of liberalism and its abstract individualism, communitarians invoke the idea of identity to strengthen the concrete, historical, embodied nature of any actual self. Writers such as Alisdair Maclntyre, Charles Taylor, Michael Sandel, Michael Walzer, Robert Bellah, and William Gallston developed their views in the service of a critique of liberalism. Liberalism's view of self, they argue, is abstracted from the concrete social forms that communalize, socialize, or integrate, such a self, that give it an ethos or, to use a monetarized and liberal term, a value-orientation. The character of the individual arises with the roles, activities, practices, and customs making humans social and political animals. Humans are embedded in a web of relations that cultivate and educate them, giving them narrative and teleological meanings. Freedom in this view is not freedom from government, but a share in the practices of ruling, which means following specific roles and becoming competent in certain practices related existentially to those roles. As Alisdair Maclntyre writes, "[W]hat is good for me has to be good for the one who inhabits these roles."

For communitarian writers like Maclntyre or Taylor, our identity is thus inseparable from our being-in-the-world in a system of intentions, from our being *agents.* This is the inescapable framework of teleology or goals that form the background picture, the narrative assumptions, of the self. Identity is irreducibly tied to humans as agents with practices. "My identity," writes Taylor, "is defined by the commitments and identifications which profile the frame or horizon which I can try to determine from case to case what is good or valuable..." Identity is tied with an individual's orientation, frameworks of meaning, "webs of interlocution," historical rootedness, religion, and tradition. Or, as Maclntyre notes, we cast ourselves, in the story of our lives, in our approach to our own circumstances, always as "bearers of a particular social identity." "I am someone's son or daughter, someone else's cousin or uncle; I am a citizen of this or that city, a member of this or that guild or profession. I belong to this clan, that tribe, this nation." Communitarians deny the existence of a malleable and universal abstract human psyche, an unencumbered or transcendental self. Ethics are thus rooted in a lived world. They are composed of strong collective goals or shared cultural goods.

The term identity in its everyday use fits a communitarian sensibility. It suggests the psychological glue holding a community together. Those shared collective or cultural goods give us meaning and recognition, make us what we are, give us a feeling of home and community. Identity in this sense designates something like a person's understanding of who he is; of his fundamental defining characteristics as a human being. Identity in this sense invokes rooted community, knowledge and confidence in friends, local parameters, sense of place, and close ties. As Jurgen Habermas has observed, the loss of orientation and the search for identity are brothers.

(iii) *Multiculturalism and Identity Politics:* Cultural studies, following an earlier focus on race, class, and sex (later "gender") developed in the universities in the wake of the 1960s and 1970s. Coincident with the shift of new-left radicalism into the academy, we see the rise of identity politics. As Todd Gitlin argues, the central meaning of identity in this sense comes from the categories of the new social movements, above all, the issues of race, class, and gender. Multiculturalism, cultural studies, colonial discourse, queer theory, standpoint theory, the critique of conquest theory—such approaches draw largely on the radical critique of subject philosophy undertaken by Derrida, Foucault, and French post-structuralist philosophy. Such perspectives make their claims to insurgency based on exposing standards and traditions as a camouflage of interests. We are all formed by our identities, all constructed or invented collectively as subject positions. Multiculturalists share with communitarians a critique of the universal and abstract character of an Enlightenment politics of commonality or abstract, universal, law-based membership. Like communitarians and cultural nationalists, they invoke difference and share the view that every claim to universality is actually a strategy of exclusion.

Cultural nationalists, multiculturalists, and communitarians all distinguish themselves from liberals by using the term identity. Communitarians can offer individuals identity and liberals putatively cannot. A person with identity contrasts critically with the abstract universalism of liberal philosophy, having a sense of place and self, whether based on ethnicity, race, gender, language, or regional culture. What is significant about the discourse of identity is that its usage or meaning in social psychological terms is shared by communitarians like Taylor with cultural nationalists and multiculturalists. They all use it to elaborate the particular and ascriptive aspects of our development or socialisation. Identities are acquired or assigned from outside—as in birth or social status. A cursory list of the most important elements or features of identity underscores this ascriptive referent. Amelie Rorty, in her theory of identity, offers a characteristic set of the modes of identification: "race, class, age, gender, ethnicity and occupation." Identity is an ascriptive concept, its appearance in recent years reflects its growing significance.

## VI. Identity Politics

Identity politics, as a mode of organising, is intimately related to the idea that some social groups are oppressed; that is that one's identity as a women, or as a subaltern, a tribal, a scheduled caste, makes one peculiarly vulnerable to exploitation, violence, marginalisation or powerlessness.

Identity politics starts from analyses of oppression to recommend the reclaiming, redescription or transformation of previously stigmatised accounts of group membership. Rather than accepting the negative scripts offered by a dominant culture about one's own inferiority, one transforms one's own sense of self and community, often through consciousness raising. The Scheduled Castes and the Scheduled Tribes in India, the woman organisations in the world (as in feminist movement) are organising themselves into a movement.

The scope of political movements that may be described as identity politics is broad: the examples used in the philosophical literature are predominantly of struggles within Western capitalist democracies, but indigenous rights movements worldwide, nationalist projects, or demands for regional self-determination use similar arguments. Predictably, there is no straightforward criterion that makes a political struggle into an example of "identity politics;" rather, the term signifies a loose collection of political projects, that each articulate a collective with a distinctively different social location that has hitherto been neglected, erased, or suppressed.

Since the twentieth century heyday of the well known political movements that made identity politics so visible, a host of people has sprung up, though 'identity politics' can draw on intellectual precursors from Mary Wollstonecraft to Franz Fanon. The fact is that the notion of identity has become indispensable to contemporary political discourse.

The concept of identity is characterised by an emphasis on inner voice and capacity for authenticity. That is the ground on which Taylor argues. "...the ability to find a way of being that is somehow true to oneself." While the doctrines of equality press the notion that each human being is capable of deploying his or her reason or moral sense to live an authentic live qua individual, the politics of difference has appropriated the language of authenticity to describe ways of living that are true to the identities of marginalized social groups. As Sonia Kruks puts it: "What makes identity politics a significant departure from earlier, pre-identarian forms of the politics of recognition, is its demand for recognition on the basis of the very grounds on which recognition has previously been denied: it is *qua* women, *qua* blacks, *qua* lesbians that groups demand recognition. The demand is not for inclusion within the fold of "universal humankind" on the basis of shared human attributes; nor is it for respect 'in spite of" one's differences. Rather, what is demanded is respect for oneself *as* different."

For many proponents of identity politics this demand for authenticity includes appeals to a time before oppression, or a culture or way of life damaged by colonialism, imperialism, or even genocide. Thus for example Taiaiake Alfred, in his defense of a return to traditional indigenous values, argues that: "Indigenous governance systems embody distinctive political values, radically different from those of the mainstream. Western notions of domination (human and natural) are noticeably absent; in their place we find harmony, autonomy, and respect. We have a responsibility to recover, understand, and preserve these values, not only because they represent a unique contribution to the history of ideas, but because renewal of respect for traditional values is the only lasting solution to the political, economic, and social problems that beset our people."

What is crucial about the "identity" of identity politics appears to be the experience of the subject, especially his or her experience of oppression and the possibility of a shared and more authentic alternative. Thus identity politics rests on unifying claims about the meaning of politically laden experiences to diverse individuals. Sometimes the meaning attributed to a particular experience will diverge from that of its subject: thus, for example, the woman who struggles desperately to be thin may think that she is simply trying to be a better person, rather than understanding her experience as part of the disciplining of female bodies in a patriarchal culture. Making sense of such disjunctions relies on notions such as false consciousness—the systematic mystification of the experience of the oppressed by the perspective of the dominant. Thus despite its conflicts with Marxism and other radical political models, identity politics shares with them the anti-liberal view that individuals' perceptions of their own interests may be systematically distorted by ideology.

We may refer to some representative aspects of identity politics, in brief, below:

(i) *Feminist Identity Politics:* Such an identity politics takes up the task of women's understandings of themselves without reducing feminity to biology. It situates women as oppressed under patriarchy. The feminists present gender as constructed and entirely separable from sex. The opponents of feminist cause attributes different metabolic systems katabolic (or energy spending) in men and anabolic (or energy-conserving) in women—and say that it is why that their participation in politics is usually deferred. But women identity in what is public is being sought in every part of the world, especially their empowerment. The movements are on for seeking equal rights of women with men; for ensuring and securring a better deal in every aspect of women's life; for giving them respect as a different class; for making them not only a class in itself but also a class for itself.

(ii) *Race, Ethnicity, and Multiculturalism:* The literature on multiculturalism takes up questions of race, ethnicity, and cultural diversity in relation to the liberal state. Some multicultural states—notably Canada—allegedly aim to permit the various cultural identities of their residents to be preserved rather than assimilated, despite the concern that the over-arching liberal aims of such states may be at odds with the values of those they claim to protect. The odds are really numerous. There would be inconsistency between defending the rights of the minority cultures and those cultural practices which the state thinks illiberal; The liberal state would hardly be able to sustain culture and value-neutrality with regard to its own cultural specificity. Defenders of the right to cultural expression of minorities in multicultural states practise forms of identity politics that are both made possible by liberalism and sometimes in tension with it.

## Conclusion

Since its 1970s vogue, identity politics as a mode of organizing and set of political philosophical positions has undergone numerous attacks by those motivated to point to its flaws, whether by its pragmatic exclusions or more programmatically as liberals, Marxists, or poststructuralists. For many leftist commentators, identity politics is something of a *bete noire,* representing the capitulation to cultural criticism in place of analysis of the material roots of oppression. Marxists, both orthodox and revisionist, and socialists—especially those who came of age during the rise of the New Left in western countries—have often interpreted the perceived ascendancy of identity politics as representing the end of radical materialist critique. Identity politics, for these critics, is both factionalizing and depoliticizing, drawing attention away from the ravages of late capitalism toward superstructural cultural accommodations that leave economic structures unchanged. Poststructuralist challenges to identity politics rests on a mistaken view of the subject that assumes a *metaphysics of substance*—that is, that a cohesive, self-identical subject can be identified and reclaimed from oppression. This subject has certain core essential attributes that define her or his identity, over which are imposed forms of socialization that cause her or him to internalize other nonessential attributes. This position, they suggest, misrepresents both the psychology of identity and its political significance. The alternative view offered by poststructuralists is that the subject is itself always already a product of discourse, that possibilities for subjecthood are set out in advance of any possible expression by an individual.

Also key to poststructuralist positions, as Connolly says, is the mutually sustaining opposition of identity and difference: "An identity is established in relation to a series of differences that have become socially recognized. These differences are essential to its being. If they did not coexist as differences, it would not exist in its distinctness and solidity. Entrenched in this indispensable relation is a second set of tendencies, themselves in need of exploration, to conceal established identities into fixed forms, thought and lived as if their structure expressed the true order of things. When these pressures prevail, the maintenance of one identity (or field of identities) involves the conversion of some differences into otherness, into evil, or one of its numerous surrogates. Identity requires differences in order to be, and it converts difference into otherness in order to secure its own self-certainty."

## SUGGESTED READINGS

1. Appiah, Kwame Anthony and Henry Louis Gates Jr., (eds.) *Identities*. Chicago, IL: University of Chicago Press, 1995.
2. Biersteker, Thomas J. and Cynthia Weber, eds. 1996. *State Sovereignty as Social Construct*. Cambridge: Cambridge University Press.
3. Bloom, William. 1990. *Personal Identity, National Identity, and International Relations*. Cambridge: Cambridge University Press.
4. Brubaker, Rogers and Frederick Cooper. 1999. "Beyond Identity." *Theory and Society*. Forthcoming.
5. Connolly, William E. 1991. *Identity/Difference: Democratic negotiations of Political Papradox*. Ithaca, N.Y.: Cornell University Press.
6. Deng, Francis M. 1995. *War of Visions: Conflict of Identities in the Sudan*. Washington, DC: Brookings.
7. Erikson, Erik H. 1968. *Identity: Youth and Crisis*. New York: Norton.
8. Gleason, Philip. 1983. "Identifying Identity: A semantic History." *Journal of American History* 6:910–931.
9. Hall, Stuart. 1989. "Ethnicity: Identity and difference." *Radical America* 23:9–20.

10. Jenkins, Richard, 1996, *Social Identity* (London: Routledge).
11. Laclaym Ernerto (ed), 1994, *The Making of Political Identities,* London Verso.
12. Laitin, David D. 1998. *Identity in Formation*. Ithaca, NY: Cornell University Press.
13. Lapid, Yosef and Friedrich Kratochwil, eds. 1996. *The Return of Culture and Identity in IR Theory*. Boulder, CO: Lynne Rienner.
14. Mackenzie, W.J.M. 1978. *Political Identity*. New York: St. Martin's Press.
15. Ringmar, Erik. 1996. *Identity, Interest, and Action: A Cultural Explanation of Sweden's Intervention in the Thirty Years War.* Cambridge: Cambridge University Press.
16. Rorty, Amelie, ed. 1976. *The Identities of Persons*. Berkeley: University of California Press.
17. Ryan, Basbara (ed) 2001, *Identity Politics in the Woman's Movements,* New Yrok: New York University Press.
18. White, harrison C. 1992. *Identity and Control: A Structural Theory of Social Action*. Princeton: Princeton University Press.
19. Young, Iris Marion. 1990. *Justice and the Politics of Difference.* Princeton, N.J.: Princeton University Press.
20. Zack, Naomi, Laurie Shrage and Crispin Sartwell (eds.). 1998. *Race, Class Gender, and Sexuality: The Big Questions*. Malden, MA: Blackwell.

## CHAPTER – 10

# Concepts: Citizenship

Citizenship, rights and duties are intrinsically connected with one another. Citizenship does not merely mean a set of rights to be enjoyed by a person. Nor does it mean that the idea of citizenship implies the existence of certain claims of a person on the state. Citizenship is, indeed, a matter of rights, but it also is a matter of duties. If we claim rights, we must also shoulder responsibilities. If, for example, we seek right to vote, we must vote for the right person or for the right political party. The one end of citizenship is a set of rights enjoyed by an individual, and the other end is, a set of duties an individual has to perform. The idea of citizenship, at one end, is what we *own,* and at the other end, is what we *owe*: rights we own; duties we owe. To think of citizenship in terms of rights only is as mistaken as is when we relate citizenship to duties only.

Citizenship also means, in addition to citizens' having rights, performing responsibilities, authority as well. It has, therefore, three things: rights, responsibilities and authority:

(i) A citizen has all of the *rights* granted to people in a given state. These are expressed in rules which specify what an individual may or may not do, and what the State may or may not do. They are usually defined in constitutions or other basic legislation. At a world level they are found in the Universal Declaration on Human Rights, one of the first links between the international system and the individual.

(ii) Citizens have *responsibilities* as well. They are expected to vote, pay taxes, obey the law, and perform voluntary public service like serving in armed forces. Some of these are codified in law, but most are part of the normal expectations of behavior. While international responsibilities are less clear than national ones, they increasingly involve expectations of behaviour: as a tourist, one should not pollute or write graffiti on national monuments; one should recycle in the interest of a global good.

(iii) And citizens have *authority*. This is the central pillar in citizenship. Slaves may have rights and responsibilities, only citizens have authority over their governments. They provide the legitimacy to most governments (absolute monarchies based on Divine Right aside), based on the principle of consent of the governed. They may change government leaders and may determine what constitutes the common good. This idea of legitimacy that was pleaded by Max Weber, as the most effective and least expensive form of power underlies democratic government. Citizen authority has, until recently, extended only as far as the nation-state; it has not reached the international system except on delegation to representatives of states.

## I. Citizenship—Meaning and Nature

The words 'citizen' and 'citizenship' owe their origin to the Latin word 'civis' which means a resident of a city. Citizen, therefore, is one who lives in a city and citizenship is the status of the citizen, a symbol that gives recognition to the fact that a citizen is a resident of a city. But this is what we understand citizenship etymologically. Such a meaning of citizen, and therefore, of citizenship is narrow and does not include in it the characteristics we normally attach to them in our times.

Citizenship implies membership of a political community called the state. We, as members of community or society, are social beings; we become political beings only after having acquired membership of the state, or having born in a state. Our membership of the state, if we extend the meaning of citizenship, grants us a legal status, a status behind which there are set and well-defined rights and duties. This is not to say that as social beings, we are without rights or are absolved of our social responsibilities. What we do not have in society and what we have in a state is the legal sanction. Our right to vote is a legally recognised right whereas our right to help the poor has a social or moral bearing.

So, citizenship is not merely the membership of the state, it is the legal recognition of the person as citizen. Social recognition implies our membership of the society; legal recognition, membership of the state, for to be a social being is one thing, and to be a political being, altogether different. All social beings are not citizens, though all citizens are social beings. A subject is a social being but he/she is not a citizen: a national is a social being, but all nationals are not citizens; an alien is a social being, but all aliens do not constitute citizen-body. A citizen is a special being, member of a state and so recognised.

Citizenship implies membership of the state and bestows a status, and grants a recognition, but with these, it demands participation in the affairs of the state. The status that turns an individual into a citizen also expects a citizen to make or unmake, and in short, participate in the activities of the state. Participation in the making, and functioning of the state by the members of a political community make them citizens and this is what distinguishes citizens from all others who are non-citizens in a state; democracy from all other forms of government. We find citizens only in a democracy; there are no citizens in a monarchy, there are only subjects there. Participation of the people, called the citizens make a system a democratic one. Citizenship and democracy go hand in hand. The growth of one means the growth of the other. As monarchies changed into democracies, so changed subjects into citizens.

Participation in the affairs of the state is a characteristic feature of citizenship. Residence within the territorial jurisdiction does not entitle one to be a citizen of that state. One has to participate in the making of the government i.e., exercise franchise, contest elections, hold public office, express opinion and so on. A subject has no such rights and so he/she is not a citizen; a national because of lower age or any other disability does not contribute in any governmental activity, and so he/she is not a citizen. An alien is not a citizen because no alien possesses any political right. An alien is a social being and in a way, is like a guest and by this logic, enjoys certain facilities not available to the citizens. But he/she remains a guest and hence is not a host. He/she is respected as a guest, but this does not bestow ownership rights on the aliens. No alien participates in building, repairing or renovating the house. So mere residence in a state does not qualify anybody to be a citizen of a state. Membership of and participation in the state constitute virtues of citizenship.

Participation in the state implies sharing and shouldering responsibilities as members of the political society. This means that those who share some responsibilities must possess certain rights which help citizens perform their duties. It is here that participation in the affairs of the state implies the existence of certain rights for the citizens. These rights are rights which help citizens participate in the formation and functioning of the government. These are the political rights—rights which include franchise rights, contesting elections, holding public offices, censuring rulers, expressing opinions and so on. These rights, in a state, are available to citizens only. This means that those who do not have these rights are not citizens. Thus, citizenship implies membership, participation, as a consequence of these, enjoyment of political rights.

There is yet another aspect which has a particular importance in understanding what citizenship really means. Citizenship implies claims that one has on others, but it also implies that there is something that state expects of a citizens—the duties. Citizenship is not only an arrangement of rights, it is also a system of duties. The quality of citizenship is both the right use of the available political rights and the faithful performance of the duties so demanded. So there is a right-based citizenship as well as a duties-based citizenship. Highlighting the rights-duties syndrome, Brigan says: "Citizenship has two aspects: (i) that every citizenship has the right to be consulted in the conduct of political society and the duty to contribute something to the general consultation, and (ii) the reverse. The citizen who has a right to be consulted is bound by the results of that consultation."

By way of conclusion, one may, for the sake of brevity, sum up the characteristic features of citizenship as under:

(i) Membership of a political community and legally recognised;
(ii) A status which is exclusive property of the citizen;
(iii) Participation in the affairs of the state;
(iv) Provision and exercise of political rights so to ensure participation; and
(v) Performance of duties as members of the state.

## II. Citizenship—Growth and Development

### *(i) Citizenship in Ancient Times*

Democracy, despite Aristotle's love for the rule of law, was a perverted form of government. If anyone is seeking the idea of citizenship in ancient Greece (from where all Western political thought is said to have begun), one may not find there all about citizenship. Aristotle's definition of citizen, as one who possesses virtues of a law-maker and a judge is insignificant to the meaning of citizenship—atleast in our times. Everyone, in ancient Greece generally and in Athens particularly, was a law-maker in so far as he participated in law-making, but each one was not a magistrate or an official. Through a system of rotation and a lot, every voter, Maclver says, "had the opportunity to be magistrate, judge or other official. ... On all political issues the citizens freely decided in their assembly." But the citizen-body, in Greek democracies, was the smallest fraction of the entire population—so it was of Attica, the territory of the Athenian state. Maclver points out: "... the citizens constituted in effect a privileged class. The citizen-roll was jealously guarded and only the sons of free Athenian parents were admitted. The outlying population of Attica, for the most part illiterate, could hardly ... exercise the rights of citizens. Resident aliens were debarred from citizenship, and below them were the slaves, constituting more than a third of the population, who had no right whatever. As for women, they were still kept ... all except the high class *hetairai* or courtesans ... in a kind of oriental seclusion." Thus, ancient Greece hardly gave the idea of citizenship, particularly where the idea of democracy was not only strictly limited (women were excluded), but had, to a great extent, an antidemocratic stance.

In ancient times, the ancient Rome including, where slavery was an inevitable part of society, the idea of citizenship could hardly find any expression worth noticing. Wherever there had existed the institution of slavery, those engaged in menial toil were regarded inferior and thus, were debarred of civil and political rights. Citizenship, then, was restricted to cities and citizens were only the city-dwellers.

### *(ii) Citizenship in Medieval Times*

The medieval age was characterised by contradictions particularly in matters relating to state-society. On the religious plane, all were considered equal—brothers because all were thought to be the sons of God. But on the social and political planes, there was hardly any equality, hardly any idea of universal brotherhood, hardly any democratic value. The medieval society was a religion-based society, hierarchical *and* rigid where lordship or serfdom was a matter of birth—hereditary. The individuals played no role in politics, for kingship was divinely ordained and King's right to rule went unchallenged. Where, despite all claims of equality in Christianity, there had existed inequality between man and man and where politics was an activity of the few, restrictively few, one could hardly imagine any democracy, and therefore, hardly any citizenship.

*(iii) Citizenship and Modern Age*

The idea of citizenship has grown with the idea of democracy. In fact, attempts at democratization preceded the franchise efforts, for much before universal male voting right, the attempts were, for example, made to make legislative bodies as representative as possible in England. Though representation, in the beginning, was not the representation of number and actually was that of interests, yet ground was being prepared for the on-coming era of democracy.

The credit must go to the medieval times for having contributed, though in a limited way, to the ideals of democracy. Christianity, highlighting the universal ethical principles, had pronounced that every human being has a value and a personality in himself. The medieval concept of the worth of human personality became the cornerstone of the basis of democracy that was to follow in the coming centuries. There was yet another development during the medieval times and this was the evolution of the representative system. Representation, in medieval times, was representation of the interests. Following the great Magna Carta (1215) of England, there was the rudimentary, discriminatory and restrictive introduction of the representation system when, in 1265, Simon de Montfort, the Earl of Leicester had summoned two citizens from every borough as well as two knights from every country to sit in the Parliament with peers and the prelates. That is how representation was introduced and the beginning—of the House of Common in England was made. Do not we recognise the English Commons as the matrix of modern democracy? The later events confirmed the introduction of representative devices, the House of Lords, representing feudal Lords, priests and the higher classes whereas the House of Commons, representing the commoners, the knights, the townsmen. As circumstances moved, the House of Lord remained as undemocratic as it was and therefore gradually surrendering political power to the commons, and the House of Commons as democratized it came to be, got all the powers, so much that the House of Commons became the Parliament in the real sense of the term. The idea of representation, medieval as it was in its origin, became an important ingredient of democracy that followed in later years.

The idea of representation did not come as a design in the history of England, the country where democracy was born and later flourished. History, as it came up in conflicts and struggles against tyranny and despotism. England provides a remarkable and in fact a representative example: the theory of two swords of medieval times not only brought religion in tune with politics, reformation following, it also abolished the trio: king, feudal lord and the priest, bringing the king-feudal lord combine as the victorious. This combine, ultimately, led to absolutism of monarchical system and the advocacy of the divine rights theory of kings. The whole Stuart period (1603-1688) was a period of civil war where the parties now were the king-feudal lords on the one hand, and the merchant and manufacturing classes on the other. The glorious revolution (1688) was the victory of the capitalists. But that was not the beginning of democracy as was the beginning of liberalism–the classical liberalism as we would call it now. The course of history in France, Germany, Italy, and other European countries was, more or less, the repetition of the English events. Macpherson, therefore, is right in pointing out that the Western system became liberal first and democratic later. As different aspects of democracy came to be introduced, so were introduced the various forms of citizenship in the West. The beginning had already been made with the French "Liberty, Equality and Fraternity" and the American declaration of "Rights of Man".

The growth and development of idea of citizenship as it came about in the writings of the great English philosophers can be summed up as under:

John Locke (1632-1704), as the forerunner of liberalism, was no democrat, and in fact, every liberal, then, was not be a democratic. His concern was his attack on political power. His whole philosophy, while justifying the English revolution of 1688, revolved around his thesis that political power was, limited because its task was limited. He had built a limited state, giving it the only task of protecting the property of the people and by this logic, advocated limited powers. Individualist as he really was, Locke declared the state as a means and the individual as an end. Thus Locke was concerned more with the functions of the state than with its structure. Hence, we do not see the introduction or the development of any democratic institutions in his writings.

Jeremy Bentham (1748–1832) lived at a time when the question of the origin of the state had lost all weight and people had turned their attention on the structuring and restructuring of democratic institutions. Non-interventionist as Bentham was, he did not go all out to give the state all functions and, therefore, all powers. Nor was he much enthusiastic about laying down the principles of representative institutions. Between 1791 and 1802, he was for a limited franchise, excluding the poor, the uneducated, the dependent, and the women. In 1809, he was for a householder franchise, one limited to those paying direct taxes on property. By 1817, he was virtually talking about universal franchise minus under age, and those who are unable to read, and of course, excluding women. By 1820, he was for manhood franchise. So, we see Bentham according no importance or less importance to either citizen or citizenship. His idea of citizen and contents of citizenship were kept changing from time to time, and from one of his writing to the other.

If Bentham was too less enthusiastic in matters relating to franchise, John Stuart Mill (1806–1873) was too eager to grant it to everyone, including women and in fact, to some, more than one vote. Participation in the affairs of the state was according to Mill, the greatest task of citizenship. In his *Thoughts on Parliamentary Reforms* (1859), Mill advocated the idea of plural voting, saying: "that a perfect electoral system required both that every person should have one vote and that some should have more than one vote." In his *Representative Government* (1861), Mill urged plural voting for some along with the exclusion of others from any vote all—the poor especially. However, in Mill's scheme what was noteworthy was the idea of plural voting. He had justified plural voting on the ground (i) that it would prevent class legislation; and (ii) that it would be beneficial by giving more votes to those whose opinion is entitled to a greater weight.

The later part of the 19th century and the first quarter of the 20th century changed the concept of citizenship, from an idea to movement. The franchise movements began everywhere in the West from England to the United States, and in the process suffrage once based on qualifications of property, education, residence, sex and so on came down to what we call universal adult franchise.

Citizenship, implying political participation with the right to franchise as the starting point had been acquired in most of the liberal world by the middle of the 20th century. In the Marxian thought, citizen and citizenship were class concepts to be found only in the class societies and in their political systems. For the Marxists, capitalist societies produce only the bourgeoisie and the proletariat: the exploiters and the exploited and that political equality, in such societies, is only a mask of bourgeois domination. The Marxists hope to find the real worth of man and his personality only in the classless society where individuals would meet as free human beings.

With advancing years, the significance of the idea of citizenship and citizenship itself has immensely increased. More we find ourselves in the state, more we realize our worth as citizens. This makes the notion of citizenship a matter of discussion as well as a debate. There are the neo-liberals, Hayek and Nozick, who are zealous of individual's rights, but do not admit a full state, much less the theory of citizenship. On the other, there are the communitarians' whose idea of citizenship, covering both rights and duties, springs from individual's membership of a community. The feminists, critics of the male notion of citizenship, urge citizenship for women as *women*. The subaltern advocates lament the progressive ill-treatment of the weakest and the most backward in the society and ask for an equally genuine citizenship for all.

## III. Theories of Citizenship: Marshall and Giddens

The concept of citizenship has been, if not neglected, a concept so well known and understood so easily that it escaped the attention of many philosophers and scholars. It is, really, easy to dismiss the idea of concept by arguing that a citizen, as a permanent member of a political society, has certain rights to exercise and certain duties to perform and that with the growth of democratic ideas, there has been a corresponding expansion of citizenship together with its contents. Citizenship is no more a set of political rights, it is also a set of social and economic rights. Its historical growth is not merely traced to the advent of democracy, but to the origin and development of capitalism. It is not merely a formal observance of laws, but is the eternal association with the society as a whole, state including.

Numerous scholars have drawn attention to various aspects of democracy. Their theories or what may be called their contribution to the concept of citizenship can be summed up below:

It is difficult to say whether *Aristotle* had any *theory of citizenship*, and if at all he had any, it is still more difficult to have its application on the modern national states. There are two reasons for that: (i) For Aristotle, citizenship was the privileged status of the ruling group of the city-state, and hence had excluded mass of the people; (ii) For Aristotle, the status of citizenship was confined to the effective participation in the deliberation and exercise of owner, and hence had excluded participation in the form of exercising franchise or of system of representation.

Over the ages, citizenship, after having its long oblivion, came to the fore with the modern period beginning since capitalism. Its area has been fairly expanded now. It, today, means that all persons as citizens are equal before law and therefore that no person or group is legally privileged. But there is a meaningful criticism against this meaning by the *Marxists* who say that despite legal membership of the state, legal equality may not help the disadvantaged people in a class society to participate in the affairs of the state fully and completely. Marx says: "The state in its own way abolishes distinctions (of) .... birth, rank, education and occupation .... where it proclaims that every member of the people is an equal participant in popular sovereignty.... Nevertheless, the state allows private property, education, and occupation to act and assert their particular nature in their way.... Far from abolishing these factual distinctions the state presupposes them in order to exist."

Marx is no enemy of the theory of modern citizenship, for he describes its achievements as a big step forward, but he insists and his thesis is that mere political emancipation in citizenship is inadequate and instead advocates a great human emancipation in which persons are freed from the determining power of private property and its associated institutions. Social revolution, Marx declares, can bring about human emancipation.

The theories with regard to citizenship arose, firstly through two-in-one question: should social inequalities be made irrelevant for membership in the status of citizenship or should these be abolished through social revolution? As Marx had suggested, and secondly through the growth of labour movements, which ultimately expanded the area of citizenship. Two opposing views, in this regard, are: one by Ossowski (*Class Structure in the Social Consciousness*, 1963) who says that as the movement for citizenship grows, it makes the class system an anachronism, leading thus to the gradual reduction of social inequalities. Another view is by Goldthorpe in his article 'Social Inequality and Social Integration in modern Britain' 1974) published in Wedderbun (ed), *Poverty, Inequality and Class Structure* who says that advances in citizenship are likely to leave class structures intact.

Marshall (*Citizenship and Social Class*, 1960) offers a systematic theory of citizenship. His general understanding of citizenship is entirely conventional. He says that (i) citizenship is a status attached to full membership of a community and that (ii) those who possess this status are equal with respect to the rights and duties associated with it. He adds that different societies would attach different rights and duties to the status of citizen, for there is no universal principle of rights and duties of citizenship in general.

Marshall provides a synthesis of the historical evolution of modern conception of citizenship and rights in Britain. He divides this process into *three* phases or elements: civil, political and social. The *first* phase, Marshall says, took place roughly speaking, in the eighteenth century and saw the consolidation of civil rights, such as 'liberty of the person, freedom of speech, thought and faith, the right to own property and to conclude valid contracts, and the right to justice. The *second* phase, occurring generally during the 19th century, witnessed the consolidation of political rights such as participation in the exercise of political power either as a voter or an official. *Finally*, the third phase, a 20th century phenomenon, involved the creation of social rights expanding from the right to economic welfare and security to share to the full in social heritage and to live the life of a civilised being according to the standards prevailing in society.

Marshall does not regard these three categories as distinct or exclusive but as complementary. Our exercise of political rights, for example, entails not only the civil rights ensuring our freedom of speech, but also a sufficient level of education. The three phases, he says, form part of a dialectical process whereby rights as privileges of feudal system are changed into universal entitlement of all the members of society. He approaches a near communitarian view when he shifts his view of citizenship from status to contract where people possess human rights as persons pursuing their own lives in their own way.

Marshall's another important contribution to the theory of citizenship, is the relationship between citizenship and social class. He notes that the development of the institutions of modern democracy coincided, as in England, with the rise of capitalism. In the early phase, capitalism tended to undermine citizenship as was found in the customary privileges of landed classes, but with its development, citizenship rights came to be ensured for the propertied (capitalist) classes. Thus Marshall says: "In undermining one type of class system, citizenship, promoted and secured a second." "During the period of the 18th and the 19th centuries, the rights of citizenship", Marshall explains, "were entirely harmonious with the class inequalities of capitalist societies," for rights were basically civil in nature. "Capitalists and workers," Marshall argues, "are indistinguishable from the perspective of civil rights in having the same right to enter into market exchanges and contracts with each other." It is only then, when citizenship comes to incorporate in itself political and social rights that conflicts in the class system come to the fore. Surveying the whole historical process of class conflict between the capitalists and the workers, Marshall says that the passing of Reform Acts, emergence of the workers in trade-unions, the Chartist movement, in England, established the claim of the workers that they, as citizens, were entitled (in addition to political rights already won) to certain social rights. The inclusion of social rights in citizenship rights meant, as Marshall says, a war between citizenship and the capitalist class system. It is therefore, argued that social citizenship has not destroyed class, nor social inequalities, but has, as Marshall concludes, "imposed modifications on' class with the result that changes are being made in the class system through the exercise of citizenship rights by the working class movement.

Barbalet sums up Marshall's contribution to citizenship in these words: "In summary then, Marshall sees the development of citizenship and of the class system in terms of interactions between them. Through their antagonistic relationship, citizenship and class inequality each contribute to changes in the other. Unlike most theorists of class structure, Marshall recognises the possible impact of citizenship on aspect of class inequality, and therefore, on class loyalty and class resentment, both of which tend to affect the nature and incident of class conflict. Marshall sees such possibilities because he understands citizenship in terms not only of its legal and political dimensions, but also of its social component."

Marshall's theory of citizenship invited more critics than admirers. Ralph Dahrendorf, for instance, while commenting on Marshall's work, refers to the gradual expansion of citizenship from the legal to the political and social sphere,' but adds that the process as 'still unfinished', for new dimensions of citizenship may, according to him, be discovered by political organisation and social groups. Anthony Giddens, no admirer of Marshall, takes strong exception to Marshall's characterisation of industrial rights. He affirms the significance of Marshall's analysis of citizenship for contemporary social and political theory, he has a number of criticism to make (see 1981, pp. 226–9; 1982. pp. 171–3; 1985. pp. 204–9). It is critical of what he sees as the teleological and evolutionary elements in Marshall's analysis (see especially 1982. p. 171). Giddens criticizes Marshall for treating the development of citizenship, as if it were something that unfolded in phases according to some inner logic within the modern world. In Giddens's account, Marshall tends to overstate the extent to which citizenship rights can be understood in terms of a threefold staged process. In addition, Giddens sees in Marshall's account an oversimplification of the role of politics and the state. Marshall, according to Giddens, understood the unfolding of citizenship rights from the eighteenth to the twentieth century as a process which is supported and buttressed by 'the beneficent hand of the state'. In Giddens's analysis, Marshall seriously underestimated the way 'citizenship rights have been achieved in substantial degree only through struggle'. The industrial rights, i.e., right to form unions or to go on strike are not mere extensions of the civil rights as Marshall makes us believe, but,

Giddens asserts, were achieved through struggle by the workers. Giddens attacks the evolutionary account of the development of citizenship for suggesting that the battle for civil and political rights has been won. According to Giddens, the battle continues into the future. Gidden's argument, as against Marshall's, is that the citizenship rights have been achieved only through struggle. He says: "the extension of citizenship rights, in Britain as in other societies, was in substantial degree the result of the efforts of the unprivileged to improve their lot and that the groups previously excluded had to struggle for attaining it."

More fundamentally, Giddens maintains that each category of citizenship right should be understood as an area of contestation or conflict, each linked to a distinctive type of regulatory power or surveillance, where that surveillance is both necessary to the power of superordinate groups and an axis around which subordinate groups can seek to reclaim control over their lives.

From Giddens's writings, the following classificatory scheme of rights, and the modes of power and institutional sites to which they are related, is suggested:

| | Types of right | | | |
|---|---|---|---|---|
| | civil | economic civil | political | social |
| Type of regulatory power or surveillance | policing | control of work-place | political | 'management' of population |
| Institutional centre or locale where rights are championed and fought over | law courts | work-place | parliament or legislative chamber | (state administrative offices?) |

Giddens is the disagreement with Marshall on the chronology of the three categories of rights: civil rights first, political rights later and social rights still later. His theory, rather, is that civil and political citizenship rights developed together, civil rights consolidating capitalist class power, and political rights adding and strengthening it. According to him, citizenship, rising from the shadow of democracy, developed with the growth and expansion of state sovereignty.

In sum, in Giddens's assessment, class conflict has been and remains the medium of the extension of citizenship rights and the basis of the creation of an insulated economy, polyarchy and the welfare state. The forging of state sovereignty was a critical impetus to the struggle for rights and to the remoulding of citizenship. The increase in state administrative power led to the creation of new aspirations and demands and to the development of institutions which were responsive to them. *Bryan Turner (Citizenship and Capitalism,* 1986), as opposed to Marshall's historical development of citizenship in terms of elements or phases, describes the development of citizenship in terms of the consequences or what he called the waves. For him, there have been four such waves: first had the consequence of removing property from the definition of citizen; the second removed sex; the third wave redefined the significance of the age and kinship ties in the family for citizenship rights; and a fourth wave, as Turner says, is currently expanding citizenship by ascribing rights to nature and the environment.

## IV. Citizenship—Rights-based and Duties-based

Citizenship, as status, characterises a set of rights. Rights are important because they attach a particular capacity to persons by virtue of a local though conventional as well, status. When persons have capacities or opportunities for particular actions, say certain powers, they are supposed to possess rights: status provides capacity, and capacity provides power and power, ultimately, a right. This, however, does not mean that all rights spring from citizenship and that citizens alone have all types of rights. There are aliens who, as aliens, possess civil and social rights. So is true about the national. What they do not possess and what all citizens, with civil and social, possess political rights? Hence, while all rights are not citizenship rights, all citizenship rights are rights.

Citizenship rights, as rights of a person in a state, are ultimately secured by the state. Barbalet writes: "Citizenship rights impose certain limitations on the state's sovereign authority." Right to vote, for example, is a citizenship right of a person, but it is a duty of the state to protect this right of the citizen.

Right-based citizenship does not specify rights to be ensured and secured by the state, it also demands a restraint on the one who exercises it and also on others in whose frame the right is exercised. Right to property is not merely a right to hold property, it is also a right to acquire it, possess it and/or dispose it of. But such a right puts a restraint on the one who enjoys property right in so far as the enjoyer of the right does not obtain or acquire property through antisocial and anti-national activities. Likewise such a right of 'A' puts a restraint on all others to demonstrate their regard for A's property. Citizenship does not mean the existence of a right as a licence, it means a claim, a social claim at that. It demands of the person who possesses it a high level of wisdom to use it in the best interests of the society as well as in his/her own. Citizenship implies an obligation as well; it is both a claim as well as a duty. Right-based citizenship does not merely mean a set of rights, it also means the provision of duties as well. This means that rights are to be enjoyed within the framework of duties.

Likewise, duties-based citizenship is citizenship high and of good quality. Such a citizenship would mean the adoption of those forms of conduct that are compatible with those of the others. Citizenship involves a right and a duty simultaneously. Liberty, Mill had said once, means pursuing our own good in our own ways provided we do not harm the like liberty of the other. 'Pursuing our own good in our own way' is a right coupled with a duty of not harming the like liberty of the other. What is a right, therefore, for a person also becomes a duty for him/her. Our rights are the duties of others and others' rights are our duties. As are our rights social, so are our duties. Rights and duties do not exist before or against society: rights are our claims on other and duties are others' claims on us. We obtain rights only after having performed our duties. Citizenship is not only the ordering of our facilities, it is also the ordering of our loyalties as well. Rights and duties put together constitute what is called citizenship. Citizenship means the right exercise of our rights; it also means the right use of our conduct as well. Both, rights and duties, are two sides of citizenship.

The concept of citizenship is both a concept of rights on the one hand, and of duties on the other. It is a citizenship with rights whose bases are the duties; a citizenship with duties whose object is individual and social welfare. In any case, the concept of citizenship is a concept about human relationships in a society. If, for example, a person has a right to something, other members of his society have an obligation to respect that right. If, again, it is a right or action such as a right to engage in political dissent, fellow citizens and the government have an obligation to tolerate expressions of dissent. But this is what we understand citizenship as rights-based.

There is the other, and perhaps more important aspect of citizenship: it is a citizenship, based on duties, on obligations of the holder of rights. We do not have a right to do any thing we like. We have rights as emanate from society and we exercise them in a social framework. We have a right to express our dissent, but in doing so, we do not have the right to block the ways which approach the hospitals, but rather, we have the duties not to do so. Citizenship, we may conclude, involves social claims as are enjoyed by the people, but they also place responsibilities on them as well. To talk of citizenship with rights and without duties is as meaningless as is citizenship with duties and without rights.

## SUGGESTED READINGS

1. Dahendrof, R., *Class and Class Conflict in Industrial Society,* (London, Routledge and Kegan Paul 1959).
2. Giddens, A., *Central Problems in Social Theory,* (London, Macmillan, 1979).
3. Greaves, H.R.G., *The Foundations of Political Theory,* (London, Bell and Sons. 2nd edition, 1966).
4. Halsey, A.H., *"T.H. Marshall: Past and Present'. Sociology,* 18(1) 1984.
5. Hindess, B., *Freedom, Equality and the Market,* (London, Tavistock, 1987).
6. Lockwood, D., *'For T.H. Marshall.' Sociology,* 8(s) 1974).
7. Marshall, T.H., *Citizenship and Social Class and Other Essays* (*Cambridge*: Cambridge University Press, 1950).
8. Marshall, T.H., *Class, Citizenship and Social Development,* (Westport, Connecticut, Greenwood Press, 1973 [First published in 1964, this differs from Marshall 1963 only through the addition of an introduction by S.M. Lipset].
9. Poggi, G., *The Development of the Modern State,* (London, Hutchinson, 1978).
10. Turner, B.S., *Citizenship and Capitalism,* (London, Allen and Unwin, 1986).

## CHAPTER – 11

# Concepts: Property

The concept of property has been a major issue in Political Science. It has affected all the ideologies and the ideologies in turn have affected it, the reason being that property constitutes the most important factor upon which the foundations of any ideology are to be built. At the same time, property also becomes a very difficult and controversial concept.

### I. Meaning of the Concept

The word property is derived from the Latin propriates which means one's own. Defined in this sense, property is the ownership of material things to the exclusion of others. The Supreme Court of India defined property thus; 'The word property must be understood in a corporal sense as having reference to all those specific things that are susceptible of appropriate appropriation and enjoyment as well as in its judicial or legal sense of a bundle of rights which the owner can exercise under the municipal law with respect to the use and enjoyment of those things to the exclusion of all others."

According to Frank Snare, in ordinary language, property and ownership are interchangeable. Following him, we can include the following in the concept of property.

1. It is a right to use things in any way which is not prohibited. Things could be immovable like land and buildings and movable like money, jewellery and livestocks.
2. It is an exclusive right to use and to the exclusion of others.
3. It also means a right to sell, dispose of or transfer to others.
4. The use of that thing by other, without the consent of its owner is unlawful and liable to be punished. The owner too cannot misuse it.
5. The unlawful use i.e. using property without its owner's consent, would invite damages to be paid to the owner.

6. The owner is responsible for any damage that his property causes to others.

Property cannot, and in fact, should not be an absolute ownership. Every legal system enunciates various restrictions on property. There is also a social and legal sanction behind property. Property cannot be conceived without state and society. It is only through state laws that property becomes a matter of right. Further, property also involves liabilities and obligations. Till now we have talked about private property. We also have public property. The public property is available for the people to use it. But that does not mean that the user becomes the owner. Those who use a public garden or public transport do not become a collective owner by virtue of its use. The title of the land vests with the local authority or state, who can sell it. Such properties are called public because (i) they are not privately owned; (ii) the local authority or state is accountable to the public; and (iii) the purpose of the property is to provide benefits to the public. Thus, in case of public property, the public is supposed to be the owner, but the state may dispose it of in public interest. Besides private and public property, we also have community property, also called common property. In India it is called panchayat's property. This property is not a public property, because its use is restricted to a specific people who live in that village, who are entitled to use, for example, land to graze animals. Thus a variety of property exists in a liberal state. The socialist states, however, do not believe in private property. They stand for its total abolition. In a socialist state, all property is owned by state and the entire economic structure is controlled and owned by the state. In developing countries, property is viewed from the angle of socio-economic justice which means the following:

(i) The citizens have a right to own, sell and dispose of property;
(ii) Property cannot be used for exploitation.
(iii) Minimum economic requirements of food, clothing and shelter should be guaranteed to all the citizens and for the purpose, the rights of the property owners may be restricted. Usually a ceiling is fixed on property with a view to avoid its monopolisation in few hands. The objective is to reduce economic disparities.

## II. Development and Growth

The concept of private property is a modern concept and its systematic development can be found at the end of seventeenth and early eighteenth century, because the particular set of economic conditions to which private property refers was not present before the arrival and consolidation of capitalism. Yet the private property in some form or the other is present from time immemorial. The description of society in the Old Testament amply proves that it possessed some of the characteristics of modern capitalism. This ancient society had private property, division of labour, market exchange and money.

Man began his life on earth in a very simple manner. The primitive societies were characterised by the simplicity of wants and their satisfaction. Human society was food-gathering pastoral society. Everything was owned by the tribe jointly. But once the tribe settled down, it came to possess land and at a later stage some dwelling units as well. The communal ownership of all the properties continued. Gradually it was accepted that the hutment in which a family was staying belonged to that family. Private property also existed in the form of consumable products like foodstuff. But as the techniques of production developed and wants became more complex, a stage arrived where new arrangements became necessary to incorporate the changing requirements of the society. The result was the extension of private property from consumable to productive goods. The old Testament describes a conflict between the tribal society with its communal property and primitive economic activity, and a more developed society characterised by class and caste divisions based on private property. Soon the primitive society disintegrated and the scope of private property grew to include land, but the individuals right over property was highly limited.

Development of private property led to domestic and foreign trade and accumulation of wealth. The Hebrew monarchy grew in this period which is marked by sharpening of class divisions between the rich and the poor. The luxury of courts was based on evergrowing enslavement and impoverishment of the masses. During this period, we also find spiritual revolt by the prophets who castigated the unjust order of the new commercial classes of traders, usurers and the land robbers. They also demanded limitations on private property. However in their protest, they could not understand the forces which were responsible for that exploitative order. Their protests remained utopian—either expecting God's wrath or arrival of some messiah who would deliver mankind from the life of sin and restore the old partriarchial society.

In Greek city states, Plato had understood the evils of private property. Therefore, he deprived the rulers from having private property. He idealised a state in which the rulers had no motive for economic exploitation; communism of property and wives followed from this assumption. Later on, his disciple, Aristotle attacked the concept of communism of property. His attack was based on incentive argument that communal property will not be looked after as carefully as private property. Aristotle also realised that conflicts are bound to take place, when men, unequal by nature, in skill and industry are not differentiated by varying opportunities of enjoyment. Aristotle also believed that private property is necessary for the development of individual personality, yet he was aware of danger of economic disparities and their contribution in revolution. However, he never advocated abolition of property. He only wanted its more enlightened and liberal use. Aristotle also justified the inhuman slavery system, which was the basis of socio-economic progress of his times.

The Roman Empire that followed the Greek City states upheld the right of private property almost without any limit and guaranteed freedom of contract. The society further witnessed the growing poverty of the general masses.

The medieval society was sharply divided in terms of social classes and groups. The society was also highly dominated by the Church. The Church sometimes condemned those economic ideas which increased exploitation and inequality and sometimes was indifferent to the miseries of the world. Trade and profits were usually condemned by the religious philosophers. However, they could not stop the organisation of society on the basis of a solid economic system which rested on private property and flourishing trade. The Church reacted by prohibiting usury. The religious philosophers also criticised it. The feudal lords rented out their landed property to tenants who would not only pay rents but also provide military services to them. Later on, the peasants were tied to their land, a new system of bondage that replaced slavery. The flourishing trade crated a new middle class or bourgeoise who were the authors of capitalism. Thus, capitalism was clearly based on the institution of private property which remains its foundation even today.

## III. The Liberal Theory of Property

We have seen earlier that liberalism is a political philosophy of the autonomy of individuals. State and society are presumed to be nothing more than a collection of individuals. The objective of state is the betterment of individual. State, by creating an order, creates conditions in the society in which individual can develop his various faculties. Therefore, they wanted the state to be hindrance to hindrances which curtail the development of individual's personality. Property, to them, is very important because without it, the individual will have no basis or incentive to develop. Men have a natural love for their property. Machiavelli, therefore, said that men will sooner forgive the death of their father than the confiscation of their property. Initially, the early liberals stood for a right to unlimited property like Locke and to a great extent Bentham. To them, state was a necessary evil which restrains the individual. With John Stuart Mill, we find the inauguration of the concept of positive state, which was a reaction to the miseries brought about by the negative state. This period also saw the rise and consolidation of socialist movement which condemned, and stood for the abolition of, property. The Marxian view of property suffers from extremity which was not welcome by the people in general, because nobody wants to lose property. It was felt that elimination of property was neither practical nor necessary. But there cannot be a right to accumulate unlimited property. What was desirable was a synthesis between the two and the democratic socialist principle sought to do the same. Yet we do have modern libertarians who, despite the accumulation of experiences by the mankind to the contrary, still believe that there should not be any restriction on property. We will take all these views one by one. First we discuss the liberal theory of property with reference to John Locke, Bentham and J.S. Mill.

### *(i) John Locke's Views on Property*

John Locke is the most vocal supporter of private property. He wrote his famous work '*Two Treaties of Government*, in the seventeenth century, in which he expounded his views on property.

To Locke, property existed even in a pre-state environment i.e. what he calls state of nature. The institution of state was absent and people were living peacefully. But unfortunately, this peace could not remain for ever and consequently people's property was in danger. Therefore, people decided to make a contract by which the state and the government were created. Thus, the state and government came into existence for the sake of perservation of property. The property is a natural right and the government has no right to abrogate it. In fact, it is the task of the government to protect and preserve property.

Locke has used the term property in both narrow and broad sense. In broad sense, property means life, liberty and estates, while its narrow sense restricted to land and goods. However, both constitute a limitation on the government.

According to Locke every individual has a right to life. For his survival and comforts, nature or God has given him the earth and its produce, which is a common stock for all mankind. Man also has a property in his own person. He says, "The Labour of his Body, and the work of his Hands, we may say, are property his." When he mixes his labour in the common stock given by the nature, he makes it his property. A flower in the plant or a fruit on a tree is the commonstock, but when I pluck them they become my property. Similarly, a piece of land becomes my property, when I till it or use it in any other way. And for this appropriation I need no permission or consent from anybody. Such an appropriation has, however, three limitations:

(i) Enough should be left for others, because every man has a right to life;
(ii) Right to appropriation does not mean right to spoil. A man can remove from the nature only as much which he can use because as Locke says, "Nothing was made by God to spoil or destroy.";
(iii) The right to appropriation is justified only when it has been accomplished by man's own labour. Only that share of common stock belongs to me and becomes my property which I have procured through my labour.

It may seem that Locke stands for a limited right to property. But this is not the case. He, very cleverly removes all the three limitations and argues for an unlimited right to property. The first limitation is removed by Locke when he says that 'he who appropriates land to himself by his labour, does not lessen but increase the common stock of mankind.' This means that the production from the acquired land is partly consumed by the man himself and the rest is left for the others to consume. Macpherson rightly points out, "Thus, although more land than leaves enough and as good for others may be appropriated, the greater productivity of the appropriated land more than makes up for the lack of land available for others." Locke now justifies unlimited accumulation of land by individual. This unlimited accumulation of property also provides to the labourer who does not own property, a living. He is better than those people who live in areas where the land has not been properly utilised; 'he lives, lodged and is clad better than the king of an Indian tribe in the empty wastes of inland America.'

The second limitation is the spoilage limitation. Nobody has a right to spoil. He can possess as much as he can consume and the rest is for others. This limitation is transcended by the introduction of money. Gold and silver do not spoil and man has, therefore, a right to their unlimited accumulation. Thus, one can sell the surplus production of his land and the money that he receives is rightfully his because it cannot spoil. The resultant economic disparity came into existence even before the state came into being. To Locke, both land as well as money is capital and the purpose of capital is to make more and more capital by profitable investment.

The third limitation on property i.e. one can have as much property as he can by using his own labour is also done away with. Every man has a property in his person which he can sell. Thus, one can sell his labour and whatever he produces is the property of that person who has bought his labour. This means I can acquire property through the doings of my servants. Locke justified the wage relationship of modern capitalist society, where labour is purchased to make more and more capital.

Locke's views on property can be summed up in following points;

(i) Right to property existed even before the state came into being.
(ii) The purpose of state and government is to protect and preserve property.
(iii) Right to property is a natural right given by God and it constitutes a limitation on state and government.
(iv) Economic disparities are also natural and pre-state. They are good for the society.

(v) Wage relationship is equally natural and property earned through it is equally justified.

*(ii) Bentham's Views on Property*

Bentham made modifications in Locke's concept of property. He does not accept the natural right to property. To him the entire concept of natural right is nonsense. Natural property rights would mean bankruptcy of the government because then the government could not impose taxes on the people. It will have to depend upon the voluntary contributions of the individuals. To Bentham, property is the product of law.

According to Bentham, property gives a sense of satisfaction. In property, we see something of ourselves. The things we have made, the house in which we have lived, the fields we have farmed, all of them are some part of ourselves. There is a personal attachment to the possessions and therefore, people are so much concerned about the security of their property.

Bentham defends property on the basis of general utility. The individual's happiness can be achieved in four things—subsistence, abundance, equality and security. The state does not have to interfere in man's work to subsistence because he has a natural desire to live and hence he takes care of procuring his means of remaining alive. But the state should see that the individuals are rewarded the result of their efforts. Otherwise, they will have no incentive to work. Bentham felt that abundance was meant for a small portion of population. The labourers would never be able to achieve abundance. But then there is nothing wrong in the abundance of wealthy. The abundance of wealthy is necessary because it provides resources to the community in times of natural calamity. No doubt abundance creates inequality. But then it is the result of the security of property. Without security, there will be no property and without property there cannot be general guarantee of subsistence.

For Bentham security of property is a major condition of achieving the greatest happiness of the greatest number. Therefore, he advocated legal protection to the distribution of property that exists at any given time. Bentham also justifies the sanctity of contract on the basis of its contribution to the maintenance and reliability of commercial transactions. Bentham is against the acquisition of property without adequate compensation. The state must respect the law of inheritance. But if an owner dies without heir, then his property should be taken over by the state for redistribution. Bentham dislikes slavery, but if there are slaves already and have been bought by their masters in good faith, the masters must not suffer the loss by the abolition of slavery. The slavery should be abolished only after the death of the masters.

Bentham defended usury and was against state regulation of economic activity. Bentham wants individuals to be left alone. That government is best which governs the least. The property right is no natural right. They are created by the state and the state should create it with a view to maximize utility. The utility is maximized, according to Bentham, when the goods and services are bought and sold at prices mutually agreed upon between the buyers and sellers and the system of property rights should facilitate such a commerce. Thus, he stood for a *laissez faire* policy or free trade against state regulation in economic activity.

However, Bentham also advocates state welfare for the weak. The policy of law should be to achieve a comparatively equal distribution of property. Atleast arbitrary inequalities should be avoided, because the greatest happiness of the greatest number cannot be achieved by unequal distribution of wealth. He also wants protection for old age people against destitution. Bentham also advocates taxing property for the unemployed and weaker people. But these taxes should be reasonable. Lastly, Bentham never believed that the property rights are absolute. Property does not mean to use it as one pleases. My knife is mine, it means that I can put it where I like, but not in your chest'. He believes in the maintenance of balance between equality and security in practice. But if there is a conflict between the two, security of property is to be given prime importance.

To sum up, Bentham's concept of property has following features:

(i) Property is not pre-state or a natural right but created by state.
(ii) Possession of property gives a feeling of personal attachment.
(iii) Bentham justifies inequality of property.
(iv) The property may be acquired only after paying adequate compensation to its owner.
(v) Bentham stands for sanctity of contract.
(vi) Law of inheritance is justified.

(vii) If there is any evil like slavery, it should be remedied without loss to the owners.
(viii) Bentham stands for non-interference of state in economic matters.
(ix) The state should help the weak.

*(iii) J.S. Mill's Views on Property*

John Stuart Mill was a follower of Bentham, yet he was a product of his times which had changed. He was the product of transition in which classical liberalism was being challenged by the philosophy of socialism. Initially he accepted Bentham's idea with, of course, his own modification but later on he became influenced by socialism. He himself became a member of Parliament with the help of his working-class followers. As a politician, he became a radical and social reformer. He became a liberal with a sharp leaning towards the later Fabian school of socialism. His objective was to remove the evils of capitalism without sacrificing its essential principles. As a result, we find a lot of inconsistencies in his views on property. The practical politician in him gave an expression that completed one epoch of early capitalism of Locke and Bentham, and inaugurated the other, the other being the epoch of socialism. To that extent, he still remains the mouthpiece of modern English liberalism. His view on property can be summed up as follows:

(i) *Defence of laissez faire:* Mill stood for autonomy of economic activity. He was a great champion of liberty of individual and there was no question of compromise. But the doctrine of liberty has nothing to do with the defence of free trade or *laissez faire*. Mill wants no restriction on trade because restrictions on trade are restraints and all restraints are evil. In fact to Mill, restraint on trade is harmful because they do not produce the results which are desired from them. Therefore, the market should be free and it should be left to the buyers and sellers to organise it. There should be free competition in the sphere of production and exchange.

Mill defended the right to form trade union on the basis of *laissez faire*. State cannot deny the workers their trade unions because it is their right based on the general rule of freedom of contract. Mill also defends competition. He did not agree that competition always lowers wages. Competition among employees can lead to higher wages. He related competition with justice which demands that the worker should understand the role of the market and he should demand neither more nor less than the worth of his work. He rejected communism because of its hostility to competition. He said, "I utterly dissent from the most conspicuous and vehement part of their (communist's) teaching, their declamations against competition."

(ii) *Mill's plea for state action:* Mill stands for reforms which would redistribute property and income. He believes that distribution of human race into employers and employed cannot be permanently maintained. This, he thinks, would ultimately be superseded by partnership in the form of 'association of labourers with the capitalists' and perhaps finally in 'association of labours among themselves.' According to him, attack on the institution of property would continue 'until the laws of property are freed from whatever portion of injustice they contain'. He also makes it clear that if the choice were to be made between communism with all its chances, and the present state of society with all its sufferings and injustices; if the institution of private property necessarily carried with it as a consequence, that the produce of labour should be apportioned..., almost in an inverse ratio' then communism is to be preferred.'

To Mill, ownership of land is a trust. Property rights are not natural rights. They are social privileges, given by the law. Trade is also a social act. Therefore, property in general demands interference from state and society. Mill advocated a theory of special taxation of 'unearned increment' and socially created values. The value of property increases as the society advances and constitutes 'unearned increment'; the owners of the property have no role in this increase and, therefore, state may take over or tax the increased portion of the property. If the state does so, it is doing no injustice to the owners because it is an unearned income created by the society and therefore, should be used for the benefit of all. For this Mill says, "The first step should be a valuation of all land in the country. The present value of land should be exempted from the tax, but after an interval had elapsed, during which society had increased in population and capital, rough estimate might be made of the spontaneous increase which had accrued to rent since the valuation was made." Thus, Mill increased the state's role in economic activity.

Mill was dissatisfied with the workers' conditions in industry. They were working in pathetic circumstances where long hours of work coupled with low wages was the rule. During his times, it was suggested that wage levels in economy reflected the size of the 'employer's wage fund' and the number of workers seeking employment and the average wage could be calculated by dividing the first by the second. The workers can improve their lot by having small families. Mill advocated for the restriction on the growing population. But then it is difficult to expect workers to restrict the size of their families because of poverty and their ignorance. However, still if the workers have to take up the responsibility of improving their lots themselves, a change in social attitudes and organisation would be needed as an incentive for them. For the purpose, Mill advocates worker's management in industry. He says that self-management in industry is a complement to self control in domestic life.

Mill deplored the employers' attitude towards their workers as feudalistic. He was sure that this could not exist for long. Once self government in industry is attained by the workers, this feudalism will go away. Mill was confident that workers would not remain content as wage earners for long. They would only be contented by being associated in the management of industry.

Mill advocated state legislation to increase wages and low working house for the workers. He wanted justice for workers. Their reward should be in proportion to the efforts they make. He wanted protection of public health, insurance against illness, industrial accidents and indigence in old age. Mill also wanted state to take up education for all children. This, however, does not mean state control over education for all children. The competition from private enterprises must also be there. State should also restrict monopolisation of economic activity.

But this does not mean that the state should interfere in every economic activity. Mill shared with Bentham that habit of putting more and more matters in the hands of the state was inimical to progress. Excessive state interference also means loss of freedom. Mill says, "If the roads, the railways, the banks, the insurance offices, the great joint stock companies were all of them branches of government.... if the employees of all these different enterprises were appointed and paid by the government, every rise in life, not all the freedom of press and popular constitution of the legislative would make this or any other country free otherwise than in name." More power to the state means more and more powerful bureaucracy. Mill is highly critical of bureaucracy which encourages an uncommendable type of ambition and it gets so entrenched that "nothing to which the bureaucracy is really adverse can be done at all... the more perfect that organisation... the more complete is the bondage of all..." Mill was very correct here. The rule of bureaucracy means the rule of file and procedures, red-tapism and corruption. As the members of bureaucracy belong to the rich class, they have no sympathies for the poor and their welfare. Mill says, "Even an insurrection or revolution, whatever else it might do, does not disturb the bureaucracy. Since there is no one else capable of taking their place." Thus, Mill is against the bureaucratic control of state which is not responsible to the people.

(iii) *Private property justified:* Mill only wants state intervention in the distribution of property. He does not want its abolition. He also accepted the liberal emphasis on competition in economic life. He had sympathies with socialist doctrine, but he never accepted communism. He said that communism should not be compared with the existing capitalist societies where the private property is not regenerative. It should be compared with a social order which contains only the best features of capitalism. In other words, as Eric Roll suggests, he envisaged a state of society in which the existing distribution of property, caused by past conquest and violence, had been corrected in which inequality of opportunity had been reduced to a minimum, in which legislation was designed to favour the diffusion of wealth, in which there was universal education and in which population was limited.' In such a society the principle of private property, Mill confidently declares, will have no necessary connection with the physical and social evils which almost all socialist writers assume to be inseparable from it." He had no objection in the accumulation of private property as a result of a person's own efforts. But he disliked the unrestricted right of inheritance. Nobody should be able to begin life at too great an advantage over everyone else.

Mill also believed that we are heading towards a stationary state. A time will come when there will be no increase in wealth. In fact there will be decline in profits. This will be due to improvements in the techniques, the law of diminishing returns, the accumulation of capital and the working of competition. Then, the conditions of working class will improve. Only thing is that the rise in population should be controlled. In such a stationary state, wealth will be more evenly divided and that will be the ideal state of private property.

To conclude, Mill's views on property are the following:

1. Mill stands for the policy of *laissez faire* and competition which is favourable to workers also.
2. He wants state action in distribution of wealth.
3. Property is not a pre-state right but created by law.
4. Unearned increment on property should be used for public benefits.
5. He wants state regulation in working conditions and workers.
6. Mill justifies private property. He only wants its evil to be removed.
7. He believes that society is heading towards a stationary state where wealth would be evenly divided.

*(iv) The Modern Libertarians and Property*

However we have modern libertarians who are highly critical of increasing state role in property.

Ayn Rand has given a moral justification of capitalism. She believes that the free market economy is the only economic system that can guarantee the dignity of man and his freedom. To Rand, ideal man is engineer, scientist and industrialist. She says "Since my purpose is the presentation of an ideal man. I had to present the kind of social system that makes it possible for ideal men to exist and to function—a free, productive, rational system, which demands and rewards the best in every man, great or average, and which demands an rewards the best in every man, great or average, and which is obviously, *laissez faire* capitalism." Rand's man is a rational being who is guided by his thinking and not by, feelings and desires and who sees his interests in terms of a life time and selects his goals accordingly". A rational man acts according to his self-interest and capitalism is the only system that provides him the basis for working. She says, "In a capitalist system, all human relationships are voluntary. Men are free to cooperate or not, as their own individual judgements, convictions, and interests dictate." Rand is highly critical of state interference in economic matters. She does not see any difference between socialism, fascism and welfare state. All of them interfere in the market activity, and are specific variants of statism". Statism is "the principle or policy of concentrating extensive economic, political and related controls in the state at the cost of individual liberty." The socialist doctrine negates private property and makes the state as the owner of property while fascism gives control of the property to the government though ownership remains in the hands of private individuals. The welfare state to Rand is also fascist because it stands for the preservation of private property with governmental control of its use and disposal. She also says, "A mixed economy is merely semi-socialised economy—which means: a semienslaved society."

However, Rand believes that 'a pure unregulated *laissez faire* never existed anywhere in the world. The political systems of the nineteenth century were not pure capitalism, but mixed economies: at the most, they were close to capitalism, and of course, there was more freedom. According to Rand, "Freedom is the fundamental requirement of man's mind" Man should be free from physical compulsions and only political power is the power of physical coercion and that freedom, in a political contest, has only one meaning; the absence of physical coercion."

Rand is against the welfare activities of the state. The state has no business to help the unemployed, aged and the weak. She declares, "Only individual men have the right to decide when or whether they wish to help others; society as an organised political system has no rights in the matter at all." She wants welfare and charity to be left to voluntary associations. She wants no restriction on right to property. She is against any limitations on inheritance. The only economic rights are property rights, and the right of free trade' and there cannot be such things like "an economic bill of rights," a right to a job or, right to a fair wage or a fair price. She also denies 'the existence of public interest.'

According to Rand, the basis of the government is the consent of governed' and the governmental function is limited to three broad categories—(i) the police to protect men from criminals, (ii) the armed services to protect men from foreign invaders; (iii) the law courts, to settle disputes among men according to objective laws.

Rand advocates free trade from international point of view. The peace in world can be maintained only by a free trade. According to her, "...the major wars of history were started by more controlled economics of the time against free countries." A statist economy logically leads to war because wealth is publically owned and a citizen has no economic stakes in peace, while war holds out the prospects of larger handouts from the government. The capitalist society, on the other hand, does not need war because (i) the principle of individual rights does not permit a man to rob another inside or outside his country. (ii) the private citizens have a stake in peace because they will have to meet the cost of war in the form of taxes. They will also suffer due to business dislocations and property destructions. Therefore, they are against war. Thus, the only way of elimination of war is to free the market and free trade among different countries. The operation of free trade would result in international division of labour, would bring people together and would make them prosperous.

Robert Nozick is another writer who favours existing inequalities in terms of property. People are justified in having property if it is not a stolen property and no fraud is involved. He dismisses all talks of egalitarianism because 'whatever is held is prima facie, justifiably held.' The existing inequalities in terms of property are the result of a long historical process and therefore, justified. The people who talk of unequal distribution in society give us a feeling that these inequalities have been deliberately created from the resources according to some specified criterion, which is not true. Further, he says, "we are not in the position of children who have been given portions of pie by some one who now makes last minute adjustments to rectify careless cuttings." Therefore any talk of egalitarianism mean paternalism at the best or at worst dictatorship. Nozick says that why should we assume that people should be treated equally and given equal shares in the common stock. Nozick wants people to keep whatever they have and it is the responsibility of the egalitarians to prove that these people should be debarred from keeping their property. However Nozick is not convinced with any argument given against property. Therefore, he is against governmental interference with existing property rights.

*(v) Liberals' justification of Private Property*

The above study of liberal views on property with reference to Locke, Bentham, Mill and Nozick demonstrates that right to private property is well justified. To Locke, private property is a natural right while Bentham and Mill accept it as a right guaranteed by the law. However, all of them regard property imperative for individuals. Other important liberals who justify private property are Adam Smith, Malthus and Herbert Spencer. The justification of private property therefore, constitutes an essential principle of liberalism. This also justifies the inequalities in the society which are consequences of property rights. In *Coppage vs Kansas* (1915) case, the US Supreme Court said the following:

"No doubt, wherever the right to private property exists, there must and will be inequalities of fortune... And since it is self-evident that, unless things are held in common, some persons must have more property than others, it is from the nature of things impossible to uphold the freedom of contract and the right of private property without, at the sometime, recognizing as legitimate those inequalities of fortune that are the necessary result of the exercise of these rights."

The liberals have justified private property on following grounds;

(i) *Property is* a *natural right:* some liberals like Locke believe that property is a natural right. By his birth, an individual acquires this right. Locke says that God has put man on this earth and given him reason to use the resources of the earth, therefore, man has a right to property so that the earth is turned into a usable commodity. He himself possesses property in his person and when he mixes his labour in the common property of earth given by God, it becomes his property. As much land a man, Locke argues, "tills, plants, improves, cultivates and can use the product, so much is his property." The liberals believe that property is a natural and inalienable right and it is the duty of the government to protect it. The U.S. Constitution also accepts this position. But all the liberals do not accept the theory of natural right. Like Bentham and Mill, they believe it is a social privilege, authorised by law.

(ii) *Psychological basis:* Liberals believe that individual is governed by his self interest and there is nothing wrong in it. He knows his interest better than others and even government, and he can do better than the government in satisfying his interest. Therefore, as Appadorai puts it, "Self-help is the best help. Psychologically, property provides incentive to individual to work. Without property there will not be any incentive to work. Further property gives him a sense of satisfaction of his living. In property he sees his achievements of life."

(iii) *Moral basis:* Morally, property is justified because it is a reward for one's ability and capacity, which he has earned by his efforts. It is only because of private property that man uses his initiative and efforts to develop his personality and he has a moral claim to the property so acquired.

(iv) *Social basis:* According to Adam Smith, "the Providence has made society into a system in which natural order prevails. Human conduct is naturally actuated by six motives—self-help, sympathy, the desire to be free, a sense of propriety, a habit of labour, and the tendency to truck, barter and exchange one thing for another. There the individual is the best judge of his own and therefore, be left alone." Further, the different motives of human action are so balanced that the benefit of one does not conflict with the good of all. Self-help is accompanied by sympathy and therefore, whatever the individual does for this development, it also helps the society. It is primarily due to natural balance of human motives. Adam Smith says, that in pursuing his own advantage each individual is 'led by an invisible hand to promote an end which was no part of his intention.' In simple words, it means that individual's development leads to common good in the society. The property is a source of social virtues like love towards family, generosity and charity. Property gives man a status in society which ultimately leads to his happiness and contentment, and only such persons can be of any benefits to the society.

(v) *Economic basis:* Liberal believes that the system of private property gives better efficiency and production. Therefore, there should be *laissez faire* and free trade. There should not be any restriction and the state should be no more than a referee in the economic world. As a referee, it should see that the participants in the economic activity should follow the rules of the market and there is no fraud and treachery. Liberals believe that market is sel-regulative and state has no role to play in economic activity. The individual should be left alone and in such a situation, a capitalist will invest his capital to his best advantage. Likewise, the labourer will also find out his job where he can get maximum wages. Thus, a free market operates on competitions and it helps both the capitalists as well as the workers. Free competitions among the producers benefit the consumers. A consumer gets cheap goods, as the producers compete to sell their goods. The right to property thus brings general happiness and common good in the economic field.

(vi) *Biological basis:* The right to property has also been justified on biological basis. Nature is characterised by a struggle for existence. In this struggle only the fittest survive. Nature has witnessed a struggle between different species for existence, and man emerged victorious because he was the fittest. The liberals have extended this argument in human society also. The government should not interfere in economic field. The natural law of struggle for existence and survival of the fittest should be the fundamental rules of the economic activity. Only the fittest will survive and the property they achieve is justified. The weak may be allowed to perish and the government should not help them because this is against nature's justice.

(vii) *Historical basis:* The institution of private property is an old system. It has existed from time immemorial, that itself proves its justification. Further, history also proves that the Western society which was based on property developed fast in contrast to the Eastern societies which were based on collective property. Now they are dominating the world.

(viii) *Pragmatic basis:* State is a man made institution created for the specific purposes of maintaining law and order. Therefore, by its very nature, it is limited. It is not designed to perform economic activities. History provides ample example when state has tried to infiltrate into economic matters and failure state has tried to infiltrate into economic matters and failure has been the result. In India most of the public enterprises are incurring huge losses. In late 1960s, the Indian Government introduced rationing system which also failed. In fact, it encouraged hoardings and other evils with regard to the distribution of food stuff. Thus experience shows that governmental interference in economic matters produces bad results. Therefore, the state should remain aloof from the economy; the demand and supply rule of the economic system is sufficient for its working. The property should be independent of state's interference.

This concept of private property and its logical conclusion of the policy of *laissez faire* or free trade was implemented in England and other parts of Europe in eighteenth and nineteenth centuries. This resulted in flourishing market and prosperity. However, it soon became apparent that right to unrestricted property and the state non-interference lead to exploitation of man by man. It also resulted in poverty for the millions. The socialist movement grew out of this phenomenon. The liberals were quick to understand this defect in liberal theory. Therefore, they modified their doctrine and accepted state regulation of property and economy.

## IV. The Marxian Concept of Property

In Marxism, the concept of private property finds a pivotal position. It is the property which is responsible for development and progress in human society. However this development has not been healthy because the property divides the society into two classes—the property owners and those who do not possess property, in other words haves and have-nots. These two classes struggle with each other as their interest in terms of property clash with each other. In this struggle, the state is always biased. It is on the side of property-owners, as they control it and use it as a means to further their interests. Property owners not only control the state apparatus, they also create or control other institutions like religion, ethics, family through their ideology. Thus, the history of mankind is a history of domination of the property owners over the have-nots. Therefore, Marxism is highly critical of private property and wants to abolish it, so that a new society is created in which there is no exploitation. In fact with the abolition of private property, there won't be any private interest and clash of interest, therefore no class and no class struggle. An ideal stateless society will follow which will be based on perfect harmoney and equality.

Thus, to the Marxists, property is a hindrance to the real development of society. This position is in contrast to the liberal theory of property which believes that property is essential for the development of man and society.

Marx differentiates two kinds of property. The first is consumable or personal property which means a property which is meant for consumption by the man. It includes food stuff, house, utensils, car etc. Marx has no obsession to their possession by the individuals. What he objects to is the producable or private property which includes land, rent, profit, cash in banks etc... Private property. The Marxists believe that it is this kind of property which is responsible for all the evils in society and therefore, it must be abolished.

The question is how the private property came into existence? Marx's friend Engels attempted to explain the origins of property in his *The Origin of the Family, Private Property and the State.* Initially there was no private property. Man was food gatherer which he used to achieve by collecting vegetables and fruits and by hunting the animals. This is also called by Marxists as the stage of primitive communism. But this stage did not continue forever. Man soon started domesticating the animals like cows and buffaloes. Later on agricultural activities also commenced. According to Engels, the domestication of animals had three effects i.e. the emergence of patriarchical family, slavery and private property. Once the private property came into existence, it changed the whole structure of the society.

According to the Marxists, the class society is always divided into two classes on the basis of property ownership. The people who own property or means of production constitute one class and who don't own them constitute another class. In the work of production people enter into definite relations and these relations of productions are the relations of property. When the property or the means of production is the land, we have the classes of feudal lords, the owners and the serfs, the non-owners. In capitalism, the machine is the new means of production, we have capitalists who are the owners of the machine and non-owners are the wage labourers or working class or as Marxists call them the proletariat. Thus, property creates relation between the people, 'the wind-mill gives you the society with the feudal lord; the steam-mill, society with the industrial capitalists.'

Property relations create not only classes but also class conflicts. The reason is that the interests of property non-owners are antagonistic to each other. The property-owners want to expand their property and this can only be achieved when they pay less to the labour while the labour demands more for its subsistence. Thus a class-struggle is unavoidable. To the Marxists, history is nothing but the history of class-struggle.

Property is also responsible for changes in the society. In the development of society a stage comes when new mode of production arises. They come into direct conflict with the existing relations of production or property relations. For example the rise of machinery as a mode of production was in direct contradiction to the then existing property relations of landlord and serfs. In such circumstances, revolution becomes inevitable. This is because property constitutes the basics of the society. The argument is very simple in Marxism. The mode of production determines the social relations of production i.e. relationship between men. This is economic relations; and these economic relations in turn determine the legal, political and other social relations. Engels says, "...that in every society that has appeared in history the manner in which wealth is distributed and society divided into classes or orders, is dependent upon what is produced, how it is produced, and how the products are exchanged. From this point of view the final causes of all social changes and political revolutions are to be sought, not in men's better insight into eternal truth and justice, but in changes in the modes of production and exchange. They are to be sought, not in the philosophy, but in the economics of each particular epoch." The introduction of machinery as a mode of production resulted in the death of feudalism and creation of capitalism.

According to the Marxists, property is also responsible for the creation of state. Engels says, "The state... did not exist from all eternity. There have been societies without it, that had no idea of any state or public power. At a certain stage of economic development which was of necessity accompanied by a division of society into classes, the state became the inevitable result of this division." This stage of economic development was that of the beginning of private property whose protection gave rise to the state. Property creates classes and class conflict, and the class conflict creates the state. The highest purpose of the state is the protection of private property. Historically the state came into being when the property of the masters was being threatened by the revolt of the slaves: the purpose was to maintain the hegemony of the masters over the slaves. Thus the state is a class organisation, an organisation of the particular class which is the exploiting class. It is merely the organised power of one class for oppressing another. Thus in ancient times, as Engels puts it, the state is "the state of slave-owning citizens, in the middle ages, the feudal lords; in our own, the bourgeoise." The ancient state checked the slaves, the feudal state oppressed the serfs and dependent farmers and the modern state is the tool of the capitalist exploiters of the wage labour. Thus, the state came into existence when the division of society into classes was brought about by a mode of production based on private property.

According to the Marxists, property is responsible for all the evils, therefore, Marxism stands for its total abolition. Marx and Engels declared in the *Communist Manifesto* that the theory of communism may be summed up in a single sentence—the abolition of private property. The Marxists are critical of capitalism because it is based upon the institution of private property. Let us now study the Marxian critique of capitalism.

*(i) Marxian Critique of Capitalism*

Modern capitalist society is a democratic society which means political power is exercised and controlled by the people for their own benefits. The Marxists do not accept this. According to them, the liberal state is just like any other state designed to protect and promote the private property and oppress the working class. However Marx's most important contribution is his analysis of capitalist society in terms of theory of alienation.

According to Marx, men are defined by their capacity to work and are different from all other creatures by their ability to produce freely. Man is not only a creator, he is also aesthetic and enjoys his work. But in capitalism with its basis on private property both the work and enjoyment are dehumanised. To Marx, property is a form of failed appropriation because we only acquire the external non-human aspect of things, and fail to acquire their richer substance. We do not enjoy it. The richer we become in conventional terms, the poorer we really are. Marx finds man's alienation in capitalist society in four ways (i) from nature (ii) from his product, (iii) from his species being and (iv) from himself. In other words man's alienation is to be viewed and understood from four different perspectives such as in relation of the workers to the product of his labour, in relation to the activity of production in terms of its impact on the worker, in relation to himself and in the context of his social life to other men. This alienation is the result of private property.

Private ownership of the means of production leads to man's alienation from his labour. Marx says "The more the worker produces, the less he has to consume; the more value he creates, the more valueless, the more unworthy he becomes; the better formed his produce the more deformed the worker, the more civilized his object, the more barbarous becomes the worker; more powerful labour becomes, the more powerless becomes the worker, the more ingenious becomes the worker and more he becomes nature's servant." The problem is that the worker himself becomes a commodity like labour; more the commodities he creates, more cheaper he becomes. Whatever he creates is not controlled by him but it is independent of him. His work becomes his enemy, like an alien power confronting him. Marx says, "Thus all the process of civilisation or in other words every increase in the powers of social production... in the productive powers of the labour itself such as results from science, inventions, division and combination of labour, improved means of communication, creation of world market, machinery etc enriches not the labour but rather capital, hence it only magnifies again the power dominating over labour; increases only the productive power of the capital. Since capital is the antithesis of the worker, this merely increases the objective power standing over labour." Thus the capital is the cause for man's alienation. The worker does not enjoy the work or the creation that he does. Marx aptly puts it." The worker, therefore, only feels himself outside his work and in his work feels outside himself. His labour is therefore not voluntary, but coerced, it is forced labour... As a result, therefore, man only feels himself freely active in the animal function—eating, drinking, procreating, or atmost in his dwelling and in dressing up and in his human function he no longer feels himself to be anything but an animal. What is animal becomes human and what is human becomes animal." All the human values are also dominated by the consideration of private property and money, and thus the basis of honesty, gentleness, beauty, powers, and wisdom is money. You are judged by your ability to amass more and more property. The capitalist is no way better than the workers. He also becomes a machine which produces money. He is forced to maximise profits otherwise he losses in the competition. He is the instrument of the power of capital in dehumanising the workers, not an independent agent. Money is a dead thing, yet it dominates the living beings. The workers and the capitalists—both think about the money always, and the object of life becomes its, more and more accumulation. Thus, according to Marx, the alienation is not limited to worker alone. The capitalist also suffers from the same kind of alienation. Capitalism is thus condemned both from the worker as well as capitalist point of view. None of them control its operations and enjoy its product.

Marx believed that alienation is due to the surplus value and the division of power which creates classes in the society. The division of power increases the wealth by raising the productive power of the labour; it also leads to inequality and private property. Alienation, automatically follows. Marx explained inequality in terms of surplus value. The capitalist wants to have more and more profit. He must get more than what he pays as wages to the workers. For the purpose he pays less to the workers and the surplus that the capitalist gets as a result is used further for the creation of private property. Thus, the surplus belongs to the labour which the capitalist usurps and creates further property. Marx concludes that property is responsible for political, economic and social evils and the only remedy is its abolition, only way of its abolition is the overthrow of the capitalist system.

*(ii) Property Under Socialism and Communism*

The overthrow of capitalism is followed by the establishment of socialist democracy or dictatorship of the proletariat. The institution of private property will be done away with. People will be rewarded according to their efforts. Nobody will receive any income without earning it. The labour will get its due and there will not be any capitalist to appropriate the surplus. This socialist society will pave way for communism, where each will get according to his needs. In communism man will really be a freeman. He will be unalienated man, which to Marx is a total man. He will be free "to hunt in the morning, fish in the afternoon, rear cattle in the evening and criticize after dinner... Without ever becoming hunter, fisherman, shepherd or critic." In communism, there is no private property, no classes, no class exploitation, no class conflicts and hence no government or state. People are happy and unalienated. It is really a heaven on the earth.

The Marxian plea of abolition of private property has been a revolutionary idea. It also alarmed the capitalists about socialism and communism. However, even during the times of Marx and Engels and also after, a different brand or shade of socialism developed which did not share many of Marxist's views including his views on private property. The evolutionary socialists, the Fabians, the guild socialists and the democratic socialists do not want the abolition of property. They shared the liberal idea of property which justifies its existence and view it necessary for the development of individual's personality. What they desired is the regulation of property, so that it is not misused for exploitation. It should be used, on the contrary, for common good.

### V. Laski's Views on Property

To Laski, there are certain advantages in having property. Property gives security; it is a safeguard against the want of the tomorrow. 'The man of property has a stake in the country. He is protected from the fear of starvation. He need not accept the work he does not desire. He can take the leisure in which most men now find the opportunity of significance. He can, if he so wills, surround himself with the environment which makes life an artistic thing. He can avoid the grim routine, and become an explorer in that intellectual hinterland where the creative faculties most readily discover their channels of self-expression. He can protect his children against the dread of want."

But the problem is that the number of property-owners is always less than those who do not possess property. People devoid of property have no meaningful life. The political system is dominated by the owners of property. Nodubt there have been major state legislation like fixing the minimum wages, yet the concept of private property perpetuates the division into the rich and the poor and separates the poor from the conditions which make possible their effective citizenship.

Laski's views of property can be understood under the following heads:

1. Criticism of capitalism.
2. Criticism of basis of private property

3. Laski's views on functionless property.
4. Laski on theories of reward.
5. Laski's theory of industrial organisation.

*1. Criticism of capitalism:* Laski is a critic of capitalism and its political ideology of liberalism. According to him, the liberal theory of state assumed a sovereign state to avoid anarchy and it was based on three functions of state. First it secured order; secondly it provided a technique of peaceful change and lastly, it enabled demands to be satisfied on the widest possible scale. The state definitely secures order but the problem is that it does not provide a technique of peaceful change and does not permit demands to be satisfied on the largest possible scale. This is because of the institution of private property. The supreme coercive power of state is used to protect and promote the interests of those who own instruments of production. Some concessions may be granted to those who do not possess property, but the last two functions of state cannot be achieved so long as the instruments of production are privately owned. Theoretically, peaceful change in a liberal state is possible through the Constitution, but in practice, the owners of the property who possess the state power always resist the change. The liberal state also fails to satisfy demands on the largest possible scale because capitalism is based on profit and therefore it cannot satisfy the demands of those who do not possess property. In other words, the distributive process in a liberal state is defective and 'the coercive power of the state is used to promote the differences in relation to the satisfaction of demand....'

Laski is against economic disparities which are the inevitable result of capitalism. To him, capital is social labour and therefore the whole society has a right over it. A small minority of capitalists cannot monopolise it.

Laski agreed with those that the state and government operate in favour of the properties class. There is ample evidence regarding this in history. " The Greek city was biased against the slave. The Roman Empire was biased against the slave and the poor. States in the medieval world were biased in favour of the owners of landed property. Since the Industrial Revolution, the state has been biased in favour of the owners of the instruments of production as against those who have nothing but their labour power to sell." He accepts the Marxian concept of economic interpretation of history. He says, "Changes in the methods of economic production appear to be the most vital factor in the making of change in all the other social patterns we know." The law the culture, the religion, the education system, styles of architecture, the character of our science, the basic framework of all that we call civilisation is, at bottom, determined by these productive relations."

A major defect in capitalism, according to Laski, is lack of planning in production. "Production is carried on wastefully and without adequate plan". Preferences are not based on social utility." We build picturesque palaces when we need houses. We spend on battleships what is wanted for schools. The rich can spend the weekly wage of a workman on a single dinner, while the workman cannot send his children, adequately fed, to school. Goods and services are produced, 'not for use', but to acquire more and more profit. To become more and more rich is the ideal, and therefore, production is done 'not to satisfy useful demands, but demands which can be made to pay.'

The profit motive dominates the scene and for this end, all means—moral and immoral are justified. For this objective, Laski says, "They will ruin natural resources. They will adulterate commodities. They will float dishonest enterprises. They will corrupt legislatures. They will prevent the source of knowledge. They will artificially combine to increase the cost of their commodities to the public. They will exploit sometimes with hideous cruelty, the backward races of mankind. They infect with their poison those who work for the wages they offer. They compel strikes which result in serious damage to the community... They may destroy the quality of political life.. They may even pervert religious institutions to the protection of their ideas." However, they cannot secure a well ordered state' because it is "historically obvious that a community divided into rich and poor is, when the latter are numerous, built upon foundations of sand."

To Laski, capitalism and democracy are contradictory. While the economic basis of power is narrow and capitalism stands for its protection and promotion, the citizens in a democracy use the political power at their disposal to increase their material well being. Yet this union of economic oligarchy and political democracy worked well so long as the capitalism was in its phase of expansion. However, after the first world war, the capitalism entered into the phase of contraction which not only limited the profits of the capitalists but also increased unemployment resulting in lower standards of life. The dissatisfied people revolted and used their political power. Their political power became a challenge to the economic power of the owning class. In such a situation arose Fascism, which to Laski, is 'nothing but simply the expedient adopted by capitalism in distress to defeat the democratic political foundation...' This analysis explains the widespread attack on principles like freedom of speech, due process in political offence (which was remarkably illustrated by Hitlerite legislation and activities) and right of labour to strike. Laski attacks capitalism from international point of view. Capitalism is organised on national basis and the capitalists use their state to further their economic interests. They also want to capture foreign markets and to them state becomes a means for protecting and extending their investments abroad. This results in competitive economic imperialism where, arms are used to secure gains, 'Fear, suspicion and hatred are born of this atmosphere. The interest of world community has to give way before the interests of powerful states. For example, the Japanese occupation of Manchuria, before the second world war, where Japan preferred to sacrifice the hope of peace and international security to the imperial ambitions of her governing class. The failure of world Economic Conference in 1933 and the Disarmament Conference in 1934 is also because of this reason. Laski declares, "Capitalism, in a word, is rooted in a system which makes power the criterion of right and war the ultimate expression of power." There can not be peace in the world in such an atmosphere.

2. *Criticism of the basis of private property:* The liberals have justified the concept of private property on various grounds. Laski criticises all the grounds as follows:

(i) *Psychological basis:* The first justification of private property has been psychological. Psychologically, the people need some incentive to work and private property provides such incentive. The desire to make property makes people work and in the process good of the community is also achieved. Laski criticises this justification on two grounds. Firstly, the good of the society is achieved only when the goods produced also bring about good for the society. But this is not the case always. For example, the people dealing in harmful drugs and narcotics may become very rich, but their goods are not for the good of the community. Secondly, people who acquire property by means of heredity may not have any incentive to work. In fact, psychologically, the private property was based on fear, and any system based on fear, cannot survive for long.

(ii) *Ethical Basis:* Liberals have justified private property ethically. The property is the result of individual's effort and hard work, and therefore, he has a moral right over it. But there are many people who work very hard, yet they cannot make property. The fact of the matter, Laski says, is that property actually is a reward for a particular kind of ability which consists in the capacity to make more and more profit. The profit motive cannot contribute to social well-being in any way. Private property is morally inadequate, because it confers rights to those who have done nothing to earn it. Thus it creates parasites in the society who deprive others the opportunity to live a decent life.

(iii) *Private Property a source of virtues:* The liberals also believe that it is the private property which provides a man such virtues like love of one's family, generosity, inventiveness and energy. But this means that the majority of people who do not have property, lack these virtues, which to Laski, is not a correct statement of fact, for these virtures have been present in persons who have never amassed property at all. People do not work just to amass property. For example, Newton's inventiveness was not due to the desire to make more property. The poor also love their family and this love has no relation with property.

(iv) *Property as the result of supplying effective demands:* The property has also been viewed as the result of supplying effective demand. Laski does not appreciate this view because it has no social utility. There may be unjust demand, for example, for obscene literature or prostitutes and property made by such efforts cannot be justified.

(v) *The historical argument:* Private property has also been justified on the basis of history. The developed societies of the West have been based on private property while the backward societies on a collective basis. The developed societies are more progressive and there is more freedom for individuals. But, according to Laski, this does not mean that they provide more happiness to individuals. The reason is that we cannot say much about the backward peoples on the basis of available knowledge which is very less. Further, historically speaking, the concept of private property has always been subjected to control. At no time in history, it was regarded as absolute. People have been aware of danger of private state property and both politically and philosophically attempts made to minimise this danger by putting control over it. Plato in fact rejected the notion of private property. The modern liberal state started with an unlimited right to property and it became a negative state. But soon it had to change its colour and become a positive state in which right to property became limited and subject to state regulation. The state saw the expansion of its operation to economic field where its obligation was to achieve common good and reduce economic disparities. According to Laski, the right to property should be related to the social needs.

*3. Laski is Against Functionless Property*

Laski is a critic of functionless property. To him, functions are related to duties and no man has a 'moral right to property except as a return for function performed. He has no right to live unless he pays for his living: To him, people who owe functionless property, are parasites upon the society. Therefore, he is critical of inherited property. According to Laski, hereditary wealth involves two things; (1) There is a class freed from the legal obligation to labour. (2) So freed, it is able to utilise its leisure in a way that taxes the productive effort of the remaining members of society. In fact, such people misuse their leisure. They devote to aimless pleasure. They dominate institution and set standards of taste. They provide employments and form the habits and ideals of the class which attains wealth by its own efforts. Their economic position involves a definite social predominance. They are able, by their prestige, to set the perspective of the state. However, this does not mean that a 'man is not entitled to provide for his immediate descendants.' Laski says security should be provided to children. Children should be given adequate education and support to enable them to enter the battle of life. "Inheritance is always justified," Laski comments, "where it means the provision of an income for widowhood, on the one hand, and the education of children on the other". Beyond that there cannot be any inheritance. Man can have a right to that property which is the result of his own personal efforts. However Laski advocates compensation to the property in the form of annual pension. Otherwise, it may result in conflicts in the polity, as Machiavelli said, men will sooner forgive the death of their fathers than the confiscation of their property.

*4. Laski on Theory of Reward*

How much a man is entitled to is the basic question before Laski. Laski discusses various theories of reward and finds them unsuitable. The first theory is the communist doctrine of equality of income. Laski says that it is not justified to reward equally where needs are unequal. A bachelor cannot be entitled to the same income as the parents who have five or six children to maintain. There can not be equal reward for unequal effort also. The second doctrine advocates the fixation of remuneration by the haggling of the market.' The operation of supply and demand fixes the reward for the labour. Laski does not agree with this theory, because such a system is based upon competition, which is unfair to labour. It leaves one-third of the average industrial community on the verge of starvation. For them it means poor health, undeveloped intelligence, miserable homes, and work in which, broadly speaking, the majority can find no source of human interest.' Therefore the state has to pass laws, such as, minimum wages Acts to protect the labour. The theory of supply and demand is essentially a capitalist norm which Laski abhors. Capitalism has failed to deliver goods to the society. Here, the motive is profit and for the purpose the demands are created irrespective of their social utility. The third theory of reward is quite attractive. 'It demands that each contributes to society according to his powers, and be rewarded by society according to his needs.' To Laski, this theory is very simple and unrelated to reality. It is difficult to measure both the 'power' of individual and his 'needs'.

According to Laski, the reward must be determined on the basis of two conditions; Firstly, it should enable the individual to develop his personality and secondly, it should preserve and develop the necessary function of society. For the purpose he advocates following things:

(i) Minimum economic requirements should be provided to all citizens. Laski calls it a common civic minimum.

(ii) The demands of weaker classes, children, old people, disabled and defective persons should be met.

(iii) Only socially useful work should be paid.

(iv) The common civic minimum or minimum economic requirements is not the same for all the members of the community. The human wants are not identical. An agricultural worker or a minor needs a more costly diet than a clerk. The minimum is to be decided according to the nature of job.

(v) The wages are to be fixed keeping in view the fact that each socially necessary occupation attracts a sufficient talent to run them adequately. Therefore, there cannot be equality of wages. A judge or a doctor should be entitled for more than a worker or minor.

(vi) The reward in terms of economic gains should not be given overemphasis. The great artist pursues his end for its own sake and not for financial gain. Similarly, scientists like Newton were not after economic gains. Laski says, "The great solider finds his reward not in the income he receives, but in the public esteem that is the measure of his repute. The average high civil servant could earn far more than his salary in the business world; but the consciousness that he has his hands on a great machine more than compensates for a comparatively modest income." Even those businessmen who have the aim of making more and more wealth do so because they want more standing and power in the commercial world.

(vii) In every society, there are people who are adventurous, and who take risk. Then there are also people who go for long training and preparations to get good positions. Laski justifies such efforts, and therefore, payment by achievement is also allowed.

(viii) The social control should be in the realm of production and not in consumption. If a worker wants to buy a piano which he cannot play, it is his business. Similarly, if a businessman wishes to have a house with endless bedrooms, it is his business and there should not be any restraint. In consumption also, class-standards should be avoided. Rules should be implemented equally to all the classes and individuals.

*5. Laski's Theory of Industrial Organisation*

Laski wants the rights of property to be well-founded in a theory of industrial organisation. There should be discipline in industries but at the sometime its aim should be general well-being of the product and the methods by which that product is attained. Laski's theory of industrial organisation can be summed up as follows:

1. The ownership of industry on the basis of inheritance is to be abolished.
2. Industry must be made a profession. The object of every profession is service. Thus industry is also a public service, where the object should not be profit. The industry must serve the community and the personal interest of the industrialists be subordinate to this end.
3. Laski suggests three changes for the industry to be professionalised. Firstly, the owner of the industry must not have a control over it. The owner renders his services by the loan of his capital to the industry and he should be paid for this service and no more. He cannot usurp the profits. Secondly, once the functionless owner is removed, the rules of the industry should be made by its workers' participation and control in the management of the industry. Thirdly, Laski wants to include more social aspects in the industry. This also means three things; (a) the profits earned must be for the benefit of the community and not for the private undertaker. The production of essential commodities may be done under cooperative production or consumer's cooperation or under state. They cannot be left in the hands of private enterprise. The socialised production may also involve nationalisation. However, other methods will also be adopted; (b) Industries, whether public or private, must have a constitution. There must be standard hours and standard rates of pay. Industry must be democratically managed and there must be absence of arbitrary and whimsical powers in

relation to hiring and dismissal of employees. Similarly, the promotion to a foreman must be based upon his ability, with the approval of those, the particular foreman is to control; (c) There must not be any chance or nepotism in industry. The head of the factory must possess required qualification. There must not be any secrecy in the matters like cost of production and rates of proft.

Thus, Laski stands for a scientific reorganisation of industry. The reorganisation should take place piecemeal and by stages, so that community learns by experience. He also wants various experiments to be undertaken in regard to the operation of industry. There may be mistakes. But, Laski declares, "there is no birth without pain; and those who would comfort the prospect of a better life, must not turn aside because there are dangers on the road."

## SUGGESTED READINGS

1. Cranston, M., *What are Human Rights*? (London; Bodley Head, 1974).
2. Laski H.J. *A Grammar of Politics*, (London, George Allen & Unwin Ltd.) 1973, 3rd print.)
3. Locke, J., *Two Treatises of Government* (Cambridge, Cambridge University Press, 1960 print).
4. Macpherson C.B. *The Political Theory of Possessive Individualism* (London: OUP, 1962).

   _______ *Property: Mainstream and Critical Positions* (Tornoto: Toronto University Press, N.D.)
5. Mount, F. *Property and Poverty: An Agenda for the Mid-80s* (London: Centre for Policy Studies, 1984).
6. Shapiro, I., *The Evolution of Rights in Liberal Theory* (Cambridge: Cambridge University Press, 1986).
7. Suvorova, m and Romanov, B., *What is Property?* (Moscow: Progress Publishers, 1986).
8. Tawney, R.H. *The Acquisitive Society* (Bombay: Orient Longmans, 1955).
9. Tully, J., *A Discourse on Property: Jolm Locke and His Adversaries* (Cambridge: Cambridge University press, 1980).

## CHAPTER – 12

# Concepts: Civil Society and State

### Introduction

Like many social science concepts, civil society is a highly contested concept. In different contexts and for different ideological purposes, the concept 'civil society' has numerous meanings. Both the diffusedness and richness of the concept of civil society reflect the deep historical sediments of meaning, which have accumulated, layer upon layer, from days as far back as those of the ancient Greece. In our times, two distinct traditions have shaped thinking about civil society: the liberal-democratic tradition and the Marxist tradition. Both traditions relate the rise of civil society to the development of capitalism and identify civil society as an arena of power that is separate from the state. Though the liberal-democratic tradition encompasses a range of perspectives on the desirability of civil society, there is a general consensus that civil society can play a politically significant role in checking the power of the state and holding government officials to account. The work of the nineteenth century thinker Alexander de Tocqueville, on associational life in the USA, and in particular, his enthusiasm for self-regulation and minimal government, underpins current discussions of civil society in the USA.

Though Marx did not undertake a systematic or comprehensive analysis of civil society, his writings underline the point that civil society is not socially neutral. For Marx, civil society represented the associational arena where the bourgeoisie consolidated its powers. These ideas were developed further in the work of the Italian writer, Antonio Gramsci, in the 1930s and 1940s. With the rediscovery of Gramsci in the late 1970s, the Marxist perspective has continued to induce debate around civil society. In particular, it has contributed towards the general recognition that civil society is a site of complex and unequal power relations, which are often challenged and renegotiated.

## I. Meaning and Definitions of Civil Society

The concept of civil society, to give it a meaning, embraces an entire range of assumptions, values and institutions, such as political, social and civil rights, the rule of law, representative institutions, a public sphere, and above all a plurality of associations. Commenting on it, David Held (*Models of Democracy*) stated that it retains "a distinctive character to the extent that it is made up of areas of social life .... the domestic world, the economic sphere, cultural activities and political interaction ... which are organised by private or voluntary arrangements between individuals, and groups outside the direct control of the state." Adding to political interaction, civil society constitutes, what Jurgen Habermas called 'the public sphere'. Enlarging the view of civil society, one may include in it the structure of modern national state, economic modernization, great interconnectedness with other societies, free enterprise and what John Dunn (*Western Political Theory*) refers to as "the modern representative democratic republic."

Neera Chandhoke (*State and Civil Society)* sums up the meaning of civil society "as the public sphere, where individuals come together for various purposes both for their self-interest and for the reproduction of an entity called society." "It is a", she continues, "sphere which is public because it is formally accessible to all, and in principle all are allowed entry into this sphere as the bearers of rights."

To what may be described as the descriptive meaning of the concept civil society, we may add a normative definition, a sociological one, stating that the "public sphere" needs to be strengthened at the expense of the state. This view can be expressed conservatively when the emphasis is laid on legality, private property, markets and the interest groups or in more leftist ways, when the emphasis is laid on empowering groups.

A classical definition of the concept 'civil society' is given by St. Augustine, who, while quoting Cicero with approval, defines 'civil society' or the commonwealth as "an assemblage of men associated by a common acknowledgement of rights and by a community of interests." The concept of civility, as a common ground shared by the state with the rest of society was traditionally grounded philosophically, notably in some concept of universal, rational human nature. In more recent times, however, especially as the philosophical derivation came under fire, this idea of civility has been used in a more simply empirical or anthropological way to describe the political culture, allegedly needed by the normative modern society, often viewed as combining the structure of the modern national state, economic modernization, great interconnectedness with other societies (as illustrated by the global economy), free enterprise, and the modern democratic system.

This brings us close to what may be called as the characteristics of the civil society and may be stated as under:

(i) considerable cultural homogeneity;
(ii) cordial trustful relations between fellow citizens who are strangers to each other;
(iii) some political consciousness, such as, a sense of nationalism;
(iv) intention to follow an abstract, unifying principle, such as, say, justice;
(v) ruler's accountability to the people;
(vi) accountability whose emphasis is on legality;
(vii) legitimization of politics where competing claims are advanced in a political market-place; and
(viii) the idea of differentiation between competing substantive demands and procedurally, formed, morally neutral 'rules of the game'.

The above characteristics of the civil society have, more or less, the liberal view of what a civil society can be. The liberal view of the civil society presupposes democratic states with their accountability towards the people, the limits on state power, the responsiveness to the spontaneous life and the interactions of civil society. For the Marxists, civil society is the arena of class conflicts, selfish competition and exploitation, the state acting to protect the interests of the owning classes. A definition of civil society, comprising the insights of both, the liberals and the Marxists, must take into account the following:

(a) The state power must be controlled and it has to become responsive through democratic practices of an independent civil society.
(b) Political accountability has to reside not only in constitutions, laws, and regulations, but also in the social fabric or what Habermas calls the competence of the 'political public' which, in turn, has the following implications: (i) it implies that

the people come together in an arena of common concerns, in debates and discussions and discourses free from state interference (ii) it implies that the discourse is accessible to all (iii) it implies a space where public discussion and debate can take place.

(c) Democratic norms and processes have to be imbibed in the social order.

(d) Civil society is the public sphere of society. It is the location of these processes by which the experiences of individuals and communities, and the expression of experiences in debates and discussions, that affirmation and constitution are mediated. It is also a theatre where "the dialectic between the private and the public are negotiated. It is the process by which society seeks to "breach" and counteract the simultaneous "totalisation" unleashed by the state" (Bayart, "Civil Society in Africa", in Chabal, P., ed., *Political Domination in Africa: Reflections on the Limits of Power*). It is a site, where the state is forbidden to shape public opinion and perceptions.

## II. Civil Society: Its Growth

The concept of civil society is associated with the Western intellectual tradition. With the epoichal changes in the West, the idea of civil society has grown progressively. Many factors have gone into developing the concept of the state as it has come to stay with us. These factors, to mention a few, include the emergence of secular authority, the development of the institution of property, the decline of the absolutist state, the growth of urban culture, the rise of nationalist and democratic movements, until the end of the nineteenth century and the rule of law. As the capitalist economy with its democratising features has developed, so has the concept of civil society.

### (a) *Civil Society: The Pre-modern Tradition*

If the idea of civil society contains in it, the idea of what relates to public, the pre-modern times may well be regarded as opposed to the concept of civil society. The Platonic rulers alone were the administrators and a large number of those who constituted 'the producing class' had no role to play in public affairs. The Aristotelian notion of '*zoon politikon*' (man as a political animal) was elitistic in the sense that (i) the political animal was a male,

(ii) he alone was a citizen and (iii) he alone was a property holder. The rest of the population, the women, the slaves etc., constituted Oikes, i.e., the private world and that could hardly be termed as constituting the civil society. As the 'private' was not 'public', it was not political, and none belonging to it had any citizenship rights. The Greek society, Chandhoke points out, did not 'possess any notion of inalienable rights of man to individual freedom which became so prominent a feature of early version of civil society. By developing the concept of rights, legally ordained, and especially relating to property of the individual, there did emerge the notion of 'civil society' in ancient Roman thinking. Indeed, the notion of 'civil society' did need such an atmosphere to shape itself, but the ancient Roman thought could hardly rise above that, notwithstanding the attempts at making distinction between 'private' and 'public' which the ancient Romans really did.

During the whole medieval period in the West, when politics took the back seat, the idea of civil society got eclipsed. What related to 'public' as 'political' was limited to a very few people called the feudal lords, barons, dukes and counts. The idea of civil society was almost unknown.

### (b) *Civil Society: The Liberal-Individualist Tradition*

The early modern period with Machiavelli and Bodin saw the emergence of politics, but the period itself did not witness the corresponding growth of the idea of civil society. The civil society, as a concept, rose with the idea of individuals with rights, individuals related to the state, and individuals related to others in society.

There is the clear reference to civil society, both in Hobbes and Locke, when the two sought to make a distinction between the 'state of nature', and the 'civil society' or the 'political society' after the contract was made. Both talk about the rights-bearing individuals; both sought the state to protect these rights. It is difficult to regard the contractualists, Hobbes and Locke, as theorists of civil society, because (i) their formulations on civil society are found in an embryonic form and (ii) their attempts, despite a rational and persuasive explanation on state and society, remained arbitrary (see Chandhoke, *State and Civil Society*).

The concept of civil society has emerged clearly between the seventeenth and the nineteenth century, especially with the classical political economy theorists such as Adam Smith. Classical political economy, echoing individual rights like *laissez faire*, freedom, equality, made the institution of state as simply irrelevant, devaluing it, and that of civil society as what Marx had said 'theatre of history'. This helped "the civil society", Chandhoke writes, "as a historically evolved area of individual rights and freedoms, where individuals in competition with each other, pursued their respective private concern."

The advent of the idea of civil society, coming from the writings of political economy theorists, was to have its shape vis-a-vis the state. J.S. Mill and De Tocqueville, who thought that the state had become much more powerful than desired, sought to limit the power of the state through the mechanism devised in the ever developing concept of civil society. Chandhoke sums up this phase of liberalism, saying: "Civil society was used as a concept, primarily for organizing state-society relations. The expansion of the state, it was perceptively recognized, would contribute to the shrinkage of the civil arena. State power could be limited only with the expansion of civil society."

The process of democratisation in the West made it possible for civil society to expand itself, and in the process, restricted the area of the state. But elsewhere, the concept of the state gained prominence restricting thus, the arena of civil society. The views of Hegel, and therefore, of Marx and Gramsci should be of some interest.

(c) *Civil Society: The Hegelian, Marxian and Gramscian Traditions*

There is a definite relationship between the state and civil society in the writings of Hegel (1770-1831). He views the state as the latest link growing out of the development of various institutions. Describing the state as the synthesis, representing universality, of the thesis of families and the anti-thesis of civil society, Hegel recognises the state as higher in kind than civil society. Hegel regards the sate as the highest, the latest, and even the final form of social institutions. For him, civil society, as the anti-thesis of the thesis of family is "an expression for the individualist and atomistic atmosphere of middle class commercial society in which relationships are external, governed by the 'unseen' hand of the economic laws rather than by the self-conscious will of persons."

So, civil society, a negative institution as it is for Hegel, belongs to the "realm of mechanical necessity, a resultant of the irrational forces of individual desires," governed, as Sabine says for Hegel, "by non-moral casual laws and hence, ethically anarchical." The thesis (the family) and the anti-thesis (the civil, the bourgeois society) merge into what Hegel calls the state (the synthesis). Thus, the state comes to have the universality of civil society and the specificity and the individuality of the family.

Thus, while the political economy and the liberal-democratic theorists had given primacy to civil society, and had given the state a back seat, Hegel reverses the position and puts the state in the position of civil society. According to Hegel, ultimately civil society is subordinated to the state, and the individual, to the whole. "Consequently, in Hegelian formulation", Chandhoke says, "there can be no interrogation of the state, of its designs for universality, or of its rationale. The resolution of the contradiction of civil society is the state, and therefore, between the people and the state, there is no dichotomy, only legitimacy and acceptance."

Marx, unlike Hegel, who had made the civil society a hostage and who had idealised the state, seeks to restore the civil society to the position of making it the theatre of history. But, the civil society. Marx argues, has failed to live up to its promises, had failed to create a situation where the individual could find freedom and democratic transformation, had to seek ways and means through which individuals could integrate into the society and the state.

Gramsci (1891-1937) following Marx, while developing his theory of state takes into account the reality of civil society. His main proposition is that one cannot understand the state without understanding the civil society. He says that the 'state' should be understood as not only the apparatus of government, but also the 'private' apparatus of hegemony or civil society. Building on the Marxian notion of the state, Gramsci makes a distinction between the state as a political organisation (the integral state, the visible political constitution of civil society) and the state as government. The integral state keeps reproducing itself in the practices of everyday life, through activities situated in civil society. It is hegemony which provides moral and intellectual leadership to practices in civil society. Hegemony, for

Gramsci, works for both, for the dominant as well as the subaltern class in civil society. Each class must, Gramsci says, before seizing power, hegemonies social relations in society.

To sum up, it may be said that for both the liberals and the Marxists, civil society is primary. While the liberals argue for the separation of civil society from the autonomy of the state, the Marxists, on the other hand, create an alternative tradition of civil society, in which, the civil society, with its all potentialities, has to keep itself always reorganised and transformed.

## III. State: Meaning and Definitions

The concept of state occupies a central place in Political Science. No discussion on political theory is complete without reference to the word 'state'. The state, indeed, touches every aspect of human life, and this is why it has, very rightly, captured the attention of all political philosophers since the days of Plato. To understand the state, as an administrative machinery ordering public life, is to know its one aspect. Important though this aspect is, it is not the only aspect which explains as to what it is. The state is where it operates on.

The state, as a word *stato,* appeared in Italy in the early part of the sixteenth century in the writings of Machiavelli (1469-1527). The meaning of the state, in the sense of a body politic became common in England and France in the later part of the sixteenth century. The word *staatskunst* became the German equivalent of *ragione di stato* during the seventeenth century and a little later, the word *staatrecht* got the meaning of *jus publican* (see Sabine, "State", *The Encyclopaedia of the Social Sciences* Vol. XIV). Thus, came the use of the term 'State'.

The state has included, from the beginning, a reference to a land and a people, but this alone would not constitute a state. It refers also to a unity, a unity of legal and political authority, regulating the outstanding external relationships of man in society, existing within society. It is what it does, i.e., creates a system of order and control, and for this, is vested with the legal power of using compulsion and coercion.

A state, thus, is found in its elaborate system. It is found in its institutions which create laws and which enforce them, i.e., in institutions, such as, the legislature, the executive and the judiciary. It is found in the bureaucratic institutions which are attached to every executive branch of the government. It is found in the institutions which are called into operation when its will is challenged, i.e., the military and the police. The state is the sum—total of these institutions. Ralph Miliband (*The State in Capitalist Society*) writes, "These are the institutions—the government, the administration, the military and the police, the judicial branch, government and parliamentary assemblies—which make up the state...". In these institutions lies the state power; through these institutions come the laws of the state, and from them spring the legal right of using physical force.

The state as governance is a system related to what may be called the political system or the political society. It includes, on the one hand, institutions such as the political parties, pressure groups, the opposition, etc., and on the other, large-scale industrial houses, religious and caste institutions, trade unions, etc. These institutions, existing outside of the state system, attempt to influence the functioning of the state, somewhere even dominating it, and somewhere in collaboration with it. Skocpol (*States and Social Revolution: A Comparative Analysis of France, Russia and China*) sums up what Neera Chandhoke calls the statist perspective of the state, "the state properly conceived....is rather a set of administrative, policing and military organizations headed, and more or less well coordinated by, an executive authority. Any state first and fundamentally extracts resources from society and deploys these to create and support coercive and administrative organizations.... Moreover, coercive and administrative organizations are only parts of overall political systems. These systems also may contain institutions through which social interests are represented in state policy-making, as well as institutions, through which non-state actors are mobilised to participate in policy implementation. Nevertheless, the administrative and coercive organisations are the basis of state power."

The other strand giving the state a meaning comes from Michael Foucault ('Truth and Power' in P. Rabinow, ed., *The Foucault Reader,* 1987) who regards the state as built on power relations already existing in society. Chandhoke writes about Foucault, "The state, he (Foucault) concluded, can only operate on the basis of existing relations of domination and oppression in society."

Rejecting both the perspectives of the state, Chandhoke says, "The statistics (Skocpol and others) concentrate on the state at the expense of society, and the theorists in the Foucauldian mode concentrate on social interaction at the expense of the state." She concludes that the state, with a view to understanding it in relation to society, and vice-versa, "is a social relation because it is the codified power of the social formation."

## IV. The State: Its Characteristics

State exists within the society. This makes the state and society analytically distinct. The two are not the same. Society is a web of social relationships and as such, includes the totality of social practices, which are essentially plural, but at the same time, are relational. The hierarchically organised and maintained social practices of a given community establish, in their turn, all kinds of power equations and relations among its members. The state comes in to give these power relations a fixity, and thereby to society its stability. The state gives legitimacy to social relationships as expressed in social practices because it recognises them and codifies them through legal acts. It is, in this sense that the state can be described as the codified power of the social formation of a given time.

The state, so considered, is itself a distinct and discrete organisation of power in so far as it possesses the capacity to select, categorise, crystallise and arrange power in formal codes and institutions. And this capacity gives to the state its status—power, power to take decisions, power to enforce decisions, and also power to coerce those who defy them. But the state so considered derives its power from society. It is, in this sense, a codified power, but within the framework of the society in which it operates.

The state, as a social relation and also as a codified power in a given society, would have certain characteristics of its own. These characteristics can be stated as:

(a) The state is a power, organised in itself. It has the power to legitimise social relations and gives them recognition through formal codes and institutions. This gives the state a distinct and irreducible status in society while making it autonomous from classes and contending factions existing in it.

(b) The state emerges as a set of specifically political practices which defines binding decisions and enforces them, to the extent of intervening in every aspect of social life.
(c) The state monopolies all means of coercion. No other organisation in the society has this power.
(d) The state gives fixity to social relations, and social stability to society. The social order, according to Chandhoke, "is constituted through the state and exists within the parameters laid down by the state."
(e) The state exists within the framework of a given society. As society responds to the changing conditions compelled by numerous social forces, the state responds to the changing society. The state always reflects the changing relations of society. As society constantly re-enacts itself, so does the state.

## V. The State: Its Growth

The state, being at the very core of political theory, has been defined differently by different political philosophers since the time of the ancient Greek. For some, it is an institution of coercion, while for others, it is the custodian of the rights of the people. While some, like the anarchists, would like to abolish the state straight away, others like the socialists of the non-Marxian shade would want it to stay to establish socialism.

Despite the fact that the state has meant different things to different people, one cannot ignore the central place the state has in political theory. One would do better, if one attempts to discuss the meaning of the state vis-a-vis society which has come to us by a host of western political philosophers.

### (a) *The State: The Pre-modern Tradition*

In all his works on political theory, there is a strong case which Plato (428/7-348/7 BC) builds in favour of an omnicompetent rule. The problem to which Plato addressed himself was not as to how best a government could be created, but as to how the best government could be installed. It is the job of the government, Plato affirmed more than once, to help people live a complete life. It is, thus, with Plato a matter of just not a government, but a just government, just not a government any how, but a perfect government, the government that was able to deliver happiness for all who lived therein. For Plato, a state is a system of relationships, in which everyone does his own business and where the job of the state is to maintain, and promote such relationships.

Following his teacher Plato, Aristotle (384-322 BC) defined the state as *polis* (the ancient Greeks used polis for the state) as a community, which exists for the supreme good. He says that the state is "an association of households and villages sharing a life of virtue, and aiming at an end which exists in perfect and self-complete existence."

Both Plato and Aristotle, and for that matter all Greeks, thought of polis as more than a state. It was an arrangement of administrative machinery, a government or a constitution, but was also a school, a church laying the guidelines for a way of life, which for them, was nothing but leading a full life. For Plato and Aristotle, there was no distinction between the state and society;: the state was an organ and a part of the society; it was submerged in the society itself. In addition, the Greeks thought of the polis as an ethical entity and that was why they assigned, ethical functions to be performed by the rulers of the state, i.e., good, happy and complete life. Barker writes, "It (the polis) is more than a legal structure: it is also a moral spirit." An ancient Greek would never imagine himself without the polis, he was only a part of the polis, a part of the whole. Barker says, "Here (in ancient Greece) were individuals, distinct from the state, yet in their communion forming the state." Wayper also says "For life to be worth living must have a meaning, and only in the polis they (the Greeks) were sure, did it acquire meaning. There was no distinction between political, social and ethical life in ancient Greece. The society was the state as the state was with Plato and Aristotle, a government: the freeman, the master was a citizen, a legislator and a member of the society; he as the ruler ruled the individual as a member of the society, all the individuals, the whole society. The slave-owing society of ancient Greek times could hardly be expected to give a theory of state, nay a theory of society, more than that of the government, precisely, the rulers."

To Cicero's writings would go the credit of giving a notion of the state which is not a polis, but a commonwealth. Like the ancient Greeks, Cicero also regards the state submerged in the society, a part, i.e., an integral part of the society. Cicero says, "The commonwealth, then, is the people's affairs, and the people is not every group of men, associated in any manner, but is the coming together of a considerable number of men who are united by a common agreement about law and rights, and by the desire to participate in mutual advantages." From this, Cicero's theory of state can be summed up as: (i) the state is differentiated from people's gatherings, i.e., society (ii) the people enter the state after they agree on certain rules, giving people a 'legal' status, which lead them to form 'legal community (iii) the state exists when people agree to participate in its affairs. In Cicero's theory, there is a theory of state different from the theory of society; he makes a distinction between the state and the society; his theory of state is the theory of government as well as a theory of political community.

The medieval political theory in the West was mainly concerned with Christianity where social life was more a religious life regulated by the dictates of the Roman Catholic Church headed by the Pope. Christendom ruled the universe and politics was controlled by the Church. The temporal power was regarded inferior to that of the ecclesiastical, the state acting as a footnote to the wider world. The state, in the medieval European world, was thought of as a means for reaching the *City of God* (St. Augustine), and the human law was to work under the divine law, natural law and ultimately, under the eternal law (St. Thomas). It was not the society that controlled the state, but those who controlled the society—the Pope, the Church priests, the monarchs and the feudal lords—who controlled the state i.e., the state machinery.

### (b) *The State: The Liberal-Individualist Tradition*

With the modern age ushering in the Western World during the fifteenth-sixteenth centuries, there appeared a definite theory of state. The liberal-individualist philosophers, with Hobbes (1588-1679) onward, came to make a clear distinction between the state and society by making the state a matter of mere governance. All liberals, basing their political theory on individuals, came to build political power, the state, as an instrument, some like Hobbes giving all powers to the state while Bentham (1748-1832) making it a non-interventionist one. All liberals argue for an autonomous individual, the degree for individual autonomy differing from philosopher to philosopher. The liberals' laurels included "individual liberties, rights as sacred as natural, property ethos, rule of law, free, competitive and market economy... all to remain free from the interference of the state. The early modern political theory could not make distinction between state, and government,.... All regarded state power as political power, and political power as the power of the government."

The Machiavellian state (credit goes to Machiavelli for introducing the word 'state' in Political Science), whether princedom or republic, is a power state, meaning thereby that it exists for power and exists because of the power, whose main interest is to maintain, enhance and enlarge its own authority. For Bodin (1530-1596), the state is "a lawful government, with sovereign powers, of different households, and their common affairs," considering the state affairs as concerning the 'public'. "The final cause, end, or design of men," Hobbes says, "is the foresight of their own preservation, and of a more contented life."

With Locke (1632-1704), the liberal theory gets impetus and the state comes to protect property, and promote a better economic life, for liberalism comes to stay as the political philosophy of the capitalist class, the democratic flavour joining it at a later stage of development. The early liberal-democratic theory restricted the role of the state to the minimal, protecting life, liberty and property of its citizens from external aggression and internal chaos on the one hand, and providing a system of justice and public works, and amenities on the other hand, with no role for the welfare of the people.

It was John Stuart Mill (1806-1873) first, and T.H. Green (1836-1882) later, who expanded the positive role of the state in preparing a conducive atmosphere where the individual could enjoy a better way of life. Mill and Green introduced democratic elements in the organisation and functioning of the state, though both could hardly leave their capitalistic shackles.

To sum up, one may therefore, conclude that the early modern political theorists such as Machiavelli and Bodin could hardly see beyond the omnipotent state. The contractualists, especially Hobbes, had thought that in order for society to come into existence, a strong state is required. The early liberals such as Locke, Smith, Bentham held the view that as the society has the capacity to reproduce and regenerate itself, the state and its power should be minimal. But the later liberals, J.S. Mill, T.H. Green, De Tocqueville felt that numerous social associations, while enhancing social ability, could become instruments through which individuals could fashion a political discourse which could limit the nature of state power. The liberal pluralists, in the third and fourth decades of the twentieth century were able to build a strong case for the numerous associations, existing in society, to control the omnipotence of the state while balancing the latter against the claims of the society.

(c) *The State: The Marxian tradition*

The Marxian theory of the state emerged, as a reaction against liberalism. For the Marxists, state and society are two distinct entities, though the state is not independent of society. The society type explains the type of state, society providing the base on which stood the superstructure. The Marxists, regarding the state as a product of a class society, believe the state to be a class institution, protecting and promoting the possessing class, and oppressing and coercing the non-possessing class. For them, the state is an engine of class rule. But, it is also an instrument of social and political change, its negative function is to destroy the remains of the earlier society, while it, through its constructive functions, builds the structure and culture of the class it is manned with.

Chandhoke discerns three theoretical moments of the Marxist theory of state. The first such moment has been when Marx and Engels, in the *Manifesto of the Communist Party* (1848) regard "the executive of the modern state" as "a committee for managing the common affairs of the whole bourgeoisie." Marx also writes in the preface to *Towards a Critique of Political Economy* (1859), "the totality of these relations of production constitutes the economic structure of society, the real foundation, on which arises a legal and political superstructure and to which correspond definite forms of social consciousness." This base-superstructure model of the state was a reaction to the liberal concept of the disembodied state standing apart from society, as also a reaction against the Hegelian model of the all-powerful state, while subordinating civil society to it. The second moment, appearing around the 1960s and with Ralph Miliband and Hanza Alvi, questions the nature of the state and its relationship with society. In it, the state emerges as a distinct theoretical object in its own right and state-centric theory emerged as the dominant stream of political theory. The third theoretical moment was made possible through the contributions of Nicos Poulantzas and Claus Off. This moment saw political theorists preoccupied with concepts and theories. Following Gramsci, who had conceptualised the state as the political consideration of civil society, the Marxist political theorists of the third theoretical moment began a spiralling interest in civil society as the sphere where meaningful practices, both hegemonic and subversive, are generalised.

## VI. State and Civil Society: Their Relationship

The relationship between state and civil society is important in so far as it suggests the comparative position of each in relation to the other. In some analyses, this relationship is depicted as a zero-sum game: the stronger the state, the weaker the civil society; the weaker the state, the stronger the civil society. Obviously, the expansion of the area of state activity would help minimise the role of civil society; the expansion of the area of civil society would help, on the other hand, minimise the role of the state. In modern liberal societies of our time, the civil society 'sphere' is larger than that of the state, while in dictatorial regimes of any sort, the state's 'sphere' is larger than that of civil society.

### (a) *State and Civil Society: Integrative Relationship*

State and civil society are not two opposite concepts. One does not stand in conflict with another. Neither is one the anti-thesis of the other. The two should not be regarded as usurping the area of each other. It is not a zero-sum game relationship between the two. Indeed, the relatively stronger state would put a premium on the role of civil society, but this, in no way, diminishes the effectiveness of civil society. The libertarian view, expressed in the writings of Hayek or Nozick, that the state is likely to oppress civil society is, more or less, ill-founded. The fact of the matter is that the relationships between state and civil society are reciprocal; the relationships are of an integrative nature, each strengthening the cause of the other. It is, infact, difficult to conceive of civil society functioning successfully without the state. We see the citizen simultaneously constrained by the state and protected by it. It is the state which provides the integrative framework within which the civil society operates; civil society cannot function properly without the state. The integrative framework, as expressed in laws and rules, is accepted as valid by all, the framework needs to be administered neutrally and in a manner consistent with the shared culture of society. We cannot imagine life without this integrative framework, which creates a degree of coherence and without which civil society is likely to become uncivil. Civil society has to open up, in the face of the all-powerful state, to challenge the bureaucratic devices lest it ends up in rigidity. It is, thus, the reciprocity between state and civil society that is significant or at least, should be considered significant. State power is to be exercised within the larger and wider sphere of civil society, and civil society has to keep state power on its toes so that it does not degenerate into absolutism.

(b) *State, Civil Society and Democracy*

The two concepts, state and civil society, are not in conflict with each other. Democracy integrates the two. The claims of the state get strengthened by civil society and civil society is made more stable through the state. The two have to work in a democratic frame: the democratic state within the framework of democratic civil society. In a democratic system, state and civil society can collaborate for effective functioning of each. The state has to be constituted democratically, wherein its powers are decentralised and its functions are performed within the rules and procedures already laid. Such a state has to respond to the ever-growing demands of civil society. Its role, more or less, is to coordinate, it has to interfere least in the social and economic life of the people; it has to be regulative in character.

Civil society has to be more open and diversified. It has to keep the dialogue continuous and constant with the state and within all the constituents making it. Its area has to be ordained freely and openly, devices making up public opinion and public discourse state-free.

In liberal-democratic state, there is a constant interplay of forces belonging to the state and civil society, each putting an imprint on the other. In dictatorial regimes, state power is used to control civil society and civil society gets integrated into the state: the state speaks for the civil society. Democracy alone unites the state with civil society. The state cannot exist for long if it is not democracy-laden; civil society cannot exist unless it is democratically structured and functions democratically.

A democratic state cannot exist if it is restrictive, coercive, prohibitive, and imposing; it cannot exist if it does not provide the civil society frame in perfect order; it cannot exist if it does not guarantee rights and freedoms to individuals. Likewise, a democratic civil society cannot exist if it does not allow every individual to act in the public sphere, it cannot exist if each and every citizen does not have equal claim on the state, if each citizen is not respected as a human being.

## SUGGESTED READINGS


1. Cohen, J.L., Arato, A., *Civil Society and Political Theory* (Cambridge, MIT Press, 1992).
2. Hall, J.A., "In Search of Civil Society" in Hall, J.A., (ed.) *Civil Society: Theory, History, Comparison* (Cambridge, Polity Press, 1995)
3. Issac, J., "Civil Society and the Spirit of Revolt", *Dissent* 29 (1), 1993.
4. Kaplan, A., *The Conduct of Inquiry: Methodology for Behavioural Science* (San Francisco: Chandler, 1964).
5. Kasfir, N., "Civil Society, the State and Democracy in Africa", *Journal of Commonwealth and Comparative Politics*, 36(2), 1998.
6. Kubba, L., "Arabs and Democracy: The Awakening of Civil Society", *Journal of Democracy* 11(3), 2000).
7. Pearce, J., "Development, NGOs, and Civil Society: The Debate and its Future", in Pearce, J., ed. *Development, NGOs, and Civil Society* (Oxford: Oxfam GB, 200).
8. Sen, Amartya, (1991). *Development as Freedom* (New York: Anchor Books, 1999).
9. Shils, E., "The Virtue of Civil Society", *Government and Opposition* 26(2), 1991).
10. Swift, J. (1999), *Civil Society in Question* (Toronto: Between the Lines, 1991).
11. Van Rooy, A., (2002). "Strengthening Civil Society in Developing Countries", in Desai, V., Potter, R.B., eds. *The Companion to Development Studies* (London: Arnold, 2002).
12. White, G., "Civil Society, Democratization and Development (I): Clearing the Analytical Ground", *Democratization* 1(3), 1994).

# CHAPTER – 13

# Aristotle on Citizenship

### I (a). Aristotle: The Man, His Times and His Works

Aristotle (384-322 B.C.) was born at Stagira, then a small Greek colony close to the borders of the Macedonian kingdom. His father, Nicomachus, was a physician at the court of Amyntas II. A longer part of his boyhood was spent at Pella, the royal seat of Macedonia. Because of his descent from a medical family, it can be well-imagined that Aristotle must have developed his, interest in physical sciences, biology particularly. Consequent upon the death of his parents, Aristotle's care fell upon a relative, Proxenus, whose son, Nicanor, Aristotle later adopted.

Although not an Athenian, Aristotle lived in Athens for more than half of his life, first as a student at Plato's *Academy* for nearly twenty years (367-347 B.C.), and later as the master of his own institution, the *Lyceum* for about twelve years (335-323 B.C.). He died a year later in Chalcis (the place to which his mother, Phaestis, belonged), while in exile, following fear of being executed for his pro-Macedonian sympathies by the anti-Macedonian party of Athens. During the intervening period of twelve years (347-335 B.C.) he remained away from Athens, his 'journeyman' period. Between 347-344 B.C. he stayed at Assus with one Hermias, a tyrant and an ex-slave but a friend of the Macedonian king, Philip. He married Hermias's niece and adopted daughter, Pythias. A little later, in 342 B.C., because of the good offices of Hermias, Aristotle became tutor to Alexander, prince of Macedonia, later Alexander the Great. He left Alexander when the latter assumed throne on his father's assassination in 336 B.C. Aristotle was now back in Athens for establishing his *Lyceum*. One may ask as to why Aristotle chose Athens as the seat for his *Lyceum*? He was not an Athenian and thus could not even purchase a piece of land there for his school. He was not selected to head the *Academy* after Plato's death in 347 B.C., the position he had expected as a reward for his long association of twenty years with Plato. A Platonic as Aristotle was known then, he was bound to receive severe opposition from erstwhile opponents of Plato, the Isocrateans especially. Inspite of all these, Athens was Aristotle's first choice where he could, he possibly thought, show his worth. Athens was then more than a city: it was a culture in itself. It was then more than one stock: it was a thought incarnate. Speaking about Athens of Aristotle's times, Barker writes, 'Mistress of the seas, she (Athjns) was also the trade-centre and the money-market of Greece, where Aristotle could study the problems of maritime trade, money and interest; but above all she was the general culture-centre of Greek-speaking world—the home of Greek drama; the home of the standard speech which was becoming common to all educated Greeks; the home of the book trade for all Greece; and above all, the home of a nascent university frequented by the Greek world. If, as the orator Isocrates said, "Hellas had become a culture," Athens was the heart of Hellas.

Like his teacher Plato, Aristotle had also kept on his association with men of ruling classes. He had seen his teacher involved in Syracusean affairs, so when he came out of the *Academy* in 347 B.C., he remained close to Hermias of Atar-neus (347-344 B.C.), Alexander of Macedonia (342-336 B.C. and long thereafter until Alexander's death in 323 B.C.) and Antipater, Alexander's regent when he was away from Macedonia on his Asian expedition. Such an association with the rulers helped Aristotle's penetrating eyes to see the public affairs governed more closely, although he could not exert much of his influence either on them or on their policies. In his relations with them, Aristotle, in fact, was mostly on the receiving end. From Hermias, he came to value the nature of one-man rule, learn something of general economics and the importance of foreign relations and of foreign policy—some references of these are found in Aristotle's *Politics.* From Alexander, he got all possible help that could improve upon his collections (Alexander is said to have utilised 800 talents in Aristotle's service and injuncted all hunters, fowlers and fishermen to report to Aristotle any matter of scientific interest). From Antipater came in Aristotle's advocacy of moderate polity and of the propertied middle class—something that he advocated in *Politics* while sketching the best practicable state. From Lycurgus, Athenian statesman during 338-326 B.C., a Platonic himself and therefore

Aristotle's mate and friend, he learnt a host of reforms which he made a part of the ideal state in his *Politics.* But this is not to say that the *Politics* of Aristotle is the result of these royal influences only. Aristotle, indeed, had his own too: his family background of looking at every thing scientifically, his Platonic impact gathered over a long period of twenty years, his keen observation on political events of the various city-states and his elaborate studies at the *Lyceum* through lectures and discussions—all these combined made Aristotle author of encyclopaedic writings. Aristotle's writings cover a variety of disciplines, almost all except mathematics. It is not certain as to when a particular work was written. W.D. Ross presumes that Aristotle's writings appeared in the order of his progressive withdrawal from Plato's influence. This is how one notes Aristotle's writings, in his period of the membership of Plato's *Academy,* on the Platonic model. The dialogues, especially *on Rhetoric* (also the *Grylus*), *On the Soul* (also the *Eudemus*), the *Protre-pticus, On Philosophy,* were those which Aristotle wrote while he was in the *Academy.* He is believed to have written the dialogues like *Alexander* and *On Monarchy* during the time or later when Alexander assumed power. To the period between 347 and 335, belong Aristotle's the *Organon,* the *Physics,* the *De Cacelo,* a part of the *De Anima* and of the *Metaphysics,* the *Eudemian Ethics* and a greater part of the *Politics*—all these are largely Platonic in character but not in the forms of dialogues. To the period of his headship of the *Lyceum* belong the rest of his works either written wholly or those to which he gave completion, notably the *Meteorologica,* the works on psychology and biology, the *Constitutions,* the *Nicomachean Ethics,* the *Poetics,* the *Rhetoric.*

Aristotle's political theory is found mainly in the *Politics,* although there are references of his political thought in the *Nicomachean Ethics.* The *Constitutions* of Aristotle analyses the system of government on this basis of his study of some 158 constitutions, notable among them is the *Constitution of Athens.* Aristotle's *Politics,* like any other work of his, has come down to the future generations in the form of lecture notes and consists of several essays, written at various times, about which the writers have no unanimity. Barker puts the order of the eight books of *Politics* on the basis of internal development of Aristotle's ideas; the first three books deal with the beginning of preliminary principles and criticism, the fourth and fifth books (traditionally arranged as the seventh and eighth books) deal with the construction of an ideal state evolved on the principles and criticism of the first three books and lastly, the last three books, i.e. sixth to eighth (traditionally, fourth to sixth) deal with the analysis of the actual states, the provision of the best possible state and the causes and cures of revolutions.

## I (b). Aristotle: His Theory of Citizenship

In his *Politics,* Aristotle discusses his theory of citizenship in Book III where he also dwells on other related topics such as the classification of states and constitutions. His views on citizenship are not only basic, they are, to some extent, important of students of Political Theory. That is what makes Book III, the central book of *Politics,* thematically atleast.

In this book, Aristotle lays out almost all of his major ideas about the purpose of politics, the virtue of citizens, the varieties of regimes and the nature of justices.

In the first five chapters of Book III, Aristotle discusses his views on citizenship, citizens, their virtues and the related questions. We give below the summary of these chapters.

### *Chapter 1*

The first matter of investigation is the definition of citizenship. Different regimes define citizenship in different ways. Some are citizens only in a qualified sense. (like children who are not old enough to participate in the affairs of the city or elders who have been relieved of their civic duties). In an unqualified sense, the citizen is one who shares in holding office and making decisions. This type of citizen in the unqualified sense really only exists in a democracy. In general, one can say that whoever is entitled to participate in an office (even if he actually does not do so) is a citizen.

### *Chapter 2*

Commonly speaking, however, a citizen is usually defined as a person whose parents are both citizens. There can be difficulty in this definition, however, as regards those who came to be citizens after a revolution. There is a question of whether such people are citizens justly or unjustly.

*Chapter 3*

The question is often raised regarding when a city as a whole actually performed action, particularly when it is a question of whether the city has a duty to fulfill public agreements after a change of regime. The deeper issue at stake in this question is what it means for a city to change. One possible criteria to look at is location, but that is rather superficial. A more serious consideration is whether a city remains the same even though its inhabitants change through birth and death. The answer is that one can only really decide whether the city is the same by looking at the regime. As long as the regime stays the same, the city is bound to uphold its commitments.

*Chapter 4*

A connected matter is the examination of the virtue of a good man in comparison with that of a good citizen. A citizen is somewhat like a sailor, one among a number of partners on a ship, each with different tasks and functions. Although each has a specific virtue according to his capacity and duty on the ship, there is also a general virtue similar to them all, which is the preservation of the ship. In a similar way, the virtue of the citizen is with a view to the regime. It is possible, therefore, for a person to be an excellent citizen yet not an excellent man. Will the virtue of the citizen ever be the same as the virtue of a human being? The virtue of a citizen is the capacity to rule and to be ruled. The virtue of an excellent man would be simply the capacity to rule, not to be ruled. However, there are different types of rule. There is the rule which is proper to a slave, but there is also the type of rule over those who are "similar in stock and free." This is political rule, which can be learned only by being ruled. Therefore, the good citizen will need to know both how to rule and to be ruled. The good person must have this same capacity as well. The only virtue, peculiar to a ruler is prudence, while all other virtues are common for both rulers and ruled.

*Chapter 5*

Are only those, who may participate in public office true citizens? If a person who is not eligible for office is considered a citizen, then the virtue of a citizen will have to vary depending on the person's status in society. There are several kinds of citizens, corresponding to the different types of regimes. In a democratic regime, laborers must be citizens, while in aristocratic regime citizenship is granted only in accordance with virtue and merit. In an oligarchy, on those, who are wealthy are citizens. In one type of city the virtue of the excellent man and the excellent citizen is the same, but in another it is not.

The above description clearly indicates that there are citizens in the qualified sense in so far as they participate in the affairs of the city, and those who do not (such as children, woman, slaves, those relieved of duties of participation) are not citizens. Furthermore, there are citizens in the unqualified sense in so far as they share public office and make decision. The above description also indicates that citizenship is not merely a legal status, or a formal symbol; it is also a function; it implies that those, having citizenship, are required to perform certain obligations and by virtue of those obligations, enjoy certain political facilities, say rights. Those who participate in politics, they can do so, Aristotle would say, if they have a share in the city's decision-making. Citizenship is not merely participation in politics or share in law-making and decision-making, it is also, additionally, preserving the city.

For Aristotle, everyone who resides in the city or polis is not a citizen. It is so because everyone does not participate in affairs of the city: women, children, slaves, aliens, diplomats are not citizens. Even all elders in the family are also not citizens, for the virtues of citizenship are possessed only by those who own capabilities of participation in law-making and also in decision-making.

So to sum up, we may say that for Aristotle:

(i) Citizen is one who has the virtues of (a) ruling, and (b) being ruled. Citizenship is participation in managing public affairs;

(ii) Citizen should have the virtue of participation in decision-making. Citizenship also means performing the job of a judge (in addition to be a legislator).

(iii) Citizen should possess the knowledge, interest and power to take decision in matters relating to politics; and

(iv) Citizen should have leisure and time to think discuss and debate in issues of public concern.

At the heart of Aristotle's views on citizenship is the idea of participation in public affairs. It is participation that legitimates decision-making; it is participation that is the key requirement of active citizenship for Aristotle. Charles Pattie, Patrick Seyd and Paual Whitely sum up Aristotle's argument: "This system required that participants should be peers or roughly equal in status, something achieved by narrowly prescribing who was and who was not a citizen. For Aristotle, the citizen had to be a male of known genealogy, a patriarch, a warrior and a property owner, where this was defined in terms of owning slaves and controlling a household. His formulation depended on a rigid distinction between the public realm, the *polis*, and the private realm, the *oikos*. Women and slaves were part of the latter and controlled exclusively by the individual householder. The *polis* was the domain of public affairs determined by active citizens and participation was regarded as a good in itself. Thus, citizens participated not merely to solve the common problems of the city state, but because such participation was an essential component of the good life." Ralph Harington too says the same thing: "Citizenship is," for Aristotle, "nothing less than the fullest fulfillment of human potential in terms of the 'good life'. In this respect, as throughout Aristotle's politics, the essence of citizenship lies in active participation. The citizen is not merely an inhabitant of the state, nor simply a member of a politically privileged class; he is the essence of the state's ability to achieve the greatest measure of happiness and virtue as a community. For this, the citizen must have the leisure to devote himself to the educative cultural pursuits which facilitate his understanding of virtue. For this reason, Aristotle is clear that 'the citizens must not live in mechanical or commercial life. Such a life is not noble, and it militates against virtue.'

Aristotle's views on citizenship and citizens, valuable as they are, emphasise on active participation in the public affairs by citizens, the virtues they should possess, the duties they should perform and the rights they should enjoy. The citizen is a law-maker, a judge, a participant in the activities of the city/state, a public servant of the city and the lover of the city; he is a member. And yet, it may rightly be said that Aristotle's views on citizenship and citizens are subject to criticism.

(a) Everyone, is Aristotle's views, is not a citizen, for everyone does not possess virtues of citizenship, which, in Aristotle's days, was both a right and a responsibility. Citizenship was a limited phenomenon, for it was denied to women, the young, the slaves, the servants, and the immigrants.

(b) Aristotle's citizen is a male member of the polis, though every male is also not a citizen; his citizen is a free man, though everyone who lives in the polis is not a free man; his citizen is one who owns property: the slaves are not citizens because they themselves constitute a property.

(c) Active participation, being a characteristic of citizenship in Aristotle's scheme of things, makes Aristotle's politics a phenomenon of direct democracy. Direct democracy, in our times, is not only impracticable, it is not even desirable.

(d) Aristotle's citizens are few and not many; a minority and excludes, thus, a multitude of people from being called citizens. To that extent, his views of citizens is against the principle of equality: including few and excluding many; few citizens, and many non-citizens.

(e) Having bestowed citizenship on those who own property, Aristotle appears to be advocating plutocracy; having bestowed citizenship only on male members of the city, he appears to be a non-feminist; having bestowed citizenship on freeman, the masters, he excludes the vast majority of slaves from citizenship and what is more and this is important, he justifies slavery, and to that extent, he becomes a great advocate of inequality.

## SUGGESTED READINGS

1. Barnes, Jonathan, *Aristotle* (Oxford: Oxford University Press, 1982).
2. Davis, Michael, *The Politics of Philosophy: A Commentary on Aristotle's Politics* (Lanham, MD: Roman and Littlefield, 1996).
3. Evan, J.D.G., *Aristotle* (Brighton: Harvester, 1987).
4. Huxley, G., 'On Aristotle's best state', *History of Political Thought,* Vol. VI, No. 1 (1985), pp. 139-49.
5. Johnson, Curtis, N., 'Aristotle's polity: mixed or middle constitution?', *History of Political Though,* Vol. IX, No. 2 (1988), pp. 189-204.
6. Johnson, Curtis, N., *Aristotle's Theory of the State* (Basingstoke: Macmillan, 1990).

7. Keyt, David and Miller, Fred D. Jr., *A Companion to Aristotle's 'Politics'* (Oxford: Blackwell, 1991).
8. Lord, Carnes, *Education and Culture in the Political Thought of Aristotle* (Ithaca, NY: Cornell University Press, 1982).
9. Mulgan, Richard G., *Aristotle's Political Theory* (Oxford: Oxford University Press, 1977).
10. Rosen, F., The political context of Aristotle's categories of justice', *Phronesis*, Vol. XX (1975), pp. 228-40.

## CHAPTER – 14

# Locke on Rights and Property

### I (a). Locke: The Man, His Times and His Works

Born at Wrington, Locke (1632-1704) was the son of a Somerset attorney, the grandson of a clothier. Locke's father had participated in the English civil war as a captain on parliament's side. Born in a storm, Locke, in fact, lived, all through, in the storm. He started his education at home and at the age of 20, he entered Christ Church College, Oxford, then managed by the fanatical and intolerant left wing of the Puritans. He did his B.A. in 1656 and M.A. in 1658 and then worked at Oxford as Philosophy tutor; his association with Oxford lasting upto 1684. His interest in sciences, particularly in medicines, was well known at Oxford. In 1666, he was introduced to Lord Ashley, later as Earl of Shaftesbury, on whom he conducted a successful operation. This brought Locke close to Lord Ashley, the founder of the Whig group and he became Lord Ashley's personal physician and his confidential secretary. From this time onward, for about fifteen years, Locke's fortune fluctuated with that of Lord Ashley. When Lord Ashley had gained the king's favour, Locke used to hold charge of important offices as he really did till about the year 1673 when he acted as Secretary of Presentations, and Secretary of the Council of Trade and Planations. In 1673, Lord Ashley lost the king's favour, so Locke also went out of public office. During the period between 1673 and 1679, Locke spent most of his time in France presumably for purposes of rest and treatment. In 1679, Charles II brought Lord Ashley back to public life, so it was time for Locke to resume office—all this till 1681, when Lord Ashley again got into trouble. Locke, fearing his arrest, this time took refuge in Holland, in 1683. There, in Holland, Locke became acquainted with William III who was to occupy the English throne in 1689. With William III as the king and with Lord Somers as Lord Ashley's successor whose friendship Locke prized too much, he was able to command respect under the new regime after the 1688 revolution. He became Commissioner of Appeals and in 1696 Commissioner of Trade and Plantations. In 1700, he resigned and thereafter, did not appear in public life. Locke's death came in 1704, and as Lady Masham, Locke's friend says, 'His death was like his life, truly pious, yet natural, easy and unaffected; nor can time, I think, ever produce a more eminent example of reason and religion than he was, living and dying.

Locke's writings were numerous. Mention may be made to *A Letter on Toleration* (1689), *Two Treatises of Government* (1690), *A Second Letter on Toleration* (1690), *Essay Concerning Human Understanding* (1690), *A Third Letter on Toleration* (1692), *Some Thoughts Concerning Education* (1693) and *The Reasonableness of Christianity* (1695).

Though Locke lived in England at almost the same period of history when did Thomas Hobbes (1588-1679), yet the two had different perception about the times they were in England. Hobbes was a great sympathiser of the royalists, in fact, he was a tutor of the Stuart child; Locke was a sympathiser of the Parliament which sought a share in the powers. Hobbes stood for the absolute powers of the kings, while Locke argued for the rights of the individual. In their mental attitudes, they were poles apart, Hobbes as rigid in arguments as robust in health while Locke as liberal in thoughts as feeble in body. In their philosophical messages, both stood for entirely different teachings, Hobbes built the case for a strong Leviathan and Locke, for a limited government.

A glance at the English history of that period shows that when Hobbes lived, and thought, the crises was still on. There was no final victory of either the king or the Parliament. In fact, the civil war was in its continuing state. Hobbes looked at this problem as a problem of division of power and he was against this division. As he said, "For these (powers) are incommunicable, and inseparable.... But if he (the sovereign) transferred the *Militia*, he retains the Judicature in vain for want of execution of the Lawes; or if he grant away the Power of raising Mony, the *Militia* is in vain.... And so if we consider any one of the said Rights, we shall presently see, that the holding of all the rest, will produce no effect, in the conservation of Peace and Justice,...". Hence Hobbes wanted the powers of the government not to be divided and not to be vested in two or more than two hands or bodies.

He would be happy if these were exercised by one, the monarch or by many, Cromwell's men. That was precisely Hobbes's problem—the problem of the division of powers. That was precisely his solution to the English civil war—the solution of entrusting sovereignty to either the king or the parliament. Locke's times were different. Locke had lived to see the fleeing of James II, the 1688 revolution, the final victory of the parliament, the incarnation of William III and the signing of the Bill of Rights (1689). His own commitments with the parliament were a matter of no secret. His passion for individual, his rights, and his autonomy was no secret. He was, thus, to defend and justify the revolution that parliament had so successfully engineered. He did this by explaining the nature and justification of political power. This is why he comes to build a theory of state which limits more than it enhances the powers of the state. To put it more crudely Locke's points: it is that the powers be limited because there are limited functions for which politics exists.

### I (b). Locke on Rights and Property

John Locke, as a forerunner of liberal theory, was a great advocate of individual, his rights, his liberties and his autonomy, and thus, in the process, made out a case for a state that is limited not only in functions, limited also in powers. His individual is an end in himself while the state serves as a means for the end, for the individual's welfare. The state, for Locke, exists for the protection and preservation of individual's rights. His views on rights and property may be stated as under:

(i) *Rights: Nature:* Rights are the domains of all human beings, because only the humans have rights. Natural rights, Locke affirms, stem from the fact that a person exists: if a person does not exist, he does not possess rights; the human existence ensures the existence of rights for the human beings. In his *An Essay Concerning Humane Understanding* and *Two Treatises of Government,* Locke argues that natural law and natural rights are inherent to man's being, while the statists, such as Hobbes, reject the idea of in born human rights. Rights only reside in the individual. Since each individual is a single human being, and separate from all others, he, as with everyone else, retains, like all other human beings, natural rights. Locke seems saying, "Either natural rights exist in each person or they exist in none."

Because society, community, state or government are not human beings, none of these have natural rights. Rights exist with individual and remain with him. As the rights remain with individual and can not be taken from him, they are inalienable. No power, Locke insists, can take them away from the individual, not the government or the state which the individuals agree to form. The state, Locke says, exists to preserve and protect the individuals's rights, which rights already exist with individuals as human beings. The state preserves, protects, maintains and guarantees rights. The individual has the right to seek protection of his rights from the state. He even has the power to overthrow the state which does not maintain or protect his rights.

To sum up, we may explain Locke's views on the nature of rights as such:

1. Only human beings possess rights by virtue of their being human beings; humans alone have rights.
2. Rights are with human beings; they remain with human beings.
3. Rights are the domains of human beings; what does not constitute human existence has no rights: Family has no rights, but the individuals in the family have rights; the state or the civil society as organisations of human beings have no rights, but the individuals in the state or the civil society have rights.
4. Rights are only individual's, guaranteed only to the individual. The state does not grant rights, it only maintains them.
5. Rights are exclusively individual's. Accordingly, they are inalienable; they can not be taken away from the individual, not even by the state which maintains them or by the society which prepares ground for them.

(ii) *Rights: Description:* Locke is convinced that individual lives, and lives by reason. To survive by reason, Locke continues, the individual must be free from the initiation of force. Society, indeed, benefits, and is beneficial to the individual became it provides him protection, division of labour and other related things. It is beneficial to that extent also from where the individual is still free to act and survive according to his own reason. Being required by man's rational nature, rights are not arbitrary or negotiable; they are absolute in the sense that they are absolute requirements for life within a society. In this background, we may state rights which Locke relates to the individuals.

1. **Right to Life**

The right to life is the fundamental right, of which all other rights are corollaries. The right to life states that you own your own body. It is your property to do with as you please. No one may force you to do anything, no one may injure you in any way, and above all, no one may take your life (without consent).

It should be noted that rights are guarantees to freedom of actions. They do not provide for anything but freedom of action. There is no right to food, for example; only the right to work and keep the proceeds with which you may buy food.

2. **Right to Liberty**

The right to liberty is a part of the right to life, specifically referring to your freedom of action. You may do what you want, when you want, provided you don't trample on the rights of anyone else. This is a necessity for man's life, because man's means of survival is reason. Survival by reason requires that you are able to act upon your reason, otherwise, your reason is of no avail. You can only act on your reason if you are free from the coercion of others.

3. **Right to Equality**

The right to equality is also a part of rights to life, especially when all human beings, as human beings, are regarded equal. The idea is to emphasise on the fact that the individual, are born free and born equal.

4. **Right to Property**

Property rights are an extension to the right to life. In order to support yourself through reason and stay alive, you must be able to own and use the product of your labour. If the tools of your survival are subject to random confiscation, then your life is subject to random destruction.

Locke's views on the description of rights as the possession of individuals as human beings indicate that as human beings, individuals have, as Locke himself says, a right to their preservation, which right no one can take away from the individuals.

**Right to Property: Locke's Theory: Analysed and Evaluated**

Among the natural rights referred to by Locke, right to property is an important one, in so far as it is the essence of his theory of rights. Property, for Locke, in the broader sense includes life, liberty and estates. In this sense, right to property includes right to life and to liberty as well. But it is property in the sense of 'estates' and 'possessions' that Locke uses the right to property in his whole political ideas.

Locke's theory of property can well be explained and analysed in his own words, emphasis added in italics:

'...men, being once born, have *a right to their preservation,* and consequently to eat and drink and do such other things as nature affords for their subsistence;....' (para 25)

'God..., has also given them reason to make use of it to the best advantage of life and convenience,.... And though all the fruits...belong to mankind in common;...; and nobody has originally a private dominion exclusive of the rest of mankind....; yet being given for the use of men, there must of necessity be *a means to appropriate* them....' (Para 26)

'...every man has a property in his own person; this nobody has any right to but himself. The labour of his body and the work of his hands, we may say, are properly his. *Whatsoever then he removes out of the state that nature has provided and left it in, he has mixed his labour with, and joined to it something that is his own, and thereby makes it his property.* (paras 27)

'And the taking of this or that part (from the nature given to men in common) does not depend on the express consent of all the commoners. (para 28)

'As much as any one can make use of to any advantage of life before it *spoils,* so much he may, by his labour fix a property in; whatever is beyond this is more than his share and belongs to others. Nothing was made by God for man to spoil or destroy.' (para 31)

'God gave the world to man in common, ...for their benefit and the greatest conveniences of life they were capable to draw from it, it cannot be supposed he meant it should always remain common and uncultivated. He gave it *to the use of the industrious and rational*...not to the fancy or covetousness of the quarrelsome and contentious.' (para 34)

'...that every man should have as much as he could make use of, would hold still in the world without straining anybody, since there is a land enough in the world to suffice double the inhabitants, had not *the invention of money and the tacit agreement* of men to put a value on it introduced—by consent—*larger possessions and a right to them.*' (para 36)

'And as different degrees of industry were apt to give men possessions in different proportions, so this *invention of money gave them the opportunity to continue and enlarge them...*' (para 48)

'But since gold and silver...has its value only from the consent of men, whereof labour yet makes, in great part, the measure, it is plain that men have agreed to disportionate and unequal possession of the earth, they having, by a tacit and voluntary consent, found out a way how a man may fairly possess more land than he himself can use the product of, by receiving in exchange for the overplus gold and silver which may be hoarded up...these metals not spoiling or decaying in the hands of the possessor. *This partage of things in an inequality of private possessions men have made practicable out of the bounds of society and without compact, only by putting a value on gold and silver, and tacitly agreeing in the* use of money;....' (para 50)

'...it is very easy to conceive how labour could at *first begin* a title of property in the common things of nature, and how the spending it upon our uses bounded it. So that there *could then be no reason of quarrelling about title,* nor *any doubt about the largeness of possession it gave.* Right and convenience went together;...'. (para 51)

'The equality of a simple, poor way of living, confining their desires within the narrow bounds of *each man's small property, made few controversies,* and so no need of many laws..., where there were but few trespasses and offenders. Since, then, those who liked one another so well as to join into society..., they could not but have greater apprehensions of others than of one another;.... It was natural for them to put themselves under a frame of government...'. (para 107)

'Nobody doubt but an express consent of any man entering into any society makes him a perfect member of that society, a subject of that government...*every man that has any possession* or enjoyment of any part...does *thereby give his tacit consent...*'.

(para 119)

'The great and chief end, therefore, of men's uniting into commonwealths and putting themselves under government is *the preservation of their property*'. (para 124)

From above, we may bring out certain characteristics of property right as they appear in Locke's writings:

1. Property, as a right, is a natural right. It exists because man exists. It is a possession of the individual as a human being.
2. Property, as a right, is a possession, a rightful possession in the sense than one owns it: it is not that one as individual possesses it, it is that he owns it, makes it, controls it. To possess it does not mean that one owns it and conversely, to own it does not mean that one possesses it: a car John owns, but he does not possess it because a thief after having stolen the car, possesses it.
3. Property, as a right, becomes property of a person who has put labour in having it: what is in the nature belongs to nature and is everyone's, but when a person has an apple by using his hand (i.e., labour), an apple becomes his property.
4. In the initial stages and until the discovery of rare metals such as gold and silver, property rights were limited. No one would take more than he required, for no one could have it or store it. Obviously then, things were left for others and in good conditions as well. Till then, all the world was America, for many, silver, gold were then unknown, and therefore, property could not be owned more than it was required.
5. With the introduction of money, gold and other rare metals, property right became unlimited, for gold or silver became not only property, but the medium of exchange of goods. Locke justifies the unlimited right to property in amassing it, for, the world, Locke would say, belongs to the entrepreneurs, and not the lazy.
6. The state comes to be established for the protection of property of those who had it in the form of 'estates', and of those who had it in the form of 'life and liberties'.

It is clear that Locke not only explains the growth of the right to property, he also justifies it. That is why the concept of property plays an important role in his philosophy. It is, as Locke insists in his scheme of things, for the preservation of property of those who have it that the state is formed through tacit consent of those who have property in the sense of goods and express consent of all who have property in the broader sense—of life, liberty and estates. The Lockean society in the state of nature, in its initial stages, is free and indeed, equal where there are few or no trespasses but as money, gold and silver are introduced, property right which was limited earlier becomes unlimited, resulting thus in a society of unequal men. As a result of unlimited property rights, on the eve of the formation of the state, trespasses increase, controversies enhance and the state is formed to protect the property of the people—of those who have possessions and of those who have only labour. The Lockean society, though free, is unequal and this inequality is taken over by the political society where the government is called upon to protect the property relations as existed in the state of nature. Locke's defence of property, though suggests for him a title of one who is advocating the case for a 'class' state as Macpherson feels, yet it goes to his credit that he is presenting a mercantilist argument in a very successful manner. He is granting unlimited right of accumulating money to the 'industrious' and 'rational' and that too in the interest of public good. William Ebenstein rightly remarks, 'When Locke defended property on the ground of individual effort and initiative, he protected the productive capacities of a new system of commercial and industrial capitalism against the restrictive traditions of a repressive state'.

Locke's theory of rights and property is not without its weaknesses. Locke has been assailed as a philosopher of inconsistencies. Some of the demerits, in his theory of rights and property, may be briefly stated as under:

1. At times, Locke insists that the rights are natural; natural because they belong to the individual as a human being; while at other times, he says that these rights are the result of his labour: property right being individual's after his having put his labour in what is common for all.
2. Locke's rights, especially property right, are limited at one stage and after the introduction of gold and silver the right to

property becomes unlimited. Locke's division of 'right as limited' and 'right as unlimited' is made with a view to justify right to property, as claimed by the capitalists in the later years.

3. Locke's theory of rights, property right including, paves the way for the rise of capitalist class in the society. He, therefore, emerges as a defender of capitalism. That is why that he has earned a name in the future capitalist society.
4. Locke's theory of rights, property right again including, earns for him the title of the forerunner of the liberal doctrine, which doctrine dominated the West in the coming centuries.
5. Locke's theory of property is a contradiction in itself. In the initial stages, property right is described limited; but in the later stages, following the introduction of gold and silver, this right is described unlimited and more so, it is defended as such.

Despite these weaknesses, Locke's theory of rights is significant in many respects. Locke regards individual as social, rational, and a moral being. He has passion for human personality and for an individual who is autonomous with rights and liberties associated with him.

## SUGGESTED READINGS

1. Bourns, H.R.F., *The Life of John Locks*, Vol. 2 (New York: Harper and Rowe, 1876).
2. Chapell V. (ed.), "The Cambridge Companian to Locke" (Cambridge: Cambridge University Press, 1994).
3. Germind, D., *Modern Western Political Thought: Machiavelli to Marx* (Chicago: University of Chicago Press, 1972).
4. Gough, J.W., *John Locke's Political Philosophy: Eight Studies* (Oxford: Blackwell, 1950).
5. Mackie, J.L., *Problems from Locke* (Oxford: Oxford University Press, 1994).
6. Macpherson, C.B., *The Political Theory of Possessive Individualism* (London: Oxford University Press, 1972 printing).
7. Parry, G., *John Locke* (London: Allen and Unwin, 1978).
8. Regun, W.L., *Locke's Two Treatises on Civil Government* (London, ..., 1965).

9. Seligar, M., *The Liberal Politics of John Locke* (London: Allen and Unwin, 1968).
10. Yolton, J., (ed.), *The Locke Reader* (Cambridge: Cambridge University Press, 1977).

# CHAPTER – 15

# Rousseau on Inequality

## I (a). Rousseau: The Man, His Times and His Works

Jean Jacques Rousseau (1712-1778) was born in Geneva (Swizerland). His father, Issac, a watchmaker was a man of erratic nature and of dubious character from whom qualities of a caring husband and a responsible father could hardly be expected. His mother, Suzanne, died a week after giving birth to him. Rousseau's childhood went by happily somehow. He had a passion for reading since his early days and used to read books left by his mother which included novels, histories, biographies, especially Plutarch's *Lives.* While still a boy, he had the occasion of spending some time in a countryside which he found so new and so enjoying that he wrote in his *Confessions,* 'I developed a feeling for it (the countryside) that was so strong that nothing has ever been able to eradicate it.' 'I felt', he continued. 'I was made for a quiet life and the countryside; it was impossible for me to live happily anywhere else.' Hermit-like living was something he never missed; the country-folks were people he gladly mixed in and liked. It was so because he found them too simple, too decent, too noble and too close to the nature. He addressed human beings when he said in his *Confessions,* 'Madmen, you who complain endlessly about nature, learn that all your evils come from yourselves.'

Rousseau's life was a life of a carefree man. He was a sort of man who had no regrets about the past and no anxiety about the future. In his active career, Rousseau tried his hand at various occupations, but did not stick to anyone. Starting as an apprentice at the age of sixteen to an engraver, Rousseau found the master too harsh for him which made him leave the master and the native place, Geneva. Rousseau came to Savoy, where he was taken in by a Catholic priest for onward handing over to one Madame de Warnes at Annecy with whom he lived for the next fourteen years. Madame de Warens, an attractive lady, was twelve years senior to him and throughout this period of fourteen years she remained, at various stages, his protectress, friend, sister, mother and mistress. It was here that Rousseau began to read men like Plato, Descartes, Locke, Leibniz, Montaigne, Voltaire and subjects like theology, anatomy, physiology, geometry, history. His interest in and study of music took Rousseau to Paris, but that did not help him much. Sometimes around here, he got, at the age of 30 or so, the post of secretary to the French ambassador at Venice. His experience of Venice with the ambassador was a complete failure except that he got to know a few pretty tunes from the Italian opera. Back in Paris after a year, Rousseau was busy in writing for the *Encyclopedia* with Diderot and D'Alembert. He was to contribute articles on music. He was in the thick of intellectual activity going on in Paris at this time. In 1745, he came to be introduced to one Therese Levasseur, a chambermaid at some hotel and a very simple uneducated peasant woman. She gave birth to five children without marrying Rousseau, all between 1746 and 1754. All the children were abandoned, a practice not very unusual in France. However, Rousseau and Therese remained together, marrying only in 1768.

Rousseau was never at ease with people. He made friends only to leave them at will. Diderot was one case, D'Alembert and later Hume other cases. His relations with women were well known, especially with Madame de Warens, Therese, Madame d'Epinay, Madame d'Houdetot, settling with Therese in a marriage just ten years before his death.

Rousseau's literary career started with articles on music for the *Encyclopedia*—1749. In 1750 he won the Dijan Academy prize on the topic 'Has the restoration of the sciences and arts tended to purify or corrupt morals?' published as his *First Discourses* (1751). In 1752 came his *Last Reply to M. Bordes* and *The Village Sorcerer.* In 1754, he completed his *Discourses on the Origin and Foundations of Inequality among Men,* published in 1575. In 1755 also appeared his article on "Political Economy" for volume V of the *Encyclopedia.* His *The New Heloise* was published in 1761 and in 1762 appeared his *Emile* and *The Social Contract. Emile* was condemned and burnt in Paris and *The Social Contract* in Geneva. He left France and settled down in Motiers which place he again left to find a refuge in the Island of Saint-Pierra. In 1766, he went to England on

Hume's invitation but suspected him of a conspiracy against himself and hence quarrelled with him. In 1767, back in France, his *Dictionary of Music* was published. By 1770, he had already worked on his *Confessions.* In 1772, he completed his work on the *Government of Poland* and began working on the *Dialogues: Rousseau—Judge of Jean-Jacques.* He also started work on the *Reveries of the Solitary Waler* in 1776. In 1778, he died at Ermenonvilla, near Paris.

### I(b). Rousseau: Origin of Inequality

Rousseau's *Discourses on the Origin and Foundations of Inequality among Men,* hereafter referred as *Inequality* is a work of immense significance. Mason says, 'If Rousseau had written nothing but this (i.e. *Inequality*) he would still be remembered today.' In the *Inequality,* Rousseau relates the tale of man's fall from his original state and attributes the cause to the origin and growth of the institutions of property and the division of labour. Mason, writing for Rousseau, says, 'Man was not naturally bad, he had become so; and the cause of this lay less in him than in the social forms in which he had become trapped.' While addressing humanity as a whole, Rousseau, in the introduction on his *Inequality,* declares thus: 'O man, of whatever country you are, and whatever your opinions may be, behold your history, such as I have thought to read it, not in the books written by your fellow-creatures, who are liars, but in nature, which never lies. All that comes from her will be true;....'

What has been the man's state in the original state? What has brought on inequality among men? What has civilisation and progress made of man? How has the state come in? How does the savage differ from the civilised man? All these questions have been discussed by Rousseau in his *Inequality* as under:

Nature nurtures man as it nurtures any other animal. It supplies for all his wants. The natural man satisfies 'his hunger at the first oak,' slakes 'his thirst at the first brook', finds 'his bed at the foot of tree' that also affords him a repast. Nature makes man strong and robust. So long as he lives under nature, lone and solitary, he is strong, but 'as he becomes sociable and a slave, he grows weak, timid and servile; his effeminate way of life totally enervates his strength and courage.' Rousseau, thus remarks, 'Let us conclude then that man in the state of nature, wandering up and down the forests, without industry, without speech, and without home, an equal stranger to war and to all ties, neither standing in need of his fellow-creatures nor having any desire to hurt them, and perhaps even not distinguishing them one from another; let us conclude that, being self-sufficient and subject to so few passions, he could have no feelings or knowledge but such as befitted his situation; that he felt only his actual necessities, and disregarded everything..., and that his understanding made no greater progress than his vanity...centuries must have elapsed in the barbarism of the first ages; when the race was already old, and man remained a child.'

As property came to be introduced and as families were established, there arose the germs of civil society. Rousseau says, 'The first man who, having enclosed a piece of ground, he thought himself of saying *This is mine,* and found people simple enough to believe him, was the real founder of civil society.' Man's very existence and his self-preservation, according to Rousseau, germinate in man, wants and needs, which compel him to grow enlightened and industrious. Man ceases to fall asleep under the first tree or in the first cave. He invents several kinds of implements, makes his hut and afterwards learns to plaster it over with mud and clay. 'This was the epoch', Rousseau says' 'of a first revolution, which established and distinguished families, and introduced a kind of property, in itself the source of a thousand quarrels and conflicts.' For him, this was the epoch of metallurgy and agriculture. As a result of it, men developed the habit of living together. So came the unity of husbands and wives, fathers and children and with it conjugal love and personal affection. A more settled manner of life resulting in the formation of tribes and nations came in gradually based not on any set of laws and regulations but on the basis of uniformity of life and common way of living. Accordingly, Rousseau says, 'As ideas and feelings succeeded one another, and heart and head were brought into play, men continued to lay aside their original wilderness; their private connections became ... more intimate as their limits extended. They accustomed themselves to assemble before their huts round a large tree; singing and dancing, the true off spring of love and leisure, became the amusement.... Each one began to consider the rest, and to wish to be considered in turn; and thus a value came to be attached to public esteem...; and this was the first step towards inequality. From these first distinctions arose on the one side vanity and contempt, and on the other, shame and envy: and the fermentation caused by these new leavens, ended by producing combinations fatal to innocence and happiness.' 'So long as men,' he continues, 'remained content with their rustic huts, so long as they were satisfied with clothes made of skins of animals and sewn together with thorns and fish-bones, adorned themselves only with feathers and shells and continued to paint their bodies in different colours, to improve and beautify their bows and arrows and to make with sharp-edged stones, fishing boats or clumsy musical instruments; in a ward, so long as they undertook only what a single person could accomplish, and confined themselves to such arts as did not require the joint labour of several hands, they lived free, healthy, honest and happy lives,.... But from the moment one man began to stand in need of the help of another; from the moment it appeared advantageous to any one man to have enough provisions for two, equality disappeared, property was introduced, work became indispensable, and vast forests became smiling fields, which man had to water with the sweat of his brow, and where slavery and misery were soon seen to germinate and grow up with the crops.'

With the introduction of private property and the division of labour, man's natural qualities came in action. His memory, imagination, wit, strength, skill and talent developed as also developed his egoism. 'It now became the interest of men, Rousseau says, 'to appear what they really were not'. So began 'insolent pomp and cheating trickery' and with that all the vices culminating thus in each becoming 'in some degree a slave even in becoming the master of other men.... In a word, there arose rivalry and competition on the one hand, and conflicting interests on the other,.... All these evils were the first effects of property, and the inseparable attendants of growing inequality'. Consequently, 'usurpation by the rich, robbery by the poor, and the unbridled passions of both, suppressed the cries of natural compassion and the still feeble voice of justice, and filled men with avarice, ambition and vice. Between the title of the strongest and that of the first occupier, there arose perpetual conflicts, which never ended, but in battles and bloodshed. The new-born state of society, thus, gave rise to a horrible state of war;....'

Rousseau feels that such a horrible state of society forced men to reflect on the whole wretched situation, the rich in particular. The rich, therefore, planned what he calls 'the profoundest plan that ever entered the mind of man.' He says, 'Destitute of valid reasons to justify and sufficient strength to defend himself, able to crush individuals with ease, but easily crushed himself by a troop of bandits, one against all, and incapable, on account of mutual jealousy, of joining with his equals against numerous enemies united by the common hope of blunder, the rich man, thus urged by necessity, conceived at length the profoundest plan that ever entered the mind of man: this was to employ in his favour the forces of those who attacked him,....' He, thus, concludes, 'Such was, or may well have been, the origin of society and law, which bound new fetters on the poor, and gave new powers to the rich, which irretrievably destroyed natural liberty, eternally fixed the law of property and inequality, converted usurpation into unalterable right, and, for the advantage of a few ambitious individuals, subjected all mankind to perpetual labour, slavery and wretchedness.' Reviewing the development and growth of inequality, Rousseau mentions three 'terms', 'the establishment of laws and of the right of property was its first term, the institution of magistracy the second, and the conversion of legitimate into arbitrary power the third and last, so that the condition of rich and poor was authorised by the first period; that of powerful and weak by the second; and only by the third that of master and slave,....

Thus came the society, the state and the law, according to Rousseau. Thus came the civilisation and the civilised man, a man much different than the 'natural' man, the savage. Thus, writes Rousseau, 'The savage and the civilised man differ so much in the bottom of their hearts and in their inclinations, that what constitutes the supreme happiness of one would reduce the other to despair. The former breathes only peace and liberty; he desires only to live and be free from labour. Civilised man, on the other hand, is always moving, sweating, toiling and racking his brains to find still more laborious occupations: he goes on in drudgery to his last moment, and even seeks death to put himself in a position to live, or renounces life to acquire immortality. He pays his court to men in power, whom he hates, and to the wealthy, whom he despises; he stops at nothing to have the honour of serving them; he is not ashamed to value himself on his own meanness.'...

Ending his *Inequality*, Rousseau says, 'It follows from this survey that, as there is hardly any inequality in the state of nature, all the inequality which now prevails owes its strength and growth to the development of our faculties and the advance of human mind, and becomes at least permanent and legitimate by the establishment of property and laws'.

From above, it is possible to count and recount the original foundation of inequality among men. Once the civil society came to be established, the foundations of inequality became in-built in the society itself. From there onward, inequality expanded in its area and in its depth. But for the causes of the origins of inequality, we may state the following:

(i) For nature-made inequality, nature itself is responsible. But the natural inequality is one that does not separates man from man; it rather unites. The cause that lies to separate man from man is man-made inequality.

(ii) Nature does not lie; it nurtures men: makes them strong. But as men move away from nature, they becomes weak and feeble; they think in other, their enemies.

(iii) The question of 'mine' and 'thine', of 'property' in other words, enhances the area of man-made inequality. Property, thus, is the major cause of inequality.

(iv) With property, we had masters and slaves; farmers and tillers; and with them, the rich and the poor—the actual (selfish) will of men dominating the real (will for others) will. The actual will, thus, created the state, and with it the whole body of laws, enchaining the man who was born free.

Rousseau's attempt at finding causes of the origin of inequality is, indeed, laudable. That property and with its evolution, because of the selfishness of man, must have what it had created in the form of possessions, is something which is hard to deny. That property must have divided men into 'haves' and 'haves-not', the rich and the poor, is again something that can hardly be disputed. That men of property must have created laws and rules helping them and that they must have created the infrastructure to man it themselves, is what history has really told us. That property is the root cause of inequality, all social evils, of all mutual conflicts is something that the future society was as it came to develop. That Rousseau's *Inequality* had served the basis for his *Social Contract* is what has been admitted by everyone. That the general will as the characteristic of the *Social Contract*, would create a free individual, a democratic polity and/or a dictatorial regime remain a matter of debate by both Rousseau's admiress as well his critics.

## SUGGESTED READINGS

1. Broome, J.H. *Rousseau: A Study of His Thought* (Oxford: Oxford University Press, 1963).
2. Grimsley, R., *The Philosophy of Rousseau* (Oxford: Oxford University Press, 1973).
3. Hall, J.C., *Rousseau: An Introduction to His Political Philosophy* (Cambridge, Mass, Harvard University Press, 1973).
4. Masters, R.D., *Political Philosophy of Rousseau* (Princeton, N.J., Princeton University Press, 1968).
5. Volpe, G. della, *Rousseau and Marx* (London: Lawrence and Wishart, 1978).
6. Vaughan, C.F., *The Political Writings of J.J. Rousseau* (New York: Wiley, 1962).
7. Watkins, F.H., *The Age of Ideology* (New Delhi: Prentice-Hall, 1961).
8. Wolin, S., *Politics and Vision* (Boston: Little Brown, 1960).

# CHAPTER – 16

# Mill on Liberty and Democracy

## I (a). John Stuart Mill: The Man, His Times and His Works

The democratic element in the liberal theory was introduced, in all earnestness by John Stuart Mill (1806-1873). John was born, in London, of a scholarly family and was the son of James Mill, himself an author in his own right. 'John would be a successor worthy of both of us', James once told Bentham, who were friends. With this in view, John's education was directed by James who acted both as John's teacher and as his companion. John studied Greek at 3 and Latin at 7, in addition to studying arithmetic and history. At the age of 12, John could read Plato, Herodotus, Xenophon, Aristotle in their original language. With these classical theorists, he added the study of recent theorists like Hobbes, while showing equal interest in algebra, geometry, experimental sciences and logic. He had his instructions on political economy from his father during their regular morning walks; studying thus economists like Adam Smith and David Ricardo. At the age of fourteen, John visited France and stayed there with General Sir Samuel Bentham, Jeremy Bentham's brother. At Montpellier in France, John studied chemistry, zoology, philosophy of science and mathematics. Next year when he returned home, he did his reading of Locke, Condillac and Helvetius. His study of Roman law and jurisprudence was completed by his father's friend and an eminent jurist, John Austin. It was all at a tender age of 15. So heavy was the dose in education for John that he became prematurely an old man, causing even a phase of depression when he was just 20. At the age of 17, he joined the East India Company and served it for a long period of thirty-five years, until 1858 when the company was closed.

John Stuart Mill was 16 when he founded a utilitarian society to discuss the ideas of Jeremy Bentham. He used to contribute articles to the *Westminster Review,* Bentham's and the *Philosophical*

*Radicalists'* official organ. He also joined the *Speculative Society* for having discussions on logic and psychology, and for economics, he became a member of the *Political Economy Club*.

John Stuart Mill, hereinafter as Mill, married at a very late age to one Hariet Taylor who was Mill's intellectual associate after his father's death, for about thirty years and his wife for eight. After their marriage in 1851, the Mills spent most of the time in seclusion and after Harriet's death in 1859, Mill was left almost alone, living mostly in his villa near Avignon, where he died in 1873. Between 1865 and 1868, Mill was a member of the House of Commons, where he advocated various measures like proportional representation, woman suffrage and the reduction of the national debt.

Mill's principal works include the *System of Logic* (1843), the *Principles of Political Economy* (1848), *On Liberty* (1859), *Considerations on Representative Government* (1861), *Utilitarianism* (1863), *The Subjection of Women* (1869), three others, published after his death, *Autobiography* (1873), *Three Essays on Religion* (1874) and *Chapters on Socialism* (1879) brought out by his step daughter.

For a man like Mill, so well read and so well experienced, the situation, as he found himself in the second half of the nineteenth century, was really bewildering. Having himself brought up in the strict discipline of Benthamite philosophical radicalism, he soon found it wanting in many respects. Himself a follower, once, of Bentham, he soon found Wordsworth, Coleridge and Carlyle more inspiring. Realising fully well the role of the state that it can play in the life of the individual, he soon found the Hegelian and Burkean theses of the state too towering. A modest critic of capitalism and the one who would recommend regulatory measures on private property, as Mill was, he soon found, the working class unequal to the tasks of a rapidly growing society. A great believer of democracy, as Mill was, he found 'one-man one-vote' system as damaging and an instance of false democracy. An enthusiastic advocate of man's freedom, as Mill was, he soon found the laissez-faire policy too harmful for the greater part of mankind. Amidst these bewildering ideas around, Mill was no follower of either Hegel or Burke in giving the state what is not state's; he was no follower of Marx in giving to the proletariat exclusive rights of governing the society; he was no follower of either Adam Smith or Ricardo in giving unhindered freedom to the propertied classes; he was no follower of Bentham in raising all the time cries of utility. His was, what Hacker calls, 'a careful and painstaking' approach'. 'When he (Mill) speaks', Hacker continues, 'of democracy, he gives close attention to the concrete political institutions which may hopefully make that form of government a reality. When he discussed human freedom, he lists the explicit consequences which may be expected if men are allowed to express themselves without hindrance'. Mill came to introduce, in the liberal theory, the humanistic and democratic values for the first time and this precisely was his distinctive contribution to liberalism and also to political theory. But his tragedy was that he could not abandon completely his bourgeois assumptions on which his whole political theory rested. George H. Sabine puts in very rightly when he says, 'His (Mill's) expressly stated theories...of human nature, of morals, of society, and of the part to be played by government in a liberal society...were always inadequate to the load that he made them carry'.

### I (b). Mill's Views on Liberty

Mill's passion for individual liberty cannot be challenged. He is rightly seen as a genuine friend of liberty. His argument in favour of liberty is that liberty helps educate public opinion so that the people are able to use their authority more responsibly.

Mill comes to define freedom or liberty in his, *'On Liberty'* as, 'pursuing our own good in our own way, so long as we do not attempt to deprive others of theirs' or impede their efforts to obtain it'. So defined, liberty is a means to the end of our own good. So considered, society appears to be a community of men pursuing good of the society, the common good. In a society where each man is to seek his own good without depriving anybody else of the same right, man has only to do actions—actions which relate to the individual himself and actions which relate to other individuals. 'The only part of the conduct of any one, for which he is amenable to society,' Mill says, 'is that which concerns others. In the part which merely concerns himself, his independence is, of right, absolute. Over himself, over his own body and mind, the individual is sovereign.' '..the only purpose,' Mill holds, 'for which power can be rightfully exercised over any member of a civilized community, against his will, is to prevent harm to others.' So far as an individual is within a sphere that concerns himself—and in this sphere Mill includes (a) the inward domain of consciousness: the liberty of conscience, of thought and feeling, of opinion and sentiment on all subjects, of expressing and publishing opinion, (b) liberty of tastes and pursuits: the liberty of framing plans of our life, of doing things; and (c) liberty of combinations: freedom to unite etc., ...society or state has no business to interfere. Mill holds, '...that the individual is not accountable to society for his actions, in so far as these concern the interests of no person but himself,... that for such actions as are prejudicial to the interests of others, the individual is accountable, and may be subjected either to social or to legal punishment, if society is of opinion that the one or the other is requisite for its protection."

Mill's account of liberty can well be understood in the light of his criticism of Bantham's utilitarianism. Mill was a utilitarian, though not a Banthamite. For Bantham, utility was the object of everything a person does; for Mill, the development of personality was the ultimate gain of an individual; living a life was Bantham's goal; living a life well, was Mill's object: 'it is better to be a Socrates dissatisfied than a fool satisfied'. Liberty is an essential ingredient necessary for attaining the heights of human personality. Liberty makes man better, wiser and more humane.

Mill's argument in favour of liberty is that it helps individual live not only for oneself, but also for others, i.e., for society. Liberty helps individual see his interest together with that of the society; pig knows only its own side whereas individual knows the side of other individuals.

For Mill, liberty is individual's greatest weapon. It is this weapon that helps him attain his own good, good of the society he is a member. It is this weapon through which he organises his own opinion, gives the opinion an expression, uses it against the law that restricts his freedoms and against the government that coerces his views. Mill is convinced that no one, not even the government, nor even the whole mankind has the power to suppress the opinion of a single person holding a view contrary to what the whole humanity has. Mill says, "Anyone who uses authority to silence an opinion on the grounds that he is certain that it is false, assumes that he is infallible. Few of us are willing to grant such infallibility to anyone."

Mill's views on liberty have been criticised on numerous grounds. It is said that the central ideas incorporated in *On Liberty* are too vague to secure liberty the way Mill hopes; in his views on liberty, Mill is too libertarian. Barker says that Mill is the prophet of empty liberty and abstract individual. He has no theory of rights, much he may speak about liberty.

## I (c). Mill on Democracy

Mill's views on democracy are found mostly in his book *Considerations on Representatives Government*. For him, real democracy is always the representative democracy. Direct democracy, being impracticable in the face of vast majority of people living over too large an area, it is through representatives that people can hopefully rule themselves so to help attain the development of their personality. To quote Mill, "...that the ideally best form of government is that in which sovereignty, or the supreme controlling power in the last resort, is vested in the entire aggregate of the community, every citizen not only having a voice in the exercise of that ultimate sovereignty, but being, at least occasionally, called on to take an actual part in the government, by the personal discharge of some public functions, local or general.' The representative government is ideal because it rests on two principles. 'The first is,' Mill says, 'that the rights and interests of every or any person are only secure from being disregarded, when the person interested is himself able, and habitually disposed, to stand up for them. The second is, that the general prosperity attains a greater height, and, is more widely diffused, in proportion to the amount and variety of the personal energies enlisted in promoting it.'

With a belief that the development of character depends on the exercise of character, Mill is a great advocate of participation. He says in the *Representative Government*, '...that the only government which can fully satisfy all the exigencies of the social state, is one in which the whole people participate; that any participation, even in the smallest public function, is useful; that the participation should everywhere be as great as the general degree of improvement of the community will allow; and that nothing less can be ultimately desirable than the admission of all to a share in the sovereign power of the state.' How the people participate? Mill's answer is that it is in the representative government that the whole people have the opportunities of participation. 'The meaning of representative government,' Mill says, 'is, that the whole people, or some numerous portion of them, exercise through deputies periodically elected by themselves, the ultimate controlling power...'. But careful as Mill is always, he cautions about the dangers of representative government being turned into a false form of democracy. He, thus, recommends, what is based on Hare's proposals, proportional representation to allay the tyranny of any majority—political, social or economic and also favours plural voting so to keep a balance of weight between the vote of an ordinary person and that of any person doing some socially useful work. Mill writes about these in the *Representative Government:* "In a really equal democracy, every or any section would be represented, not disproportionately. A majority of the electors would always have a majority of the representatives; but a minority of the electors would always have a minority of the representatives. Man for man they would be as fully represented as the majority. Unless they are, there is not equal government, but a government, of inequality and privilege: one part of the people rule over the rest; there is a part whose fair and equal share of influence in the representation is withheld from them; contrary to all just government, but above all, contrary to the principle of democracy, ...,."

Or at another place, he says: 'Democracy is not the ideally best form of government ...; unless it can be so organised that no class, not even the most numerous, shall be able to reduce all but itself to political insignificance, and direct the course of legislation and administration by its exclusive class interest.'

This is what is Mill's argument for proportional representation. For *plural voting,* Mill's argument runs asunder, also in his *Representative Government:* 'In all human affairs, every person directly interested and not under positive tutelage, has an admitted claim to a voice, and when his exercise of it is not inconsistent with the safety of the whole, cannot justly be excluded from it. But though one ought to have a voice—that everyone should have an equal voice is a totally different proposition.... If with equal virtue, one is superior to the other in knowledge and intelligence—or if with equal intelligence, one excels the other in virtue—the opinion, the judgement, of the higher moral or intellectual being, is worth more than that of the inferior.... One of the two, as the wiser or better man, has a claim to superior weight.'

'...two or more votes might be allowed to every person who exercises any of these (say, socially useful) superior functions..., in this direction (of plurality of votes) lies the true ideal of representative government.'

'The plurality of votes must on no account be carried so far, that those who are privileged by it, or the class...to which they mainly belong, shall outweigh by means of it all the rest of community.'

The *object* of the government, in Mill's views, being the attainment of values and virtues in men, their self-development, it is essential that the government should be of those whose self-development is being sought. This is possible only when the people participate in the making and working of their government or when the government is truly representative. True political education can not be imposed on the people as Plato had suggested. Nor it means the habit of obedience as Burke had recommended. Political education is the participation of the people in the process of self-government. Trials and errors, commissions and ommissions can teach an individual a lot. Hacker writes for Mill when he says, '...political education can only be meaningful if every citizen is encouraged to participate in the process of self-government. An individual learns best in the course of making and correcting his own mistakes. Virtue and intelligence should become genuine attributes of character in a citizen and not simply a catalogue of catch phrases he has memorized.' And then, through participation, people, at large, would be able to control their rulers by influencing the character and direction of public policy. This would also help the people to exercise their pressure in pushing their own demands as against the rulers' selfish demands, for in the absence of the right of participation, the realisation of the peoples' interests can not be imagined. *Participation based on Proportional representation and plural voting,* as Mill suggests, can be of *immense help in furthering the interests of the people* as it is in strengthening the foundations of representative government.

Mill's all hopes lie on the *individual.* He therefore, insists that the individual should exercise his ballot in a responsible manner, casting his vote in the right manner and should be able to know for himself as to who has to be his representative. He has to be, as Mill suggests, 'active, self-helping,' character. Mill's views about representatives are not appreciative. He thinks that the representative is no better than an average voter. The representatives only check and supervise those who make the nation's crucial decisions i.e. cabinet. 'It (the representative assembly) should...control the operations of government,' Mill says. 'That alone,' he continues, 'which it can do well, it ought to take personally upon itself. With regard to the rest, its province is not to do it, but to take means for having it well done by others.' Parliament, accordingly, Mill would say, 'is not expected, nor even permitted, to originate directly either taxation or expenditure. All it is asked for is its consent, and the sole power it possesses is that of refusal.' 'But a popular assembly,' Mill continues, 'is still less fitted to administer, or to dictate in detail to those who have the charge of administration. Even when honestly meant, the interference is almost always injurious.' With regard to matters like the legislation, Mill says, '...a numerous assembly is as little fitted for the direct business of legislation as for that of administration.' If this is all which a representative assembly is not supposed to do in Mill's opinion, what and for what, then, it actually exists? Mill has a heavy agenda for the representative assembly. 'Instead of the function of governing for which it is radically unfit, the proper office of a representative assembly is to watch and control the government: to throw the light of publicity on its acts: to compel a full exposition and justification of all of them which any one considers questionable, to ensure them if found condemnable, and, if the men who compose the government abuse their trust, or fulfil it in a manner which conflicts with the deliberate sense of the nation, to expel them from office, and either expressly or virtually appoint their successors.... In addition to this, the Parliament has...to be at once the nation's Committee of Grievances and its Congress of Opinions;....' With such functions as stated here, the representative assembly, in Mill's opinions, can usefully employ itself only if it 'talks'. The actual administration is carried on by the Cabinet, chosen from the parliament, with the help of the permanent public services appointed through the competitive examinations.

This, in short, is the framework of Mill's structure of representative government. Participation, based on the devices of proportional representation and plural voting, makes the government not only representative and thus democratic, it also gives men sufficient opportunities to attain political education. But Mill warns that for the successful working of representative government, there should be people (a) willing to receive the representative government; (b) willing and be able to do what is necessary for its preservation, and (c) willing and be able to fulfil the duties and discharge the functions which it imposes on them. Wherever, Mill holds, the representative government is practicable, it is the best government and wherever it is impracticable, it is the worst.

That Mill is a democrat is something that cannot be lightly dismissed. He is democrat because at the heart of his whole philosophy lies his passion for human personality. He strongly feels, and none before him had felt so strongly, that democracy alone helps individual attain his interest, his prosperity. This Bentham also felt. But whereas Bentham was interested in a happier man, Mill, on the other hand, is interested in a better man too. Mill is a democrat because he feels, and here again he has no parallel amongst all the earlier liberal thinkers, that man's participation in the process of government generates in man, a process of development as well, for it is he who believes that the development of character depends upon the exercise of character. Mill is a democrat because he is so well aware of democracy's shortcomings—peoples' illiteracy, their apathy, their ignorance, their passiveness—that inspite of all these weaknesses, he is ready to give democracy a fair trial. He is a democrat, because he is able to make a distinction between false and true democracy, between the rule of either ignorant or of elite and the rule of the competent, between the rule of quantity and that of the quality. He is a democrat because he wants to give franchise to each and all, male and female, aristocrat (one who gives to life more than he takes out of it as Mill thinks) and manual labourer. But in giving this right, Mill recommends his concept of plural voting, *i.e.* one vote each to every citizen but more than one votes to those citizens who are doing socially useful functions. He is a democrat because he neither wants the tyranny of majority nor the attack on minorities. His answer to these evils is the proportional representation. But one must note that Mill is a democrat only from the standards of the nineteenth century point of view. His own country, after having tried plural voting particularly, abandoned his recommendations. His speeches, favouring proportional representation and woman surffrage, in the House of Commons when he was its member, went without any particular heed.

If Mill is a democrat, he is also a liberal. It will be well to call him a liberal-democrat rather than a democratic liberal. Such a proposition means that he is first a liberal and only afterwards, a democrat. He builds 'democratic' elements on the already assumed liberal foundations. His is an attempt to find ways and means as to whether there is any possibility of making a liberal society also a democratic one. But in making such an attempt, he accepts all the liberal ethos of the earlier liberals. He accepts the assumptions of the capitalistic society. He accepts the class interests and class inequality. He accepts man's right of property and also accepts thereby the autonomy of the individual and limited area of state operation. On these assumptions, the assumptions which Mill is in no mood to leave, he creates a democratic model, the model of representative government, the model in which he gives one vote to each and several votes to some, the model where no class is to dominate the other class, the model of an active citizen, a talking assembly and a powerful executive. Honest as Mill is in creating the democratic model, he is equally adamant in not leaving his bourgeois assumptions. The result is anybody's guess. Obviously the two should not and actually can not, go together. No one can build equality on inequality. Mill also does not do this exercise. What he does is that he introduces certain changes in his bourgeois assumptions on the one hand and on the other shifts emphasis in his democratic model in the name of what he calls 'True' democracy. Mill's this attempt is also honest, indeed. But even this also puts Mill nowhere. He remains, among the liberals, a rebel liberal and among the democrats, a 'reluctant' democrat as C.L. Wayper feels.

## SUGGESTED READINGS

1. Barlin, I., *John Stuart Mill and the Ends of Life* (London: Edgar G. Dunstan and Co., 1959).

2. Cook, I., *Reading Mill: Studies in Political Theory* (London: Macmillan, 1998).
3. Cowling, M., *Mill and Liberalism* (Cambridge: Cambridge University Press, 1963).
4. Gray, J., *Mill on Liberty: A Defence* (London: Routledge, 1983).
5. McCloskey, J.H., *John Stuart Mill: A Critical Study* (London: Macmillan, 1971).
6. Rees, J., "A Re-reading of Mill on Liberty," *Political Studies*, VIII.
7. Ryan A., *The Philosophy of John Stuart Mill* (London: Macmilan, 1970).
8. Ten, C.L., *Mill on Liberty* (Oxford: Clarendon Press, 1980).

## CHAPTER – 17

# Marx on State

### I (a). Karl Marx: The Man, His Times and His Works

Karl Marx (1818-1883) was born at Trier (a place in the Rhinaland area of Germany) on May 5, 1818, where he finished his secondary education in 1835. His father, a middle class Jew (later converted to Protestantism) lawyer, sent him to the universities of Bonn and Berlin. At Berlin, he obtained his Ph.D. on the thesis titled as 'The Difference between Democritus' and Epicurus' 'Philosophy of Nature' from the University of Jena in 1841. By this time, Marx had started shaping his view of the world outlook. He was a young Hegelian with leftist leanings. It was because of this that he could not get a university job and thus turned to journalism and started editing *Rheinische Zeitung*. In 1843, he had to leave the journal following its closure for his criticism against the then German government. This year, he married Jenny and was now a socialist. He came to Paris in 1843, and got acquainted with French materialism. Hence, with German philosophical background, he added the French materialism, Thus he wrote his *Introduction to a Critique of Hegel's Philosophy of Right* in 1844 (first published in 1927) in which he condemned Hegel's idea that the state was, in its origin and value, quite independent of the empirical individuals who composed it. Rejecting he Hegelian thesis that the state was the embodiment of men's general interests, he held that the purpose of the true state was not that each citizen should devote himself to the general cause as though to a particular one, but that the general cause should be truly general, i.e. the cause of every citizen. Marx also did not agree with Hegel that the state was a mediator between particular interests and held, on the contrary, that it was itself a tool of particular interests. In this book, he also disclosed the historic role of the proletariat and explained the inevitability of revolution as a fulfillment of history's innate tendency. In the year 1844, Marx also wrote *Economic and*

*Philosophic Manuscripts* (first published in 1932), a work in which Marx expounded socialism as a general world-view and not merely a programme of social reform, and also related economic categories to a philosophical interpretation of man's position in nature, i.e. his theory of alienation. Now in Paris, he came under the influence of communist theory, particularly the role of the working class in history. His meeting with Friedrich Engels in Paris turned into a life-long association between the two. After 1845, Marx spent sometime in Brussels and studied economics and economic theory. Marx and Engels wrote together *The Holy Family* (1845), *Theses on Feuerbach* (1845) and *The German Ideology* (1845-46). *The Holy Family* was a polemic against the Bauer brothers who looked down upon the proletariat as an uncritical mass. While rejecting the idealism of Hegel and those of the young Hegelians, Marx and Engels attempted to show the idea of the social relations of production and the view that the struggle of the working class against their exploiters was the central feature of all history. *These on Feuerbach,* a polemic against Feuerbach, was a work in which Marx and Engels expounded the ideas (a) that the social life is mainly practical; (b) that man is the product of his own labour; (c) that he is essentially social by nature and (d) that the ideological phenomena depend on the conditions of society's existence and development. *The German Ideology* (1845-46) was a work written against the views expressed by the young Hegelians and those of Feuerbach and also of the anarchist Stirner. In this book, (which appeared in 1932), Marx and Engels developed the ideas they had expressed in *The Holy Family* and *Theses on Feuerbach,* especially the view that idealism as a theory had to be associated with classes against the proletariat and that the establishment of the communistic system was to be inevitable consequence of the operation of the economic laws which worked independent of man's will. In 1847, Marx wrote *The Poverty of Philosophy,* a polemic against Proudhon's *The Philosophy of Poverty,* and indeed, a work of mature Marxism. In 1848, Marx and Engels both wrote for the Communist League *The Communist Manifesto,* the first programmatic document of scientific communism, the one that expounded the foundations of Marxism. In February, 1848, the troubles arose and Marx participated in the struggle in Rhineland (Germany). On failure of these events, he returned to Paris only to be expelled from

France. He came to London in 1849 and lived there until his death in 1883. Thick in the proletarian movement, Marx was active fighting for the workers. After the dissolution of the Communist League in 1852, Marx founded the First International in 1864. This gave him the opportunity to follow closely the progress of the revolutionary movements in all the countries. In 1850, he wrote *The Class Struggles in France*, a work in which he emphasised the alliance of the workers and the peasants. In his *The 18th Brumaire of Louis Bonaparte* (1852), he predicted that the bourgeois state machinery would be destroyed ultimately. In 1871, he wrote *The Civil War in France*, the experiences of the Paris Commune, a work in which Marx expounded his views on the state form of the dictatorship of the proletariat. *The Grundrisse* (1857-58), published in 1941, was his wide-ranging work with special reference to the study of economics. In the *Critique of the Gotha Programme* (1875), he developed further the theory of scientific communism. Marx's works on economics are highly exhaustive. In his *The Critique of Political Economy* (1859) he set forth the essence of the materialistic understanding of history. This theme and the working of the capitalistic society were worked out in his *Capital* Vol. I (1867), Vol. II (1885) after the death of Marx, by Engels and Vol. III in 1894. In his *Theories of Surplus Value* (1862-63), he discussed mainly the theories of Adam Smith and Ricardo.

### I (b). Marx on State

Marx's views on the concept of state are scattered over his vast writings spread over a long period of about forty years. As Marx advanced in years, he kept on developing his thought with extreme consistency. It may be noted that once Marx formulates his views on a specific subject (formulation itself being based on intensive readings and knowledge), he continues to maintain them all through his later days. As Leszek Kolakowski rightly puts it, 'From 1843 onwards he (Marx) developed his ideas with extreme consistency, and all his later work may be regarded as a continuation and elaboration of the body of thought which was already constituted by the time of *The German Ideology*'. This is true about his views on the concept of the state.

(a) *Hegel and Marx on State*

Marx commences his views on state by discussing the nature of the state and its relations to society. His views on the state, in the formative years of his intellectual development, bear, of course, very little of the Hegelian imprint. In an article written in May, 1842 and published in the *Rheinische Zeitung,* Marx regards law necessary for freedom. He says, 'There are no preventive laws at the present time. Law only prevents by forbidding. It becomes active law as soon as it is transgressed, for it is only true law when in it the unconscious natural law of freedom becomes the conscious law of the state.' In another article, published also in the *Rheinische Zeitung,* he says, that modern philosophy 'considers the state as the great organism in which juridical, moral, and political liberties must be realized and in which each citizen, by obeying the law of the state, only obeys the natural laws of his own reason, human reason.' But even at this stage what is important for Marx is freedom and not law, true state and not merely a state, true law and not merely a law. In the same May, 1842, article, he says, 'Where law is true law, i.e., where it is the existence of freedom, it is true existence of the freedom of man.' In the same article for the *Rheinische Zeitung* cited above, he says, '...a state that is not a realization of rational freedom is a bad state.' In an another article, 'On the Estates Committees in Prussia,' he describes as to what constitutes a true state. 'Representation should not be conceived of as the representation of some stuff that is not the people itself, but only as its self-representation, ...In a true state there is no landed property, no industry, no material stuff that can, as such elements, strike a bargain with the state; there are only spiritual powers and it is only in their resurrection in the state, in their political rebirth, that natural powers are capable of having a political voice.'

Marx differs with Hegel. He finds the actual state much different than it appears in hegel's writings: Hegel's 'exalted view of the state' seems opposite to what it really is, Rejecting Hegel's abstract idea of the state in the "Critique of Hegel's *Philosophy of Right,'* Marx says, '...the family and civil society are real parts of the state, ...the modes of being of the state; family and civil society make themselves into the state. They are the initiators. According to Hegel, they are, on the contrary, created by the actual idea; ..." Thus, the two view the state differently. For

Hegel, the state is independent of the individuals who compose it; for Marx, the state owes its existence to actual human needs. For Hegel the functions of the state are connected with individuals only in an accidental manner; for Marx, there is an essential link between the functions of the state and the needs of the individuals. For Hegel, the individual man is a subjective and secondary form of the existence of the state; for Marx, the individual man is an objectified man: "Hegel starts from the state and makes man into the subjective aspect of the state; democracy starts from man and makes the state into objectified man. Just as religion does not make man, but man makes religion, so the constitution does not make the people, but the people make the constitution.... Man is not there for the benefits of the law, but the law for the benefit of man.' For Hegel, the states exist as an embodiment of the general interest and as such, in the Hegelian scheme, man must devote himself to the general cause of the state; for Marx, the state, though exists for the general interest should exist for a cause which is truly general, i.e. the cause of every citizen. For Hegel, the civil society gets reconciled in the state and its contradiction with the state is removed in its representation in the state; for Marx the state removes from the civil society what is real in it and detaches from man his real private condition, for, 'the real man is the private man of the present constitution of the state.' For Hegel, the state works through bureaucracy, bureaucrats being, for him, the spirit of the state as expressed in the consciousness of officialdom; for Marx, 'bureaucracy is a web of "practical illusions" or "the illusions of the state." The bureaucratic spirit is...a Jesuitical, theological spirit. The bureaucrats are the Jesuits and theologians of the state. Bureaucracy is the republic as priest.' For Hegel, the state, synthesises the particular interests of the individual; for Marx, the state, instead of being a mediator is 'a tool of particular interests of a special kind.'

In the initial years, Marx rejected the idealist notion of the state as advocated by Hegel. But he does want the state to do adopt democracy and seek political emancipation. He writes, "Democracy is the solution to the riddle of all constitutions...All other constitutions of the state are a certain, definite, and particular form of the state. In democracy, the formal principle is at the same time the material principle. Thus, it is first the true unity of universal and particular..., in a true democracy, the political state disappears.' He writes in "On the Jenith question: 'Political emancipation is of course a great progress. Although it is not the final form of human emancipation in general, it is nevertheless the final form of human emancipation inside the present world order.'

(b) *Marx: State as a Means*

By the year 1844, when Marx wrote his *Economic and Philosophic Manuscripts,* his views on the state began taking a direction, if not a shape. The state, for Marx, is no abstract concept and as such is not independent of the civil society. Nor it is an embodiment of any general cause, but, in fact, is one that exists as an instrument for the protection of interests of the propertied classes. Critical, as Marx is, of the role of the state, he visualises an immediate democratic order and a farthest socialist system in which each individual's life is identified with the life of the community and where individual's private, selfish interests are eliminated in favour of a sense of absolute community with the whole. Kolakowski puts Marx's case when he says, 'He (Marx) also formulated at this early stage the idea of socialism...as the abolition of politics altogether. In articles published in the Paris journal *Vorwarts* in the summer of 1844 he declared that there could not be a social revolution with a political soul, but there could be a political revolution with a social soul...Marx's ideal was that every man should be fully aware of his own character as a social being, but should also, for this very reason, be capable of developing his personal attitudes in all their fullness and variety.'

*The German Ideology* (1845-46), written by Marx and Engels, does highlight their views on the state. Now, they do not consider the state to represent the interests of community. Nor the struggles between democracy, aristocracy and monarchy and the struggles for franchise are the real struggles. The fact of the matter, for Marx, is just the opposite. 'Just because individuals seek only their particular interest, which for them does not coincide with their communal interest, the later will be imposed on them as an interest "alien" to them, and "independent" of them,....' 'The material life of individual,' Marx continues, 'which by no means depends merely on their "will", their mode of production and form of intercourse, which mutually determine each other—this is the real basis of the State and remains so at all the stages at which division of labour and private property are still necessary, quite independently of the will of individuals. These actual relations are in no way created by the State power; on the contrary they are the power creating it.'

In *The Poverty of Philosophy* (1847), which is his polemic against Proudhon's *The Philosophy of Poverty,* Marx says, '...it is the sovereigns who in all ages have been subject to economic conditions, but they have never dictated laws to them. Legislation, whether political or civil, never does more than proclaim, express in words, the will of economic relations.'

In their famous work, *Manifesto of the Communist Party* (1848), Marx and Engels describe the executive of the state as 'a committee for managing the common affairs of the whole bourgeoisie.' 'In political practice,' they continue, 'therefore, they (the bourgeoisie) join in all coercive measures against the working class;....'

That the political power rests with the economic lords is evident from Marx's *The Class Struggles in France* (1850). He writes, while describing the France of 1848-49. 'It was not the French bourgeoisie that ruled under Louis Philippe, but one faction of it: bankers, stock-exchange kings, railway kings, owners of coal and iron mines and forests, a part of the landed proprietors associated with them—the so-called finance aristocracy. It sat on the throne, it dictated laws in the Chambers, it distributed public offices, from cabinet portfolios to tobacco bureau posts.' And then in *The Eighteenth Brumaire of Louis Bonaparte* (1852), he describes as to how the economically-strong groups attempt to use the state power to strengthen and benefit themselves. He says, '...in its struggle against the revolution, the parliamentary republic (dominated by the bourgeoisie) found itself (as in France during 1848-51) compelled to strengthen, along the repressive measures, the resources and centralisation of governmental power. All revolutions perfected this machine instead of smashing it. The parties that contended in turn for domination regarded the possession of this huge state edifice as the principal spoils of the victor.'

*The Civil War in France* (1871) is Marx's that work which explains the state form during the period between capitalism and communism, the period of the dictatorship, of the proletariat." ...the working class," he declares, "cannot lay hold of the ready-made state machinery, and wield it for its own purposes.' Retaining the old state machinery of the bourgeoisie would amount to having 'the national power of capital over labour, of a public force organised for social enslavement, of an engine of class despotism.' What is important for Marx is the abolition of the class rule. Only the proletarians, he says, '...were the men to break the instrument of that class rule...the State, the centralized and organised governmental power usurping to be the master instead of the servant of society.' This explains that for Marx the state is but only a means which should serve the society rather than controlling it as is the form of the state in most of the capitalist societies of the Western Europe of Marx's own days. In his *Critique of the Gotha Programme* (1875), he says, 'Freedom (of the state, i.e., the Free State) consists in converting the state from an organ superimposed upon society into one completely subordinate to it,....'

Marx's writings on economics also indicate his views on the state. In the *Grundrisse* (1857-58), he regards state 'as a means to the production of wealth.' In the preface to *A Contribution to the Critique of Political Economy* (1859), he writes, 'In the social production of their existence, men inevitably enter into definite relations of production appropriate to a given stage in the development of their material forces of production. The totality of these relations of production constitutes the economic structure of society, the real foundation, on which arises a legal and political structure, and to which, correspond definite forms of social consciousness. The mode of production of material life conditions the general process of social, political and intellectual life. It is not the consciousness of men that determines their existence, but their social existence that determines their consciousness.' In the *Capital* Vol. I, Marx explains how ruthlessly the economically dominant class uses political power.

These text-by-text illustrations from Marx's writings covering a long period of about forty years should make it clear that Marx does have his views on the state and that he does develop them as and when he discusses various events of his times. Engels and later Lenin contribute much to the Marxist theory of State.

Of what has been said in the preceding pages on Marx, one can sum up Marx's views on the state.

(a) Society and state, for Marx, are two distinct realities, the type of society explains the type of state, the society thus furnishes the basis over which is constructed the superstructure of the state.

(b) The state is not independent of society and those who make it, as Marx thinks that Hegel has so made, independent, make the state only a fiction, an illusion and thus, Marx believes, impose it on the society.

(c) The state is, for Marx, a means for the fulfillment of the ends of those who control the society. Thus, the slave-owning society serves the masters; the feudal state serves the feudal lords and the capitalist state serves the capitalists, the bourgeoisie.

(d) The class society produces a state that serves the economically dominant class and becomes, in the process, an instrument of exploitation which exploits the economically weak one, such antagonistic classes originating because of the institutions of private property and of division of labour.

(e) The state, for Marx, is, thus, an engine of class-rule. The seizure of power by the proletariat from the capitalist signifies the dictatorship of proletariat, which dictatorship abolishes the roots of class antagonism, i.e., private property is the means of production and division of labour in the process in which the production is made.

(f) The dictatorship of proletariat is not the abolition of the state as is the existence of the state. The proletarian state, like any state of the class society, is also a means, a means that serves the workers, a means that establishes socialism and a means that leads to its own abolition, its own "withering away" as Engels uses the words.

(g) Regarding the state as a 'parasite feeding upon and clogging the free movement of society,' as Marx believes, the Marxists think that state's destiny is its own abolition. 'The first step is the overthrow of the existing State, the bourgeois State, by revolution of the proletarian class. The next task is the establishment of a transitional State, the proletarian dictatorship. This new State, however, is to be abolished not by the revolution, nor by force, but through its own withering away.'

(c) *Historical Evolution of the State*

Marx and Engels are convinced that the state is not natural as the society is Engels says: "The state, then, has not existed from all eternity. There have been societies that did without it, that had no idea of the state and state power. At a certain stage of economic development, which necessarily involved the split of society into classes, the state became a necessity because of this split." He, therefore, predicts, "we are now rapidly approaching a stage in the development of production at which the existence of these classes has not only ceased to be a necessity but becomes a positive hindrance to production. They will fall just as inevitably as they arose at an earlier stage. Along with them the state will inevitably fall. Society, which will reorganise production on the basis of a free and equal association of the producers, will put the whole state machinery where it will then belong: into the museum of antiquities, by the side of the spinning-wheel and the bronze axe."

Marx and Engels are of the view that the state did not exist in all societies, and as such, it appeared at a particular stage of the development of society.

The 'primitive communist' society knew no private property, nor division of labour, nor antagonistic classes and hence no state. It was a classless society, a communal community. But the evolution, as in the West, of private ownership on animals and lands, and development of labour and exchange, there appeared the organisation called the state, owned and manned by the masters and for their welfare, and against those without the means of production, the 'haves-not,' the slaves. Thus having become economically stronger and dominant on the basis of new production relations the big landowners and slave owners started to reorganise society according to their rules. Although they were wealthy and powerful from an economic point of view, they constituted a minority. In order to be able to preserve their economic superiority they needed another organisation apart from their economic organisation. An organisation that would defend the common interests of the big landowners and slave owners and assure the permanence of their economic superiority. Thus, special political organisation of the ruling class, which is called state, came out.

The feudal society of the medieval ages of the West created a feudal economy, rural in nature, where the feudal lords dominated not only the society but also the state power. It was a system where the lords, as masters of the slave-owning society, exploited the peasants, the serfs particularly.

In the case of the Western type of development of civilisation we see first the emergence of the private property and exchange (commodity relations) and then, on the basis of these, the division of society into classes, and finally the coming onto the stage of history of the state as the instrument of political rule. Yet, in the case of Eastern type of development of civilisation, the formation of the ruling class and state, developed on a completely different basis. Those states in the ancient ages of the East (for instance, Sumer, ancient Egypt, India, China, Persia, etc.) arose not on the basis of individual private property and relations of individual exploitation (exploitation of slaves) as in the West, but of collective communal property and the relations of collective exploitation. The ruling class of the Eastern society emerges as a result of the fact that those functions, which had been just public functions at the beginning, were turned into standing posts and that those servants turned their authority of function into authority of exploitation.

The modern Western society begins with capitalism, one that is as class society as was feudal and the slave-owning ones, with different antagonistic classes: the capitalists on the one hand, and the workers on the other. Lately, the societies in the East, too became capitalistic. The capitalist society provides a history of wage labour and capital, and the modern state becomes the instrument of exploitation of wage labour by capital. Marx wrote in *A contribution to the critique of Political Economy:* "The bourgeois mode of production is the last antagonistic form of the social process of production—antagonistic not in the sense of individual antagonism but of an antagonism that emanates from the individual's social conditions of existence—but the productive forces developing within bourgeois society create also the material conditions for a solution of this antagonism. The prehistory of human society accordingly closes with this social formation."

The bourgeois society, following the proletarian resolution, would be abolished and the dictatorship of the proletariat would establish the socialist society based on the principle 'from each according to his abilities to each according to his work.' The socialist classless society will eventually lead to the communist classless and stateless society based on the principle 'from each according to his work to each according to his needs.' It would be a society without the state, when the state would wither away: no state would mean no exploitative machinery, no state-apparatus and no oppression. Engles, thus, pronounces: "As soon as there is no longer away social class to be held in subjection; as soon as class rule and the individual struggle for existence based upon our present anarchy in production, with the collisions and excesses arising from these, are removed, nothing more remains to be repressed, and a special repressive force, a state, is no longer necessary. The first act by virtue of which the state really constitutes itself the representative of the whole of society—the taking possession of the means of production in the name of society—this is, at the same time, its last independent act as a state. State interference in social relations becomes, in one domain after another, superfluous, and then withers away of itself; the government of persons is replaced by the administration of things, and by the conduct of processes of production. The state is not "abolished". *It withers away.*"

In conclusion, we may say that for Marx, the state:

(i) is a class institution, for it is the product of the class society;

(ii) is a made institution, of it came into being when the classless society changed into a class society as a result of the birth of antagonistic classes, one having the ownership of the means of production, and another, without them;

(iii) is an instrument in the hands of the dominant class (the masters, the feudal lords, the capitalists in the class society, and the proletariat in the socialist society);

(iv) is a means which exists for the class that dominates: the masters in the slave-owning society; the feudal lords in the feudal society; the capitalists in the capitalists society; the workers in the socialist society;

(v) is an instrument of oppression; the state exploits the opposing class: the slaves, the serfs, the workers, the capitalists respectively;

(vi) does the destructive functions by abolishing the structure, the laws, the values, the culture and the like, and also the constructive functions by establishing the structure, values, laws of the class that comes to power;

(vii) is transitional in so far as it exists in the socialist society till the capitalist is abolished completely and the communist society is established in full. Thereafter, the state withers away.

Marx's theory of state has its peculiar limitations. Based as the idea is on materialism, Marx's theory of state suffers from its materialistic base. The material factor is an important factor, it can not be described as the solitary factor. His theory that the struggle between classes is the characteristic of a class society, paving for the future socio-economic formation is not a fact in so far as the evolution of history is concerned. The fact is that the state, as an institution, has developed through the cooperation among the classes which exist at any point of time. To describe the state as a class institution, granting him only the oppressive tasks is to take a very small view of the state: the state does exist for performing the welfare functions as well. Again, to imagine that the state will wither away in the complete communist society is merely an imagination.

## SUGGESTED READINGS

1. Bottomore, T., *Karl Marx* (Oxford: Social Blackwell, 1973).
2. Carr, E.H., *Karl Marx: A Study in Fanaticism* (London: Dent, 1934).
3. Cohen, G.A., *Karl Marx's Theory of History: A Defence* (Oxford: Oxford Universtiy Press, 1979).
4. Heilbroner, R., *Marxism: For and Against* New York: Oxford University Press, 1980).
5. Laski, H.J., *Karl Marx: An Essay* (London: Cluarin Books, 1922).
6. Mandel, E., *Introduction to Karl Marx* (London: The Capital, 1976).
7. Mallan, I., *The Thought of Karl Marx* (London: Macmillan, 1971).
8. Miliband, R., *Marxism and Politics* (Oxford: Oxford University Press, 1977).
9. ......, R., *Marx and the State* (*The Socialist Register*), pp. 278-290.
10. Miller, R., *Analysing Marx* (Princeton, N.J., Princeton Universtiy Press, 1984).

11. Wayper, C.L., *Political Thought* (Bombay: B. I. Publications, 1977).
12. Popper, K.R., *The Open Society and Its Enemies,* Vol. 2 (London: Routledge and Kegan Paul, 1945).
13. Singer, P., *Marx* (Oxford: Oxford University Press, 1980).
14. Wolfe, B., *Marxism: One Hundred Years in the Life of Doctrine* (New York: Avon, 1969).
15. Wolin S., *Politics and Vision* (Boston: Little Brown, 1960).

# CHAPTER – 18

# Kautilya on State

## I (a). Kautilya: The Man, His Times and His Works

Kautilya[1] lived during the period 350-275 B.C. The most of the details about Kautilya's life are uncertain and in fact, hazy. He is also known as Vishnugupta[2] and Chanakya[3], and traditionally known as the author of the *Arthashastra.* The ancient Indian tradition describes Kautilya as a native of Taxila (near Peshawar in modern Pakistan) as the *Mahavasma Tika* (the Buddhist literature) mentions it, though the Jain scriptures (the *Adbidhana Chintamani*) mention his place of birth as South India around the present Kerala. However, Kautilya's birth place will continue to remain a controversy.

What is certain about Kautilya is the fact that he was a man of strong will and a man with an unparalleled determination. That is why that he made up his mind to avenge insult inflicted on him by Nanda, the king of Patliputra. After leaving the city humiliated, he met the young Chandragupta on his way. He found Chandragupta a promising young man with all traits of a king. He worked hard for Chandragupta's installation and the throne of Magadha. After having met with a failure in the first attempt, Chandragupta regrouped his forces and kept launching his onslaughts on the Nanda kings, ultimately killing the Dhanananda in 322 B.C. and establishing a new dynasty, the Maurya one. Chandragupta Maurya was enthroned as the king of Magadha in 321 B.C. and ruled upto 298 B.C. All through, it was Kautilya who had masterminded the attacks first and continued as the king's advisor in statecraft.

[1]Because he was born in 'Kautala' gotra, he was, thus, called Kautilya.

[2]His parents gave him the name Vishnugupta, following the 'namkaran' ceremony.

[3]Chanaka was the name of the village where he was born; hence he was known as Chanakya.

The scholars differ with regard to the date when the *Arthasastra* was written, some contesting even the authorship. There is a school of thought which describes the time of the *Arthasastra* somewhere around the fourth century B.C. while the other, to the third or fourth century AD. What is usually agreed is that it was the Mauryan Kautilya who had written the *Arthasastra* and someone else rewrote his work or compiled a text from his teachings.

Kautilya's *Arthasastra,* containing the essence of the ancient Indian political thought, was discovered as late as 1904, when an anonymous priest of Tanjore district, handed over the manuscript of the monumental work written by Bhattasvamin to Dr. Sharma Shastri, who got it published in 1909 in Sanskrit, in the book form and it was published later in 1915 in English. R.P. Kangle refers to seven different manuscripts of the *Asthasastra* published in different languages. Kautilya's *Arthasastra* is described to be a compendium of all *Arthasastras* penned down by the ancient teachers. Hence, it has been portrayed as the culmination of the earlier *Arthasastra* literature embording its essence. In fact, the *Arthasastra* is the only treatise which has preserved the old political ideas. U. N. Ghoshal writes, "Kautilya makes a closer analysis and expresses a sounder judgement on the points at issue and reconstructs the science of politics."

The *Arthasastra* was not a work on political philosophy which it treats incidentally, but a manual of instructions on the administration of a state, and the way it meets challenges. Kautilya is a thorough going political realist. He views the state as a seven-limbed organism which grows in war and whose purpose is to destroy its enemies, and extend the territory under the control by all means.

The *Arthasastra* is divided into 15 books. These are:

1. Concerning discipline;
2. The duties of Government superintendents;
3. Concerning law;
4. The removal of thorns;
5. The conduct of courtiers;
6. The source of sovereign states;
7. The end of the six-field policy;
8. Concerning vices and calamities;
9. The work of an invader;

10. Relating to war;
11. The conduct of corporations;
12. Concerning a powerful enemy;
13. Strategic means to capture a fortress;
14. Secret means and
15. The plea of a treatise.

It is believed that the *Arthasastra* had two major objectives: (1) to discover the ways through which a ruler is able to protect his domain; (2) to discover the ways through which he is able to add new territories to his domain. For the first, Kautilya discusses, in his work, the basis of state administration, and for the second objective, he explains in details the foreign policy of the state in relation to other states. Thus, the two objectives constitute the whole range of state's activities. That is why that Kautilya views his *Arthasastra* as "the science of statecraft, of politics, and of administration."

## 1 (b). Kautilya on State

### (i) *What is a State?*

Kautilya's state is a state organised in people with the king or the ruler exercising full authority over his subjects but subject, above him, only to the divine power. It is a kingdom in which all lead a disciplined life. There is the king who is wise and virtuous; there are the officials who advise the king in his administration, every official performing his duties honestly. There are the people, as subjects, who demonstrate their loyalty to the king: for them, the king and the kingdom are the same; the king personifying the domain of the kingdom. The security of the kingdom and its protection constitute what may be called the king's *dharma.* The king is himself under the law which he is supposed to obey himself. He is a public servant, for, as Kautilya says, "In the happiness of his subjects lies the king's happiness, in their welfare, his welfare. He shall not consider as good only that which pleases him but treat as beneficial to him whatever pleases his subjects."

Thus, for Kautilya, the kingdom is the state; the state headed by the king; the people headed by the king; the king rules, but he himself is ruled by the law above him; the rulership is a duty, it is a *dharma;* the kingdom is a trust, a trust administered in trust whose breach tantamount to violating the *dharma.* In the Kautilyan state, there lies divinity: the *dharma* at work.

(ii) *Origin of the Kingship*

There is a contractual reference to the origin of the kingship, though not of the state. The authority of king finds justification on the ground that it is the consequence of a contract. R.S. Sharma writes, "...overtaken by a state of anarchy, the people elected Manu Vaivasvata as their king and undertook to pay 1/6 of their grain, and 1/10 of their articles of merchandise, in addition to a portion of their gold." In return for these taxes, Sharma continues, "the king guaranteed social welfare to the people by undertaking to suppress acts of mischief, afflicting the guilty with taxes and coercion."

For Kautilya, the kingship originated as a result of the contract; the king came to overtake anarchy; he came to give people protection; he came to provide people their welfare. On their count, the people agreed to pay taxes; they agreed to burden themselves the expenses of their ruler so to enable him maintain his officers and army as well as police; they agreed to pay full regards to their king. The contractual nature of the authority, as propounded by Kautilya, was two-fold: the king and the people agreeing to certain conditions; the king was powerful but powerful within limits, the people admitted the king's authority, but the admission was to their welfare; the king had possessed powers, powers because he was to perform certain duties, the people had duties, but duties because they had a regard for his authority. The Kautilyan king had possessed power as that of the Hobbesian *Leviathan,* but he was one whose powers were limited as that of the Lockean State.

The contractual references in Kautilya did contain the anarchical situation, a situation of the state of nature before the contract was concluded. But such a state appeared to be Lockean rather than Hobbesian. It was a situation where there was society, though there was no state (king); there was the *Dharma,* though there was no authority to ensure its application; there were moral values, though there was none to enact it. The contract was concluded so to create a situation of security, protection, welfare, *dharma.* That was what John Locke was to argue for in late seventeenth century England.

(iii) *Nature of the State*

From whatever has been discussed above, it is possible to highlight certain characteristics of the Kautilyan state. Some of these features are as under:

1. The king is the keystone of the political arch. All authority revolves around the king;
2. The king's powers, though are absolute, are held within the proper limits of the *Dharma;*
3. The *Dharma* guides all activities of the king. The king himself is bound by the dictates of the *Dharma* which finds expression in the ancient sayings and works;
4. The king functions through his subordinate officials, a disciplined lot with duties performed in all loyalty;
5. The king rules to enable him safeguard and protect his subjects;
6. The king governs in the interest of the subjects, the welfare of the subjects is his welfare; their happiness, his happiness;
7. The Kautilyan state is totalitarian in so far as it has no limitations on what it does; and
8. The protection of the subjects at home and the expansion of the territory of the state supported with all diplomatic avenues abroad constitute the very objectives of the Kautilyan state.

(iv) *The Elements of the State*

*Kautilya's Saptanga Theory:* The Kautilyan state has seven constituents, so described as the Saptanga theory. These elements can be discussed as under:

(a) *Svami:* Literally *svami* means the master, the lord. But as an element of the state, it refers to the headship in both monarchies and republics, the *raja* for monarchical systems, and the *vairajya* for the non-monarchical systems. As head, he enjoys an exalted position with all state powers vested in him. As head, he has to have certain qualities, such as, native of the territory, noble by birth, easily accessible, truthful and pious, person of sharp intellect, brave, and of strong mind, one who has the virtues of inspiring confidence in others, and one who takes prompt and quick decision.

(b) *Amatya:* Amatya is usually translated as a minister. In the *Arthasastra,* the amatyas constitute "a regular cadre of service,"

R.S. Sharma says, "from which all high officials such as the chief priest, ministers, collectors, treasurers, officers engaged in civil and criminal administration, officers in charge of harm, envoys and the superintendent of various departments are to be recruited." Thus, for Kautilya, amatyas constitute the whole body of executive which operates the laws of the State. The actual ministers' number is very small, called as *mantrins*. The *amatyas* are also "men of noble birth, trained in the arts, possessing eyes, intelligence, dexterous, bold, eloquent, persons with a ready wit, endowed with energy and power, able to bear troubles, upright, friendly, firmly dewled, endowed with character, strength, health, and spirit, devoid of stiffness and fickleness, amiable and not given to creating animosities," as the *Arthasastra* describes them.

The king's *mantrins* or let us say, *mantris* are his advisors, the former may or may not go by their advice. The number of the *mantris* is limited only to 3 or 4, depending upon the needs of the domain.

(c) *Janapada:* The *Janapada* as another element refers to both the territory as well as population. The nature of the *Janapada* defined in the *Arthasastra,* as R.S. Sharma explains, "indicates territory which should have a good climate, should provide grazable land for cattle and should yield grain with little labour," and population "inhabited by industries peasants who are capable of bearing the burden of taxes and punishments." "Finally, it should contain," Sharma continues, "intelligent masters and be predominantly populated by members of the lower classes and its people should be loyal and devoted."

(d) *Durga:* The expression *durga* is understood in the sense of fortress, and in the sense of fortified capital, if we include in it the sense of *pura* as well. *Durgavidhava* and *Durganivasa,* the two terms used, refer to 'fortress' and the fortified capital respectively. In the sense of fortified capital, the emphasis is laid on the planning of the capital which includes, among other things, the areas where people of varnas live in their respective apartments.

(e) *Kosa:* Kosa, as the fifth element of the Kautilyan state, refers to the treasure. According to Kautilya, the treasure accumulated by righteous and legitimate means should be under the control of the svami, the king, filled with gold, silver, precious jewels, and gems, the treasury should be able to meet the strains of expenditure caused during the times of adversity: famines, wars, flood, or any calamity. Kautilya states that without treasury, the army can not be maintained and can not become loyal.

(f) *Danda: Danda* or force, in the form of army, is another element of the state. It is sometimes bracketed with *kosa*. This element, according to Kautilya, consists of hereditary, hired, forest and corporation soldiers comprising of infantry, chariots elephants and cavalry. He says that the army should consist of the Ksatriyas, though vaisas and sudras can be enlisted on considerations of their numerical strength. The army has to be equipped with weapons, and has also to be skilled, patient and always ready at the call of the king.

(g) *Mitra: Mitra* means ally. According to Kautilya, the ally should be hereditary, not artificial, one with whom there is no possibility of rupture, and one who is ready to come to help when occasion so demands. His *mandala* theory clearly states the kind of role an ally has to play. He wants to increase the number of allies in relation to other states.

(v) *Role of the State*

Kautilya's theory of the functions of the state and its role can be summed in general terms as: "The state exists to provide order; the order is not merely for the sake of order, it is for the sake of protection; protection for the sake of development; the state exists to conserve and develop so to distribute the social benefits among the people."

In Kautilyan terms, the role of the state relates to two main domains: (a) Acquisition of Dominion; (b) Preservation of Dominion. Hence he has to offer two distinct policies:

(a) Policy of acquision of the dominion, (b) Policy of preservation of dominion. The functions of the king, as the repository of authority, may be summed up as under

(a) *Policy of Acquision of Dominion:* Kautilya refers to five-fold method of achieving the policy of acquision of dominion. These are: by creating disaffection among the enemy's partisans (*uprajapa;* by getting rid of the·enemy through recret tactics (*yogavamana*); by setting spies on the enemy's kingdom (apasarpa); by sieze (parypasana); and by assault (avanarda).

The policy of acquisition of dominion is supplemented by Kautilya's statement of the policy of pacification of the acquired kingdom. An acquired territory, according to Aristotle, is of three kinds: (i) Newly acquired by a king from his enemy, (ii) that which had belonged to him formerly and now has been recovered, (iii) that which has inherited from his father. The measures of pacification with regard to the first should include king's efforts to display enemy's faults, to double his merits as against those of his enemy, to do good to the new subjects by performing his *dharma* and *karmas,* and to bestow gifts and honours, to keep his promises, to show favour to the floor, the helpless and the diseased, to identify himself with his subjects. The additional measures of pacification with regard to the second should include the king's efforts to renounce those faults which cost him the kingdom and strengthen those virtues which helped him regain it. With regard to the third, the king should suppress the faults of his father and proclaim his virtues.

(b) *Policy of Preservation of Dominion:* This can be studied under the following headings:

1. *Policy of Security of the king and the community:* The king needs to be protected from princes, while the ill-controlled should be banished or imprisoned, the self-controlled should be appointed to the official post. The king needs to be protected from his own officials as well as of his enemies through an elaborate system of espiouage. The king needs to be protected against the enemy's wiles corrupting his loyal subjects through his policy of conciliation. He needs to protect the *dharma* and the territory of the state through a loyal and disciplined army. He needs to protect his people, rich and poor and those belonging to numerous varnas, living in both rural and urban areas from 'thorns' (human such as violaters of laws, animals, such as rats and wild ones, and natural calamities such as floods, earthquakes and famines).
2. *Policy of Regulation:* The regulative functions of the state, through the king, include regulation of contractual relations between the employees and the employers, weights and measures, of trade and of commerce, of market forces, of social system and societal relations, of health services and the like.
3. *Financial Functions:* The state has certain financial functions as well. For guarding the treasury, the king is justified in applying the use of force and farced. The king possesses the power to tax people, ask for peoples' benevolences to strength his territory. He has to be very careful in spending the state's

money. He has to protect the natural resources and has to see that the state-owned industries are carefully run.

4. *Welfare functions:* The state's welfare functions include:
   (i) building of dams, tanks, irrigational works, opening trade routes, developing pastures, cultivation of virgin lands, protection of citizens;
   (ii) help the poor, the orphans, the aged, the infirm, the helpless, the pregnant women, the newly born babies;
   (iii) health care;
   (iv) recreational and entertainment;
   (v) social insurance through strengthening the family structure for the widows, minor kids, the aged, the unmarried daughters.
5. *Policy of Inter-state Relations:* Kautilya shows how his six-fold policy produces efforts for achieving a work and for securing the desired results. The six-fold policy is: *sandhi* (treaty), *asna* (armed neutrality), *vigraha* (state of hostility), *yana* (a position of preparedness so to march against the enemy), *samsraya* (an alliance with a superior power), and *dvaidhibhava* (a policy of peace with me and war with another).

Kautilya says that the successes (the siddhis) can be achieved if the king has three powers: the power of the king's counsel, the power of the king's material resources, the power of the king's energy: *mantrasakti* (the strength of knowledge), *prabhusakti* (the strength of revenue), *utsahasakti* (the prowess). The test of a strong, a weak and an equal king, Kautilya says, is the possession of the above powers, the king receiving the successes in relatively varying degree.

U.N. Ghoshal views the Kautilyan state as one which has "...the personal safety of the king within his own household, the protection of the people against anti-social elements as well as providential calamities, the suppression of secret criminals and enemies of the state, state-planning of the rural and urban areas with the object of meeting the military and economic needs of the administration and the requirements of a developed administrative organisation respectively, and lastly, the alignment of foreign policy with the avowed end of achieving a complete programme of power and success as well as of progress at the expense of the enemy. Summing up the above we may say that the Kautilyan polity is essentially a human institution, controlled by a highly trained ruler with his staff of officials especially recruited and selected for the purpose. At home, it partakes of the joint characteristics of a collectivist and a totalitarian state, while abroad, it is inspired by a passionate zeal for expansion with the goal of universal rule in view. In the branches of internal and foreign administration, it uses the weapons of diplomacy and force with such a strong preference for the former in all its forms as to make the state administration essentially a work of art requiring the exercise of the highest qualities of intellect and character on the part of the ruler."

(vi) *Conclusion*

The study of Kautilya's views on the state and polity explains the versatility of his formulations with regard to polity. His views with regard to the origin of the kingship, his guidelines for maintaining the security of the king and his kingdom and the promotion and welfare of the people, as well as his definite proposals regarding the inter-state relations have left imprint on the well-administered ancient polity.

Yet Kautilya's state was more Brahminical than secular; more monarchial than republican; more about the king than about the kingdom; more about the expansion of the kingdom than about its maintenance; more about the security of the king than about the security of his kingdom; his king was more totalitarian than absolute; more collectivistic than authoritarian.

## SUGGESTED READINGS

1. Bandyopadhaya, N.C., *Kautilya or An Exposition of His Serial and Political Theory* (Calcutta: National Publishing House, 1927).
2. Ghoshal, U.N., *A History of Indian Political Ideas* (Oxford: Oxford University Press, reprint 1996).
3. Jayaswal, K.P., *Hindu Polity* (Calcutta: Butterworth, 1930).
4. Law, N.N., *Aspects of Ancient Indian Polity* (Bombay: Oriental Longman, 1921).
5. Mabbett, J.W., *Truth, Myth and Politics in Ancient India* (Delhi: Thompson Press, 1972).
6. Prasad, Beni, *The State in Ancient India* (Allahabad: The Indian Press, 1928).

## CHAPTER – 19

# Gandhi on Swaraj

### I (a). Mahatma Gandhi: The Man, His Times and His Works

Mohandas Karam Chand Gandhi (M.K. Gandhi, herein after Gandhi) was born on October 2, 1869 in an average family, and in an obscure town (Porbandar) in Kathiawad. He was the sixth child and the youngest of all in the family. His father was 48 and mother in her early twenties when Gandhi was born. His father had studied till about three classes, but rose to become a Diwan in a small state of Gujarat province. His mother was illiterate.

Gandhi was very shy and timid in his childhood. As a student, he was an average one. At the age of 13, he was married to Kasturba. The early marriage did affect his studies, but he soon was able to catch up. He was the first in his family to have passed 10th class. Though he failed poorly in the college, yet he sought to go to England for his law degree. The money for his England education was made available after selling a part of the family land and the permission to go abroad was given by the mother after his having made promises not to touch meat, women and wine. He left India in September 1888 when he was 18. After three years, he came back to India with the Barrister's title, in 1891. In 1893, at the age of 23, he went to South Africa to help contest a case. He was to stay in South Africa for a year or so, but spent about 22 years there. Gandhi returned to India as a great champion of social equality with his techniques of *Satyagraha* and *non-violence.*

Between 1915 and 1948, Gandhi worked in India for country's freedom. He was much more than the liberator of his country. As a nationalist, Gandhi was no less a patriot like Washington, Mazzini, and Sun Yat-Sen, but his achievements went far beyond independence. He stood for truth, humanity and world peace. In many respects, he was a citizen of the world. Though born a Hindu, Gandhi was, in more than one way, a member of humanity. Though he was a politician, he was in fact, a saintly person.

Gandhi's greatest strength, in politics, was his power to convince others, especially his opponents. No other person was as friendly with the adversaries as he was; no other person could win his enemies so easily as he could. With his weapons of non-violence and with his objectives of truth, he fought the mighty British empire.

Gandhi was a leader; he made the Congress movement as the nationalist movement; he turned the national movement of India into a mass movement. Millions of his countrymen stood behind him, his political opponents in the front. With each movement that he launched from the Champaran Satyagraha (1917) to the civil disobedience movement (1930-1934) and the initiation of the Quit India (1942), Gandhi rose as a taller leader, the tallest of all.

Gandhi, though claimed to have no 'ism', was one who had 'Gandhism', for he had said himself, "Gandhi can die, but Gandhism can never." Gandhi was more than Plato and Aristotle, he was a Socrates; he was more than Mill and Marx, he was a great humanist like Buddha. He had, in him, the mixture of so many ideologies: he was an individualist among the socialists, socialist among the individualists; a Marxist among the socialists, and a socialist among the Marxists. He was a great champion of the poor, the lowly, the outcastes, the weak; he was a great advocate of unity: social or political. He was a great man, the greatest among the great, the parallel of him is born after ages. It is a matter of pride for those Indians who lived during the age of Gandhi.

Gandhi was assassinated by a fanatic Hindu on January 30, 1948. Nehru had said, then, "The light has gone out of our lives and there is darkness everywhere," "a pillar of strength and a source of inspiration to the nation," as Sardar Patel had described Gandhi.

It is said that during his lifetime Gandhi wrote about 10 million words. That means that he wrote about 500 words everyday over a period of about 50 years. More than half of that writing went into the editorials of his newspapers. A person who writes so much on moral, political, economic, social, religious matters, is bound to develop an extraordinary character.

Gandhi's works included *An Autobiography or The Story of My Experiments with Truth, Non-violence in Peace and War, Non-violent Satyagraha, Satyagraha, Young India.* The papers he edited were the *Harijan, the Young India.* His writings and speeches, in *Gandhiana,* run into about 125 volumes.

Gandhi was a saint and a revolutionary, saint in so far as he stood for spiritualisation of all aspects of individual life; a revolutionary in so far as he worked through *satya* and non-violence. In his political ideas, Gandhi advocated a morally-based and ethically-oriented politics, a decentralised polity starting from individual onward, a duty-based scheme of rights, a state with minimum functions; in his economic ideas, he was for trusteeship, swadeshi, socialism where the basic needs of human beings are taken care of, and an economy which is self-reliant with its direction toward growth. In his social ideas, he was for a well-knit society with unity made up of diversities. In his technique, he was for techniques such as satyagraha and non-violence.

## I (b). Gandhi on Swaraj

The concept of *Swaraj* was developed during the Indian freedom struggle. In his book *Hind Swaraj* (1909), Gandhi was emphatic that swaraj was 'much more than simply wanting the English rule without the Englishmen, *the tiger's nature but not the tiger.*' What he meant was that the English rule, in its institutions relating to politics, economy, bureaucracy, legal system, military arrangement, and educational scheme, were inherently unjust, exploitative and alienating. Gandhi believed that *Swaraj* was "infinitely greater than and includes independence. So for Gandhi, swaraj was two-dimensional:

(i) It involved self-rule for India as an independent nation;
(ii) It involved self-rule for each individual.

The first was to be the natural outcome of the latter.

With regard to self-rule as independence for India, Gandhi wrote as follows: "...the independence should be political, economic and moral. 'Political' necessarily means the removal of the control of the British army in every shape and form. 'Economic' means entire freedom from British capitalists and capital, as also their Indian counterparts. In other words, the humblest must feel equal to the tallest...'Moral' means freedom from armed defense forces..."

Thus, political *swaraj* means self-government, and not good government. For Gandhi, good government is no substitute for self-government. What swaraj, in the sense of self-rule, means is that the people participate in the formation, and functioning of the government; it means continuous efforts to be independent of governmental control, whether foreign government or national government; it means a power with the individual to improve their lot, a power through which people make their destroy, a power to combat a corrupt polity, a power that controls absolute authority.

Independence involved more than just the expulsion of British political and economic institutions from India. Gandhi expressed this when he said that "*swaraj* means not mere political awakening, but an all round awakening—social, educational, moral, economic, and political." Gandhi declared that the English would leave India "only when we reform ourselves." Independence from British rule would only come, when individual Indians uprooted British culture from themselves and their communities. Essentially, *swaraj* was "a movement of self-purification", for the Indian people. Gandhi stated, "If we become free, India is free... It is *swaraj* when we learn to rule ourselves."

There is, therefore, *swaraj* at the individual level. On this level, the call for swaraj represents a genuine attempt to regain control of the 'self' - our self-respect, self-responsibility, and capacities for self-realization - from institutions of dehumanization. As Gandhi states, "It is *swaraj* when we learn to rule ourselves." The real goal of the freedom struggle was not only to secure political independence from Britain, but rather to gain true *swaraj* (liberation and self-rule). Gandhi writes, "At the individual level, *swaraj* is vitally connected with the capacity for dispassionate, self-assessment, ceaseless self-purification and growing swadeshi or self-reliance." *Swaraj* is the sovereignty of the people based on pure moral authority. For Gandhi, *swaraj* of the people means the sum-total of the *swaraj* of individuals and so he clarified that for him, *swaraj* means freedom for the meanest of his countrymen. And in its fullest sense, swaraj is much more than freedom from all restraints; it is self-rule, self-restraint, and could be equated with *moksha* or salvation.

To sum up, we may say that Gandhi's concept of *swaraj*, in its use of the word with regard to national movement, means independence of India from the British rule. But in its use of the word as a political concept, it is more than mere independence of the country; it is the power to rule one-self, to form one's government, to support the government if it works for the people, and oppose if it abuses the trust posed in it by the people, to resist the authority if it violates its mandate. And in yet another sense, *swaraj* is related to the individual, in what it raises individual's capacity to rise above all temptations, each performing his duty to the service of all mankind, cultivating, as Gandhi had said, "the spirit of service, renunciation, truth, non-violence, self-restraint, patience."

### I (b) (i). How to Realise Swaraj?

Gandhi was more serious in finding ways and means of realising *swaraj*. He used to say that swaraj will not drop from the clouds, but it would be the fruit of patience, perservance, ceaseless toil, and courage. He also insisted that *swaraj* means vast organising ability, penetration into the villages solely for the service of the villagers, i.e., through mass education. In the Gandhian scheme, education of the masses means conscientization, mobilisation and empowerment, making people to stand up to face bravely to the powers that be. He said, "Real swaraj will come, not by the acquisition of authority by the acquisition of the capacity by all to resist authority when it is abused. In other words, swaraj is to be attained by educating the masses to a sense of their capacity to regulate and control authority."

Indeed, political independence was an essential pre-condition, and in fact the first step towards the realisation of the goal of *swaraj*, but it was only a first step. For political independence, Gandhi worked with and through the Indian National Congress. Foreign domination was one form of domination. There were, Gandhi felt, numerous other ills with which India was suffering from. He, therefore, wanted an internal cleansing through self-motivated voluntary action in the form of constructive work. That was why that Gandhi attached much importance to the constructive work in all his movements. He used to dovetail it into his movement for freedom. *Swaraj* of Gandhi's dream was to be built from below, brick by brick. *Swaraj*, for Gandhi, meant the elimination of all forms of domination, oppression, segregation and discrimination through the use of active non-violence and through programmes, such as, the revival and propagation of khadi and other related rural schemes. For translating these constructive programmes, organisations were necessary. Gandhi, therefore, founded voluntary organisations to carry out constructive programmes, organisations such as the All India Spinners Association (AISA), All India Village Industries Association (AIVIA) and the Harijan Sewak Sangh (HSS). Though constructive workers were debarred from directly taking part in political struggles, Gandhi did enlist them for political mobilisation. For example, the 79 volunteers who constituted the Dandi march were all constructive workers; Gandhi's Individual Satyagraha (1940) had Vinoba Bhave the first Satyagrahi, was a constructive worker, who later was engaged into sarvodaya movement in which Jayprakash Narayan also took part in 1960s.

### I (b) (ii). Gandhi's Opposition to the Centralised State

Gandhi was a philosophical anarchist. He was of the opinion, like all individualists that more of the state amounts to less of the individual. The state laws oppose the spirit of '*swaraj*' in the individual. That was why Gandhi had defined the western type of state as the most organised and concentrated form of violence and called it an impersonal entity, a soulless machine, which lay at the roots of all progress. Gandhi never thought that the route can be moulded into an instrument of serving the people. In giving more functions to the state, we find the state abrogating the rights of the citizens and in the process, it would arrogate to itself the role of grand protector and would demand people's obedience. This would, Mathai, in his article "What Swaraj Meant to Gandhi," says "create paradoxical situation where the citizens would be alienated from the state, and at the same time, enslaved to it which, according to Gandhi, was demoralising and dangerous." Gandhi's close acquaintance, Mathai continues, "with the working of the state apparatus in South Africa and in India strengthened his suspicion of a centralised, monolithic state, his intimate association with the Congress and its leaders confirmed his fears about the corrupting influence of political power and his skepticism about the efficacy of the party systems of power politics and his study of the British parliamentary system convinced him of the utter impotency of representative democracy.... So he thought it necessary to evolve a mechanism to achieve the twin objectives of 'empowering the people' and 'empowering the state," by developing, "two progned strategy of resistance (to the state) and reconstruction (through voluntary and participatory social action."

**I (b) (iii). Swaraj as Relatedness**

Preferring *swaraj* to independence, Gandhi emphasised that swaraj means the rule of the self, where the self is not an isolated phenomenon, but a related entity: related to the nature, to others. Here, self is not an isolated normal subsisting in itself and for itself. Here self is self of the self which is the transcendent immanent reality, that is the self of the inner self, the truth in him. *Swaraj* presupposes that all individuals are related to each other, for all of them are related to their respective self and hence there is interdependence or relatedness among them. This interdependence and relatedness of the individual is not arrived at through any social contract for the sake of socialisation; it is in-born; it is related one. In Gandhian system, this relatedness in the individual operates and operates through the principle of non-violence which gives relatedness its legitimacy. The individual, Gandhi says, should not violate the truth in others. This respect for truth in others, and this relatedness with others non-volatile is the path of *swaraj*. It is the very striving after *swaraj* that takes care of *swaraj*.

As relatedness, *swaraj* is not isolation; it is rather a feeling of fellowship, of companionship and not that of alienating desires. As one that is an object of search truth and finding truth in everyone else, *swaraj* is a situation of non-domination, i.e., freedom from all kinds of domination. As interdependence, *swaraj* is mutual help, mutual assistance, and therefore, freedom from oppression and exploitation.

**I (b) (iv). Swaraj Structurally Devised**

*Swaraj* as self-dependence and as interdependence, following the spirit of relatedness means, structurally for Gandhi, that every village would be a republic having full powers as self-sustained and self-dependent body. In such a self-regulated body, individual is the basic and ultimate unit who would render his cooperation freely and willingly. The ultimate basis of the individual and the village—society, Gandhi explains, is truth which is both transcendent and immanent concept having non-violence as its operational principle.

In this structure, composed of innumerable villagers, George Pattery says, for Gandhi "there will be ever-widening, never ascending circles. Life will not be pyramid with the apex sustained by the bottom. But it will be an oceanic circle whose center will be the individual, always ready to perish for the village, the latter ready to perish for the circle of village, till at last the whole becomes one life composed of individuals never aggressive in their arrogance but ever humble, sharing the majesty of the oceanic circle for which they are integral unit."

The outermost circumference, Pattery says, "in this design would not wield power to crush the inner circle, but would give strength to all within and derive its own strength from it. Machinery would not displace human labour, nor would there be concentration of power in a few hands." *Swaraj* is decentralised polity; it is power in devolution, always devolving.

### I (b) (v). Swaraj, Swadeshi and Sarvodaya

*Swaraj,* in Gandhian system, implies swadeshi, i.e., homeness. Swadeshi may be described as something routed in one's immediate surroundings. As the whole universe, each nation in the universe and each region in the nation is linked, the correct mode of relating is to remain related to one's immediate surroundings. As Gandhi had said about *swadeshi* "...that spirit in us which restricts us to the use and service of our immediate surroundings, to the exclusion of the more remote. I restrict myself to my ancestral religion; if defective, I purge it from within. In politics, I use of indigenous institutions, if defective, I improve upon them; in economics, I use the immediate surroundings."

*Swaraj,* as total freedom is a true home-coming. *Swaraj* also means sarvodaya: the welfare of all. Gandhi's social theory envisages well-being for all, well-being that is oriented to self-realization of one and all. In this new society economic relations are not controlled by market-forces, but by social affections. Political economy gives way to 'affective economy'; a mother, though hungry, may go starving in order to feed her son. Accordingly, Gandhi argued that affective resources could enter into all economic equations, and produce the maximum. If the spirit of the worker is brought to its greatest strength by the motivating forces of affection, it can produce more. Labour, with stable wages and constancy of numbers in employment, functions in terms of service, not in terms of profit, the wages being a necessary adjunct, not the object of life.

In the construction of a civil society, Gandhi introduces the quest for liberation or self-realization as the basic component. Search for liberation gives all the members a transcendent reference point and enables them to relativize everything else, and, at the same time, to be related to one another on a basis that is above themselves. By introducing a transcendent referentiality in the construction of civil society, Gandhi visualizes a civil society that is eco-friendly and theandric, not narrowly anthropocentric. It gives civil society a primordial character.

### I (b) (vi). Swaraj as Fearlessness and Self-Suffering

*Swaraj* as the individual level means one's capacity to rise above all temptation; it is self-realisation; it is renunciation and not greed; it is search for truth, and not running after material satisfaction; it is self-restraint. *Swaraj* demands an individual who is non-violent, disciplined and fearless. Fearlessness, for Gandhi connotes freedom from all external fear, fear of disease, bodily injury and death, of dispossession. Self-suffering creates a selfless individual. In the Gandhian scheme, it means:

1. Suffering undertaken in the form of fast or self-discipline purifies the heart and makes one unattached: "Without inward purification, work cannot be done in a spirit of non-attachment."
2. In satyagraha, suffering would convince the agent of the power of injustice against which the struggle is undertaken and of the earnestness of the demand.
3. Suffering is the dynamics of human love. "Love does not burn others, it burns itself."
4. "Non-violence in its dynamic condition means conscious suffering. It does not mean meek submission to the will of the evil-doer, but it means putting one's whole soul against the will of the tyrant." Suffering is a program of transformation of relationship.

5. Suffering is a more efficacious and more manly method of representation. "My faith in the efficacy of quiet but continued suffering is much greater than in negotiation and public agitation, though I am aware that both are part of the struggle, in so far as the struggle represents strong and weak parties alike."
6. The fearless self-suffering for a righteous cause overflows into infinite compassion (karuna) and benevolent friendship (maitri), doing good even to evil-doers and reaching out to all in love.
7. Fasting, as a protest against an injustice, awakens the sleeping conscience either of the loved ones, of the society or of the ruler (tapas = heat produced from single-minded devotion). Fasting is not a means to force someone into action. A genuine fast is a direct act of resistance to untruth; it is an immediate appeal to the conscience of the wrong-doer; it relies on one's inner spiritual strength. In this sense fasting epitomizes the meaning of suffering in non-violent resistance as an eminently "transformative pedagogic act." The therapeutic value of suffering and of bodily inscriptions of freedom is matter important in itself.

## Conclusion

Gandhi's concept of *swaraj* had, in it, the expression of more than political independence. It had its meaning stretched to the domains of individual, economy, politics, and to those aspects which relate to life. *Swaraj* was, for him, both a means as well as an end; as an end, it was Truth; as a means, it was the principle of non-violence. It was freedom, inner freedom; it was what came from one's inner voice.

## SUGGESTED READINGS

1. Bose, N.K., *Selections from Gandhi* (Ahmedabad: Navjivan, 1948).
2. Dhawan, G.N., *The Political Philosophy of Mahatma Gandhi* (Ahmedabad: Navjivan, 1962).
3. Gandhi, M.K., *An Autobiography* (Ahmedabad: Navjivan, 1956).
   ________, *Non-violence in Peace and War,* 2 vols. (Ahmedabad: Navjivan, 1948)

________, *Non-violence Resistance* (New York: Schocken Books, 1967).

________, *Satyagraha* (Ahmedabad: Navjivan, 1951).

4. Ghose, Sankar, *Modern Indian Political Thought* (New Delhi: Allied Publishers (P) Ltd., 1984).
5. Jha, M.N., *Modern Indian Political Thought* (Meerut: Meenakshi Prakashan, 1975).
6. Sharp, Gene, *Gandhi Wields the Weapon of Moral Power: Three Core Histories* (Ahmedabad: Navjivan, 1960).

   ________, *Gandhi as a Political Strategist* (Boston: Porter Sergant Publishers, 1979).
7. Tendulkar, D.G., *Mahatma: Life of Mohandas Karamchand Gandhi* (Delhi: Publication Division).

## CHAPTER – 20

# Ambedkar on Social Justice

### I (a). B.R. Ambedkar: The Man, His Times and His Works

There are evils such as slavery, apartheid, caste system, gender bias and the like which are creations of possessive people. There are evils which are man-made created by man for the exploitation of man. Those who raise their voice against such evils and give a relentless fight against them go down in history as immortal personalities. Among these personalities, mention can be made about Buddha, Jesus Christ, Guru Nanak and in our days, Dr. Bhimrao Ramjee Ambedkar.

Dr. B.R. Ambedkar, a great crusader of social justice was born on April 14, 1891 in Mhow Cantt in Madhya Pradesh, the fourteenth child of his parents, and in an 'untouchable' Mahar family. His father, Ramji and grandfather Maloji were in the British army and the government of those days had required all army personnel and their children to be educated. Thus, the Ambedkar family was able to see its children receive a good education.

When Bhim was six years old, his mother died, and he was brought up by his father's sister Meerabai until Ramji remarried. His father was a strict, pious man, and avoided meat and drink. Along with his children, he often sang devotional songs composed by Namdev, Tukaram, Moropant and Mukteshwar, and read stories from the *Ramayana* and the *Mahabharata.* When he retired from the army as a Subedar-Major of the Second Grenadiers after 14 years of service, the family moved to Dapoli in Konkan and then to Satara. Bhim and his older brother Anand were enrolled in the contonment school, Government High School.

Despite the opportunity that education permitted, Bhim began to taste the bitter reality of his birth. He had to sit on the floor in one corner in the classroom. Teachers would not touch his notebooks. If Bhim felt thirsty, he could only drink water if someone else poured water into his mouth. Once provoked by an uncontrollable fit of thirst, Bhim drank from the public reservoir. He was found out and beaten by the higher caste Hindus. These experiences were permanently etched onto his mind. He realised that this was the fate of everyone who was born "untouchable."

In the year 1908, young Bhimrao passed the Matriculation examination from Bombay University with flying colours. Four years later he graduated in Political Science and Economics from Bombay University and got a job in Baroda. Around the same time his father passed away. Although he was going through a bad time, Bhimrao decided to accept the opportunity to go to USA for further studies at Columbia University for which he was awarded a scholarship by the Maharaja of Baroda. Bhimrao remained abroad from 1913 to 1917 and again from 1920 to 1923. During this period he had established himself as an eminent intellectual. Columbia University had awarded him the PhD for his thesis, which was later published in a book form under the title "The Evolution of Provincial Finance in British India." But his first published article was "Castes in India—Their Mechanism, Genesis and Development." During his sojourn in London from 1920 to 1923, he also completed his thesis titled "The Problem of the Rupee" for which he was awarded the degree of DSc. Before his departure for London he had taught at a College in Bombay and also brought out Marathi weekly whose title was 'Mook Nayak' (meaning 'Dumb Hero').

By the time he returned to India in April 1923, Dr. Bhimrao Ambedkar had equipped himself fully to wage war against the practice of untouchability on behalf of the untouchable and the downtrodden. Meanwhile the political situation in India had undergone substantial changes and the freedom struggle in the country had made significant progress.

While Bhimrao was an ardent patriot on the one hand, he was the saviour of the oppressed, women and poor on the other. He fought for them throughout his life. In 1923, he set up the 'Bahishkrit Hitkarini Sabha' (Outcastes Welfare Association), which was devoted to spreading education and culture amongst the downtrodden, improving the economic status and raising matters concerning their problems in the proper forums to focus attention on them and finding solutions to the same.

The problems of the downtrodden were centuries old and difficult to overcome. Their entry into temples was forbidden. They could not draw water from public wells and ponds. Their admission in schools was prohibited. In 1927, he led the Mahad March at the Chowdar Tank at Colaba, near Bombay, to give the untouchables the right to draw water from the public tank where he burnt copies of the 'Manusmriti' publicly. This marked the beginning of the anti-caste and ant-priest movement. The temple entry movement launched by Dr. Ambedkar in 1930 at Kalaram temple, Nasik is another landmark in the struggle for human rights and social justice.

In the meantime, Ramsay McDonald announced the 'Communal Award' as a result of which in several communities including the 'depressed classes' were given the right to have separate electorates. This was a part of the overall design of the British to divide and rule. Gandhiji wanted to defeat this design and went on a fast unto death to oppose it. On 24th September 1932, Dr. Ambedkar and Gandhiji reached an understanding, which became the famous Poona Pact. According to this Pact, in addition to the agreement on electoral constituencies, reservations were provided for untouchables in Government jobs and legislative assemblies. The provision of separate electorate was dispensed with. The Pact carved out a clear and definite position for the downtrodden on the political scene of the country. It opened up opportunities of education and government service for them and also gave them a right to vote.

Dr. Ambedkar attended all the three Round Table Conferences in London and each time, forcefully projected his views in the interest of the 'untouchable'. He exhorted the downtrodden sections to raise their living standards and to acquire as much political power as possible. He was of the view that there was no future for untouchables in the Hindu religion and they should change their religion if need be. In 1935, he publicly proclaimed, "I was born a Hindu because I had no control over this but I shall not die a Hindu."

After a while Dr. Ambedkar, organised the Independent Labour Party, participated in the provincial elections and was elected to the Bombay Legislative Assembly. During these days he stressed the need for abolition of the 'Jagirdari' system, pleaded for workers'.

In 1947, when India became independent, the first Prime Minister Pt. Jawaharlal Nehru, invited Dr. Ambedkar, who had been elected as a Member of the Constituent Assembly from Bengal, to join his Cabinet as a Law Minister. Dr. Ambedkar had differences of opinion with the Government over the Hindu Code Bill, which led to his resignation as Law Minister. The Constituent Assembly entrusted the job of drafting the Constitution to a committee and Dr. Ambedkar was elected as Chairman of this Drafting Committee.

In the beginning of 1948, Dr. Ambedkar completed the draft of the Constitution and presented it in the Constituent Assembly. In November 1949, this draft was adopted with very few amendments. Many provisions have been made in the Constitution to ensure social justice for scheduled castes, scheduled tribes and backward classes. Ambedkar laid special emphasis on dignity, unity, freedom and rights for all citizens as enshrined in the Constitution. He advocated democracy in every field: social, economic and political. For him social Justice meant maximum happiness to the maximum number of people.

On 24 May 1956, on the occasion of Buddha Jayanti, he declared in Bombay, that he would adopt Buddhism in October. On October 14, 1956 he embraced Buddhism along with many of his followers.

Dr. Ambedkar's patriotism started with the upliftment of the downtrodden and the poor. He fought for their equality and rights. His ideas about patriotism were not only confined to the abolition of colonialism, but he also wanted freedom for every individual. For him freedom without equality, democracy and equality without freedom could lead to absolute dictatorship.

Dr. Ambedkar died in 6th December, 1956. In 1990, he was bestowed with Bharat Ratna, and the year 1990-1991 was observed the "Year of Social Justice" in India in the memory of Dr. Ambedkar.

Dr. Ambedkar's works, among others, include *Annihilation of Caste* (1935), *Federation vs Freedom* (1939), *Mr. Gandhi and the Emancipation of the Untouchables* (1942), *Ranade, Gandhi and Jinnah* (1943), *What Congress and Gandhi have done to the Untouchables* (1945), *Who Were the Shudras?* (1946), *The Untouchable* (1948), *Buddha and His Dhamma* (1957).

## I (b). Ambedkar on Social Justice

Lalit Mansingh, one time the High Commissioner for India in Britain had said: "Dr. B.R. Ambedkar was seen to be a man of the stature of Mahatma Gandhi and a great man of India. He has been influenced by history: he studied Thomas Jefferson's 1776 US Bill of Rights and the events of the 1789 French Revolution.... Dr. Ambedkar realised that the Indian Constitution must incorporate the four elements: equality, liberty, fraternity and justice. But above all he knew the absolute necessity of Social justice.... His status was equal to that of Dr. Martin Luther King. 250 million people look upon Ambedkar as a shining light. He was a great democrat, a great patriot and a great man of his people." Vijay Chintaman Sonawane writes, "Dr. Babasaheb Ambedkar was truly a multi-faceted personality. A veritable emancipator of Dalits, a great national leader and a patriot, a great author, a great educationist, a great political philosopher, a great religious guide and above all a great humanist with out any parallel among his contemporaries."

Dr. Ambedkar was indeed a saviour of the downtrodden for whose upliftment he lived. His views with regard to social justice stem from his understanding of the Indian society based on caste system leading to the plight of the dalits.

(a) *Anti-caste system:* Dr. Ambedkar was of the opinion that the Hindu society was based on caste system which has ultimately led to the establishment of inequality. Caste system breeds inequality and inequality leads to the exploitation of the shudras. Caste system emerging from the *varna* system had the support of the Hindu religion and the Hindu scripts: *the Manu Smriti, the Bhagavad Gita, Vedanta the Mahabharata, the Ramayana, the Puranas.* The Brahamins, Dr. Ambedkar was convinced, as the highest in the caste ladder, indulged in high-handedness towards the untouchables and forced them to live as outcastes.

Dr. Ambedkar was opposed to all that which perpetuated caste system. That is why that he felt that the end of *varna* system could only help reform the untouchables. That was why that he opposed *Manusmriti,* making bonafire of it in September 1927 at Mahad. That was why that he opposed the nasty caste system, pointing out its ills and evils as under:

1. Caste system has been responsible for the destruction and downfall of the Hindu society;

2. The Hindu society's division into four classes has led to exploitation of one caste by another, the Brahamins exploiting all the other classes;
3. Inequality based on caste system is unscientific and illogical, and as much had no utility;
4. The Hindu society, divided into numerous castes, often opposing one another, has been harmful in so far as it demoralised people by denying same the facilities of education; and
5. Society based on caste system is opposed to all principles of liberty, equality, justice, brotherhood.

Dr. Ambedkar had held the view, "The caste difference destroyed the Hindu *vansh*. It drew out the Hindu society into deep darkness and now it has remained as a powerless and weak society."

(b) *Perpetuation of Untouchability:* Caste system is the role factor that perpetuates untouchability. Dr. Ambedkar had said: "The root cause of untouchability lies in caste system. In a message to the first issue of the *Harijan* weekly, he had pointed out, "...The out-caste is a by-product of the caste system. There will be outcastes so long as there are castes and nothing can emancipate outcaste except the destruction of the caste system." He rose as the leader of the untouchables for those who had no right to pull water from the well; for those who had no right to enter the temple; for those who had no right to get education; and for those who had no socio-political rights. His Bahishkrit Hitkarini Sabha of 1924 had aims such as:

1. to establish hostels for the spread of education for the down-trodden;
2. to start reading for cultural development;
3. to open industrial and agricultural school for economic development;
4. to start movement for eradicating untouchability;
5. to remove bad traditions of higher classes.

Dr. Ambedkar led a movement of about 500 untouchables to use the water of chawtar tank in Mahar village in March 1927. Addressing the untouchables, he had remarked, "You have to establish your right. If you do not do so, then there will be no difference between you and the cattle." And at another place, he had said, "My final words of advice to you is: educate, agitate and organise; have faith in yourself. With justice on our side, I do not see how we can lose our battle. For our battle is a battle not for wealth or for power. It is a battle for freedom. It is a battle for the reclamation of the human personality." He wants the untouchables to rise and abolish their slavery. He says, "You must abolish your slavery yourself. Do not depend for its abolition upon God or a superman." He was sorry to note that despite all efforts to abolish, untouchability remains, so remain the untouchables. To quote Dr. Ambedkar, "There have been many Mahatmas in India whose sole object was to remove untouchability, and to elevate and absorb the depressed classes, but everyone has failed in their mission. Mahatmas have came, Mahatmas have gone, but the untouchables have remained as untouchables." The loss of the untouchables has been, Dr. Ambedkar would say, the gains of other classes. So he says, "What you have lost, others have gained. Your humiliations are a matter of pride for others. You are made to suffer wants, privations and humiliations, not because it was pre-ordained by the sins committed in your previous birth, but because of the overpowering tyranny and treachery of those who are above you. You have no lands because others have usurped them; you have no posts because others have monopolised them. Do not believe in fate; believe in your strength."

(c) *Women's Rights and Human Rights:* In his political ideas, Dr. Ambedkar stood for equality: social, economic and political; he stood for justice: social, economic and political. He had remarked, "Justice has always evoked ideas of equality, of proportion, of compensation. Equity signifies equality. Rules and regulations, right and righteousness are concerned with equality in value. If all men are equal, then all men are of the same essence, and the common essence entitles them of the same fundamental rights and equal liberty.... In short justice is another name of liberty, equality and fraternity."

It is, in this spirit, that he wanted rights for women, especially the protection of their rights. His sponsored Hindu Code Bill which was "killed, buried, unwept and unsung" as he had remarked had the following points, favouring the womenfolk: (i) abolition of the doctrine of rights by birth; (ii) absolute rights over property to women; (iii) a share in the property to the daughter; (iv) provision for divorce. He was of the view that a society which did not give due respect and due rights to women was a society most traditional, most backward, and most undemocratic. For him, "Democracy is not a form of government, but is a form of social organisation." Again, he says, "It (democracy) is primarily a mode of associated living. ...It is essentially an attitude of respect and reverence towards our fellow men," especially women. For him, democracy is incompatible and inconsistent with isolation and exclusiveness resulting in the distinction between the privileged and unpriviledged.

Dr. Ambedkar was a great advocate of rights, human rights at that. He thought of the state as an institution which maintains, as Laski also had once said, rights: (i) the right of every person to life, liberty, and pursuit of happiness; (ii) the right of every class, the depressed class especially, to have social, economic and political equality; (iii) the right of everyone to enjoy freedom from want and freedom from fear. To him, true freedom was not a mere political freedom, but it was also social, economic, intellectual and spiritual. He said, "Freedom of mind is the real freedom. A person whose mind is not free though he may not be in chains, is a slave, not a free man. One whose mind is not free, though he may not be in prison, is a prisoner and not a free man. One whose mind is not free though alive, is no better than dead. Freedom of mind is the proof of one's existence."

Rights to be protected must have an atmosphere of the rule of law. It is law that helps maintain peace and social justice; it is law that is guardian of liberty and equality. Dr. Ambedkar was convinced that law has not created man, but man has "created law for his own happiness, emphasising that law must be social and human, shall discriminate between the wolf and the sheep, should protect the sheep against the wolf. This is what lays behind the idea of 'protective discrimination.'

Rights to be protected must have remedies. Unless the rights are legally protected, they have no meaning at all. According to him, "Rights are real only if they are accompanied by remedies. It is no use giving rights if the aggrieved person has no legal remedy to which he can resort to when his rights are invaded." In the absence of legal remedies, one should expect rights being protected, especially from usurpers. In such cases, victims are always the poor, the downtrodden, for "goats are used,"

Dr. Ambedkar said, "for sacrificial offerings and not lions." He was keen that the individuals need to be free from the shackles of old dogmas and rituals. To quote him, "Make every man and woman free from the thraldome of the *shastras,* cleanse their minds of the pernicious notion founded on the *shastras.*" An ideal society, for him, was one that is based on equality, liberty, justice and fraternity.

(d) *Justice for All:* Dr. Ambedkar argued for giving justice to all, especially to those who have been denied for centuries: right done for those wrongs, is justice. This was the spirit behind Dr. Ambedkar's concept of justice. His concept of social justice advocated a social system which is based on right relations between man and man; between class and class. According to him, "the strength of a society depends upon the presence of points of contacts, possibilities of interaction between different groups that exist in it. There are what Carlyle calls 'organic filaments', i.e., the elastic threads which help to bring the disintegrating elements together and to rewrite them. "It is a society where there are neither the beasts of burden and nor the beasts of prey."

Dr. Ambedkar's use of the term 'social justice' is one that advocates the organisation of society on the principles of equality, liberty and justice, which, in turn, necessitates the preferential treatment for the weaker sections of society. That is why that such clauses relating to protective discrimination were made part of the constitution in whose making Dr. Ambedkar presided, especially in the provisions relating to the Fundamental Rights and the Directive Principles of State Policy. Dr. Ambedkar entertained hatred for those who debarred the entry of the outcastes on public platforms. He had once remarked with regard to the opening of temples for the untouchables, saying "To open or not to open the temples is a question for you to consider and not for me to agitate. If you think it is bad manners not to believe in the sanctity of human beings, then throw open the doors and be a gentleman, but if you wish to remain an orthodox Hindu then shut the doors and damn yourself, for I don't care to come."

Dr. Ambedkar's concept of social justice was related to religion, religion of his own thinking. It was not the religion of a particular sect or community. It was the religion of humanity. He had emphasised: "I tell you, religion is for man and not man for religion. If you want to organise, consolidate, and be successful in the world, change this religion. The religion that does not recognise you as a human being, or give you water to drink, or allow you to enter in temples, is not worthy to be called a religion. The religion that forbids you to receive education and comes in the way of your material advancement is not worthy of the appellation 'religion'. The religion that does not teach its followers to show humanity in dealing with its co-religionists is nothing but a display of a force. The religion that teaches its followers to suffer the touch of animals but not the touch of human beings is not a religion but a mockery. The religion that compels the ignorant to be ignorant and the poor to be poor is not a religion but a visitation!" He said, "I like the religion that teaches liberty, equality and fraternity."

## SUGGESTED READINGS

1. Aloysius, G. (2004). "Transcendence in Modern Tamil Buddhism: A Note on the Liberative in Popular Religious Perceptions." In S. Jondhale and J. Beltz (Eds.) *Reconstructing the World: B.R. Ambedkar and Buddhism in India.* New Delhi: Oxford University Press.
2. Ambedkar, B. (1987-) *Dr. babasaheb Ambedkar Writing and Speeches* [BAWS] (Vol. I-XVIII) Mumbai: Education Department, Government of Maharashtra.
3. Brazier, D. (2001), *The New Buddhism.* London: Constable Robinson.
4. Chakravarti, U. (1987). *The Social Dimensions of Early Buddhism.* New Delhi: Oxford University Press.
5. Nanda, M. (2002). *Breaking the Spell of Dharma and Other Essays.* New Delhi: Three Essays Press.
6. Sangharakshita. (1986). *Ambedkar and Buddhism.* Glasgow: Windhorse Publications.
7. Sponberg, A. (1996). "TBMSG: A Dhamma Revolution in Contemporary India." In C. Queen and S. King (Eds.), *Engaged Buddhism: Buddhist Liberation Movements in Asia* (pp. 73-120). Albany, NY: State University of New York Press.
8. Rhys Davids, T.W. (1903). *Buddhist India.* London: T. Fisher Unwin.

## CHAPTER – 21

# Nehru and Lohia on Democracy

### I (a). Nehru: The Man, His Times and His Works

Jawaharlal Nehru was born on November 14, 1889 in Allahabad to Motilal Nehru and Swaroop Rani, his parents. His father was a famous lawyer of a high nobility, who wanted to give him the best education possible. He did not undergo any formal schooling, though he had his early education at home through tutors, especially Ferdinand T. Brooks. He was sent to Harrow, a boarding school in England, in 1905, a school famous for educating most of the to be Prime Ministers of England, with him there, the would be Prime Minister of independent India. Later, he attended the Trinify College at the University of Cambridge. He studied law at the Inner Temple in London, a profession which he practised for about seven years after he came back to India. He married Kamla Kaul in 1916 and both had a daughter, Indira, in 1917 who also became the Prime Minister after the death of Lal Bahadur Shastri in 1966. Two years later, Nehru joined the Indian National Congress in 1919. From 1920 to 1947, Nehru was very active in nation's liberation struggle. During these twenty seven years, Nehru spent about 10 years in prison (his *Glimpses of World History, the Discovery of India* were written during these years). During this period, he was elected the President of the Indian National Congress for four times: in 1929, 1936, 1937, and 1946.

Nehru was a versatile genius who possessed the rare qualities of head and heart. He was a staunch patriot, a great statesman, a constructive politician, a true democrat, a distinguished writer, a freedom fighter, a lover of peace, a maker of modern India, a humanist par excellence, a nationalist of first order, an internationalist without parallel, and a symbol of Asia's awakening and an architect of Non-aligned Movement.

He headed the Indian government for 17 long and brilliant years. He wanted India to develop into a world-recognised nation. He supported technological and scientific progress and encouraged art and literature. He wanted to eliminate discrimination from the face of the world and encouraged peaceful co-existence. Nehru did not believe in aligning himself with the military political blocks and wanted to end the cold war. He was awarded the Bharat Ratna in 1955.

Not only was he a brilliant orator, a charming, warm and noble thinker and philosopher, but also a prolific writer. He has written a few wonderful books *Discovery of India, Glimpses of World History, Letters from a father to a daughter* and *Autobiography.*

On May 27, 1964, India lost a great influence. In the words of Dr. Radhakrishnan "As a fighter for freedom he was illustrious, as a maker of a modern India, his services were unparalleled. His life and works have had a profound influence on our mental make-up, social structure and intellectual development." Indeed, Nehru lived up to his own words, "Life is like a game of cards. The hand that deals represents determinism, the way you play it is free will."

In the language of psychoanalysis, Professor V. P. Varma says, "Jawaharlal was the son of his father...." Motilal Nehru's spirit of independence and courage, as well as his pride, had been inherited by Jawaharlal. The strength of determination and the capacity to take risks that characterised Motilal had deeply influenced his son. When Nehru met Gandhi for the first time at the Lucknow Congress session of 1916, he found him 'very distant, and different and impolitical,' though after three years, 1919 onward, Gandhi's influence on Nehru became so imprint that the former declared him his political heir.

With his concern for the poor and downtrodden and with his association of the Fabian-socialists, Nehru was a socialist of non-Marxian type. His sympathies for Marxism was well-known, but he never called himself a communist. He was, indeed, a materialistic and was, in no case, a theocrat. He disliked communalism: both Muslim and Hindu. Religion had no attraction for Nehru. He remarked, "Of religion, I had very hazy notions. It seemed to me a woman's affair." He also said once, "Nor am I greatly interested in the after life, in what happens after death. I find the problem of this life sufficiently absorbing to fill mind. It is the Tao, the path to be followed and the way of life that interests; how to understand life, not to reject it but to accept it, to confirm it and to improve it."

## I (b). Nehru on Democracy

Nehru's views on democracy are neither well-worded nor do give any clear-cut meaning. These are different in different situations. At times, some of his views describe democracy as opposed to authoritarianism, sometimes contrary to fascism. While he talks of democracy as a system of rights and liberties, including freedom of speech at one point of time, he refers to democracy as a form of representative and responsive form of government at another time. Democracy, for Nehru, is a political concept, though on other occasions, it has to have an economic and social content. Nehru describes democracy as a form of governance here, and a way of life there. He holds the view that democracy is a procedural system of administration at one time while at another, he insists on its humanistic spirit. Thus, we find numerous meanings given about the term democracy by him at different times. During the British rule, democracy means 'self-rule', his later socialistic ideas interpret it as a form of social organisation. In his interview to Cousins, Nehru had said, "...Democracy is not only political, not only economic, but something of mind.... It involves equality of opportunity to all as far as possible in the political and economic domain. It involves the freedom of the individual to grow and to make the best of his capacities and ability. It involves a certain tolerance of others and even on other's opinion when they differ from your's.... It is dynamic, not a static thing.... It is mental approach, applied to our political and economic problems." The analysis of this definition of democracy clearly shows as to what democracy is and what it is not in Nehru's views: while equality of opportunity is democratic, inequality among the people is undemocratic; while freedom of expression is democratic, its suppression is undemocratic, while opportunities which help individuals grow is democratic, denying people such opportunities is undemocratic; while tolerance of other's opinion is democratic, intolerance is undemocratic; dynamism is democratic while staticism is anti-democratic; democracy is a thing of mind; what does not constitute a thing of mind is not democracy; the non-violent approach is democratic while violent approach is anti-democratic; for Nehru, democracy is a scheme of values and moral stands in life. Self-discipline and social discipline are values and as such they constitute values of democracy.

Nehru had a vast vision of democracy, one that had included an all-comprehensive aspects of what democracy can really mean. D.E. Smith has summed up Nehru's views on democracy projected by him from time to time. These are:

(i) Democracy defined in terms of the freedom in which human values can be realised;
(ii) Democracy defined in terms of certain government institutions and procedures;
(iii) Democracy defined in terms of a structure of society in which economic and social equality will gradually be attained;
(iv) Democracy defined in terms of a certain attitude and approach to problems on the part of the individual and society.

*I (b) (i). Democracy and Individual Freedom*

For Nehru, the essential assumption of democracy is an autonomous individual, a free being and a self-growing personality. Like the individualist-democrats, Nehru's democracy involved a passion for individual. He says, "...more and more the individual is giving way to the crowd...the crowd seldom places the reins on itself that the individual often feels compelled to do. The crowd dominates the individual but lacks a conscience of its own. Almost everywhere today, the individual is giving himself over to the crowd or is being seized by it. The crowd is brute. The crowd terrifies me."

Nehru is for individual; he argues in favour of a free individual. Individual freedom is a value in itself. In his numerous speeches, he makes a powerful case for freedom of thought, of writing, of speech, of conscience. The Objective Resolution moved by Nehru in the Constituent Assembly in late 1946 laid emphasis on guaranteeing and securing to all the people of free India "freedom of thought, expression, belief, faith, worship, vocation, association and action." Nehru's love for individual freedom was unparalled. B.K. Ahluwalia (*Jawaharlal Nehru: India's Man of Destiny*) writes, "He (Jawaharlal Nehru) had a love of liberty not merely for his own people but for all the peoples of the world. ...He believed in the liberty of all without distinction of class, creed or country." With John Stuart Mill before him, Nehru thought of individual liberty as "pussing one's own good in one's own way" without harming the like liberties of others.

Indeed, Nehru was all for the liberty of the individual, but his freedom was not a licence; for unrestricted liberty is no liberty or is liberty of the stronger. In a debate in the Indian Parliament, Nehru had remarked, "In a democratic society, the concept of individual freedom has to be balanced with social freedom and the relation of the individual with the social group. The individual must not infringe on the freedom of other individuals." In his *Discovery of India,* he expressed the same views: "It seemed to me obvious that in a complex social structure, individual freedom had to be limited and perhaps the only way to real freedom was through some such limitation in the social sphere." In another interview to R.K. Karanjia, he had said: "Freedom and democracy have to be limited, of course, lest they injure others."

Nehru was well aware of the fact that in the interest of nation's security, freedom of the individual would have to be balanced: the protection of the nation's security is as important, rather more important than that of the individual, for if nation is insecure, no individual can feel secure.

Nehru also knew that for a country like India whose modernisation can be sought through national planning, there is a need to have a balance between the forces of centralised planning and individual initiative. But above all, he was convinced that individual freedom is the essence of a democratic polity. He used to say, "Democracy will cease to exist if individual is not assured freedom for the realisation of human values." Ashoka Mehta writes, "His (Jawaharlal Nehru's) faith in his fellowmen made him a confirmed democrat. He never hesitated to endow the people with wider powers and responsibilities because he never doubted their ability to use them widely...."

*I (b) (ii). Democracy and Representative Government*

Nehru thought of democracy as a form of government as well. Democracy as a form of government implies representative democracy which, in turn, implies popular sovereignty, majoritarian rule, responsible political parties and responsive leaders. Democracy as government of the people, by the people and for the people means that the people participate in the foundation of the government, help in the functioning of the government and one that takes care of the people. Direct democracy, being impracticable, is not what is government of the people: democracy, today, is representative government: people rule through their elected representatives. The people have the ultimate power, i.e., sovereignty, to decide and determine as to who could rule and to what extent and in what manner. This is what is known as the rule of the people through their representatives. The *Hindu* quotes Nehru (August, 1946), "The details of Constitution are for lawyers to make, but the fundamental basis of a constitution for a state, or for the whole of India can only be decided by its people and that the power and responsibility and ultimate sovereignty must rest with the people." Representative democracy implies:

(i) that political power lays with the people and is exercised through the elected representatives;
(ii) that all the adults possess franchise equally, without any distinction of caste, creed, colour, place of birth, sex or region;
(iii) that the people have the equal power to seek redressal of their political grievances;
(iv) that all possess freedoms and liberties.

The concept of representative government, as one aspect of democracy, involves the principle of majoritarian rule as well. Nehru remarked, "If a government is in line with the thought of a majority of the people, it is a democracy given vent." However, he insisted that while the majority has the right to rule, of it also has the duty to protect the interests of the minority groups. He writes in the *Discovery of India,* "...in a vast and varied country like India, a simple type of democracy gives full power to a majority to curb or over-rule minority groups in all matters was not satisfactory or desirable even if it could be established."

It is admitted that no democracy can function without elections and no elections can ever be held without political parties. Nehru was well aware of the indispensability of political parties for any democratic set up. He, therefore, insisted on the existence of more than two political parties. He was not very appreciative of the British two-type of party-system and used to say that such a party system restricts and limits the choice of the people, for, there would never be too many candidates to choose from. He was also of the view that a strong opposition always benefits democratic polities, though he would always express love for the Congress, over which he practically presided for 17 years after independence. Smith says, "Nehru's over-emphasis on national unity through one political party (i.e. the Congress) may be considered a weakness of his democratic theory."

Democracy does not function on its own; it functions through people, their elected representatives, their political parties and through leadership. The success or the failure of any democratic polity, largely, depends on the character or efficiency of its devoted and responsive leaders, either in power or in opposition. Nehru knew the obligations which the leaders owed to their people. That is why that he always emphasised on the responsive character of the leaders in a democracy. According to Nehru, democracy needs, if it has to stay, to have responsive leadership which alone serve the people and deliver goods.

### *I (b) (iii). Democracy and Equality: Economic and Social*

Nehru was a socialist of Fabian type. To that extent, he was more close to men like Laski and Tawney. His idea of democracy was akin to socialism spreading its wings to equality, both economic and social. For Nehru, democracy was not merely political equality; it was also social and economic equality; it was also socialism-oriented. In his *Glimpses of the World History*, he wrote, "Democracy means equality and democracy can only flourish in an equal society." It is in socialism that equality can flourish. For Nehru, democracy, socialism and equality constituted a perfect order.

Democracy means equality: political, economic and social. Political equality is not what complete democracy is. If there is no economic equality and social equality, democracy and political equality have no meaning. One-person, one vote is political equality, but if there are rich and poor, and if there are caste barriers, what is the worth or utility of political equality. In course of his talks with Norman Cousins, Nehru had observed: "Political democracy is the very basis on which you build up other qualities. At the same time, political democracy may cease to have meaning if there is gross economic inequality. Where people are starving, the vote does not count." That is why he emphasised that political democracy must, therefore, be supplemented by economic democracy.

Nehru was not a Marxist. He did not advocate a classless and a stateless society, but he did insist on a classless (rich and poor) and a casteless society. In a debate in the Lok Sabha (June, 1951), Nehru had remarked, "...anything that perpetuates the present social and economic inequalities is bad." Nehru condemned the structure of society based on social divisions and castes. In the *Discovery of India,* he writes, "In the context of society to-day, the caste system and much that goes with it, are wholly incompatible, reactionary, restrictive and barriers to progress. There can be no equality in states and opportunity within its framework nor can there be political democracy and much less economic democracy."

Nehru maintained that no ideology other than socialism could fit into the democratic pattern. Capitalism does not ensure democracy, and if it ensures anything, it is inequality, a system of privileges and powers concentrated at one point. It is only socialism which helps establish a society of equals, a decentralised polity and a society of fellowship and companionship. Socialism, Nehru was convinced, served to put an end to the "acquisitive factor in society," and therefore, the socialist way alone was the way, as he had observed, "...of ending of poverty, the vast employment, the degradation and the subjection." He, therefore, argued that the practice of socialism was the only way to the realisation of democracy in a hungry and starving country like India. India, he would urge, would have to accept the socialist philosophy of social processes if democracy had to become a reality. If socialism was not adopted in a country like India, Nehru had predicted, democracy would be the first victim, development and progress, second socialism, for Nehru, was not an end in itself, but was only a means, a means for the maximisation of democracy. It was not centralisation of economic power, but was, in fact, its decentralisation.

### *I (b) (iv). Democracy as a Way of Life*

Nehru had viewed democracy more than a form of government; it was a social organisation in that it involved an equalitarian and socialist kind of society. It is, with Nehru, the way of life, the way the life has to be lived. It is an attitude in that it involved individual's committed toward his/her society; an attitude of fellowship, of friendliness, of tolerance towards those who are with him/her or those who are opposed to him/her. It is an approach, an approach towards life, an approach towards others. It is both self-discipline as well as social discipline: the way one conducts oneself, and also the way one conducts oneself as a member of the society; more are these types (of discipline), more is the development of democracy; higher are these forms of discipline, higher is the quality of democracy.

Democracy implies people living together in harmony, in peace and in order; it also implies people's attitude towards problems as they emerge in their behaviour with one another—the way they look at the problems, the way they take on the problems, the way they resolve the problems. Democracy is, thus, a method, a solution, a dialogue, a conversation, a negotiation, conciliation, and a persuasion. For Nehru, democracy prescribes a way of life and also way as to how one should live it. Summing up the whole argument of Nehru's views on democracy, Smith observes, "In practice, democracy would not be in operation if, for example, representative institutions were used to trample over the rights of the non-conformist individual or to perpetuate an economic structure of vest inequality or if institutions were not used according to the established procedures and with a measure of self-discipline."

## II (a). Ram Manohar Lohia: The Man, His Times and His Works

Ram Manohar Lohia was a vaish (his kinsmen dealing in iron-Loha, so were described as Lohia) born on March 23, 1910 in a village, Akharpur (Faizabad – U.P.). His father, Hira Lal was a Gandhian-nationalist; his mother, Chanda, died when he was very young. He got introduced to freedom struggle at an early age, when he organised a small hartal on the death of Bal Gangadhar Tilak. His father took him to Gandhi whose influence remained throughout his life, both as an inspiration and as a guide. Ram Manohar Lohia remained a true Gandhian, a socialist Gandhian throughout his life. He met Nehru and over the years, they developed a close relationship, though they disagreed over numerous key issues. Lohia was Nehru's great critic, spending a good number of years (twelve years) in free India's jails. Lohia was a revolutionary by temperament, a rebel to some extent. Jail was Lohia's another home; it is said that he was imprisoned forty times during the days of India's struggle for freedom.

Lohia completed his intermediate from the Banaras Hindu University. In 1929, he completed his B.A. from Calcutta University. He decided to attend Berlin University, Germany. He wrote his PhD thesis paper on the topic 'Salt Satyagraha' (1932) focussing on Gandhi's socio-economic theory.

Lohia returned to India in 1933. He became a founder member of the Congress Socialist Party in 1934 and was the first editor of the weekly "Congress Socialist." He also became secretary of the Foreign Department of the Indian National Congress. The approaching shadows of World War II led him, along with some other younger leaders to propose the launching of a Satyagraha for Indian independence, He was arrested by the British Government for obstructing the supply of the material for the war.

Ram Manohar Lohia took an active part in the Quit India Movement in 1942, and was one of the leaders who went underground. He set up secret radio stations in Bombay and Calcutta and also worked for "Azad Daste" in Nepal territory. He was arrested in 1944.

On release from prison in 1946, he was offered the Secretaryship of the Congress Party but he declined as he did not agree that the Congress President should also be the Prime Minister or that any member of the Working Committee should be a minister.

He along with certain other socialist leaders, finally left the Congress in 1948. In 1952 they merged with the Kisan Mazdoor Praja Party and formed the Praja Socialist Party. However, he resigned the Secretaryship of the party as a protest against the refusal of Pattom Thanu Pillai, Chief Minister of Travancore-Cochin, to quit office on the issue of police firing on language agitators in 1954.

He formed the Socialist Party at Hyderabad and himself became Chairman and editor of its organ, "Mankind", in 1956. He was elected to the Lok Sabha in 1963. In 1964, the Socialist Party merged with the Praja Socialist Party, which then came to be known as Samyukta Socialist Party. However, strong difference continued on account of insistence of the followers of Ram Manohar Lohia on Hindi as the national language, the rights of untouchables and the principle of no compromise with either the Congress or the Communists.

As a member of the Parliament, Dr. Lohia contributed a lot, especially in the field of advocating the cause of women and the downtrodden.

Dr. Lohia died on October 12, 1967. He left behind no property or any bank balance. In the words of N.C. Mehrotra, "Dr. Lohia was not only a politician but also a philosopher having his own thinking, a social reformer pressing to the end the caste system and social discrimination and to improve the lot of women adivasis and backward communities; an economist, suggesting a number of steps for the economic progress of an under-developed country. ...After his death, the way he received praise from all the sections of leaders and people remind us of Lohia's views on the aspect on Indian history that worship a Man Singh in his life time and a Rama Pratap after death." Madhu Limaye says, "Dr. Lohia was an original thinker, a unique leader and a rebel. He played an important part in the making of modern India. But Ram Manohar was not an ivory tower philosopher. He was essentially a man of action."

The works of Dr. Lohia included the *Wheel of History, Aspects of Socialist Policy, Will to Power and Other Writings, Towards the Destruction of Castes and Classes, Marx, Gandhi and Socialism, the Culprits of the Division of Bharat, Power Determination.*

## II (b). Lohia on Democracy

Dr. Lohia was a staunch democrat, lover of democracy and of socialist democracy at that. Gandhian, as Dr. Lohia was through and through, his democracy is the democracy of the common man, of the poor and the downtrodden, one in which the weaker sections of society have their say in the governance and which takes care of such sections of people. A close associate of Jayaprakash Narayan, Dr. Lohia did not entertain any significant view of representative democracy and of one based on party systems. For him, as well as Jayaprakash Narayan, it was individual who constituted the very basis of democracy and it was decentralisation through which democracy can really work as a way of life and as a way of governance. Both, of course, found fault with the functioning of democracy as it actually operated in the West.

*II (b) (i). Weaknesses of Western Kind of Democracy*

Like Gandhi, Dr. Lohia condemned the Western kind of democracy which had been adopted by the newly independent countries of Asia and Africa, India including. Dr. Lohia was of the opinion that the so-called free individual is not, in reality, free to elect his representative; the representative is more representative of the political party that makes him contest elections than the constituency he represents; the legislatures hardly represent their electorates; they hardly make the ministers accountable to them; it is the ministers who control the legislature rather than the legislatures, controlling the ministers; political parties rule both the ministers as well as the legislative bodies; the centralised party system rules the people.

Dr. Lohia was no admirer of the Western form of democracy which democracy he described as the democracy of the rich. He was not appreciative of the Western type of democratic functioning which functioning he described as one where the individual remains sovereign in the rhetorical sense of the term. He had no liking of the Western kind of state which state he described as one with powers centralised at one point, something of a force with all body and no soul. The Western democracy has no equality at its base, but has only liberty to fly with and grow further with the rule that reigns, is the survival of the fittest.

Dr. Lohia was a great advocate of democracy, one that, as a method, works through peaceful means for arriving at any decision. As a method, democracy is discussion, dialogue, conversation, participation, involvement. It is also an effort, an attempt to create an equalitarian society, one that seeks to remove inequalities, distinction, discrimination, exploitation, injustice.

Democracy, for Dr. Lohia, was much more than a form of government. It is an end that brings about equality and justice for all; it is a means that lays down the method as to how one lives a full life; it is an effort that seeks to achieve a world of peace and prosperity for each and for all, a world without distinction and a world without discrimination.

Dr. Lohia was a true democrat. When no one dared to face Pt. Jawaharlal Nehru, he used to fight election against him. He made every person stunned when he stated that in the Parliament that 27 crore people in India live on 3 annas and Rs. 3 is spent on a dog of Prime Minister and Rs. 25-30,000 per day on security. He stated that labour earned 12 annas daily, whereas, an industrialist earns three lacs per day. Dr. Lohia challenged in the Lok Sabha to prove untrue, he will resign as MP. He deprecated the Government undertaking when he found TB vaccination costing only 2 annas is sold for 12 annas.

Whatever Dr. Lohia spoke for others, used to follow himself. The government money was never misused by him. When he attended seminars, and meetings, he avoided use of hotels and stayed at houses of some known persons. Once, he was found sleeping on the board of a boat at the Ganges banks when he visited Varanasi on government duty.

Regarding caste as a strumbling block, Dr. Lohia thought that the caste system was India's misfortune and as long as it existed, democracy, in India, would not find a place in the country. 'Caste', Dr. Lohia had said, "was a congealed class. Class was mobile caste," the Brahmins dominating the intellectual arena, and the Baniyas, the business. He was sorry to note that caste restricts opportunity; restricted opportunity constricts ability; constricted ability further restricts opportunity. Where castes prevail, opportunity and ability are restricted to ever-narrowing circles of the people." To eliminate caste, his aphoristic prescription was: "Roti and beti," the people would have to break caste barriers to eat together (Roti), and be willing to give their girls in marriage to boys from other castes (Beti).

For democracy, bridging the rich-poor divide, and the elimination of caste, Lohia's list included tackling man-woman inequality, banishing inequality based on colour and the like.

### *II (b) (ii). Democracy as Dr. Lohia Viewed it*

Dr. Lohia's concept of democracy had its own peculiar features. Some of these can be, briefly, summed up as under:

(a) There can be no real democracy without *socialism;* socialism alone ensures democracy. Dr. Lohia, though, was influenced by Marx, was a Gandhian socialist. He was not a socialist of orthodox type to which he had described as 'a dead doctrine' and 'a dying organisation.' He was a Gandhian socialist to which he described as an open doctrine. His six-point plan is one that aims at strengthening democracy:

   (i) Maximum attainable equality towards which nationalization of economy may be one necessary step.

(ii) A decent standard of living throughout the world.
(iii) A world parliament elected on adult franchise, leading to world government.
(iv) Collective and individual practice of civil disobedience.
(v) Freedom of the individual against unjust encroachments of public authority and securing an area of free speech and association and private life over which no government may exercise control.
(vi) Evolution of a technology consistent with these aims and processes.

(b) Democracy can thrive on the ethos of *equality.* Equality comes through socialism alone. Accordingly, democracy, equality and socialism supplement and strengthen one another, Dr. Lohia refers to certain kinds of equality:
(i) equality between men and women;
(ii) abolition of inequalities based on colour;
(iii) elimination of inequalities of birth and caste;
(iv) economic equality through increased production.

(c) Dr. Lohia's socialism is akin to individual attaining his real self. He argued that only a person could have a will and the state, not being a person, does not have a will of its own. "Though it was the function of the socialist state," Jha writes, "to help an individual realise his rational will while it kept the irrational will from the social processes, the anvil for testing the rationality of an individual will could not be the collective will of its rulers, but the will of the community in its entirety." Only a rational will has a chance of being realised.

(d) *Socialism* alone helps India remove her poverty and backwardness and in the process bring her people to enjoy the *fruits of democracy.* Where there are poor, there can be no democracy; where there are poor, socialism alone can ensure them a decent living: right to work must precede right to govern. In his paper, 'the Farmer in India', Lohia formulated a thirteen-point plan to end the rampant poverty and backwardness in the country, paving, thus the way for a socialist democracy:

1. Lowering of prices on the basis of parity between agricultural and industrial prices.
2. Austerity and sacrifice to be shared by all so that no income or salary exceeds Rs. 1000 a month.

3. Industrialisation with the help of small-unit machines, the invention and manufacture of which to be promoted by the state.
4. Any factory running below capacity to be taken over by the state, and immediate nationalisation of basic industries.
5. Anti-corruption commissioners in every state and at the centre with departments independent of the government.
6. Land to the tiller and redivision of lands—12½ acres minimum and 30 acres maximum. Correction of wrong entries in Patwaris' registers.
7. Cultivation of 1 crore acres of new land by a state-recruited food army.
8. Decentralisation of administration and of economy so as to achieve the four-pillar state. Repeal of discriminatory laws including the criminal tribes Act.
9. Housing programmes and other economic activity to provide full employment.
10. Establishment of polytechnic schools and people's high schools and centres for youth and women for cultural activities.
11. Immediate adult franchise elections in unrepresented areas, that is, merged states and unions.
12. Pursuit of a positive policy of world peace through promoting full freedom and right for all nations; social and economic equality among a people and between nations, and a peace bloc which can dictate truce to warring Power blocs.
13. Volunteer bands for agriculture, irrigation, road-making and the like.

(e) Democracy and decentralisation go together. So did Dr. Lohia argue, "All the political power is concentrated in the hands of the Central Government today. The states are left with very little power; there is no self-government at the district, taluk and village levels. The citizens of the country elect representatives to the Lok Sabha and the state assemblies once in five years. Once elected the representatives cannot be questioned by the common man. Lohia felt that this state of affairs was unsatisfactory in a democracy. He suggested a different solution. The suggestion was that there should be decentralization of power at all the four stages – at the center and the state, the district and the village levels. He wanted that there should be minimum power at the center and that at the village level there should be maximum power in the conduct of the affairs of the village. The Panchayat administration in charge should also have power over the police. It should also have power to collect taxes. The village Panchayat should get a share of the taxes collected by the state and the center. The progress of a village ought to be planned by the village itself. He called this organization the four-pillared state. According to this arrangement Swaraj begins at the village level and stretches up to Delhi. This provides an opportunity for the common man to participate in the administration."

More than half of our population comprises women. Their condition is pathetic. Cooking food, breeding children and being a slave to her husband—this is woman's fate. A woman is not considered equal to a man, such is the blind belief sustained through the ages. The law has guaranteed equality to women, but that is only on paper. Equality has not been practiced. Hence jobs must be reserved for women in all walks of life. They must be freed from the tyranny of homework. The latent talent of women should be brought to the limelight. Society does not progress as long as women remain oppressed. Society must be rid of deep-rooted beliefs and old practices. Beginning with women in villages every woman should be given justice. Lohia strove for this cause. According to him the *emancipation of women* was the foundation of social revolution; without this there can be neither any democracy nor any propriety.

## SUGGESTED READINGS


1. Arora, V.K. and Rathore L.R., *Ram Manohar Lohia and Socialism in India* (New Delhi: Deep and Deep, 1984).
2. Bhagwan, Vishnoo, *India Political Thinkers* (Delhi: Atma Ram and Sons, 2002).
3. Breeher, Michael, *Nehru: A Political Bibliography* (Oxford: Oxford University Press, 1959).
4. *Jawaharlal Nehru's Speeches* (Publications Division, New Delhi, 1946, 1949, 1949-57).

5. Jha, *An Modern Indian Political Thought* (Meerut: Meenakshi Prakashan, 1975).
6. Nehru, Jawaharlal, *Letters from a Father to His Daughters* (Allahabad: Kitabistan, 1938).
   _________, *Glimpses of World History* (London: Linday Drummond, 1938).
   _________, *Autobiography* (London: John Lane, the Bradley Head, 1936).
   _________, *The Discovery of India* (Calcutta: The Signet Press, 1946).
7. Patil, V. C., *Studies in Nehru* (Delhi: Sterling, 1987).
8. Sinha, Sachidananda, *A Short Life Sketch of Jawaharlal Nehru* (Patna: Law Press, 1936).
9. Smith, Donald Eugene, *Nehru and Democracy* (Calcutta: Orient Longmans, 1958).
10. Verma, Rajni Kant, *Lohia* (Allahabad: Rasim Prakashan, 1969).

## CHAPTER – 22

# Periyar on Identity

### I (a). Periyar: The Man, His Times and His Works

E.V. Ramasami Naicker, also known as Periyar, EVR, Thanthai Periyar (the great sage) or Periyar Ramasami was a rationalist, atheist, freedom-fighter, activist, founder of Dravilar Kazhagam and founder of Self-respect Movement. Though born in an upper caste family, Periyar fought against untouchability, the rituals of Hinduism and the caste system, describing him/her a fool who had created god, a scoundrel who had spread his name, and a barbarian who would worship him.

Periyar was born in an affluent family at Erode (Tamil Nadu) on 17th September 1879. His parents were deeply religious and they frequently arranged religious discourses to be given at a temple or in other public places. While all the other members of the family listened to the discourses with great devotion, even in his early teens, Ramasami displayed a keen rationalistic tendency and ridiculed the pundits who gave the talks, by pointing out the contradictions in their statements and also their incredible exaggerations. Referring to this early experience of his, Periyar wrote later in one of his autobiographical articles: "It gave me extraordinary pleasure to fling at the pundits their own contradictions and thus, perplex them. It also gave me the reputation, among our neighbours of being a clever speaker. I believe that it was this experience which deprived me of faith in castes and communities, in religion, in *puranas*, in *sastras* and in god." It is an irony that the religious discourses, which were intended to kindle piety and religiosity in all listeners, produced the opposite effect on Ramasami. As he grew up, he became convinced that some people used religion only as mask to deceive innocent people. That was why he took it as one of the duties in his life to warn people against superstitious and priests.

Periyar believed that all men and women are equal and should have equal opportunities to develop their physical, mental and moral faculties; all have the right to live in dignity. That is why that he wanted to put an end to all kinds of discrimination. There is, he believed, a need for promoting social justice and rational outlook among all.

Periyar joined the Indian National Congress in 1919. He participated in the Non-cooperation Movement, launched by Gandhi. He resigned from 29 public posts which he held at that time and undertook whole heartedly the constructive programme by spreading the use of Khadi, picketing toddy shops, boycotting the shops selling foreign clothes and eradication of untouchability. He also courted imprisonment in Erode in 1921.

Periyar's vigorous and spirited role in the Vaikom Satyagraha (1924-25) contributed in no mean measure for the triumph of that first historic social struggle in the history to use public roads without any inhibition and for other prospective egalitarian social measures.

Since 1919, Periyar kept on seeking reservations for different social groups, but having failed in his efforts, he resigned from the Congress in 1925 and parted company with Gandhi, for not having, in his views fought against the evils of caste system. It was here that he founded the Self-Respect Movement in 1925, whose objectives were already being taken care of by the Justice Party and which changed its name to Dravidas Kazhagam in August, 1944. These organisations, at their respective period, fought against untouchability, Brahminism, caste system and stood for a casteless equalitarian society.

As the leader of the Justice party, Periyar had opposed all programmes of imposing Hindi language in the southern dravidan speaking states. He also campaigned against the casteistic politics, especially one that undermined the position of the non-brahmin classes. He also fought for human rights for all. At one point of time, he even worked on independent state of Dravida Naadu and had called the 15th August, 1947 and 26th January, 1950 dates as the mourning days, for the transfer of power meant change from the British to the Brahmins-Baniyas combine. His fight against the caste system and the Hindu religion and against the imposition of the Hindi language went on uninterruptingly. In 1949, Periyar married, at the age of seventy, to one Maniammai (his second marriage) 30 year old, to guard his health and promote his movement.

The UNESCO conferred on Periyar, a glorious title the citation of which read as 'Periyar—the prophet of New Age', 'Socrates of South East Asia', 'Father of the Social Reform Movement', and 'an Arch enemy of ignorance, superstitions, meaningless customs and base manners' in June, 1970.

Periyar died on December 24, 1973.

Periyar published a Tamil Weekly under the title *Kudi Arasu* in 1925 to spread the principles of Self-Respect for awakening of the Dravidian Race against the oppression by the Brahmins, calling it *Brahminocracy.* He published an English magazine under the title *Revolt* in November, 1928. By 1937, he was publishing "Viduthalai", a Tamil Daily Newspaper. In 1938, he wrote his book called *The World to Come,* visualising many scientific inventions including the possibility of the "Test Tube Baby". His another work was *The Ramayana: True Reading,* (1959). His followers were known as 'Blackshirters'. A bi-monthly the *Unmai* (Truth) was started by Periyar in 1970, and also inaugurated an English monthly the *Modern Rationalist.*

His views, social, economic, political, are found in his speeches and articles.

Periyar Ramasami was known as the Voltaire (1694-1778) of South India, particularly, in Tamil Nadu. Both were rationalists who aroused their people to realize that all men are equal and it is the birthright of every individual to enjoy liberty, equality and fraternity. Both opposed religion virulently because the so called men of religion invented myths and superstitions to keep the innocent and ignorant people in darkness and to go on exploiting them. In one of his articles, Voltaire said, "They (the religious men) inspired you with false beliefs and made you fanatics so that they might be your masters. They made you superstitious, not that you might fear god but that you might fear them."

The "revolution", which Periyar brought about, was a bloodless one and he had to spend more than fifty years of his life opening the eyes of people to their want of education and consequent backwardness, their faith in superstitions, the deception and exploitation to which they are subjected by cunning people and also on the need for them to develop self-respect and self-confidence. It is interesting to note the term 'self-respect' as used by Periyar, includes the three concepts liberty, equality and fraternity, which Voltaire and other French revolutionists exhorted their countrymen to acquire. Periyar, repeatedly and feelingly spoke about women's liberation.

## I (b). Periyar on Identity

Identity refers to a type of recognition: how are we recognised?; how are we identified in the society we live?; what makes us different from others?; should our different identity accord us differential treatment?; how does different identity lead to ill-treatment, exploitation, oppression?; how does it deny our self-respect and dignity? All these questions and those related to those questions bring issues associated with degradation, deprivation, inhuman treatment, which social groups confront in a society divided socially. In the Indian context, numerous thinkers, reformers, intellectuals have toiled to find out causes responsible for ill-treatment, and exploitation of the socially identified as deprivate ones. Periyar spent all his life to seek recognition and identity for those people who were victims of denial of social justice and dignity. Periyar's call, therefore, was: "Man must hold his personal respect and dignity as precious as his life."

### *I (b) (i). Identity as Dignity*

Periyar thought of man's dignity as the sole characteristic of his identity. Identity and dignity supplement each other. It is dignity which gives human beings self-confidence and self-respect. "Man must," Periyar says, "remove by himself his feelings of inferiority, the feeling that he is lesser born than other beings, and attain self-confidence and self-respect." "He who does not care for dignity," he says, "is no better than the prostitute, however highly educated he is. His education will only endanger those that care for dignity." The Self-Respect Movement which Periyar had founded in 1925, sought equal rights for all sections of society so to enable them enjoy the fruits of the resources and development of the country. It aimed to give recognition of each individual as an existence for one-self; each group as an equal one along with others, giving every one a self-respect. The provincial conferences of the Self-Respect Movement held in 1929, 1930, 1931 and 1933 infused the feelings of self-confidence among the people fighting against the tyranny of Brahmins, Brahminocracy as

Periyar called it.

*I (b) (ii). Brahminocracy as the Root-cause of all Evils*

Periyar condemned the Indian caste system, and more furiously its Brahminical aspect. He held Brahmins responsible for all tyranny inflicted on non-Brahmins, the Dravidian race in particular. Addressing a non-Brahmin conference in Kancheepuram in November, 1925, Periyar insisted on the compelling need of the Dravidians to preserve the self-respect of their race, language and culture which had been degraded by the Brahminical dominance by nursing caste system and superstition of Hindu religion. He launched an agitation against Brahminism. The Brahmins used to inscribe the name in the hotel name-board as 'Brahmin Hotel' to spread the impression that they were the superior race. Periyar asked his followers to erase the name of 'Brahmin' in the hotel name-boards in Tamil Nadu in 1958. The Vaikom Satyagraha (1924-25) was against the Brahminical dictate debarring the Dravidians to walk in the streets around the temple, defying, thus, the prohibitory law order. Basically, Periyar's anti-Brahminical struggle was based on the Brahmins' assumptions that all Brahmins belonged to upper-class while, all non-Brahmins, the lower-class Dravidians, accusing the Brahmins for destroying the Dravidian identity.

*I (b) (iii). Rationalism as Anti-religion and Anti-god*

Periyar was an atheist and a rationalist at that. It is reason that reduces our ignorance; it is reason that brings us out from superstitious. Periyar was sorry to note that we, Indians, build temples whereas people, in other lands, fly in space. He was for rationalism and humanism. He thought that religions divide people. Explaining this, he would cite the celebrations of festivals such as Ganapathi puja: people make a lot of noise and take processions carrying huge idols, choosing purposely, a route where people belonging to other religions have their place of worship. In this way, they create communal disharmony. He would ask people to give up their faith in the efficacy of such idols. He used to campaign against idolatary so to show that there was no divine power in idols. He broke in public places idols of Ganesa and Pillaiyar (Vinayaka). He used to ask: "How can a god who is not able to protect himself, be able to protect you."

Rationalism does not admit the existence of god. Periyar was an atheist, in fact, he was anti-god. He thought that the man who invented the deity in primitive times was ignorant; he was only a fool to think of and believe in god in ancient days, when the scope of acquiring knowledge about the natural phenomena was limited. But those who propagate the faith in god in these days are not ignorant. They know god does not exist. Still they try to make people to have faith in god out of selfishness, to deceive and exploit the common masses. Periyar and his followers used to take anti-god stand. They used to argue that those who are god-men, they do activities which are anti-god. People, for example, worship Agni Bhagwan (the fire god). But when fire breaks out, the god-men call the fire services to put out the fire and stop it from spreading. Thus, on the stance of god-men, the government and such people themselves act against Agni Bhagwan. To take another instance: god-men think and in fact, propagate that child-birth takes place according to god's will. People cannot do and should not do anything about it. We should not interfere in the work of Brahama, the god of creation. But now we adopt various measures to control birth. Is this not strictly speaking, acting against the will of god? Isn't birth-control an anti-god measure if we go by orthodox faith?

### *I (b) (iv). Evils of Caste System*

Periyar was well aware of the evils of caste-system with which the Hindu society suffered, at times, making him an anti-Hindu. He thought of Hinduism inimical to equality, antagonistic to liberty and opposed to fraternity. It is Hinduism which, through *chaturvarna*, had created the caste-system which was responsible for the deprivation and degradation of the classes, lower in the ladder. Caste system breeds untouchability, denies the lower caste people their human existence; their identity even.

Periyar was of the opinion that caste system has only evils, with all minuses and no pluses. As a scheme of distribution, caste system has failed miserably, producing only inequality of wealth, immense wealth side by side extreme poverty; producing people of higher castes on the one side and of lower castes on the other, one the exploiters, other the exploited. Caste system only creates conflicts and clashes and disunity, both of the nation and of the purpose.

K. Veeramani, Periyar's associate, highlights the following evils of the caste system:

1. Caste divides labourers; it is also a division of labourers and not the division of labour; the division of labour accompanied by the gradation of labourers. It is a division not based on aptitude or abilities or capacities, but is one based on birth, on the dogma of predestination.
2. Caste disconnects intelligence from manual labour; it disassociates intelligence from work and creates contempt labour. The Brahmin is permitted to cultivate his intellect but is not permitted to cultivate labour; rather he looks upon the labour. The Shudra, on the other hand, is required to do only labour and lead the life of a slave.
3. Caste devitalises a man; it is a process of sterilisation. There is all wealth and all education for the higher castes; there is only the wages, and quite often no wages for the labour.
4. Caste prevents mobilisation. It does not permit all the classes to face an aggression or a war like situation. It does not allow the vaish or the shudra to take arms. General and military mobilisation is not permitted within the framework of caste system.

If these conclusions are sound, Veeramani says, how can a philosophy which dissects society in fragments, which dissociates work from interest, which disconnects intelligence from labour, which expropriates the rights of man to interests vital to life and which prevented society from mobilizing resources for common action in the hour of danger, be said to satisfy the test of social utility.

In the entire caste system, the ideal, it is argued, is neither the individual nor society; it is the class—the class of supermen called the Brahmins. The ideal of the caste system teaches that what is right for the superman is the only thing which is called morally right and morally good, one that is found in Nietzsche; one when the superman is worshipped and the common man damned. Self-respect demands the end of the distinction between superior and inferior castes. Periyar said, "The caste system that teaches notions of superiority, inferiority, high and low, depending on birth should be scotched at the very base."

*I (b) (v). Social Reforms Directed Towards Equality and Social Justice*

Periyar's ideal society is one which perpetuates and promotes equality: equality between the rich and the poor, absence of distinction among the numerous castes and classes, equality between man and woman. Periyar was a great advocate of women's rights. "If the man has the right to claim a woman, then," he used to say, "a woman also should have right to claim a man." He was pained to learn to deteriorating conditions of women in India. "Women in India," he said, "experience much suffering, humiliation and slavery in all spheres, than even the untouchables." He, therefore, held the view, "the terms 'husband' and 'wife' are inappropriate. They are only companions and partners. One is not slave for other. They both have equal status." Social justice should be the aim of any social reform. "To discard what is unwanted and to retain what is needed," he said, "is what reform means." "The proper task of social reform, "according to Periyar, "is to remove poverty from society and to ensure that people do not sell their conscience to make a living."

## SUGGESTED READINGS

1. Periyar, E.V. Ramasami (Madras: D.K. Publications, 1984), *Periyar and His Ideologies* (Madras: Periyar Self-Respect Propaganda Institute, 1983).
2. Diehl, Anita, *E.V. Ramaswami Naicker: A Study of the Influence of Personality in Contemporary South India.*
3. Internet Links.

# CHAPTER – 23

# Introducing Political Argument

### I (a). Understanding Political Argument

Political Science is no moral science in the sense that it does not preach and nor does it prescribe. It is also not history in so far it does not describe what had already happened. It is neither economy in so far it does not go into the details of what has been achieved and what has been lost in matters relating to our material life. It is about politics, about state, about government and about a political life. In Political Science we do not discuss what is good or what is bad, what we discuss is as to what is relevant and what is not. To know about what good government is the job of an idealist or a moralist. The domain of Political Science is the domain of what is real or can be real in terms of its practicability. Political Science is, by its nature, a practical phenomenon.

Political Theory, as the essence of Political Science, is what explains, analyses, enquires, assesses, examines, and evaluates any political phenomenon. It is an argument, a dialogue, a debate and a conversation. In Political Theory we discuss and debate over an argument, explain and analyse our point of view, examine and evaluate where have we faulted and where we should have gone. The importance of a political theorist, as Brecht had said, is "to see, sooner than others, and to analyse, more profoundly than others, the immediate and potential problems of the political life, to supply the practical politician, well in advance, with alternative causes of action..., and to supply him... a solid block of knowledge on which to build." Political Theory, as Rorty says, "...exploratory, conversational, open-minded...."

Understanding political argument involves seeking to know the political issues, participation in the discussion of such issues, arguing on the viability and feasibility of the position one takes in the argument. When we discuss political concepts, we go into the details of their past, we go into the circumstances which gave them a particular meaning and what led the writers to assume and adopt a new definition of the concept. Justice, for example, as Plato understood was not to be the one, his disciple, Aristotle thought of it or what came to be known, centuries after, by John Rawls. The argument on the concept of justice has continued and shall continue in future.

Political argument seeks to state the potentiality of a particular point an issue possesses. We seek to build a case for or a case against bicameral legislature, for we never argue on whether it is good to have the second chamber or not. We know democracy, as a form of government, is not what a monarchy or aristocracy or a dictatorship, is; when we put forward conditions that help democracy a success, we do so on the argument that if a government for the people has to survive, it ought to be a government of the people. Political argument is what makes a science of politics as science.

Political argument is the very basis on which the fabric of our discipline in general and political theory in particular stands. It sustains political theory; it helps its growth and development. In the absence of continuing of political argument, it would not be possible to see political theory grow. Aristotle took the political argument further and added the science aspect to what Plato had made a philosophy of politics: Plato's political idealism came to be followed by Aristotle's political realism, all through the continuing argument. There are numerous examples, when a later theorist adds in the realms of political theory through debates, he choses to participate. This is true if we see the argument Locke offered against Filmer, Bentham against Blackstone, John Stuart Mill against Jeremy Bentham, Marx against Hegel and Proudhon. Understanding political argument means understanding political theory.

## I (b). Is Democracy Compatible with Economic Growth?

The essence of political argument is the essence of understanding a particular political position in the argument. Which position one takes is irrelevant, what is relevant is the participation in the debate.

One such debate revolves around the issue as to whether democracy is compatible with economic growth or not?

(i) *Democracy and Economic Growth are Compatible*

There is a point when one insists that democracy is difficult to be built on empty stomachs. The point is that democracy flourishes and thrives in a society which is economically sound. Studies have shown (Przeworcki and Limongi) that a democratic country with $1500 per capita income is likely to survive for a life of 8 years; between $1500-$3000 per capita income, 18 years while with per capita income of above $6000, democracy is likely to have stability in that country. The argument is that democracy survives in the domain of plenty and not amidst that of poverty. The failure of the democratic model in most countries of Asia and Africa following their liberation victories may have numerous reasons, but one potent reason can be attributed to their poverty. The argument is that economically developed countries strengthen democratic politics while the reverse is also true, i.e., democratic systems alone prepare and provide an atmosphere where economic growth is possible. A report on Democracy and poverty covering four regions, the former Soviet Union, South Asia, Latin America and Sub Saharan Africa (2001) has described the state of democracy in the region as "a facade that initiates democracy" and "a show of elections", saying that "for the ordinary person, democracy was considered to be the reason for all problems, the cause of unemployment and poverty." What is being emphasised is that poverty is not the place where democracy can breathe; it is where democracy gets weakened. In the face of poverty, unemployment and degradation, there can be no democracy. Democracy develops in economically developed societies. The fact is that democracy is an expensive form of government and it flourishes where people are able to pay for it. This is not to say that democracy is plutocracy. Democracy requires an atmosphere where economically well-of people elect their representative and control them.

The opposite is also true. It is democracy which helps economic growth. The following reasons can be advanced to substantiate this argument.

1. Only governments with some legitimacy will be able to implement and sustain policies that may bear high short-term costs.
2. Various of the institutional characteristics of a democracy, like an independent legal system, are also required for a successful

liberalisation. As North puts it, "well specified and enforced property rights, a necessary condition for economic growth, are only secure when political and civil rights are secure; otherwise arbitrary confiscation is always a threat."

3. Democratisation may limit rent-seeking due to its system of checks and balances. Recently, Rodrik has argued that democratic institutions—political parties, elected representatives, free speech, and the like—can be viewed as the ultimate institutions of conflict management, as they allow for differences among social groups to be resolved in a predictable, inclusive, and participatory manner.

On the contrary, the authoritarian regimes may and actually do harm the process of economic growth. These regimes do mean arbitrary rule and undue interference which usually hinder economic growth.

The fact of the matter is that democracy and economic growth go together; they do not pull their forces in opposite directions. A well-to-do nation, S.M. Lipset had rightly held the view, is more likely to maintain democracy than that which is relatively a poor one. The economically advanced country is also a politically developed country; its economic development makes ground for its political development; its social development is its test of economic development. We must remember that political development and economic development or even social development do not exist in isolation and function separately; they all work in relation to one another; they supplement and strength the cause of each else.

The growth of economic progress and that of democracy, in Europe, has gone together. As the capitalist class came to dominate the political arena in the West European countries, they introduced certain features, though slowly, relating to what is now known as the liberal democracy, features such as the extension of franchise rights, the system of elections and the mode of electioneering. The right to property, its sanctity, its protection is, in fast, the very essence of liberal-democracies. Locke's state came into existence for the protection of the property of the people; the propertied classes came to control the state and its apparatus in due course of time and the democratic polity they came to build was capitalist-oriented democracy. Democracy, in the West, is democracy founded on economic growth: more a state grows in growth terms, more its democratic institutions work effectively.

(ii) *Democracy and Economic Growth are not Compatible*

The other side of the argument is that democracy and economic growth are not compatible. This means that democracy does not help economic growth. There are nations which have grown, in economic field, without adopting democracy. The argument runs that democracies do not lead to economic growth: they may lead to policies which may hamper growth (rich-to-poor redistribution, large public sector, high taxes). The argument runs that democracy may lead to poverty: with more number of democratically governments around there has been more increase in global poverty. In most developed countries, poverty and its related problems continue to pose serious challenger to the democratic project.

Empty stomachs do not build democracies. Democracy does not flourish in poverty; the poor are never democrats, they only eat the fruits of democracy. The argument is: Historically, governments have not been", Meghad Desai of London School of Economics says, "friends of the poor, indeed, very much the opposite. Governments have normally been part of the structures of power and inequality that have oppressed the poor rather than helped them. The growth of democracy in the 20th century has begun to change this. Governments are increasingly exposed to public scrutiny and need to renew their mandate to gain public support at periodic elections. Even now, structures of governance are barely friendly to the poor."

Democracy is no guarantee for economic growth. Some non-democratic nations have attained economic growth. Among these, mention may be made with regard to countries like Singapore, South Korea, Taiwan, Indonesia and Malaysia. Lee, the Prime Minister of Singapore, had shown through his "Lee thesis" that the democratic rights hamper growth and that if people are given choice to choose between political freedom and fulfillment of economic needs, they would choose the latter. The point being emphasised is that the economic growth does not require the democratic foundation, and that the authoritarian polities may attain heights of economic growth. The following reasons can be advanced:

1. Only an authoritarian government is in a position to introduce unpopular measures; electorates often turn down economic reform even when it is known in the end that they would benefit a majority of voters. Policies that would be popular ex-post are often not implemented in a democratic regime.
2. The demand for comprehensive state action requires strong state: there has been no case of successful economic development during this century without comprehensive political action, involving massive state intervention in the economy.
3. Supporters of this view often refer to the experience of countries such as Chile, South Korea and Taiwan, Singapore.

Italy and Germany, the latter in particular, developed in terms of economic growth during the fascist dictatorship more than the democratic regimes such as Great Britain and France did. Economic growth needs a larger measure of discipline if material development is to be sought. Democracy flourishes on the gain of economic growth, as has been the case in the West. Economic growth can be attained through non-democratic regimes as has been the case in some former socialist countries of the Eastern Europe and in some South Asian states. These two types of cases suggest that economic growth is both compatible and non-compatible with democracy.

In conclusion, it may, therefore, be said that there can be economic growth with democracy, and there can be economic growth despite democracy. To that extent, there is no essential relationship between democracy and economic growth. What is important to note is the fact that democracy functions slowly, but functions assuredly whereas non-democracies, authoritarian and dictatorical regimes, operate hurriedly, but operate disastrously. The USA is an example relating to the former; the former USSR, of the latter.

### I (c). Is Censorship Justified?

Censorship is usually described as the restriction of public expression of the views believed to be those which undermine law and order, security, moral norms, social values and the like. It is always the power that be, who fling censorship and it is they, who decide on the extent of censorship. Censorship is a device that brings about order, system and discipline in the society. There is a point in the argument that those who are responsible for running a system, they should be empowered to make the system work properly and effectively. They are, so far and to that far, justified in imposing censorship, for the security of the country is more important than that of an individual.

Censorship is not a new concept. It has been in force in all times. The philosophers knew the utility of censorship; Plato's ideal state would not permit poetry, literature, drama. In ancient Rome, censorship was related to cultural realm. During the medieval Europe, especially in the Christian era, the church did not permit literature opposed to faith. The early modern age was one where the liberal-capitalist philosophers, Locke, Adam Smith, Bentham, Mill exposed the evils of censorship. These philosophers sought freedom in all field—political, economic religions etc. The American and the French revolutions sought freedoms and liberties from those who had power. In the latter centuries, censorship was justified in rare circumstances.

Censorship is the suppression of ideas and information which certain people—individuals, groups, or government officials—find it objectional, offensive or dangerous on others. Censorship is essential to eliminate discrimination on the basis of race or sex, to maintain stability and restore moral values. It occurs when expressive materials like books, magazines, movies, videos, music or work of art are restricted.

(i) *Censorship is Justified:* All censorship is not bad. It is justified if it helps *curb communalism.* Any material—book, magazine, film, music or work of art exciting one group of people against another should be curbed. Communalism is the perversion of religion in which religion is misused to gain some political and petty advantage. It attacks on the unity of the people; it creates communal tensions and conflicts. If certain print media indulges in such communal activities, if certain people—leaders of officials—resort to excite people on communal issues so to attain small or big gain, if certain political parties use religious places for political purposes, they may be held responsible for violating censorship, rules and be severely punished.

Censorship is justified if it helps curb *castiest tendencies.* Any activity or any expression of views which perpetuates and promotes divisive forces need to be censored casteism is a divisive force; it divides people; it separates them. It violates, as in the case of India, the very principles of the Constitution—principles such as liberty, equality, justice, fraternity, integrity, dignity, social justice and the like. It harms not only the polity, but also the society. It is also an attack on the unity of the country. Censorship is justified, if laws help curb castestic activities.

Censorship is justified against *anti-social, anti-national* and *terroristic activities.* If anti-social activity is a war against society; anti-national, a war against nation; terrorism is a war against humanity. Strict laws should be imposed on people indulging in such activities through any means—published or vocal.

Censorship is justified if an opinion, idea, expression or an activity describes people of certain *caste* or *race* in *derogratory terms,* dubbing all blacks as lazy or violent or unpatriotic. Censorship is justified if people belonging to a particular sex, i.e., women- folk, are made to suffer for being people of that sex: no civilized society permits women to be insulted.

Censorship is justified on *music that corrupts the youth.* The Pop and Rock music in the USA, for example, has influenced a lot of youths and being subjected to these types of songs, children and teenagers are committing crimes, drinking alcohol, using drugs and forming racist or sexist opinions. Rap music is a powerful source for young people. These people are expressing the reality of their lives and their culture, which includes drug use, sexual activity and violence. Generally foul language has rapidly increased with modern popular song lyrics. An increase in explicit violence and misogyny in popular music has been recorded. Song lyrics have been judged to be inspirations for violent, suicidal and other criminal acts.

Censorship is justified if it helps *curb pornography.* Pornography leads to crime and sex discrimination and it has no positive effect on the society. About 81 percent of criminals (in USA) rate pornography as their highest sexual interest. This means a majority of criminals love pornography and find it highly interesting. Psychologist Edward Donnerstein (University of Wisconsin) found that brief exposure to violent forms of pornography can lead to anti-social attitudes and behaviour.

Pornography, if not censored, can lead to sex discrimination. It is mainly the graphic, sexually explicit subordination of women or women presented as sexual object who enjoy pain or humiliation. This suggests the viewer whether a male or female that women are inferior and hence causing sexual discrimination.

Censorship should also be imposed on the work of art if it is related to any sexually expressive materials because it shows the women as a sexual object, which will lead to gender discrimination. In the article "Perils of Pornophobia" the writer Nadine Strossen does not feel the need of censorship on the work of art. In the third paragraph, she finds nothing wrong with a nude picture on the classroom wall. However, the picture will surely distract students. The teacher and the female students feel uncomfortable. As there were no men in nude pictures, this would make the women feel inferior. This could also cause gender discrimination. Another point, which she emphasized, was that a greater availability of sexually explict material seems to co-relate with higher indices of gender equality. But, when the sexually explicit material shows the subordination of women or women presented as sexual object who enjoy pain or humiliation, how can they be equal as men when the men are shown as the gender that enjoys subordinating women. Feminist author Diana Russell, notes in her book *Rape and Marriage* the correlation between deviant behaviour (including abuse) and pornography. She also found that pornography leads men and women to experience conflict, suffering, and sexual dissatisfaction.

Censorship is essential in order to maintain peace and stability in the society. It will decrease the crime rates. Children can be exposed to sexual matters in school in a different manner as education. Excessive amount of sexual explicit material would surely be harmful.

(ii) *Censorship is not Justified:* All censorship is not good as well. Censorship means restriction and suppression of ideas, opinions and expression. At times, it is not justified as well.

Censorship, is not justified if the power that be seeks to curb opposition. Though opposition for the sake of opposition is not good for democracy, it is always constructive when it helps build a democracy. If the ruling authority censors all that opposition does, spies its activities, keeps it in awe, endangers it by throwing the draconian laws on its leaders, it does not justify what it does. If it does, it only establishes its absoluteness, it only seeks to maintain itself in power. Censoring opposition leads to weakening the forces of democracy. Soli Sorabjee gives instances of such mindless censorship.

"During the spurious 1975 Emergency, some of the Censor's decisions were farcical. Quotations from Mahatma Gandhi, Tagore and Nehru were banned. So was news of Begum Vilayat Mahal, squatting at New Delhi railway station, the junior lawyers' march to Delhi High Court and similar news which had no bearing on the security of the state or public order." "Our Supreme Court has," he continues, "ruled that freedom of expression cannot be curtailed because of the hyper-sensitivities of excitable persons who resent any legitimate criticism of their beliefs or their leaders. Again, freedom of expression cannot be suppressed on account of threats of violence because that would tantamount to negation of the rule of law and surrender to blackmail and intimidation. Freedom of expression cannot be held to ransom by an intolerant group of people."

Censorship is not justified if the foreign rules inflict censorship through some seditious Meetings Act (1980) or the later Rowlatt Acts on people seeking to non-cooperate with the authorities. Civil disobedience is justified if the Salt Act is violated (1930).

To rise against injustice is not an act of rebellion. We do not call those men as revolteers who stood against the absolute French monarchs, nor those who fought for liberation of their nations; they are described as revolutionaries. Censorship against revolteers is justified, censorship against revolutionaries is not.

## I (d). Does Protective Discrimination Violate Principles of Fairness?

The concepts such as justice and equality are not opposing ones. The claims of justice and of equality do not clash with one another. To give special facilities to those who were denied such facilities for centuries do not stand against the principles of justice; they, rather, seek to build the properties of justice. To grant and provide social justice to the deprived people, amounts to strengthen the claims of equality, for they seek to bring hitherto unequals on parity with the to-day's equals.

(i) *Protective Discrimination does not Violate the Principles of Fairness:* In any society, there are people who are not equal: the rich is not equal to the poor; the weaker is not equal to the stronger; the lower caste people are not equal to people who belong to higher caste. In a society of unequals, it is the weaker who needs protection; it is the downtrodden who needs special care; it is the poor who needs security. We should and in fact, need to discriminate, discriminate in favour of the weak, for we need to distinguish between a wolf and a lamb. Who needs protection? Obviously, it is the lamb who is in need of protection. The concept of protective discrimination is a characteristic of the Indian Constitution. Our Constitution provides protection for the poor, the weak, the downtrodden—socially as well as economically. It discriminates in favour of the socially and economically weaker section of society by providing them certain special facilities. The idea behind the US affirmative action is the same as that of the protective discrimination—both do not violate any claim of equality, nor any principle of fairness.

The Scheduled Castes and Scheduled Tribes have been, for centuries, the most neglected, marginalized and exploited people. The scourge of untouchability was a blot on the Indian civilization. Despite its abolition under Article 17 of the Constitution, it persists in many subtle and not so subtle ways. It has been a tale of prejudice, discrimination and exploitation. At stake, in the ultimate analysis is the very integrity and survival of Indian society. Without transforming vertical inequality in society into horizontal equality, democracy will have no meaning. If the law does not favour the disadvantaged, they will never achieve true equality of opportunity and freedom of choice. The nation's unity will be at risk. In some form or the other, overt or covert, in many subtle ways, the prejudice against these weaker sections persists. This is perhaps because of the mindset of certain sections of the society. Indeed to refer to the Scheduled Castes and Scheduled Tribes and other backward classes as mere 'sections of society' is a grave misuse of words. They together constitute the vast and not merely a section. 24% of the whole population as per the 1991 causes. The injustices heaped on them and also on the other backward classes (OBCs) for no other reasons than the pure birth or their situation of poverty have few parallels in the history of civilisation.

The Constitution of India provides an elaborate constitutional mechanism for the upliftment of the people belonging to the Scheduled Castes, the Scheduled Tribes and the OBCs. Article 17 abolishes untouchability. Article 46 requires the State 'to promote with special care the educational and economic interests of the weaker sections of the people, and, in particular, of the Scheduled

Castes and the Scheduled Tribes, and to protect them from social injustice and all forms of exploitation. Article 335 provides that the claims of the members of the Scheduled Castes and the Scheduled Tribes shall be taken into consideration, consistently with the maintenance of efficiency of administration, in the making of appointments to services and posts in connection with the affairs of the Union or of a State. Article 15(4) refers to the special provisions for their advancement. Article 16(4A) speaks of "reservation in matters of promotion to any class or classes of posts in the services under the State in favour of SCs/STs, which are not adequately represented in the services under the State'. Article 338 provides for a National Commission for the Scheduled Castes and Scheduled Tribes with duties to investigate and monitor all matters relating to safeguards provided for them to inquire into specific complaints and to participate and advise on the planning process of their socio-economic development etc. Article 300 and Article 332 of the Constitution respectively provide for reservation of seats in favour of the Scheduled Castes and the Scheduled Tribes in the House of the People and in the legislative assemblies of the States. Under Part IX, relating to the Panchayats and Part IXA of the Constitution relating to the Municipalities, reservation for Scheduled Castes and Scheduled Tribes in local bodies has been envisaged and provided.

Part IX and Part IXA of the Constitution respectively permit the legislature of a State to make provision for respectively permit the legislature of a State to make provision for reservation of seats in Panchayat and Municipalities in favour of backward classes of citizens. Article 340 of the Constitution provides for appointment of a Commission to investigate the conditions of Backward classes. Article 16(4) and 16(4A) respectively permit reservation of appointments or posts and in matters of promotion in favour of backward classes not adequately represented in the services under the State. Article 15(4) permits the State to make special provision for the advancement of any socially and educationally backward classes of citizens. In addition to these, there are also other Constitutional provisions for the welfare and socio-economic empowerment of the Scheduled Castes, the Scheduled Tribes and other backward classes.

The Governments, both at the centre as well as at the state levels, have done a lot to help these classes attain a measure of respectability and a status equal to those above their ladder. Giving them special rights is paying them for the insults and the ill-treatment done towards them for centuries. It is not something of any concession towards the people belonging to these classes; it is respecting the constitutional rights granted to them by the Constitution; it is a kind of correcting a wrong; it is something that helps them rise higher to stand in equality with those who were hitherto higher than them. It is, in no way any breach of equality rights; it is in a way a phenomenon that strengthens equality; it is in a way being fair to the people of these classes. Obviously, a type of protective discrimination as has been incorporated in our Constitution, is no violation of the principles of fairness.

(ii) *Protective Discrimination Violates the Principles of Fairness:* There is a school of thought, especially among the neo-liberals—Hayek, Nozick and Dworokin—who hold the view that giving special rights to the disadvantaged is against the principles of fairness. It is not fair to be unfair towards those on whose cost the disadvantaged would enjoy special rights.

The following are some of the major arguments which state that the protective discrimination violates the principles of fairness the essence of which lays emphasis on giving special rights to the weaker sections of the society.

(a) Protective discrimination creates a parasite class which finds one or the other excuse to keep obtaining special care. Once the special care is taken care of through some facilities, it becomes and is made to become a right for all time to come for those classes called as the weaker section of society. It makes them ultimately lazy.

(b) In the absence of any adequate and proper mechanism, which help know the results of such assistance given to the poorer sections of society, to help them or to continue helping them, is a wastage of resources, particularly when such resources are limited. It is really unfair to cost the national purse.

(c) Political theorists like Hayek and Nozick contend that it is unfair to tax the advantaged for meeting the demands of the disadvantaged. Besides being unjustified, protective discrimination punishes the advantaged for their talent, initiative and intelligence.

(d) The very idea of protective discrimination is faulty. It is faulty in the sense that through it, the attempt is made to seek equality amidst differences. There is a point when Hayek says, "...from the fact that the people are very different, it follows that if we treat them equally, the result must be inequality in their actual position. The desire of making people more like...is a justification for further discrimination and coercion."

(e) To provide people equal opportunities is something perfectly in order and it is in no case the denial of the principle of fairness and to that extent such a claim of equality is not antagonistic to the claim of justice. But when the attempt is made to extend from 'equality of opportunities' to 'equality of conditions', the results are injustices and unfairness, violating all norms and values.

(f) The idea of protective discrimination is described as the idea of correcting a wrong done in the past against the weaker sections of society, especially the people belonging to the Scheduled Castes and the Scheduled Tribes. This idea amounts to asking for a compensation for the wrongs committed by one's forefathers. To keep compensating decades after decades with no indication of any final decade is really unfair.

(g) The claims of protective discrimination seek to increase the functions of the state, followed by the increase in state's powers. This, in itself, restricts the liberties and rights of the people in general, and of the advantaged in particular.

It may be said, in conclusion, that there should be a distinction between a wolf and a lamb, and it does mean that the lamb be protected. It is, therefore, necessary to devise ways and means that it is the lambs who are being protected, and not that the wolves who are being made more powerful. The special facilities given under the framework of protective discrimination should reach those who deserve them and the resultant outcomes need to be scrutinised from time to time.

### I (e). Should the State Intervene in the Institution of Family?

There is no doubt that the institution of family is the basic and primary institution of the society. Internally, it helps its members attain social virtues: cooperation, tolerance, assistance sacrifice, unity, interdependence close relationship and what not. It is, therefore, rightly called the school of social virtues. Externally, it creates society, creates other families: clans, tribes, races, villages, cities, states, societies. Maclever was right when he had said that kinship (family) creates society and society creates the state. The institution of family is necessary to constitute a society and the state comes to serve the relationships that spring from society.

Whereas the institution of family is described as something 'domestic', 'private', 'personal', 'internal', therefore, it is kept in the domain of the sphere of 'within'. The society, the state, on the other hand are described as 'public', 'universal', 'external', and therefore, kept in the domain of 'without'. It is in these contexts that there are different ways, means, attitudes, customs and rules regarding what are related to the 'private' and 'personal' and entirely different with regard to what is 'public' or 'external'. Accordingly, different perceptions govern them: the institution of family differently than the institutions of the state and society differently. What is important to note is that these institutions are separate, are separately described, are separately viewed. The question that seeks an answer is: should the state or society intervene in the institution of family by making rules for it and for its functioning or should they not? Feminism, as an ideology and also as a movement, has its definite perception about it.

(i) *State should intervene in the institution of family:* Sex and gender are two different phenomena. Sex is the method of classifying people on grounds of biological structure; gender is a method of classifying people on grounds of sex. Gender is a 'social' classification whereas sex is 'biological' classification. It is made, whereas sex is born. It reflects nurture whereas sex, nature. It is gender discrimination against which feminism has arisen. Nobody, not even the radical feminist, oppose sex-inequality.

What the feminists object is the gender discrimination. They say that women are women and they have to be mothers, but why should they be blamed to have given birth to the she-babies? They argue that as women why should they be kept within the four walls of the house, doing household jobs, rearing and nurturing children, wait for their men and not eat until they come home late night, suffer all cruelties, be beaten and be burnt, be regarded as a means of men's enjoyment, be discriminated as against their brothers in education, be confined to what is called 'private'?

The discrimination against women has a long history, beginning from the days of patriarchy, and of male dominated society. Patriarchy, as is understood, means the male ruling the female,

male heading the family, male holding the 'outside', 'the external', 'the public' domain. With patriarchy gaining ground and with passage of time, attained power, made women as secondary members in the family and entrusted to them secondary functions and confining them to the household activities and in the process, relegated in the background for all public activities and made to serve men. Its essential characteristic is, as Millett says, male dominating female.

The society that came up, following the patriarchal families, was male dominated society. All its rules, customs, values favoured men. The state that such a society builds, also favoured men, as against women. The state is in patriarchal system from days immemorial. Bryson (*Feminist Political Theory*) says, "but one manifestation of patriarchal power, reflecting other deeper structures of oppression and women, well-documented exclusion from its formal institutions as a system of gender inequality." The state, the feminists think, being a part and product of the over-all patriarchal system, perpetuates male domination. It may support reforms relating to women's upliftment (the abolition of Sati in 1829, the Widow Remarriage Act, 1856) and in doing so, it may hail the efforts of Kabirs, Nanaks, Gandhis, but it remains, in ultimate analysis, an instrument of the patriarchal society.

The liberal feminists (beginning with Wollstonecraft's *Vindication of the Rights of Woman,* Mill's *The Subjection of Women,* Friedan's *The Feminine Mystique*) lament man's domination over woman and hope, as Wollstonecraft does, that the distinction of sex would become unimportant in political and social life as women would gain education and would be regarded as rational creatures in their own right. The liberal feminists are social reformers and wish to seek state intervention to help win, for women, a situation of respectability. They seek to open up public life to equal competition between men and women rather than challenge the patriarchal structure of society itself. In fact, they do not wish to abolish the distinction between the public and the private; they even insist on the privacy in the institution of family—making personal as personal and private as private. They argue for equal rights in all fields of life, seeking their entry in public life as well. They urge on state laws so to make women secure against dowry atrocities, male's right of divorce, and secure their right to inheritance, especially property rights.

(ii) *State should not intervene in the institution of family:* The feminists, more particularly the radical ones, regard the institution of family as the root factor responsible for the exploitation of women by men. They even think that the state has legalised the male domination as the characteristic feature of the institution of family. Some feminists, Firestone ( *The Dialectic of Sex*), go to the extent of rejecting patriarchy as neither natural nor inevitable. They contend that women can only achieve emancipation if they transcend their biological nature and escape from the curse of 'Eve': pregnancy can be avoided by artificial reproduction in test tubes through modern technology; child-rearing responsibilities can be transferred to men or some social institutions. The radical feminists believe that women's liberation requires that sexual differences between men and women be diminished and eventually abolished, for, as they feel, the true nature of the sexes is equal and identical. Some feminists believe that women's values are superior to those of men, for the former possess qualities of creativity, sensitivity and caring. While others such as Susan Browinmiller (*Against Our Will*) are of the opinion that men are devilish and animalish. She says, "Men have created an 'ideology of rape' which amounts to a 'conscious process of intimidation by which all men keep all women in a state of fear'." She, therefore, argues, "...men rape because they can, because they have the 'biological capacity to rape'."

Although it is difficult to go alongwith the radical feminists to abolish the institution of family and argue in favour of free 'family' system, freeing particular 'male' to a particular 'female', it can be suggested that the patriarchal rules be purged from the institution of family through some kind of social revolution and a new system be built on a relationship based on the principles of equality, dignity and reciprocity recognised each by man and woman. The institution of state need not be a party to such a relationship and the arrangement be made with the help of the state if possible, and without and despite the state if necessary.

## SUGGESTED READINGS

1. Aparjit, Jayant, *Equality and Compensatory Discriminations* (Nagpur: Dattason, 1999).
2. Fred, Rigges and Daya, Krishan, *Development Debate* (Jaipur, Printwell Publishers, 1987).

3. Larner, G., *The Creation of Patriarchy* (New York: Oxford University Press, 1989).
4. Negel Thomas, *Equality and Patriarchy* (Oxford: Oxford University Press, 1991).
5. Tawney, R.H., *Equality* (London: George Allen and Unwin, 1931).
6. Wolin, S., *Politics and Vision* (London: George Allen and Unwin, 1965).

# Index